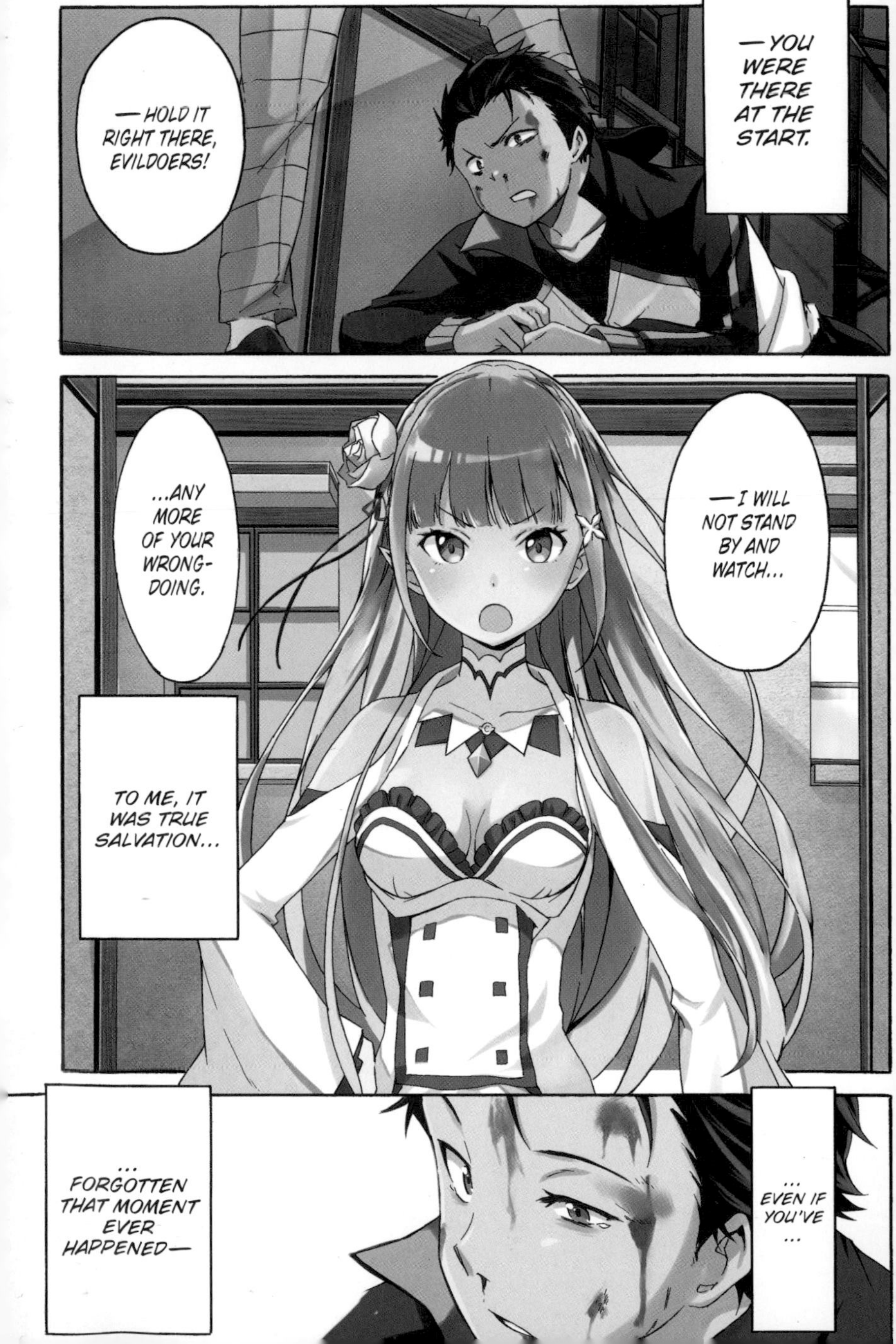
—YOU WERE THERE AT THE START.
—HOLD IT RIGHT THERE, EVILDOERS!
—I WILL NOT STAND BY AND WATCH...
...ANY MORE OF YOUR WRONG-DOING.
TO ME, IT WAS TRUE SALVATION...
... EVEN IF YOU'VE ...
... FORGOTTEN THAT MOMENT EVER HAPPENED—

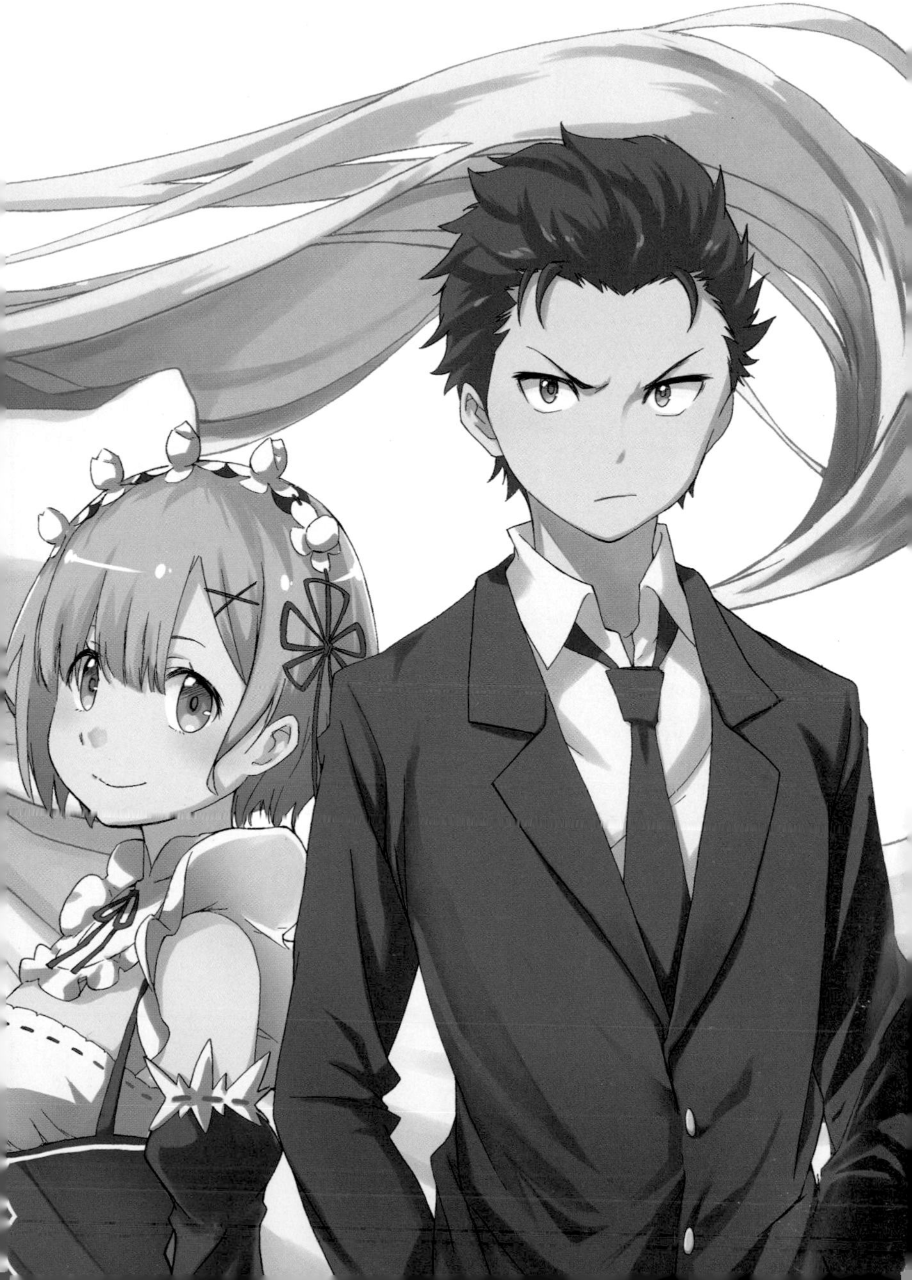

Episode 1 A Gentle, Early Morning

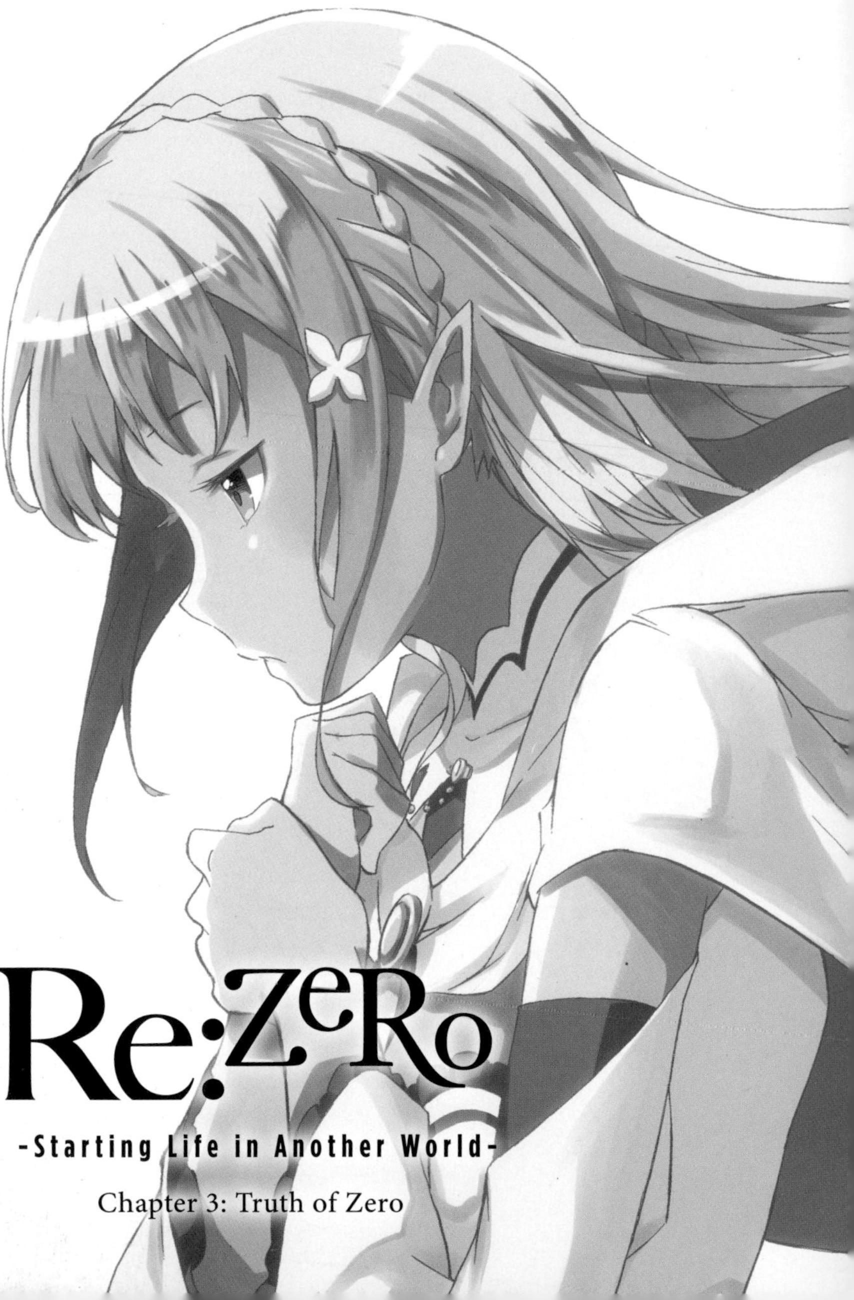
Re:ZeRo
-Starting Life in Another World-
Chapter 3: Truth of Zero

Re:ZERO -Starting Life in Another World-

Chapter 3: Truth of Zero

The only ability Subaru Natsuki gets when he's summoned to another world is time travel via his own death. But to save her, he'll die as many times as it takes.

Contents

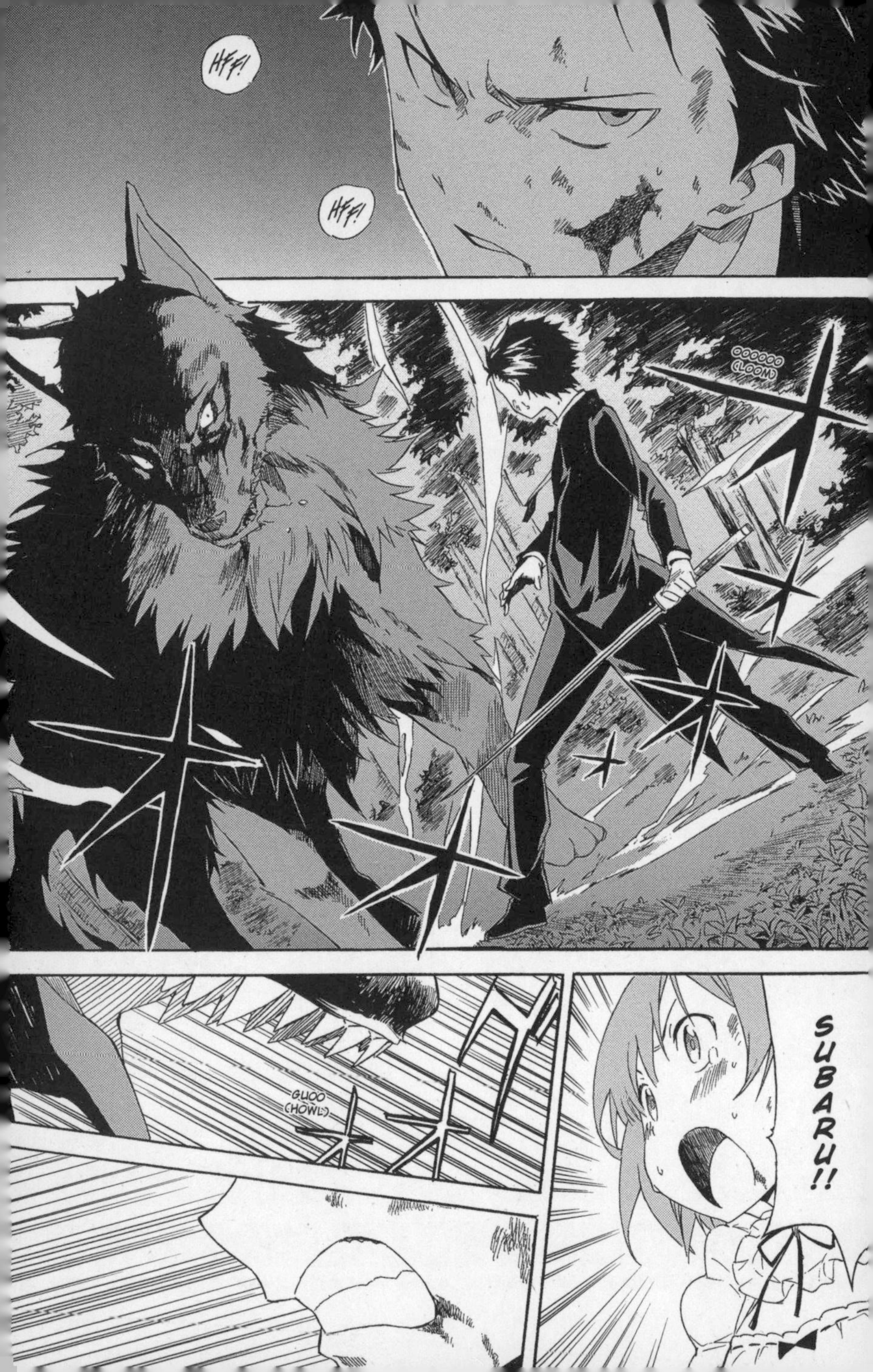
HFF!
HFF!
OOOOOO (LOOM)
SUBARU!!
GUOO (HOWL)

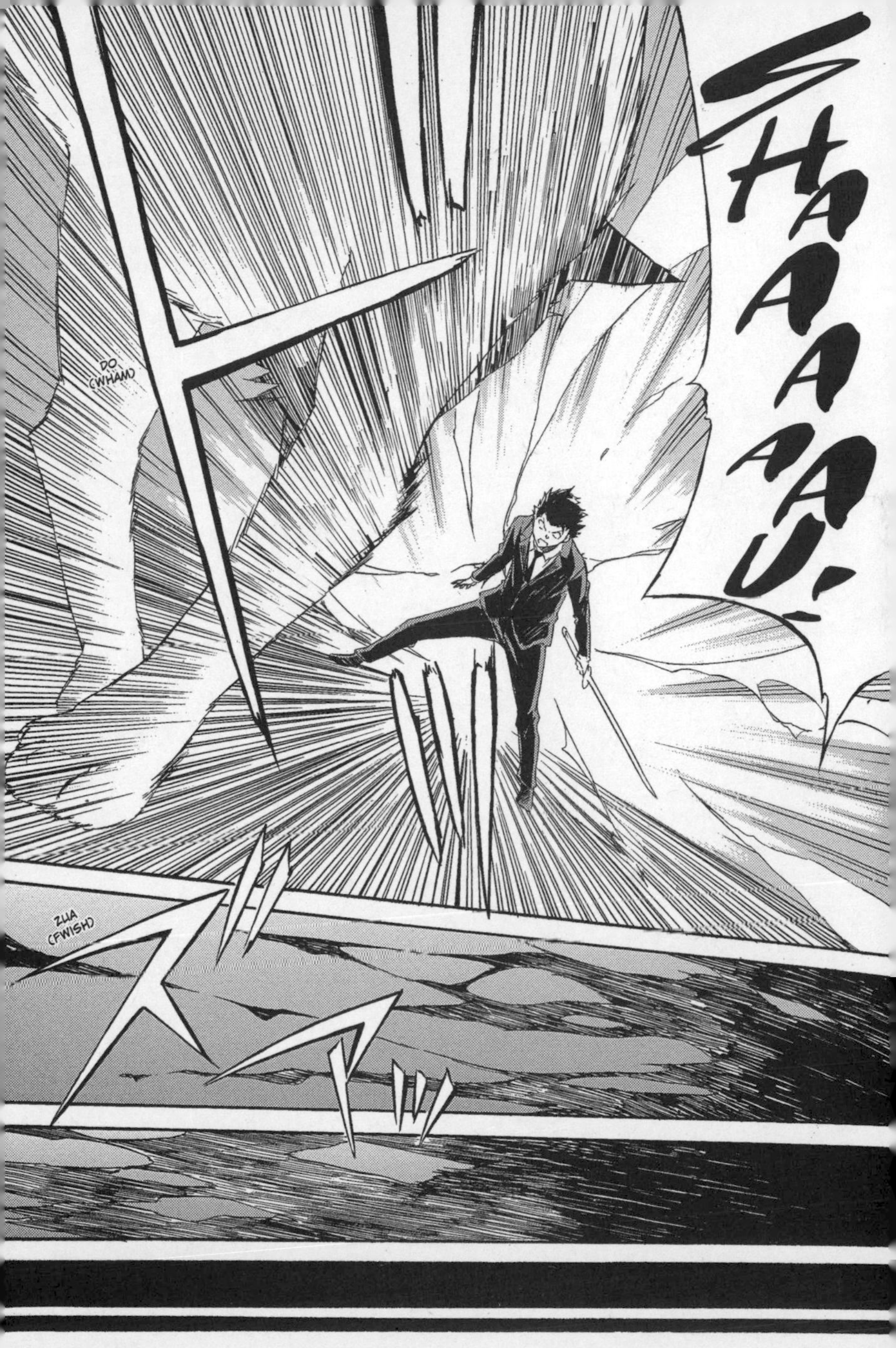
SHAAAAAU!
DO (WHAM)
ZUA (FWISH)

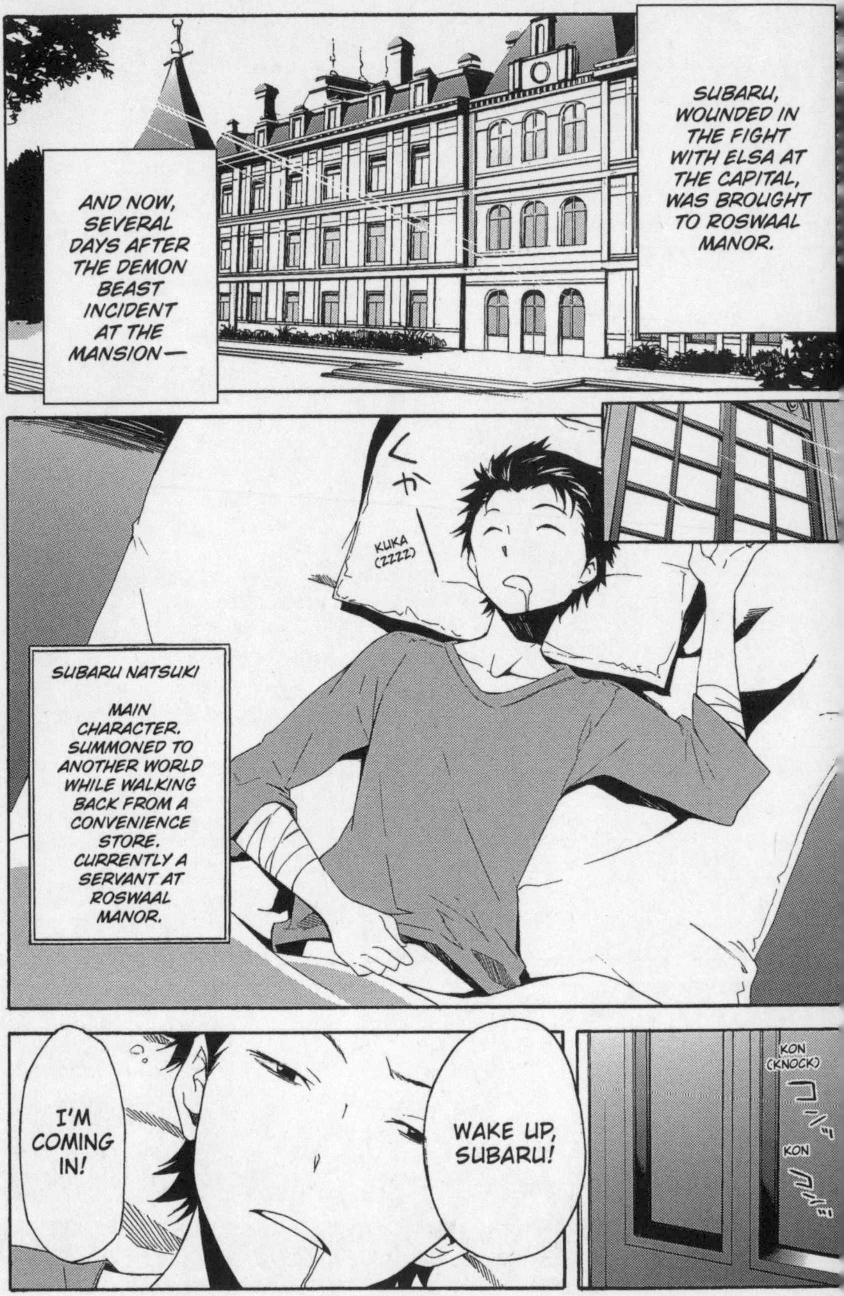
SUBARU, WOUNDED IN THE FIGHT WITH ELSA AT THE CAPITAL, WAS BROUGHT TO ROSWAAL MANOR.
AND NOW, SEVERAL DAYS AFTER THE DEMON BEAST INCIDENT AT THE MANSION—
KUKA (ZZZZ)
SUBARU NATSUKI
MAIN CHARACTER. SUMMONED TO ANOTHER WORLD WHILE WALKING BACK FROM A CONVENIENCE STORE. CURRENTLY A SERVANT AT ROSWAAL MANOR.
KON (KNOCK)
KON
WAKE UP, SUBARU!
I'M COMING IN!

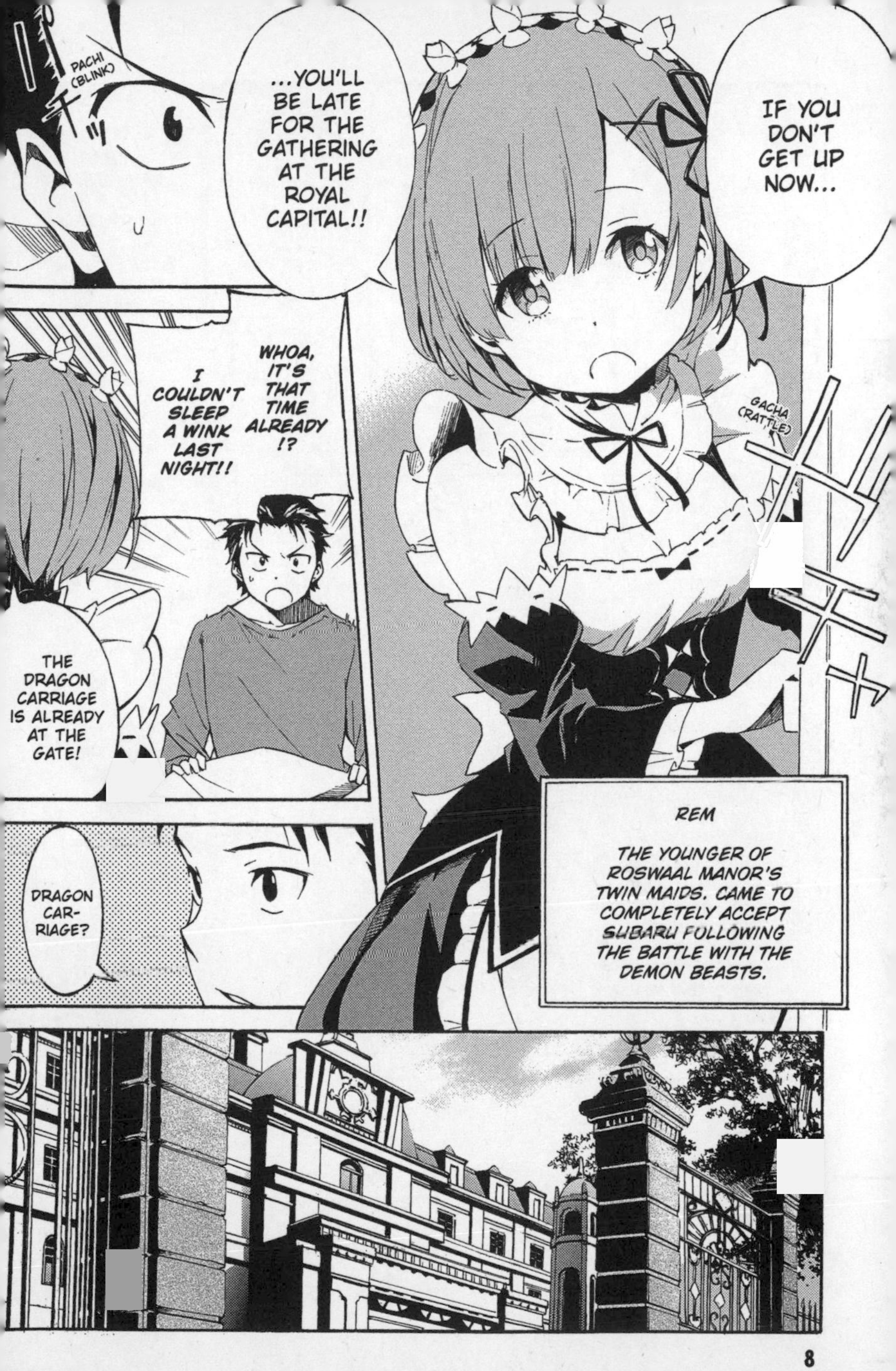
IF YOU DON'T GET UP NOW...
...YOU'LL BE LATE FOR THE GATHERING AT THE ROYAL CAPITAL!!
GACHA (RATTLE)
REM
THE YOUNGER OF ROSWAAL MANOR'S TWIN MAIDS. CAME TO COMPLETELY ACCEPT SUBARU FOLLOWING THE BATTLE WITH THE DEMON BEASTS.
PACHI (BLINK)
WHOA, IT'S THAT TIME ALREADY!?
I COULDN'T SLEEP A WINK LAST NIGHT!!
THE DRAGON CARRIAGE IS ALREADY AT THE GATE!
DRAGON CAR-RIAGE?

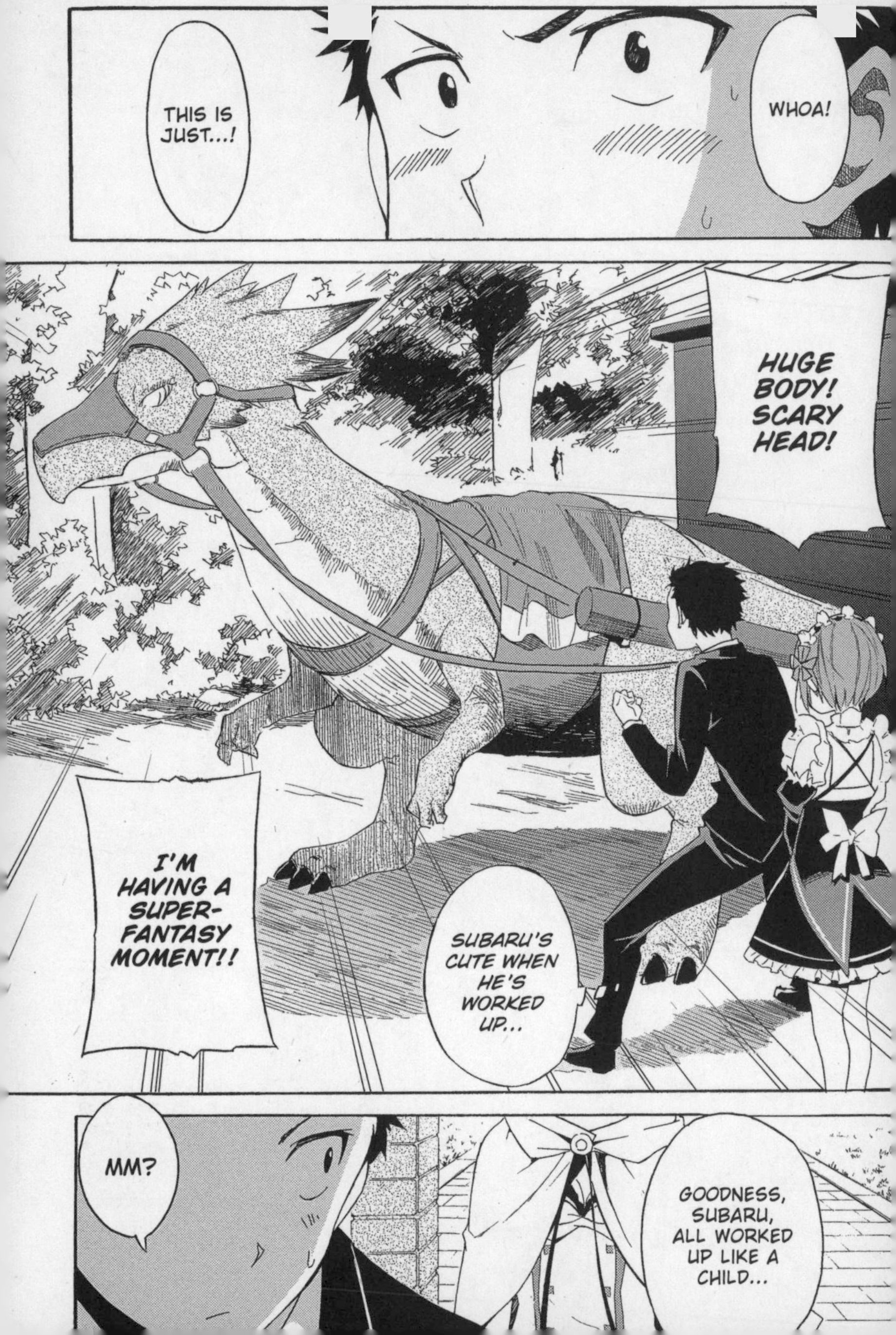
WHOA!
THIS IS JUST...!
HUGE BODY! SCARY HEAD!
I'M HAVING A SUPER-FANTASY MOMENT!!
SUBARU'S CUTE WHEN HE'S WORKED UP...
GOODNESS, SUBARU, ALL WORKED UP LIKE A CHILD...
MM?

WE'RE NOT GOING THERE TO PLAY AROUND!!

EMILIA-TAN!!

I GET IT, GEEZ!! IT'S AN IMPORTANT SUMMONS, RIGHT!?

YES...!

IT'S A REAAALLY IMPORTANT ROYAL SELECTION CONFERENCE!

EMILIA

SILVER-HAIRED HALF-ELF. THE GIRL WHO SAVED SUBARU WHEN HE FELL INTO ANOTHER WORLD.

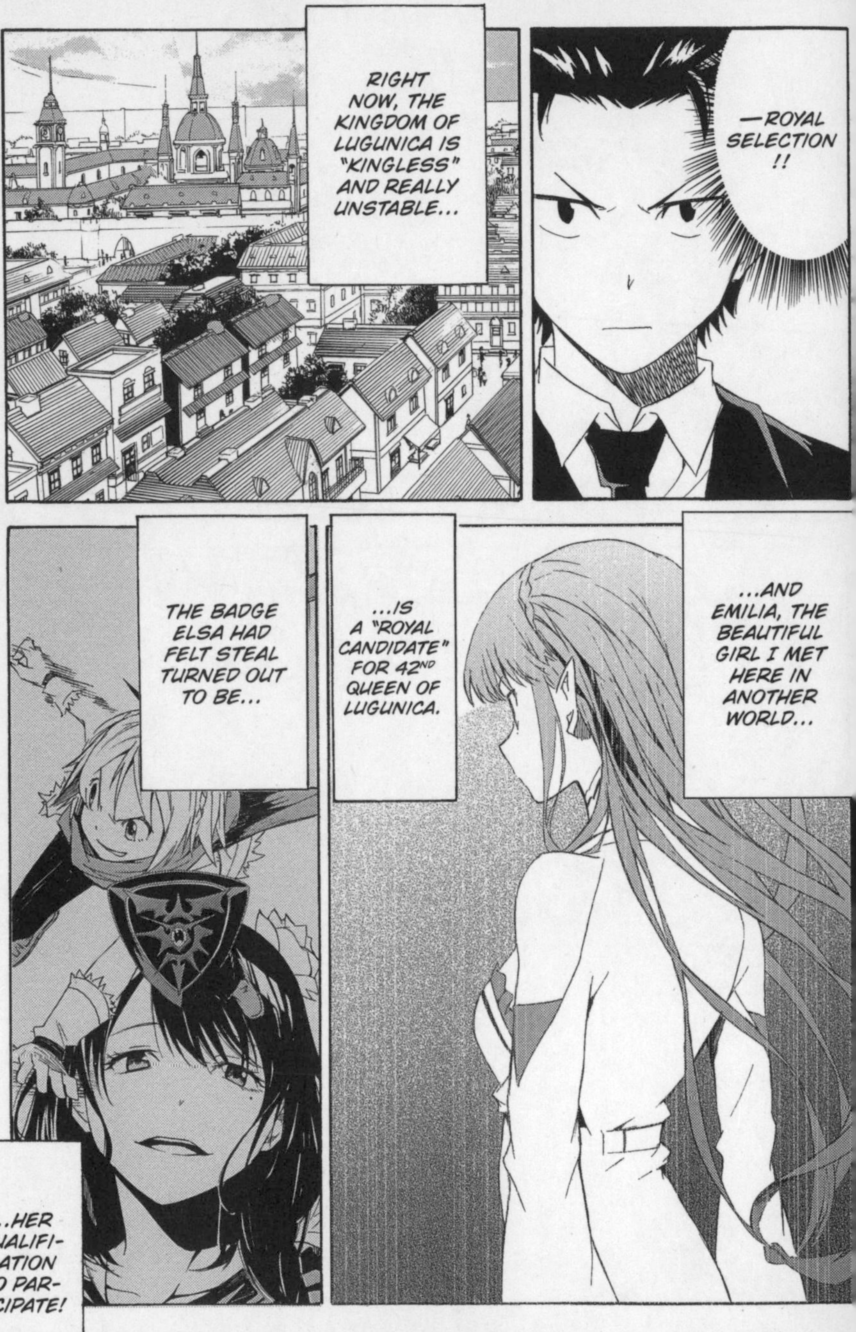
RIGHT NOW, THE KINGDOM OF LUGUNICA IS "KINGLESS" AND REALLY UNSTABLE...
—ROYAL SELECTION!!
...AND EMILIA, THE BEAUTIFUL GIRL I MET HERE IN ANOTHER WORLD...
...IS A "ROYAL CANDIDATE" FOR 42ND QUEEN OF LUGUNICA.
THE BADGE ELSA HAD FELT STEAL TURNED OUT TO BE...
...HER QUALIFICATION TO PARTICIPATE!

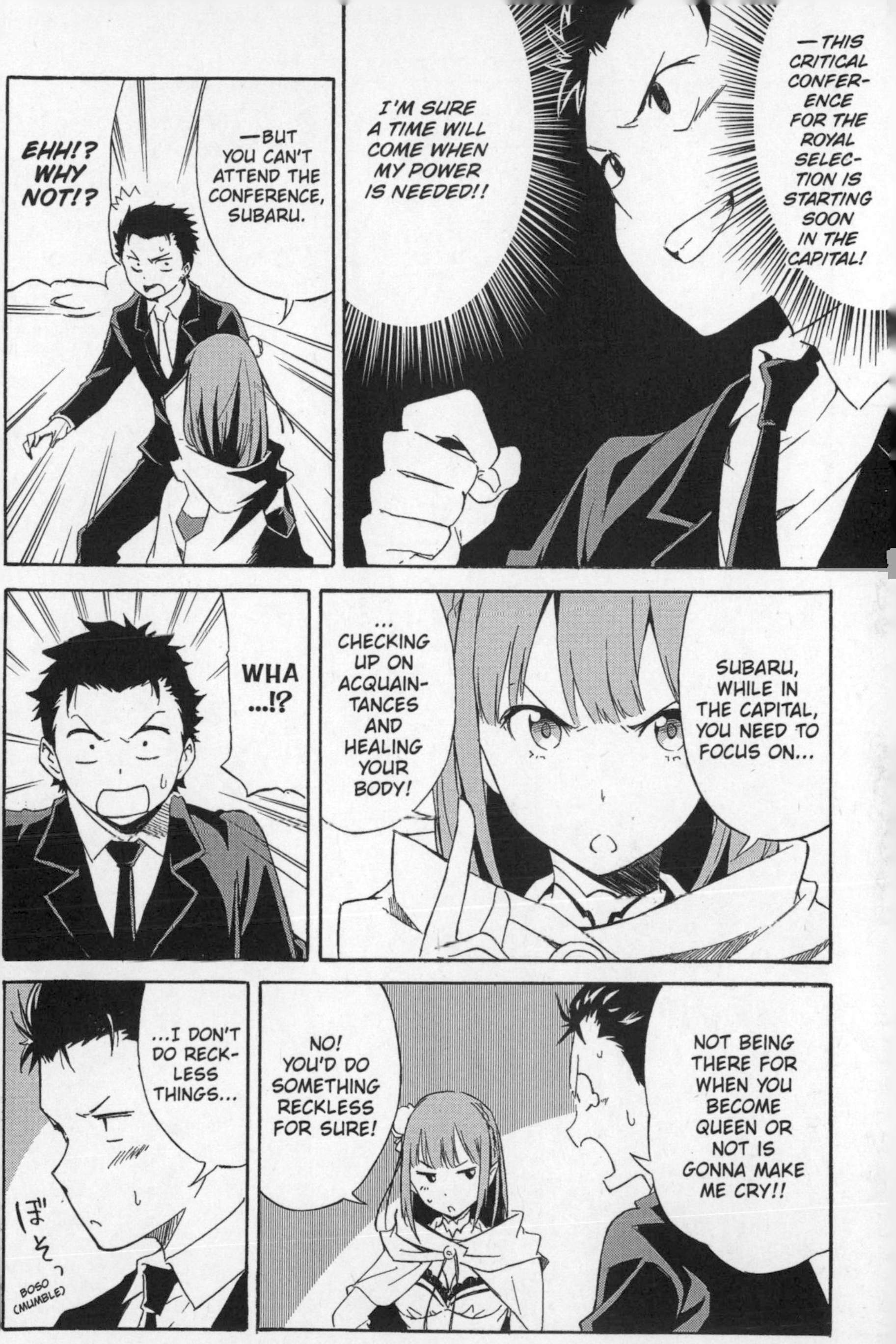

—THIS CRITICAL CONFERENCE FOR THE ROYAL SELECTION IS STARTING SOON IN THE CAPITAL!
I'M SURE A TIME WILL COME WHEN MY POWER IS NEEDED!!
—BUT YOU CAN'T ATTEND THE CONFERENCE, SUBARU.
EHH!? WHY NOT!?
SUBARU, WHILE IN THE CAPITAL, YOU NEED TO FOCUS ON...
...CHECKING UP ON ACQUAINTANCES AND HEALING YOUR BODY!
WHA ...!?
NOT BEING THERE FOR WHEN YOU BECOME QUEEN OR NOT IS GONNA MAKE ME CRY!!
NO! YOU'D DO SOMETHING RECKLESS FOR SURE!
...I DON'T DO RECKLESS THINGS...
ぼそっ
BOSO (MUMBLE)

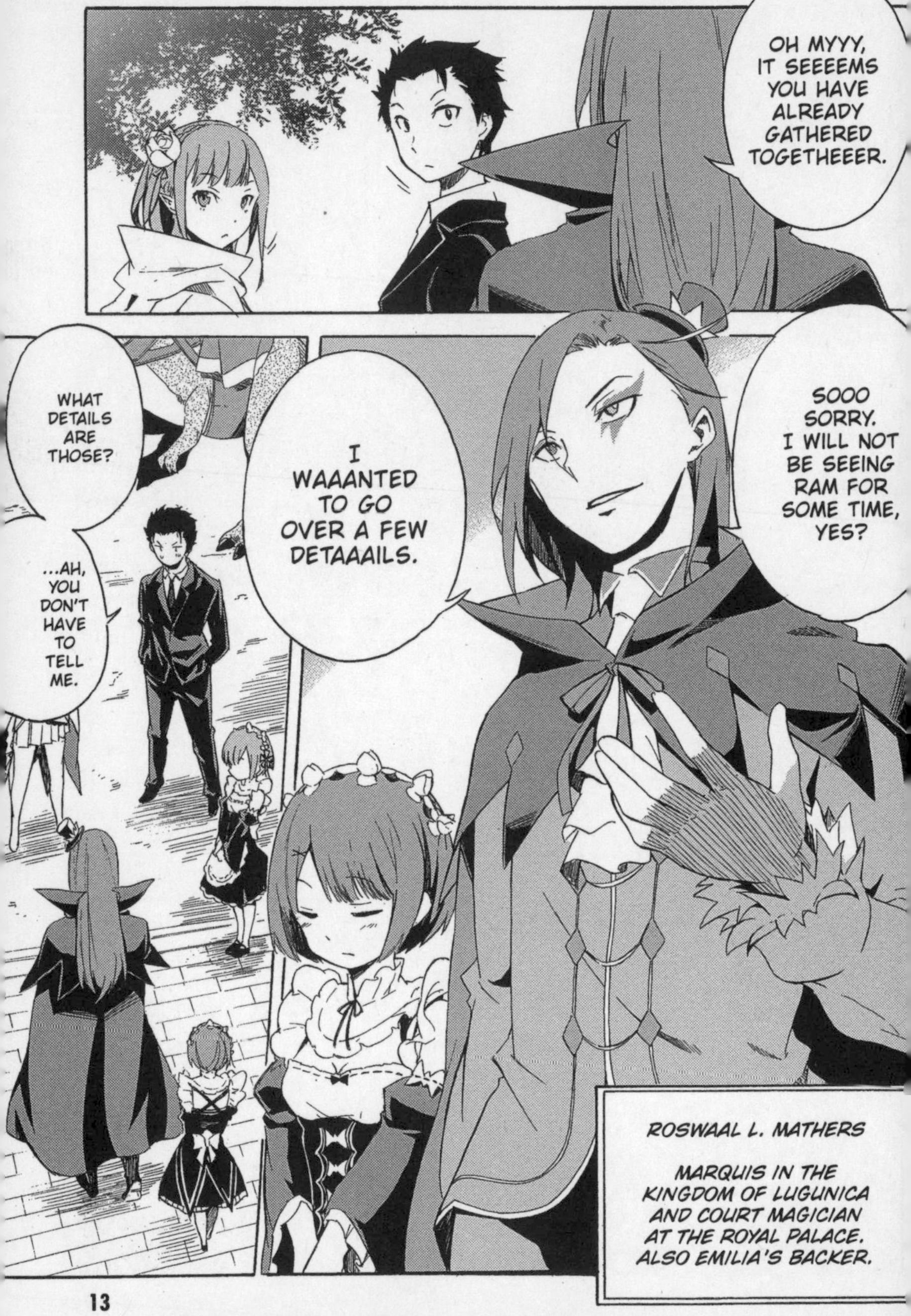
OH MYYY, IT SEEEEMS YOU HAVE ALREADY GATHERED TOGETHEEER.
SOOO SORRY. I WILL NOT BE SEEING RAM FOR SOME TIME, YES?
I WAAANTED TO GO OVER A FEW DETAAAILS.
ROSWAAL L. MATHERS
MARQUIS IN THE KINGDOM OF LUGUNICA AND COURT MAGICIAN AT THE ROYAL PALACE. ALSO EMILIA'S BACKER.
WHAT DETAILS ARE THOSE?
...AH, YOU DON'T HAVE TO TELL ME.

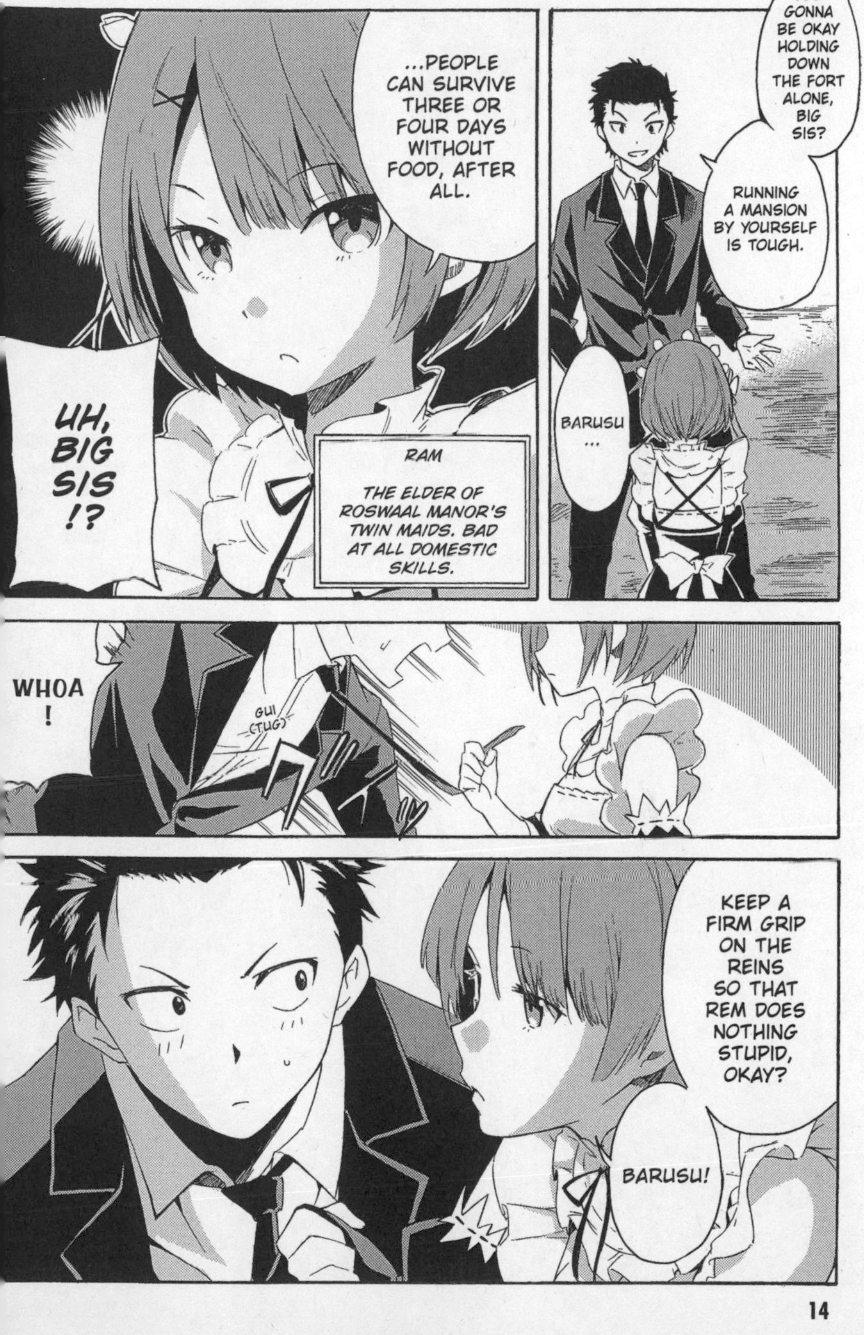
YOU GONNA BE OKAY HOLDING DOWN THE FORT ALONE, BIG SIS?
RUNNING A MANSION BY YOURSELF IS TOUGH.
BARUSU ...
...PEOPLE CAN SURVIVE THREE OR FOUR DAYS WITHOUT FOOD, AFTER ALL.
RAM
THE ELDER OF ROSWAAL MANOR'S TWIN MAIDS. BAD AT ALL DOMESTIC SKILLS.
UH, BIG SIS !?
GUI (TUG)
WHOA !
KEEP A FIRM GRIP ON THE REINS SO THAT REM DOES NOTHING STUPID, OKAY?
BARUSU!

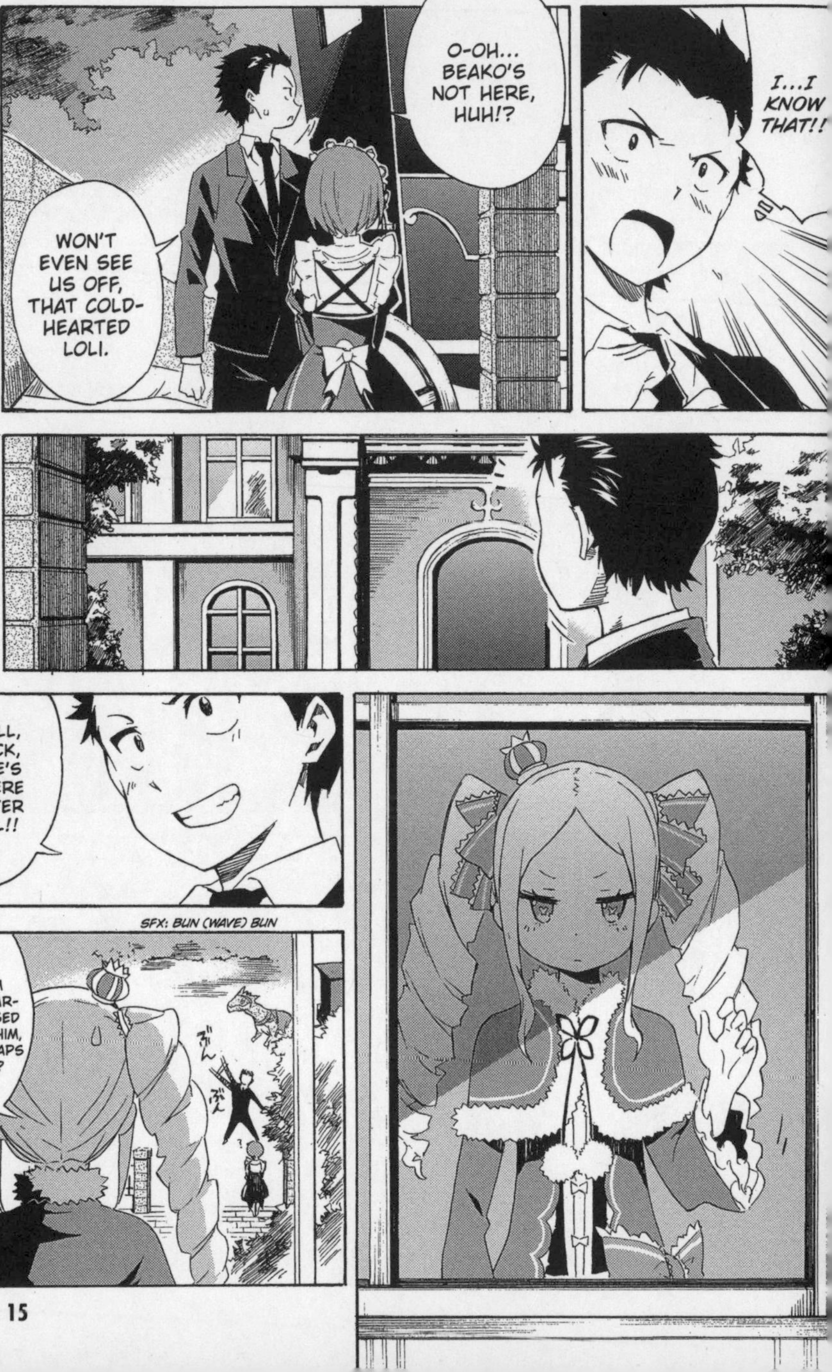
I...I KNOW THAT!!
O-OH... BEAKO'S NOT HERE, HUH!?
WON'T EVEN SEE US OFF, THAT COLD-HEARTED LOLI.
WELL, HECK, SHE'S THERE AFTER ALL!!
SFX: BUN (WAVE) BUN
I'M EMBAR-RASSED FOR HIM, PERHAPS...?

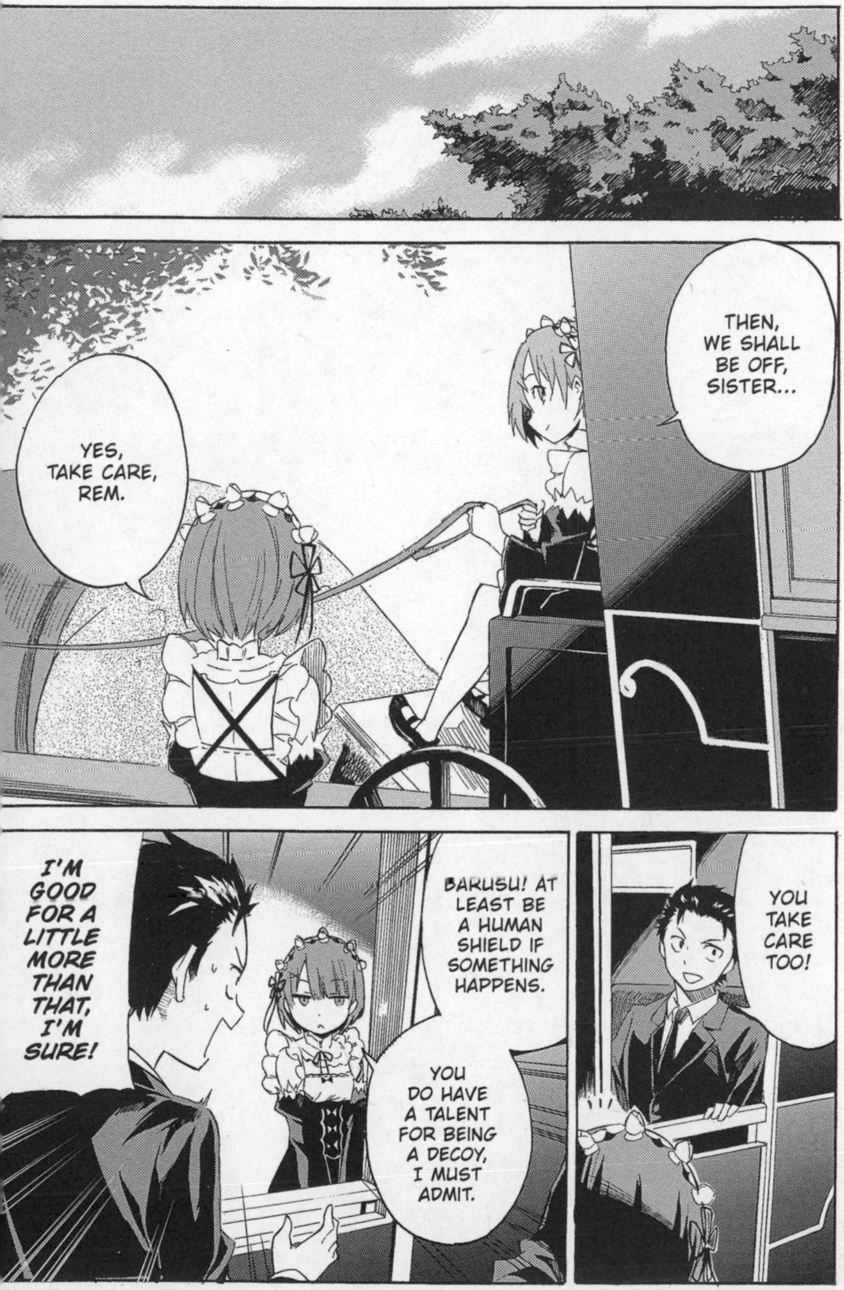
THEN, WE SHALL BE OFF, SISTER...
YES, TAKE CARE, REM.
YOU TAKE CARE TOO!
BARUSU! AT LEAST BE A HUMAN SHIELD IF SOMETHING HAPPENS.
I'M GOOD FOR A LITTLE MORE THAN THAT, I'M SURE!
YOU DO HAVE A TALENT FOR BEING A DECOY, I MUST ADMIT.

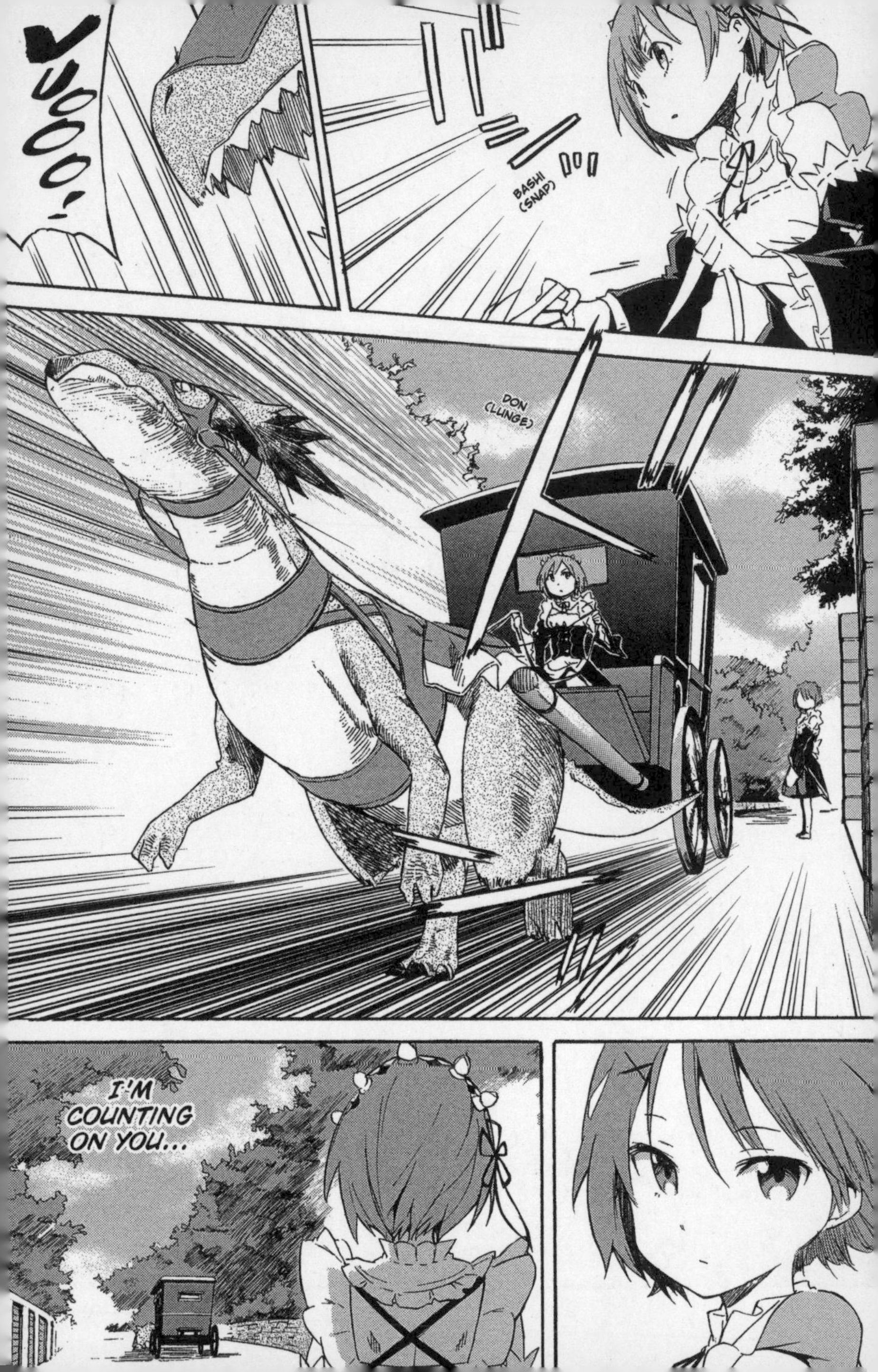
BASHI (SNAP)
VUOOOO!
DON (LUNGE)
I'M COUNTING ON YOU...

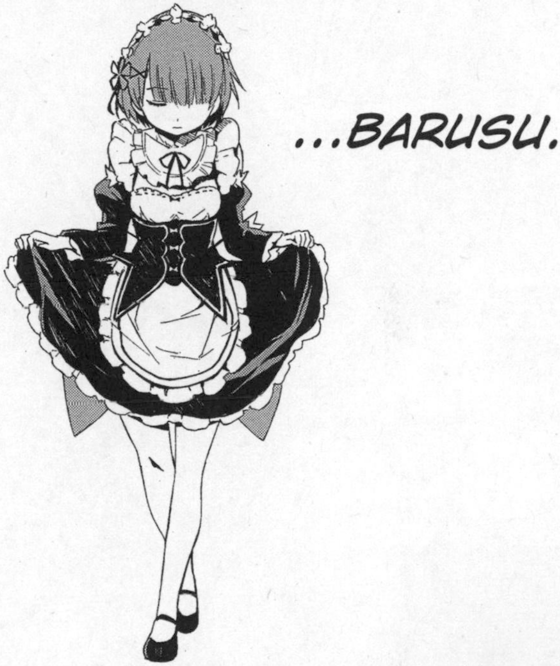
...BARUSU.
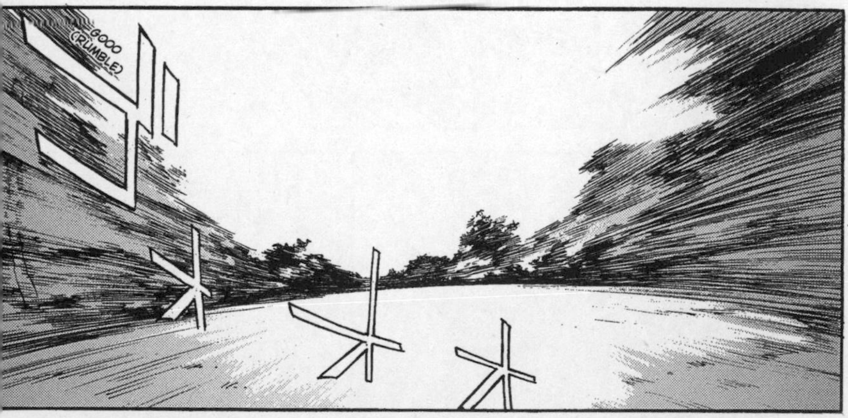
GOOO
(CRUMBLE)

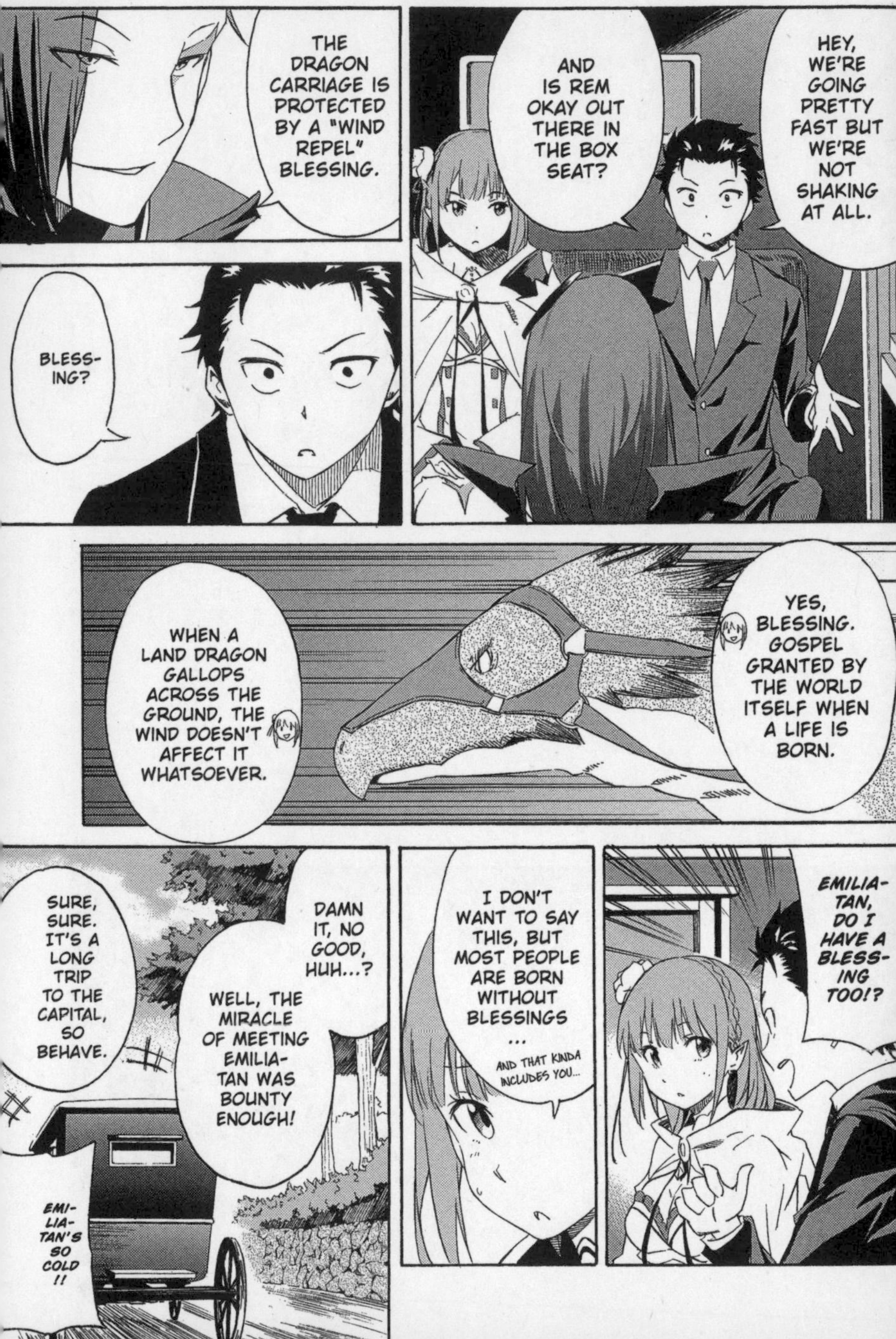
HEY, WE'RE GOING PRETTY FAST BUT WE'RE NOT SHAKING AT ALL.
AND IS REM OKAY OUT THERE IN THE BOX SEAT?
THE DRAGON CARRIAGE IS PROTECTED BY A "WIND REPEL" BLESSING.
BLESS-ING?
YES, BLESSING. GOSPEL GRANTED BY THE WORLD ITSELF WHEN A LIFE IS BORN.
WHEN A LAND DRAGON GALLOPS ACROSS THE GROUND, THE WIND DOESN'T AFFECT IT WHATSOEVER.
EMILIA-TAN, DO I HAVE A BLESS-ING TOO!?
I DON'T WANT TO SAY THIS, BUT MOST PEOPLE ARE BORN WITHOUT BLESSINGS...
AND THAT KINDA INCLUDES YOU...
DAMN IT, NO GOOD, HUH...?
WELL, THE MIRACLE OF MEETING EMILIA-TAN WAS BOUNTY ENOUGH!
SURE, SURE. IT'S A LONG TRIP TO THE CAPITAL, SO BEHAVE.
EMI-LIA-TAN'S SO COLD!!

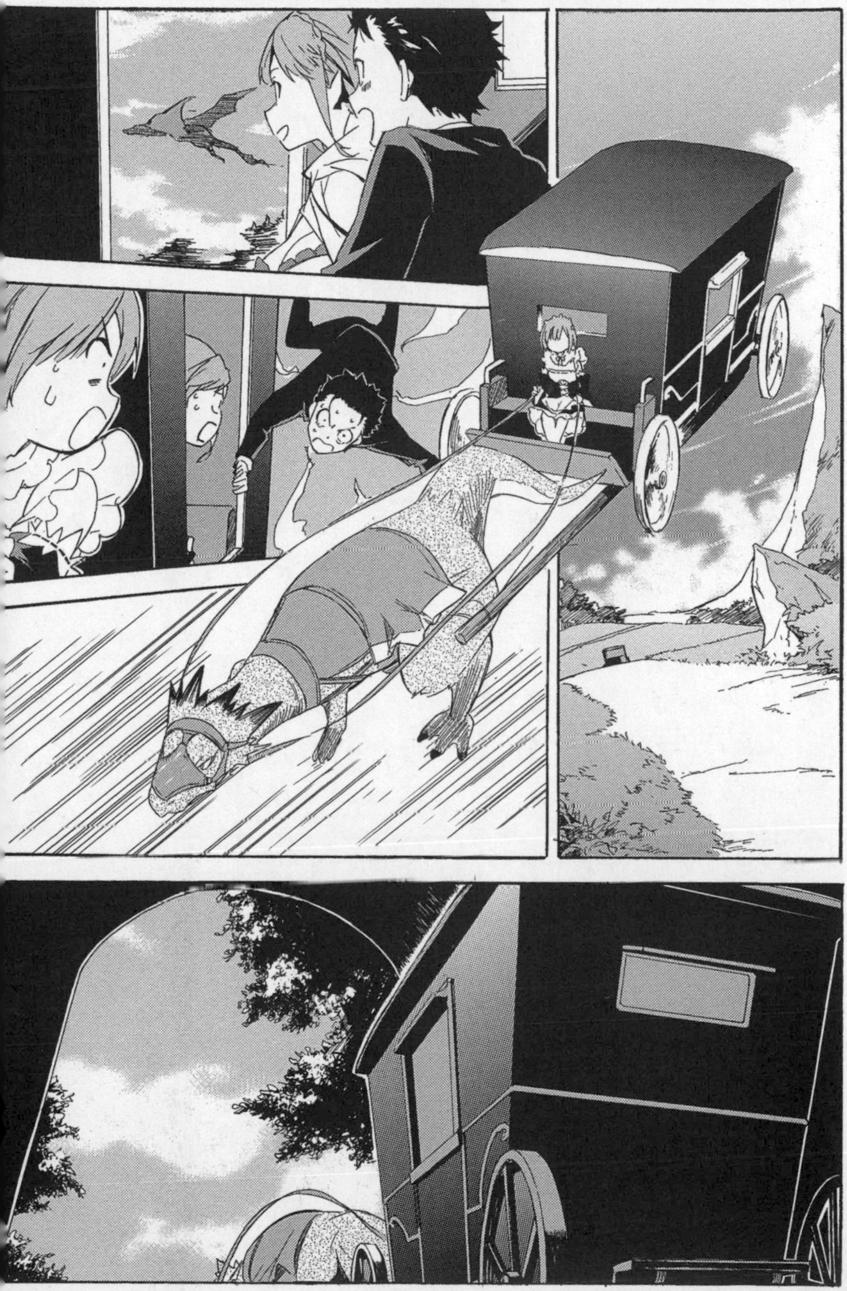

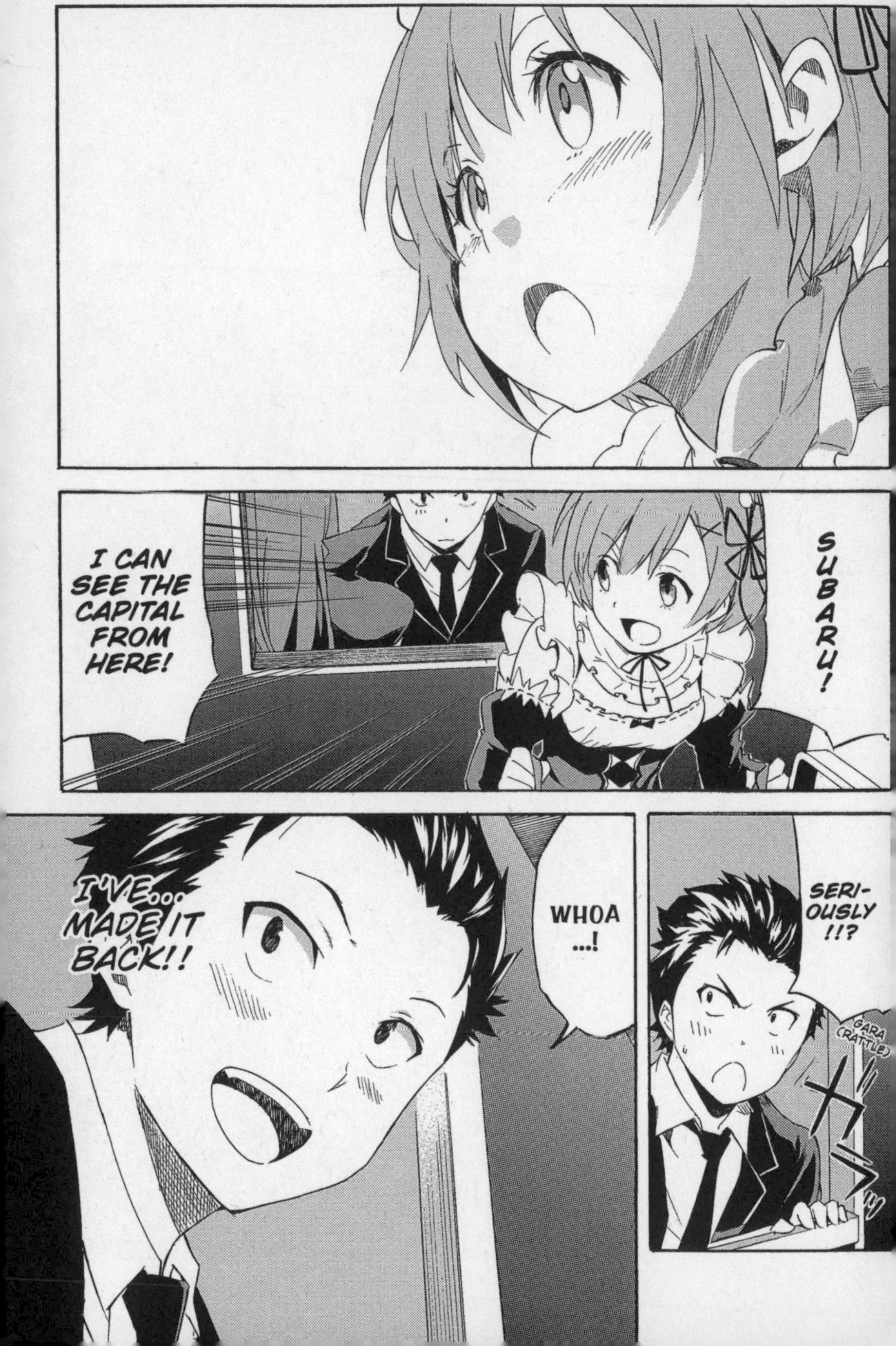
SUBARU!
I CAN SEE THE CAPITAL FROM HERE!
SERI-OUSLY!!?
GARA (RATTLE)
WHOA...!
I'VE... MADE IT BACK!!

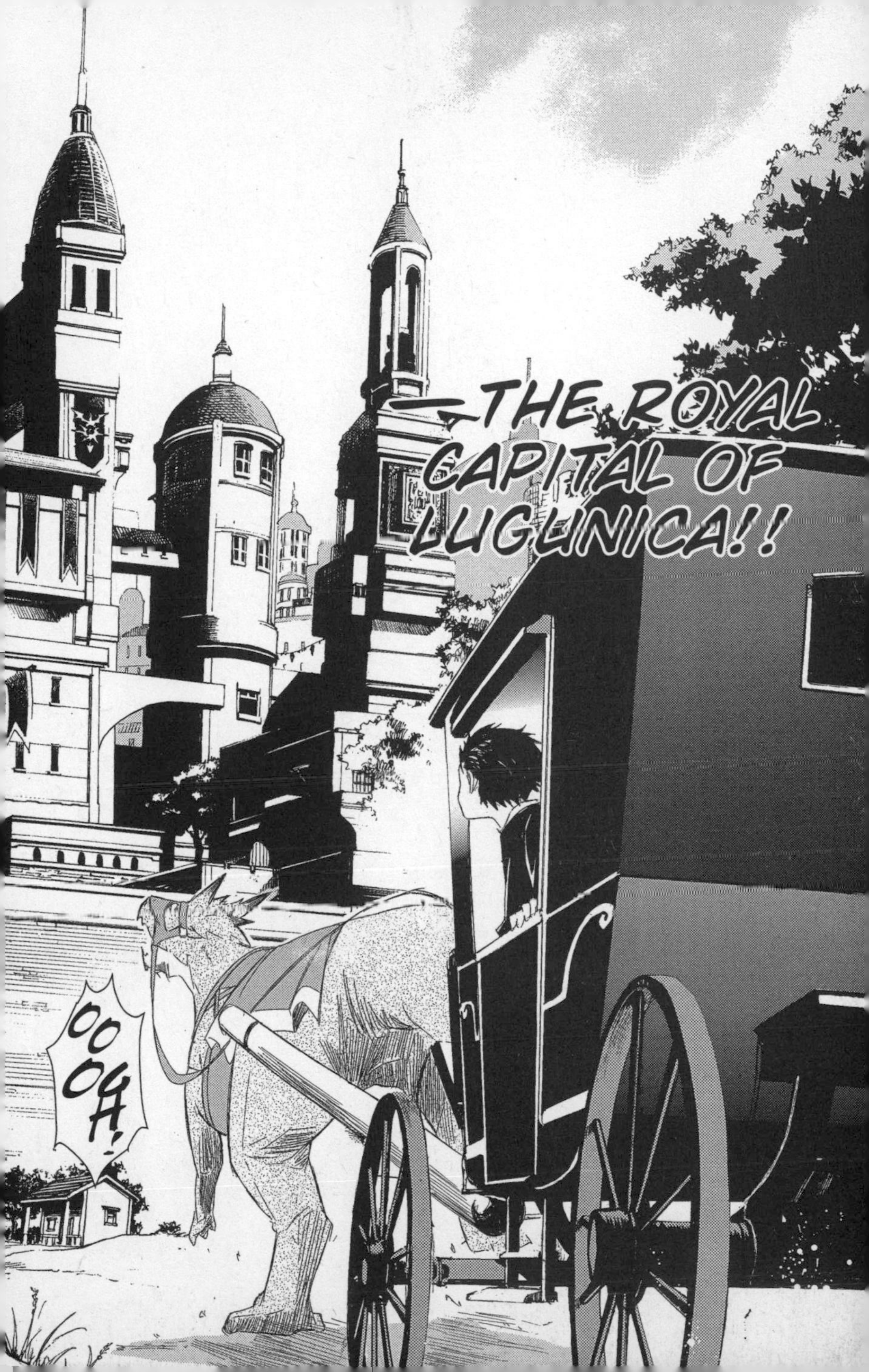
—THE ROYAL CAPITAL OF LUGUNICA!!
OOOOH!

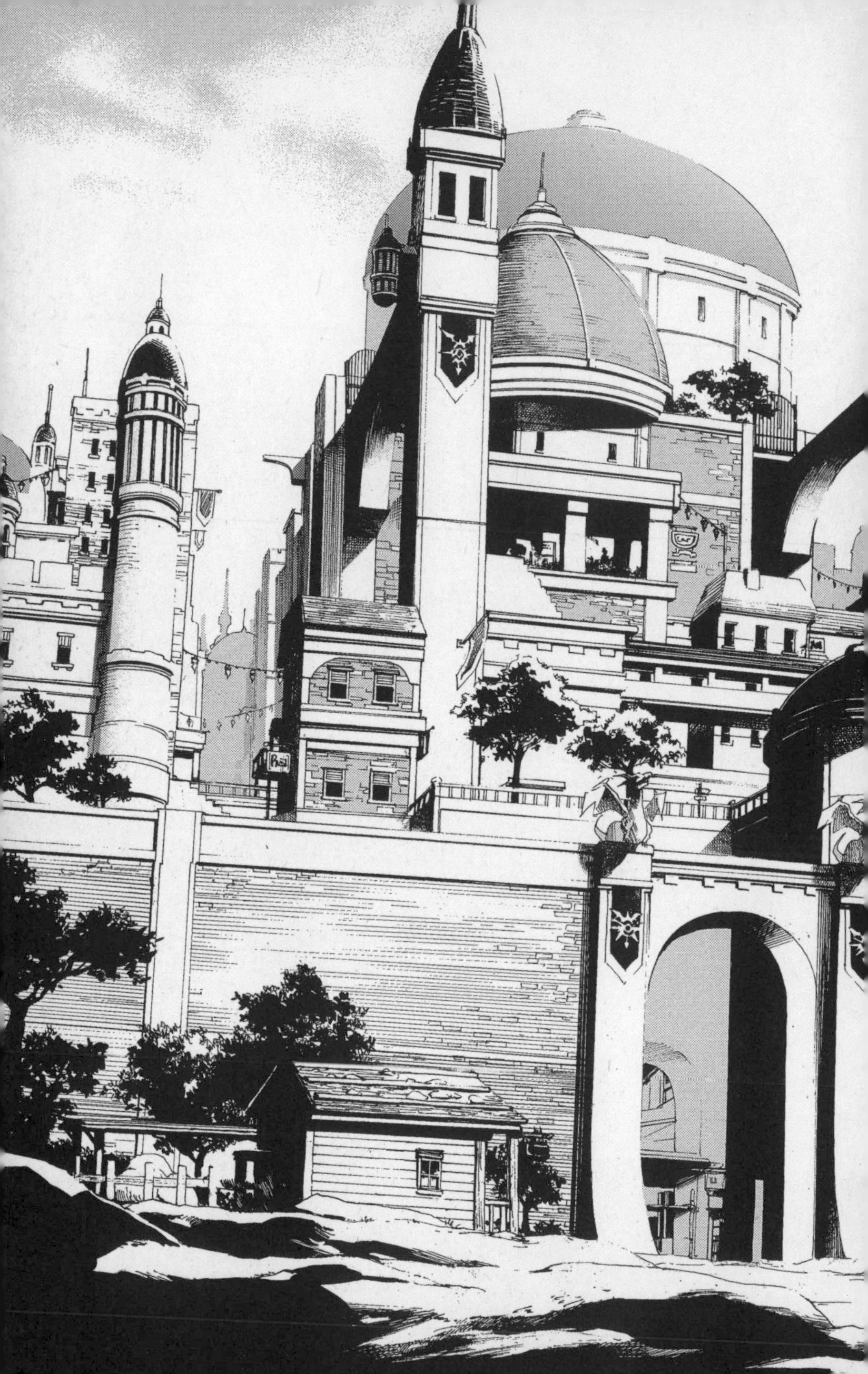

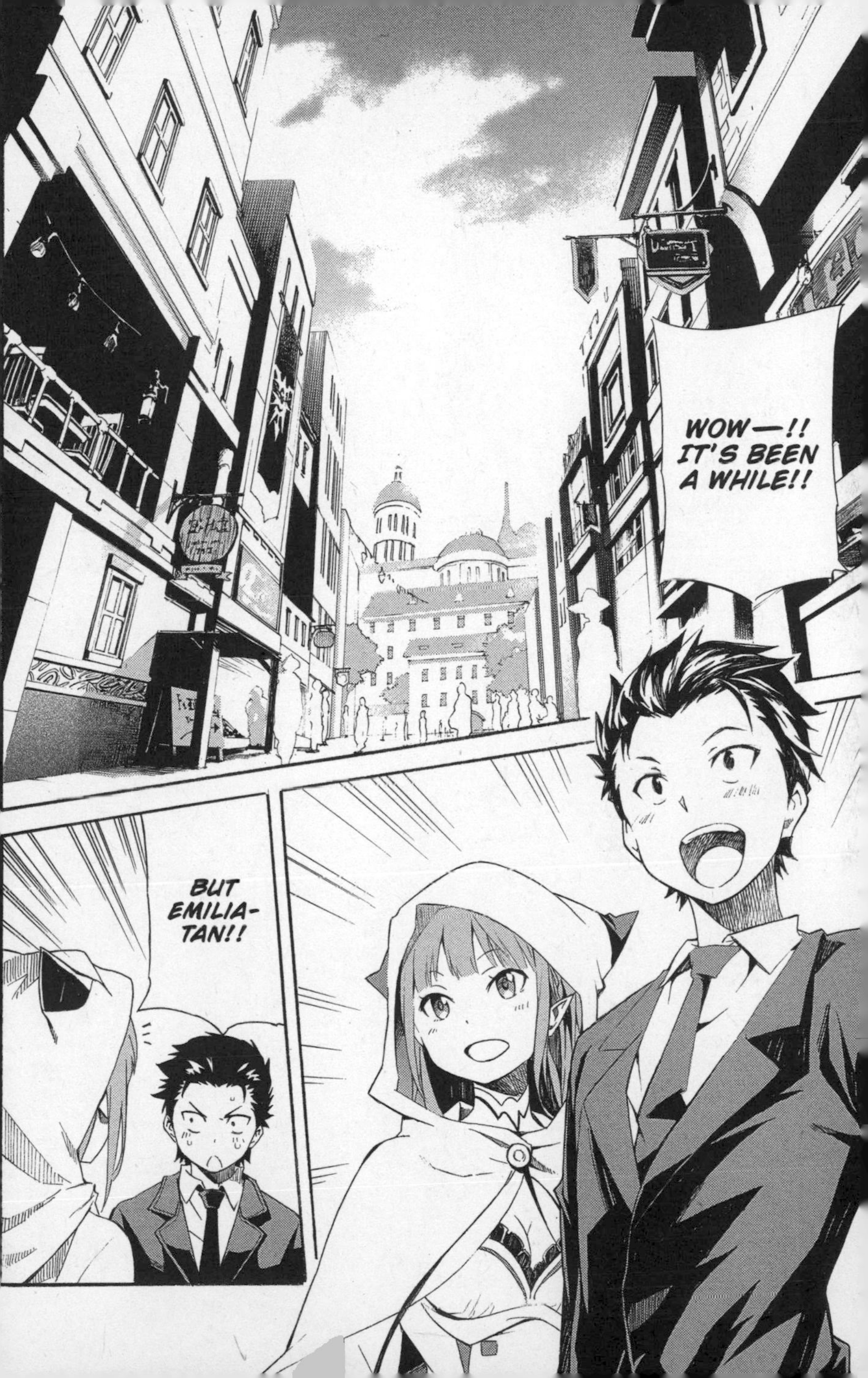
WOW—!! IT'S BEEN A WHILE!!
BUT EMILIA-TAN!!

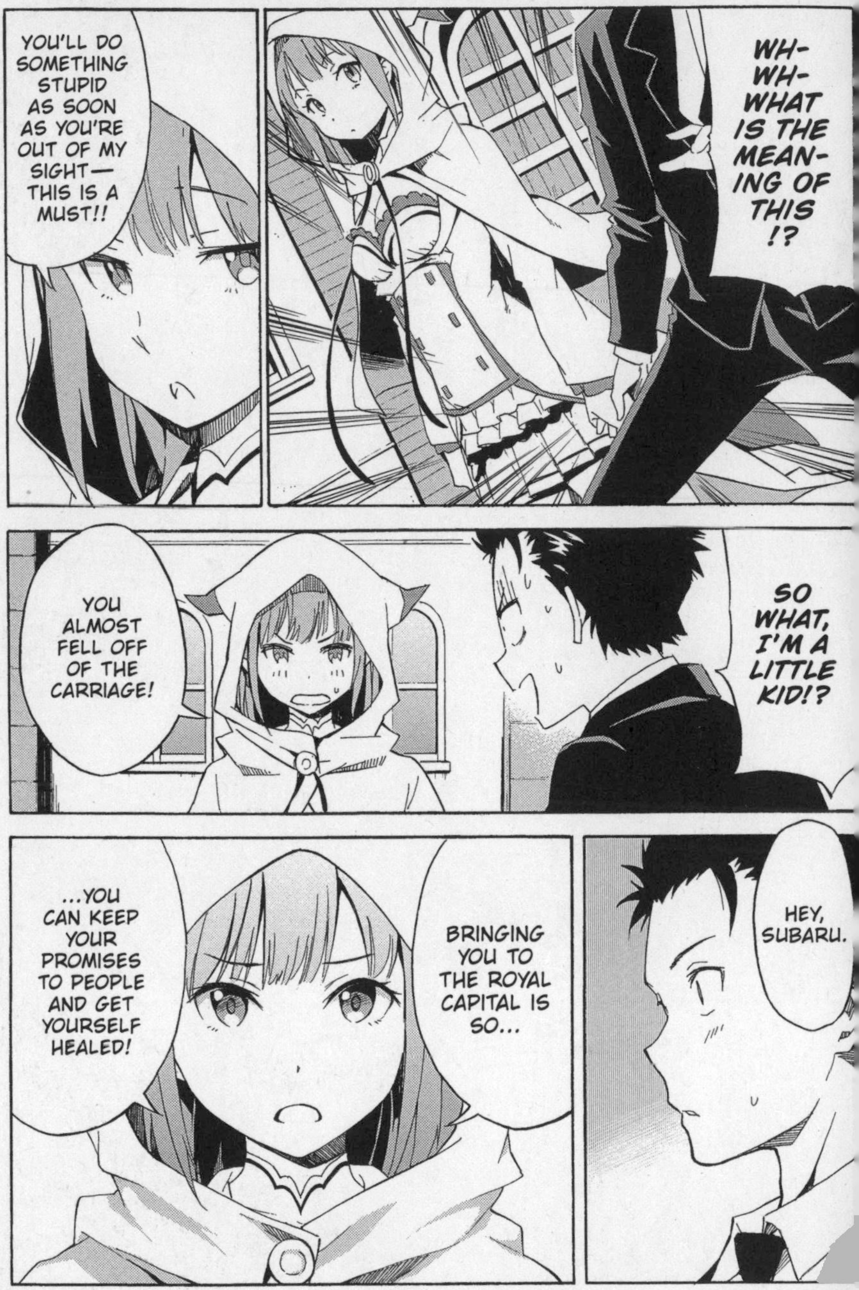
WH-WH-WHAT IS THE MEANING OF THIS!?
YOU'LL DO SOMETHING STUPID AS SOON AS YOU'RE OUT OF MY SIGHT—THIS IS A MUST!!
SO WHAT, I'M A LITTLE KID!?
YOU ALMOST FELL OFF OF THE CARRIAGE!
HEY, SUBARU.
BRINGING YOU TO THE ROYAL CAPITAL IS SO...
...YOU CAN KEEP YOUR PROMISES TO PEOPLE AND GET YOURSELF HEALED!

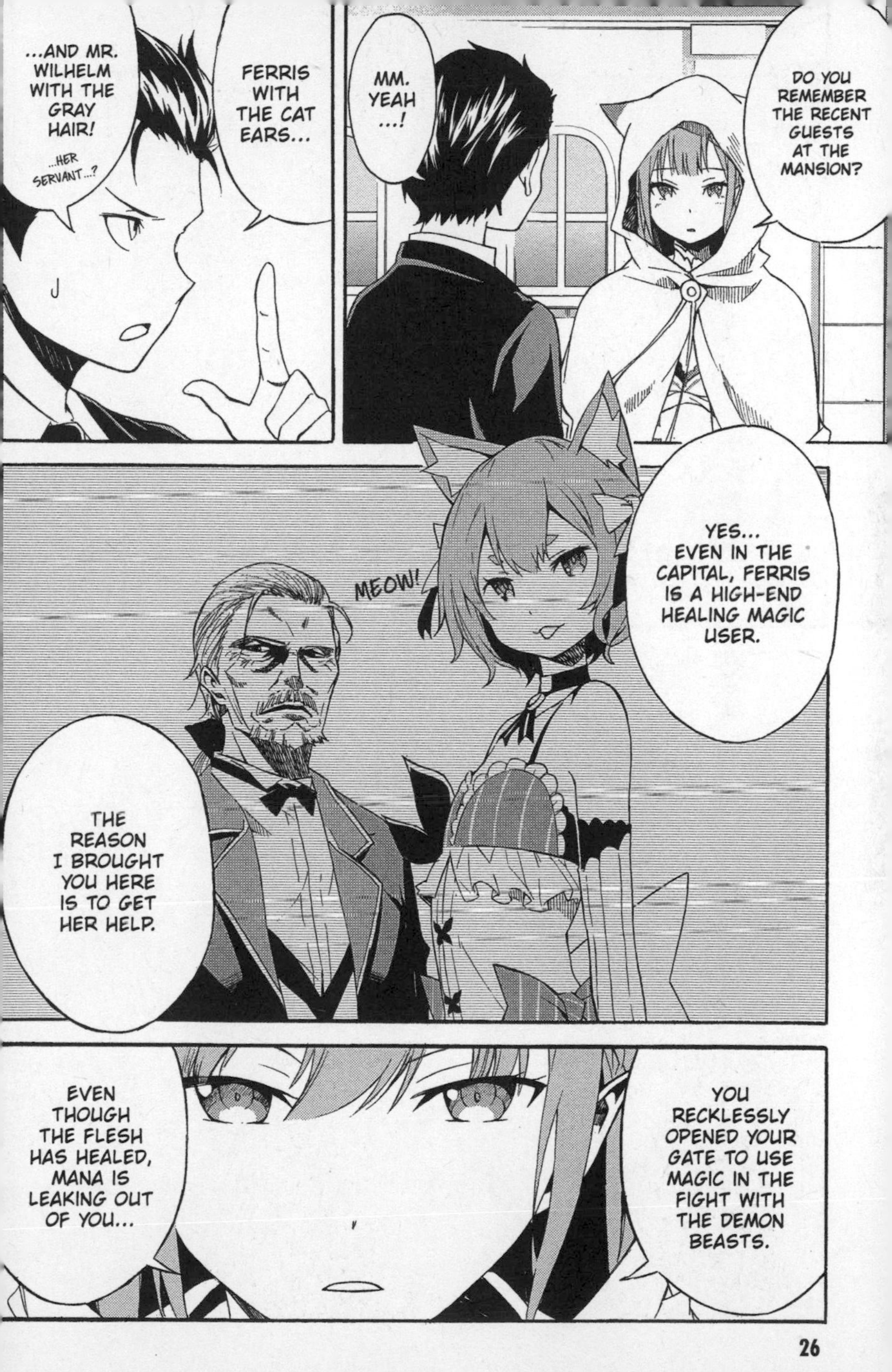
DO YOU REMEMBER THE RECENT GUESTS AT THE MANSION?
MM. YEAH ...!
FERRIS WITH THE CAT EARS...
...AND MR. WILHELM WITH THE GRAY HAIR!
...HER SERVANT...?
YES... EVEN IN THE CAPITAL, FERRIS IS A HIGH-END HEALING MAGIC USER.
MEOW!
THE REASON I BROUGHT YOU HERE IS TO GET HER HELP.
YOU RECKLESSLY OPENED YOUR GATE TO USE MAGIC IN THE FIGHT WITH THE DEMON BEASTS.
EVEN THOUGH THE FLESH HAS HEALED, MANA IS LEAKING OUT OF YOU...

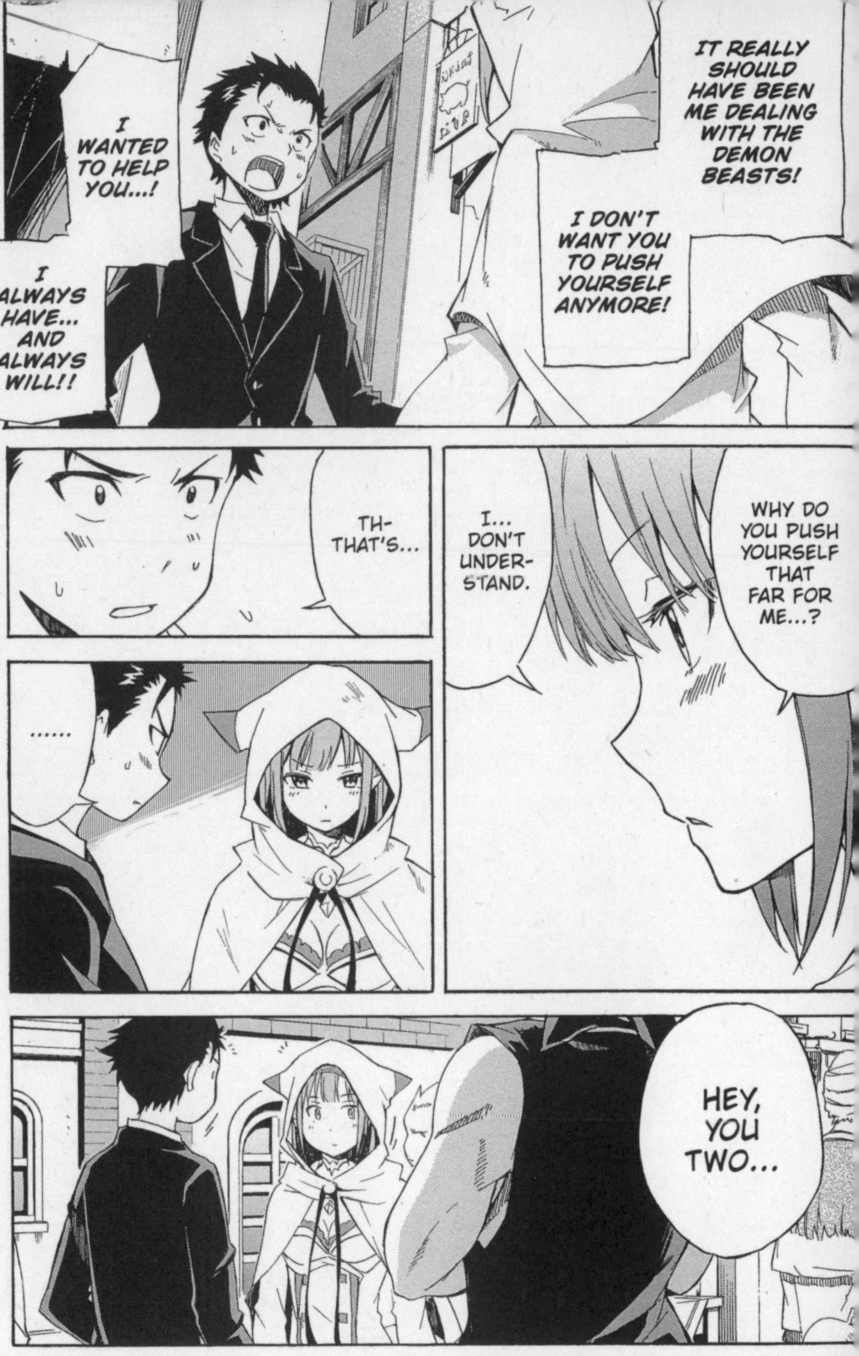
IT REALLY SHOULD HAVE BEEN ME DEALING WITH THE DEMON BEASTS!
I DON'T WANT YOU TO PUSH YOURSELF ANYMORE!
I WANTED TO HELP YOU...!
I ALWAYS HAVE... AND ALWAYS WILL!!
WHY DO YOU PUSH YOURSELF THAT FAR FOR ME...?
I... DON'T UNDER-STAND.
TH-THAT'S...
......
HEY, YOU TWO...

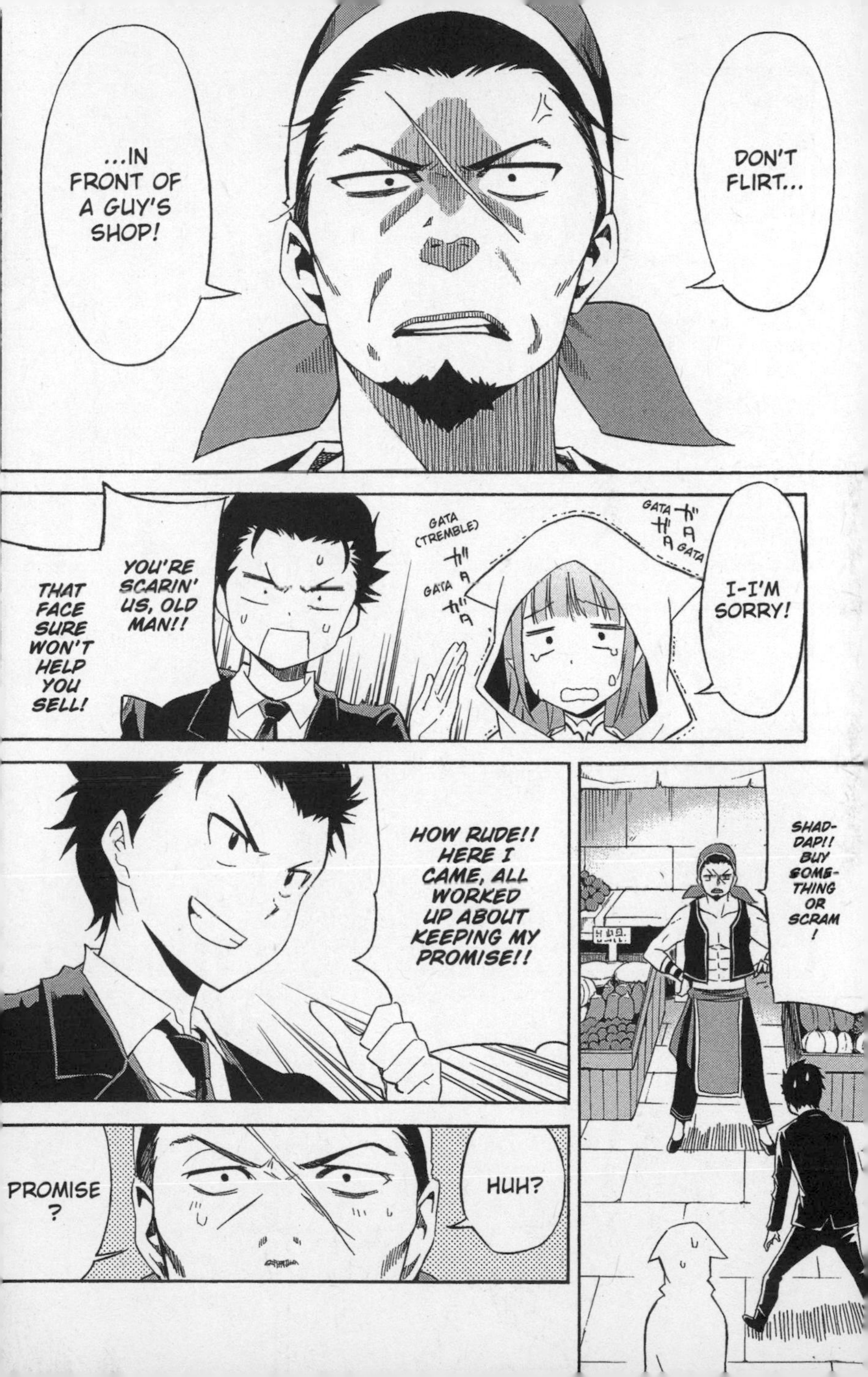
DON'T FLIRT...
...IN FRONT OF A GUY'S SHOP!
I-I'M SORRY!
GATA GATA
GATA (TREMBLE)
GATA
YOU'RE SCARIN' US, OLD MAN!!
THAT FACE SURE WON'T HELP YOU SELL!
SHADDAP!! BUY SOMETHING OR SCRAM!
HOW RUDE!! HERE I CAME, ALL WORKED UP ABOUT KEEPING MY PROMISE!!
HUH?
PROMISE?

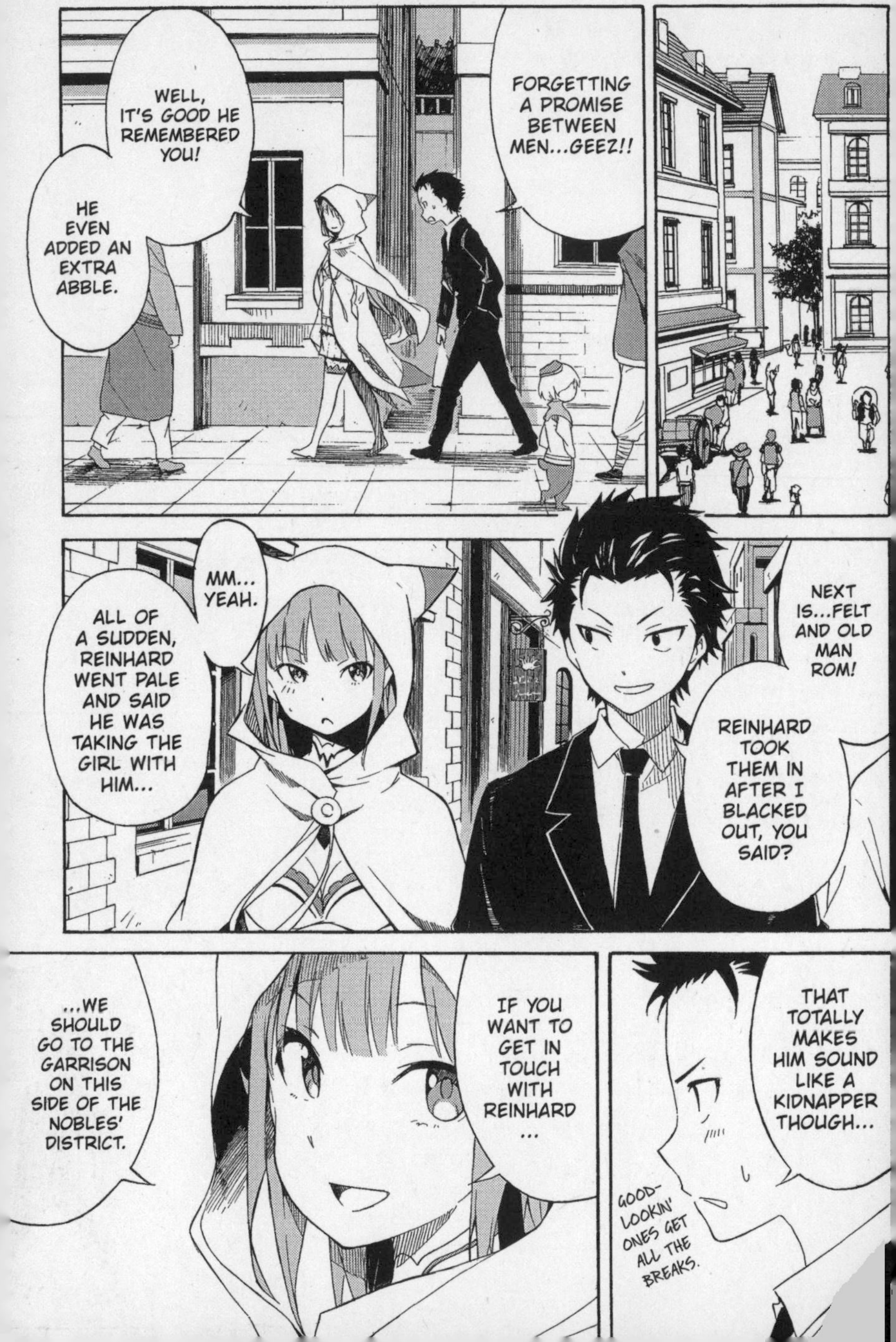
FORGETTING A PROMISE BETWEEN MEN...GEEZ!!
WELL, IT'S GOOD HE REMEMBERED YOU!
HE EVEN ADDED AN EXTRA ABBLE.
NEXT IS...FELT AND OLD MAN ROM!
REINHARD TOOK THEM IN AFTER I BLACKED OUT, YOU SAID?
MM... YEAH.
ALL OF A SUDDEN, REINHARD WENT PALE AND SAID HE WAS TAKING THE GIRL WITH HIM...
THAT TOTALLY MAKES HIM SOUND LIKE A KIDNAPPER THOUGH...
GOOD-LOOKIN' ONES GET ALL THE BREAKS.
IF YOU WANT TO GET IN TOUCH WITH REINHARD...
...WE SHOULD GO TO THE GARRISON ON THIS SIDE OF THE NOBLES' DISTRICT.

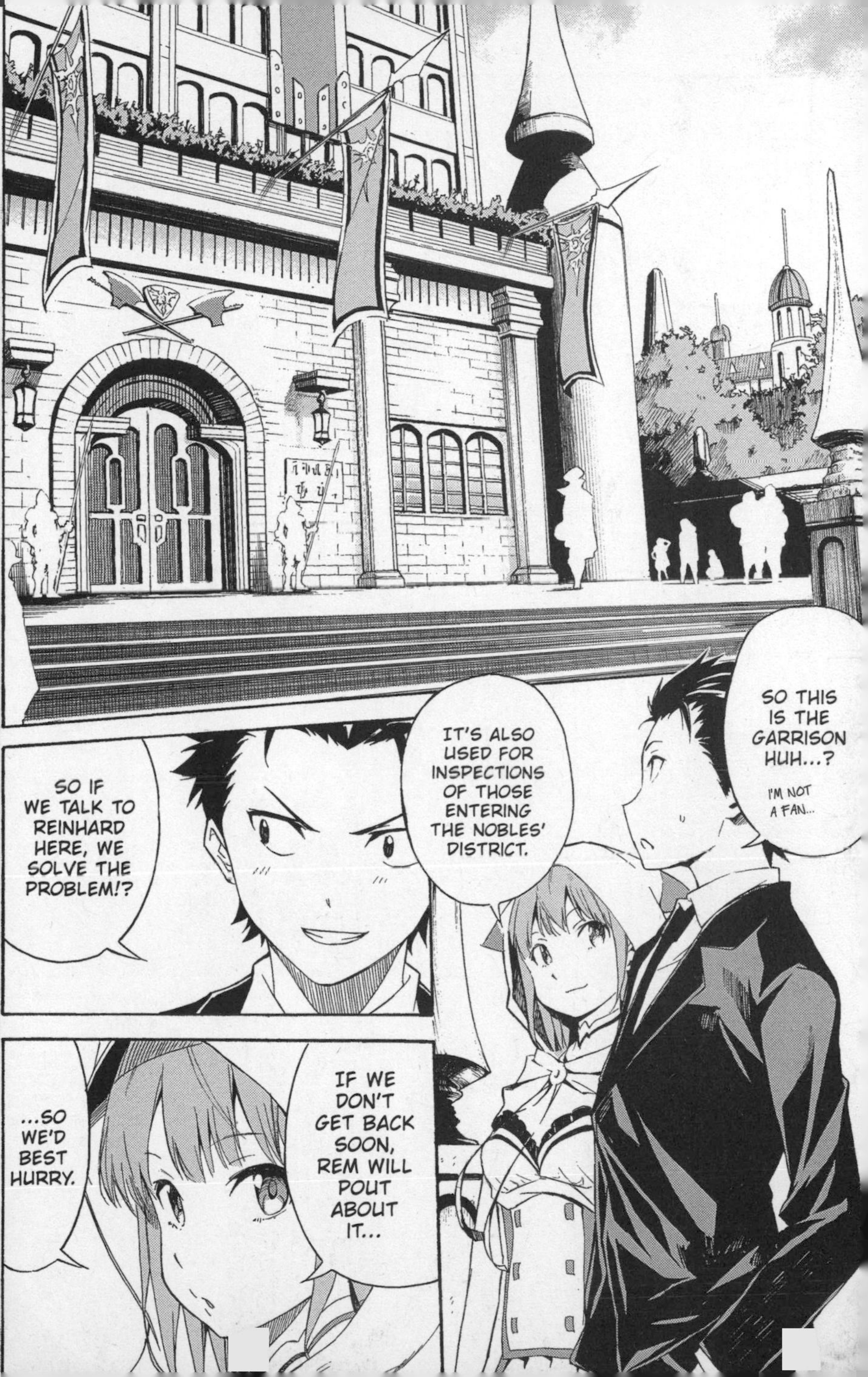
SO THIS IS THE GARRISON HUH...?
I'M NOT A FAN...
IT'S ALSO USED FOR INSPECTIONS OF THOSE ENTERING THE NOBLES' DISTRICT.
SO IF WE TALK TO REINHARD HERE, WE SOLVE THE PROBLEM!?
IF WE DON'T GET BACK SOON, REM WILL POUT ABOUT IT...
...SO WE'D BEST HURRY.

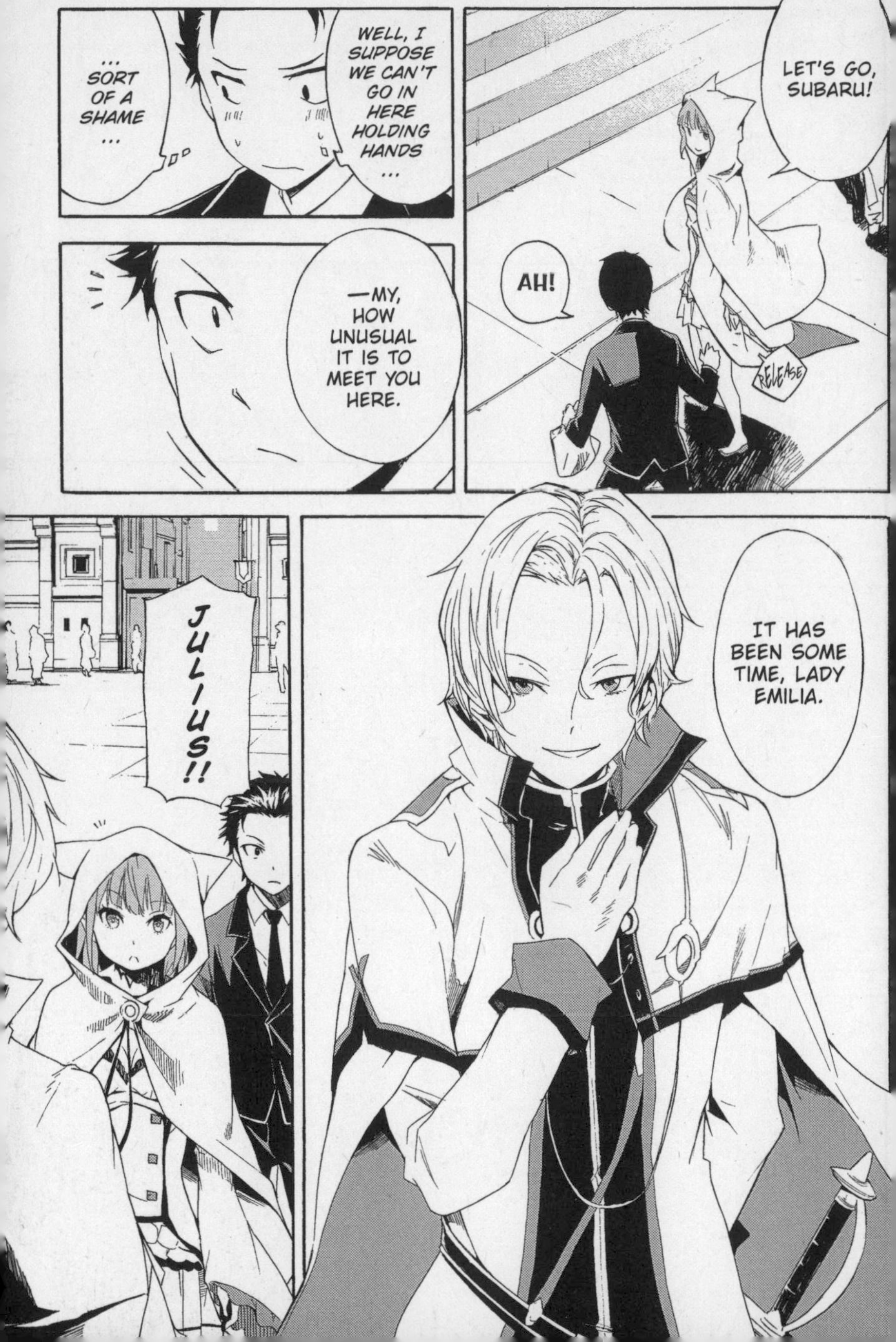
LET'S GO, SUBARU!
AH!
RELEASE
WELL, I SUPPOSE WE CAN'T GO IN HERE HOLDING HANDS ...
... SORT OF A SHAME ...
—MY, HOW UNUSUAL IT IS TO MEET YOU HERE.
IT HAS BEEN SOME TIME, LADY EMILIA.
JULIUS!!

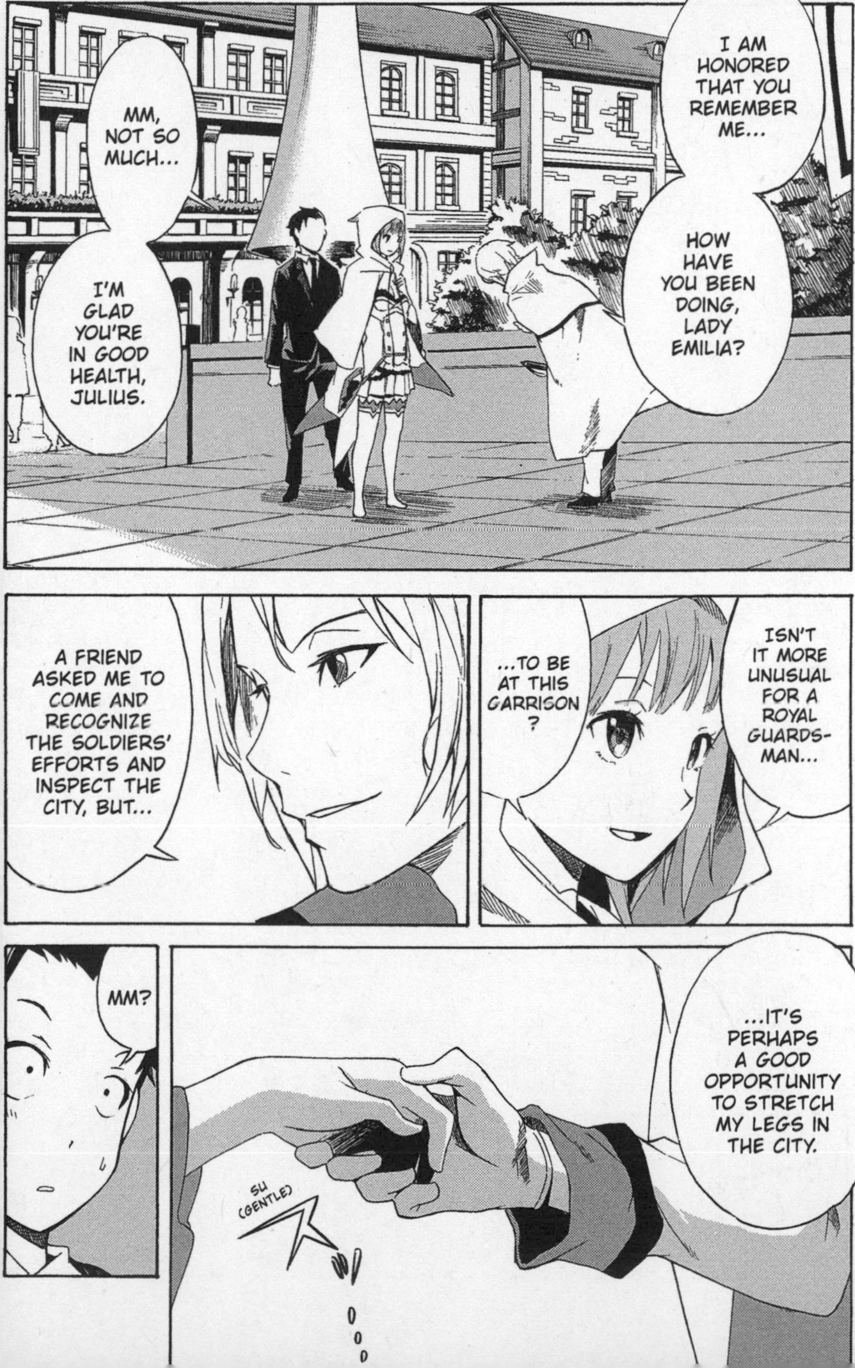
I AM HONORED THAT YOU REMEMBER ME...
HOW HAVE YOU BEEN DOING, LADY EMILIA?
MM, NOT SO MUCH...
I'M GLAD YOU'RE IN GOOD HEALTH, JULIUS.
ISN'T IT MORE UNUSUAL FOR A ROYAL GUARDSMAN...
...TO BE AT THIS GARRISON?
A FRIEND ASKED ME TO COME AND RECOGNIZE THE SOLDIERS' EFFORTS AND INSPECT THE CITY, BUT...
...IT'S PERHAPS A GOOD OPPORTUNITY TO STRETCH MY LEGS IN THE CITY.
SU (GENTLE)
MM?

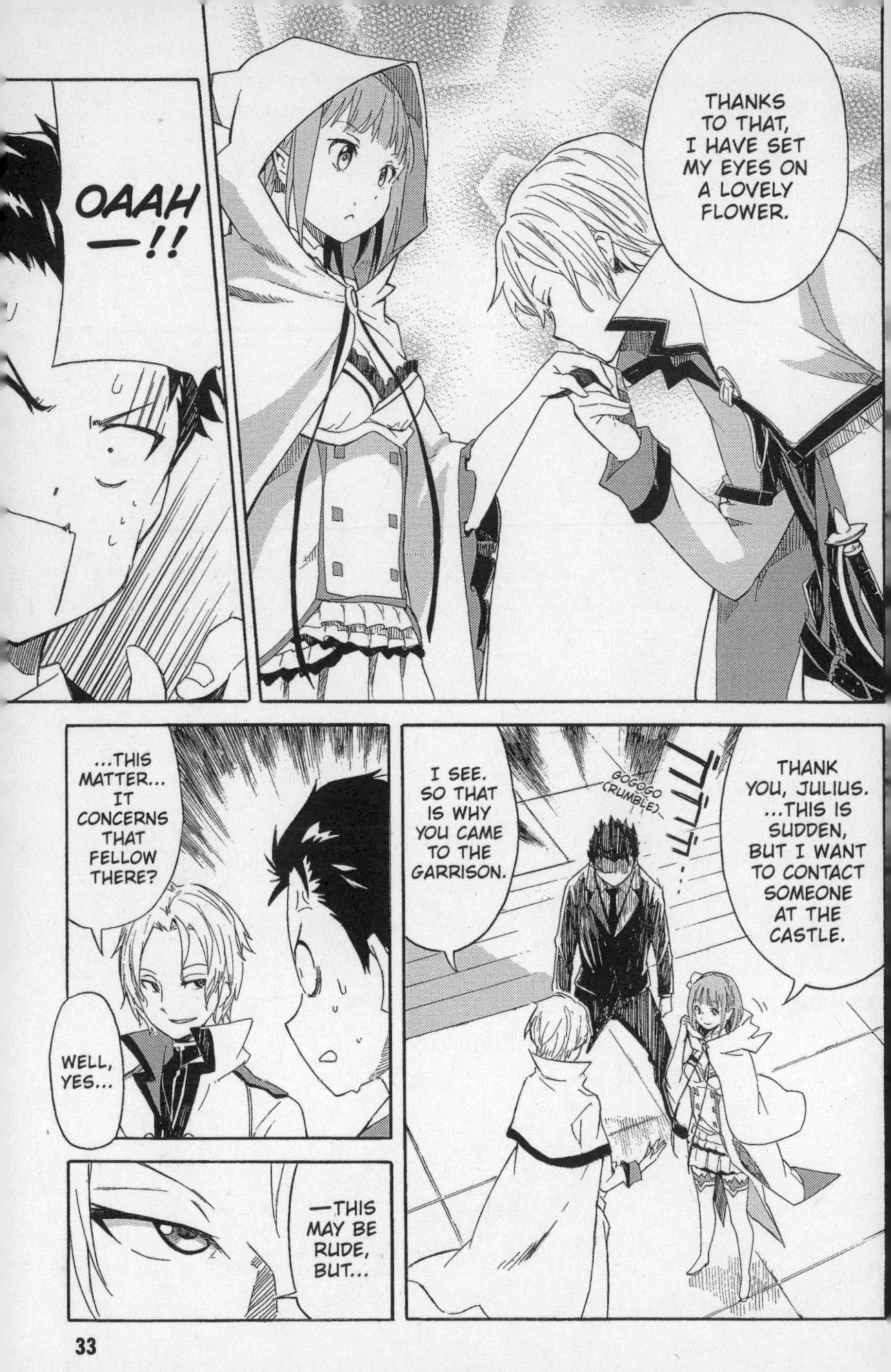
THANKS TO THAT, I HAVE SET MY EYES ON A LOVELY FLOWER.
OAAH—!!
THANK YOU, JULIUS. ...THIS IS SUDDEN, BUT I WANT TO CONTACT SOMEONE AT THE CASTLE.
GOGOGO (RUMBLE)
I SEE. SO THAT IS WHY YOU CAME TO THE GARRISON.
...THIS MATTER... IT CONCERNS THAT FELLOW THERE?
WELL, YES...
—THIS MAY BE RUDE, BUT...

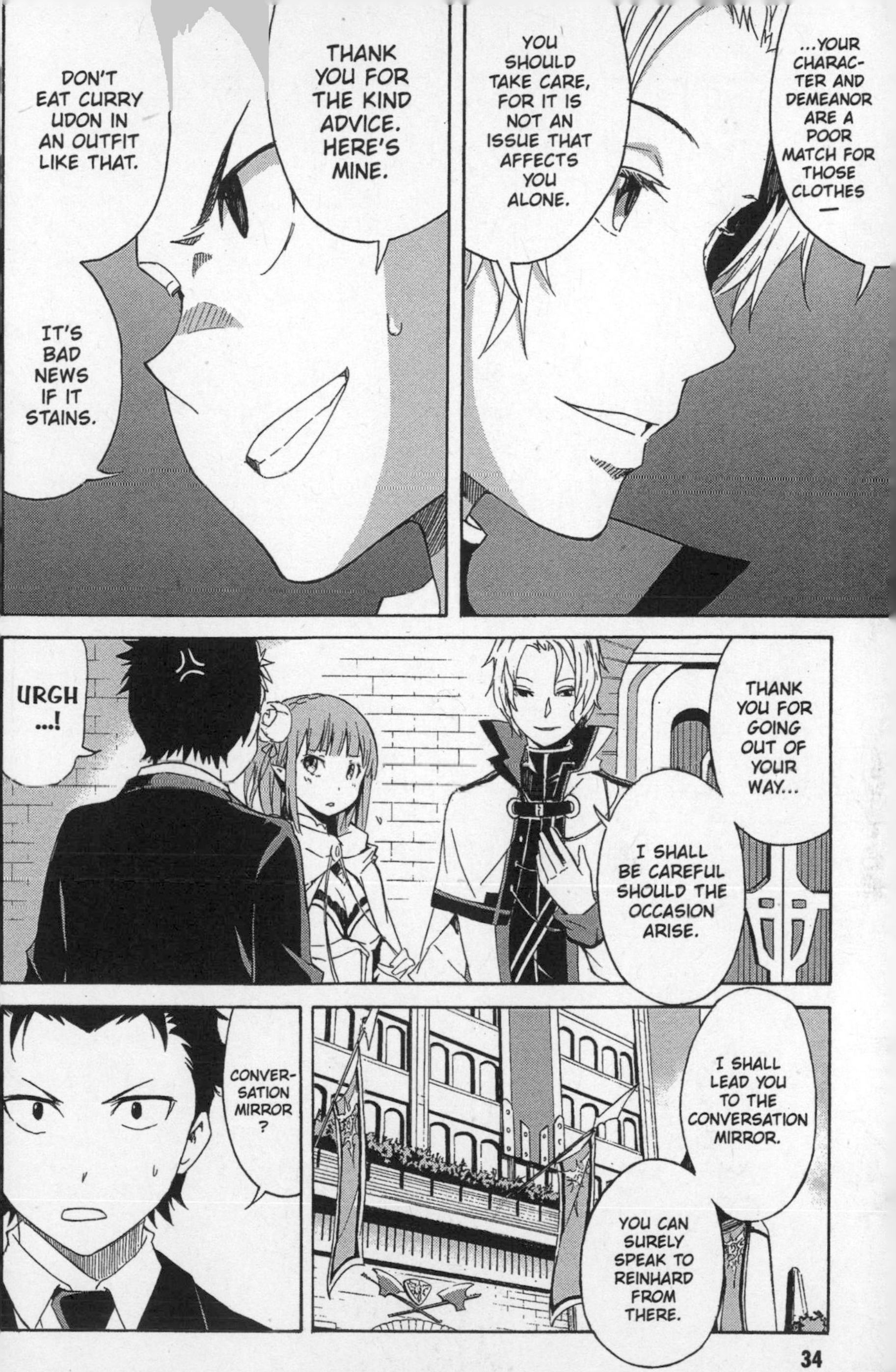
...YOUR CHARACTER AND DEMEANOR ARE A POOR MATCH FOR THOSE CLOTHES—
YOU SHOULD TAKE CARE, FOR IT IS NOT AN ISSUE THAT AFFECTS YOU ALONE.
THANK YOU FOR THE KIND ADVICE. HERE'S MINE.
DON'T EAT CURRY UDON IN AN OUTFIT LIKE THAT.
IT'S BAD NEWS IF IT STAINS.
THANK YOU FOR GOING OUT OF YOUR WAY...
I SHALL BE CAREFUL SHOULD THE OCCASION ARISE.
URGH ...!
I SHALL LEAD YOU TO THE CONVERSATION MIRROR.
YOU CAN SURELY SPEAK TO REINHARD FROM THERE.
CONVERSATION MIRROR?

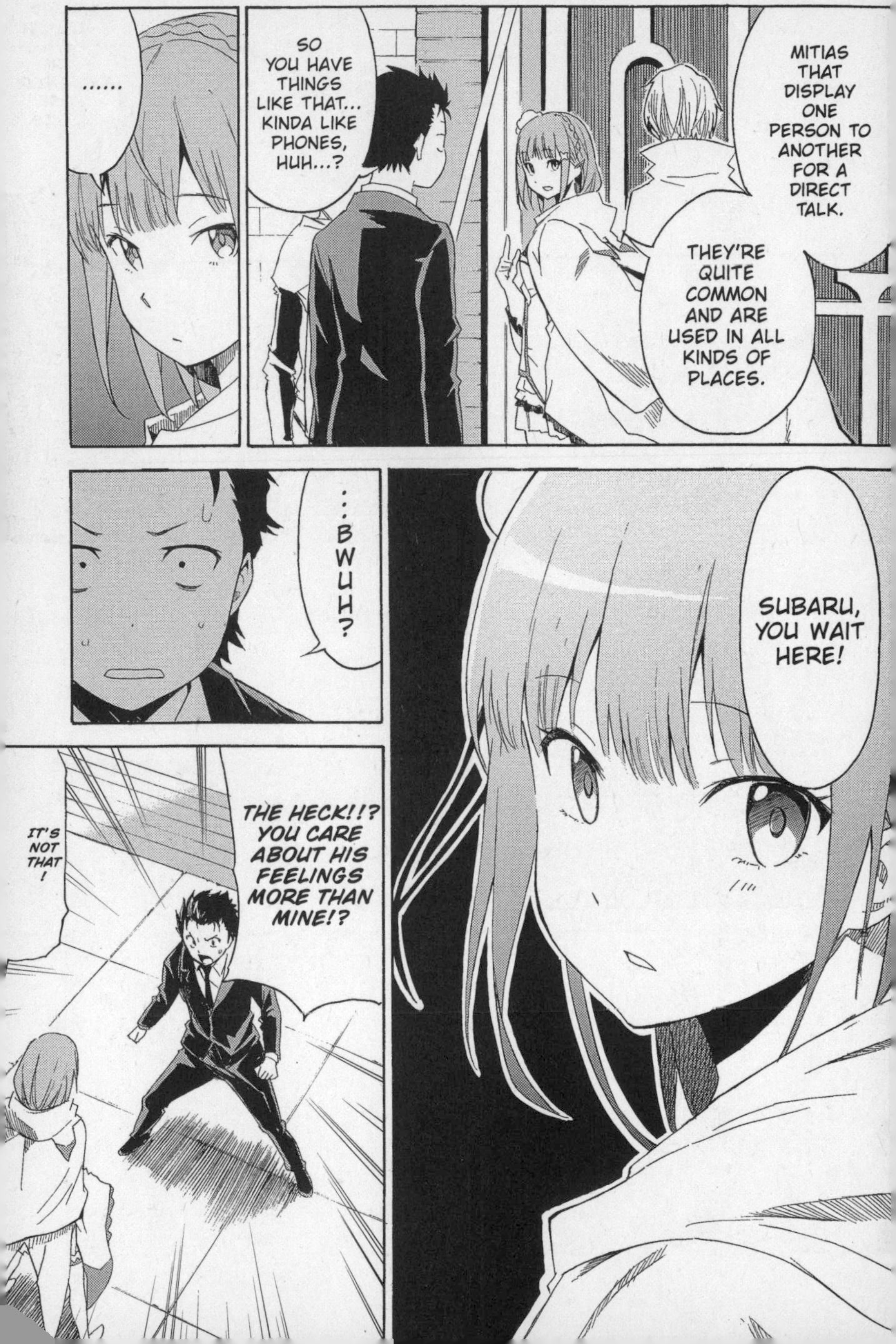
MITIAS THAT DISPLAY ONE PERSON TO ANOTHER FOR A DIRECT TALK.
THEY'RE QUITE COMMON AND ARE USED IN ALL KINDS OF PLACES.
SO YOU HAVE THINGS LIKE THAT... KINDA LIKE PHONES, HUH...?
......
SUBARU, YOU WAIT HERE!
...BWUH?
THE HECK!!? YOU CARE ABOUT HIS FEELINGS MORE THAN MINE!?
IT'S NOT THAT!

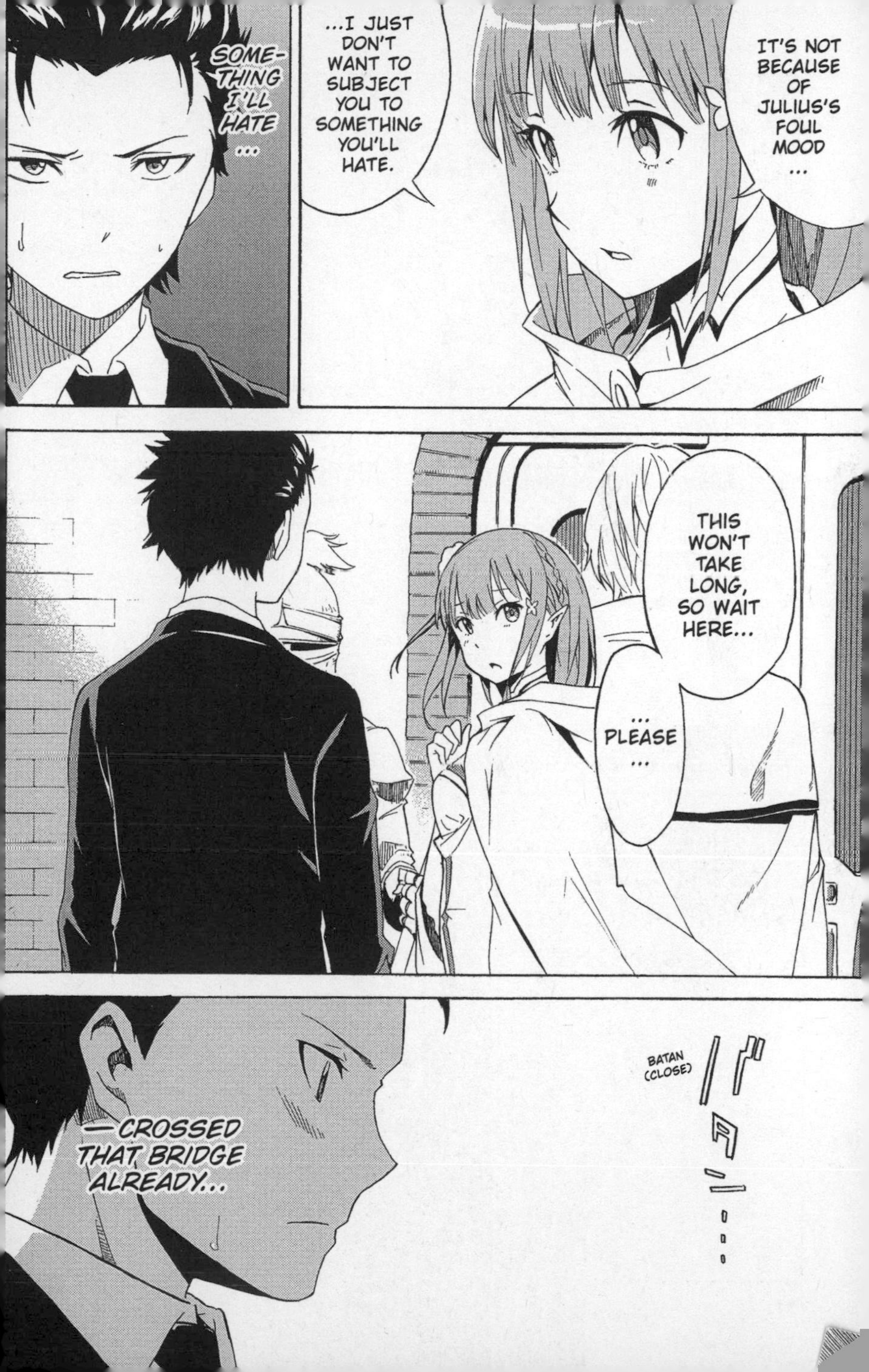
IT'S NOT BECAUSE OF JULIUS'S FOUL MOOD ...
...I JUST DON'T WANT TO SUBJECT YOU TO SOMETHING YOU'LL HATE.
SOME-THING I'LL HATE ...
THIS WON'T TAKE LONG, SO WAIT HERE...
...PLEASE...
BATAN (CLOSE)
—CROSSED THAT BRIDGE ALREADY...

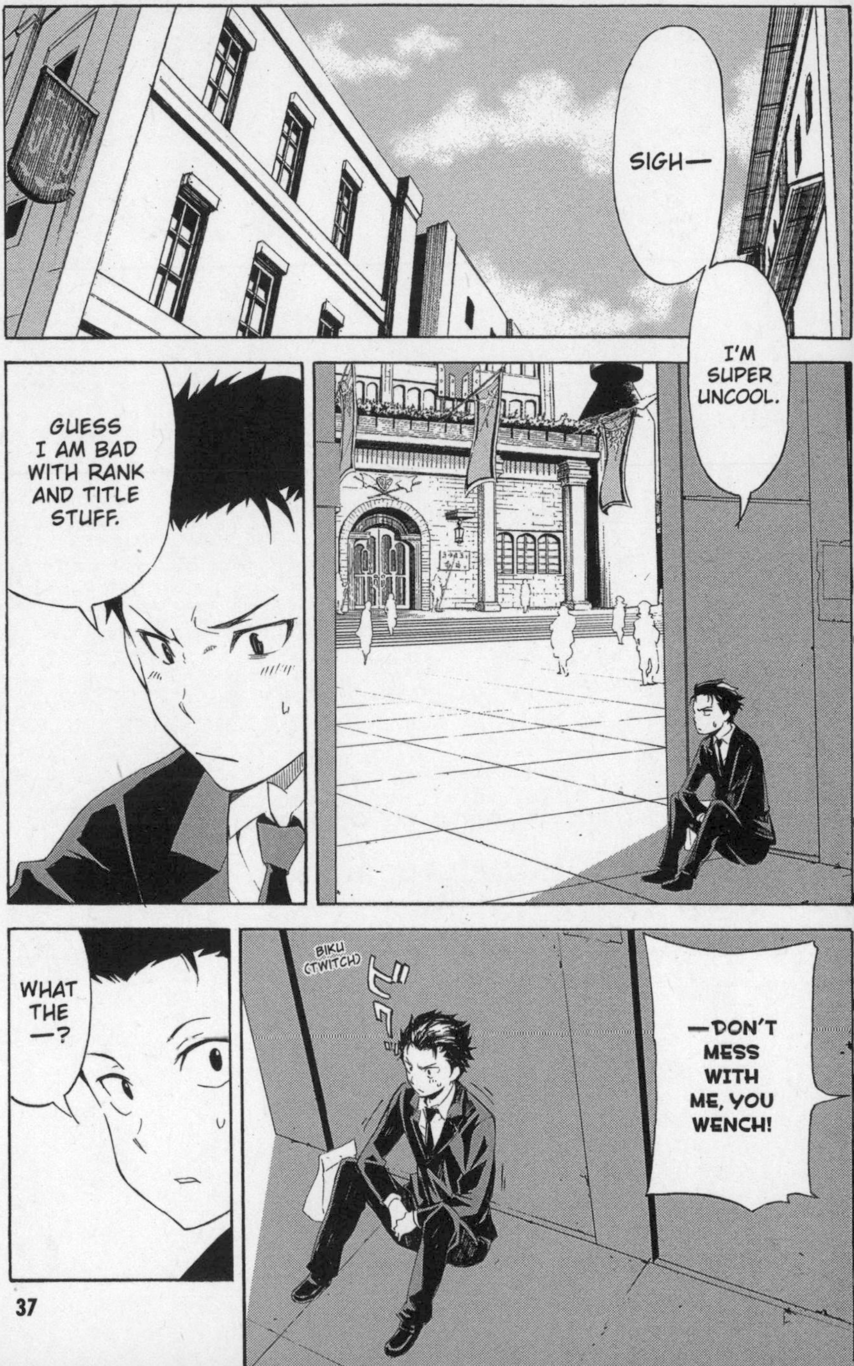
SIGH—
I'M SUPER UNCOOL.
GUESS I AM BAD WITH RANK AND TITLE STUFF.
—DON'T MESS WITH ME, YOU WENCH!
BIKU (TWITCH)
WHAT THE—?

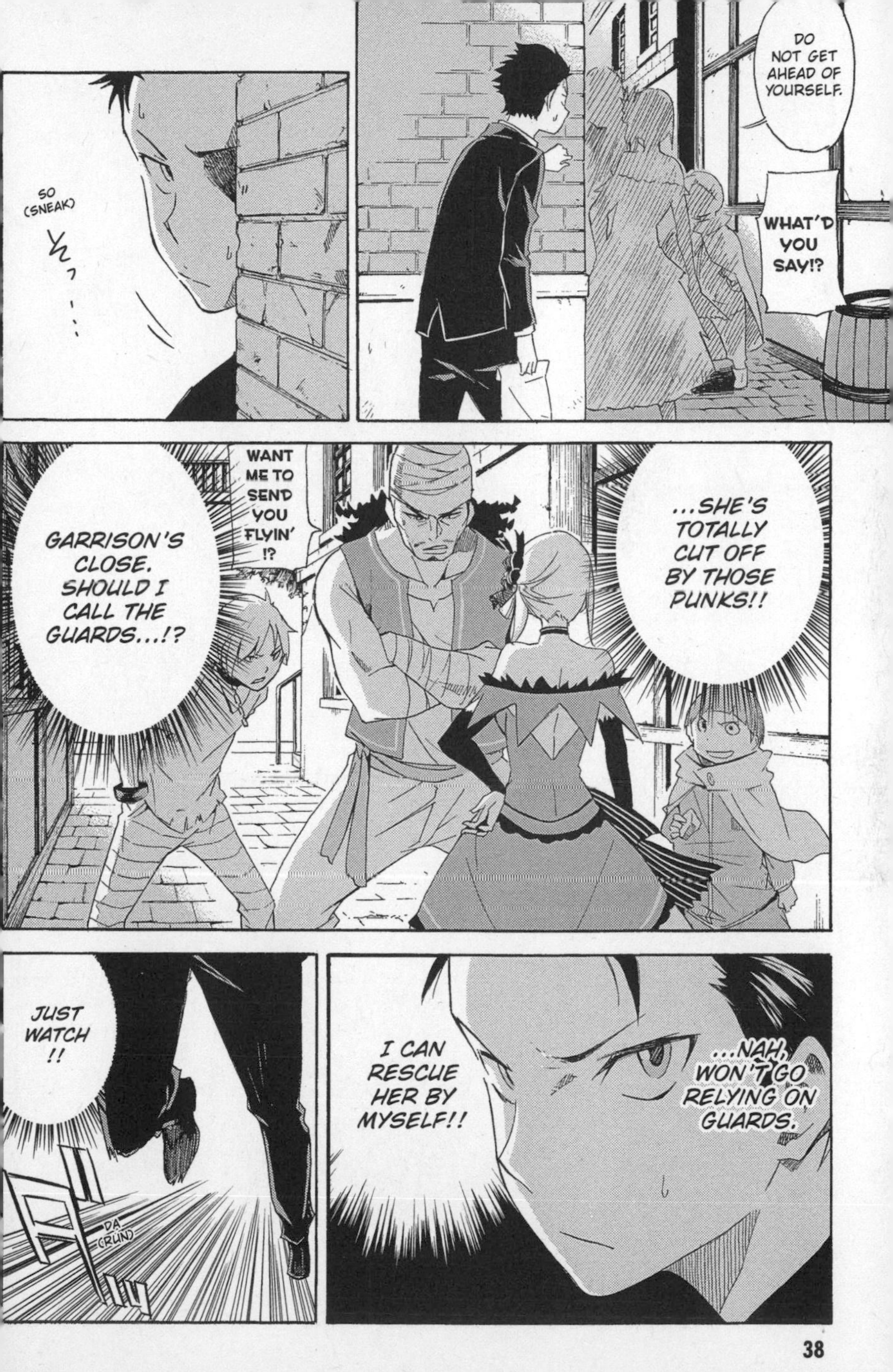
DO NOT GET AHEAD OF YOURSELF.
WHAT'D YOU SAY!?
SO (SNEAK)
...SHE'S TOTALLY CUT OFF BY THOSE PUNKS!!
WANT ME TO SEND YOU FLYIN'!?
GARRISON'S CLOSE. SHOULD I CALL THE GUARDS...!?
...NAH, WON'T GO RELYING ON GUARDS.
I CAN RESCUE HER BY MYSELF!!
JUST WATCH!!
DA (RUN)

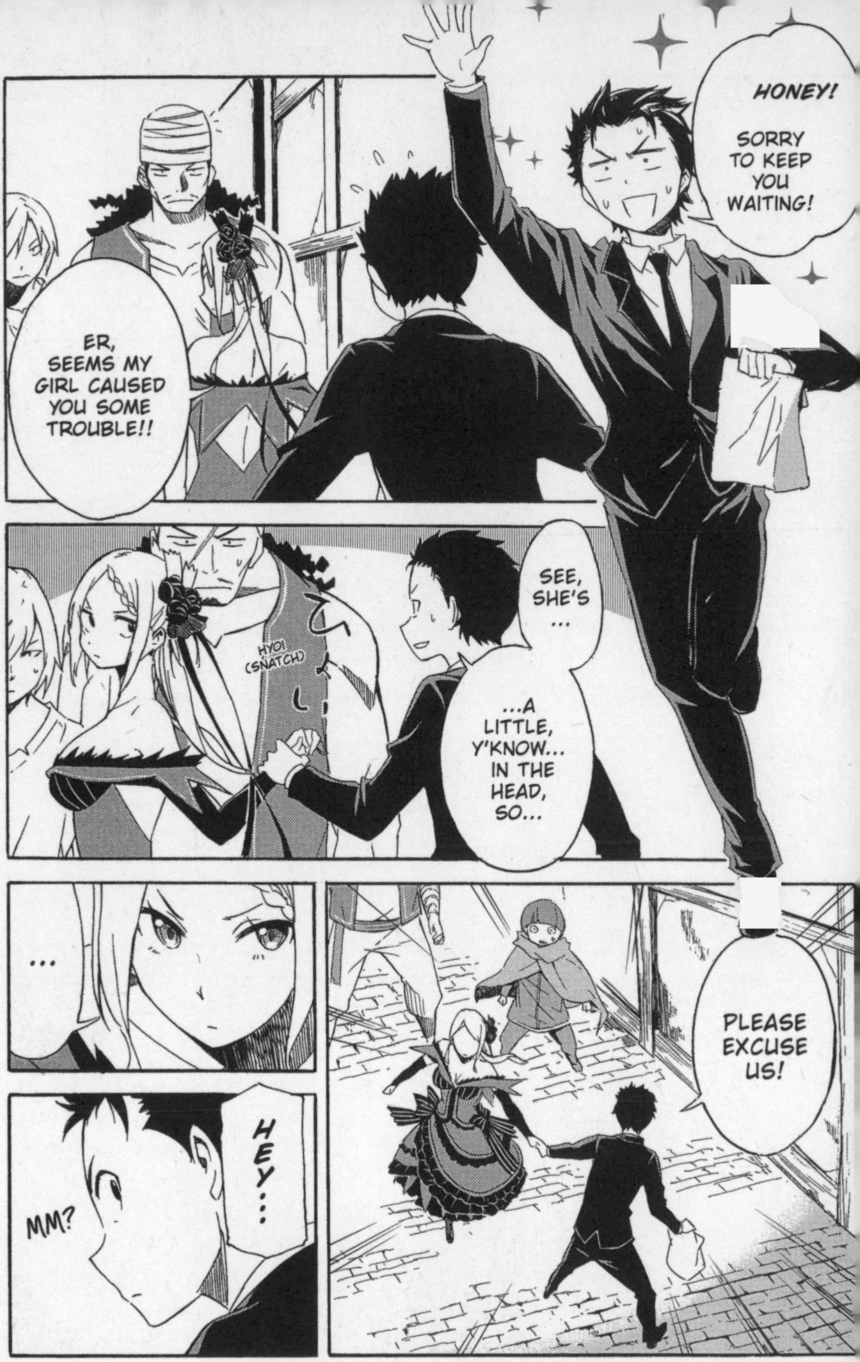
HONEY!
SORRY TO KEEP YOU WAITING!
ER, SEEMS MY GIRL CAUSED YOU SOME TROUBLE!!
SEE, SHE'S ...
...A LITTLE, Y'KNOW... IN THE HEAD, SO...
HYOI (SNATCH)
PLEASE EXCUSE US!
...
HEY...
MM?

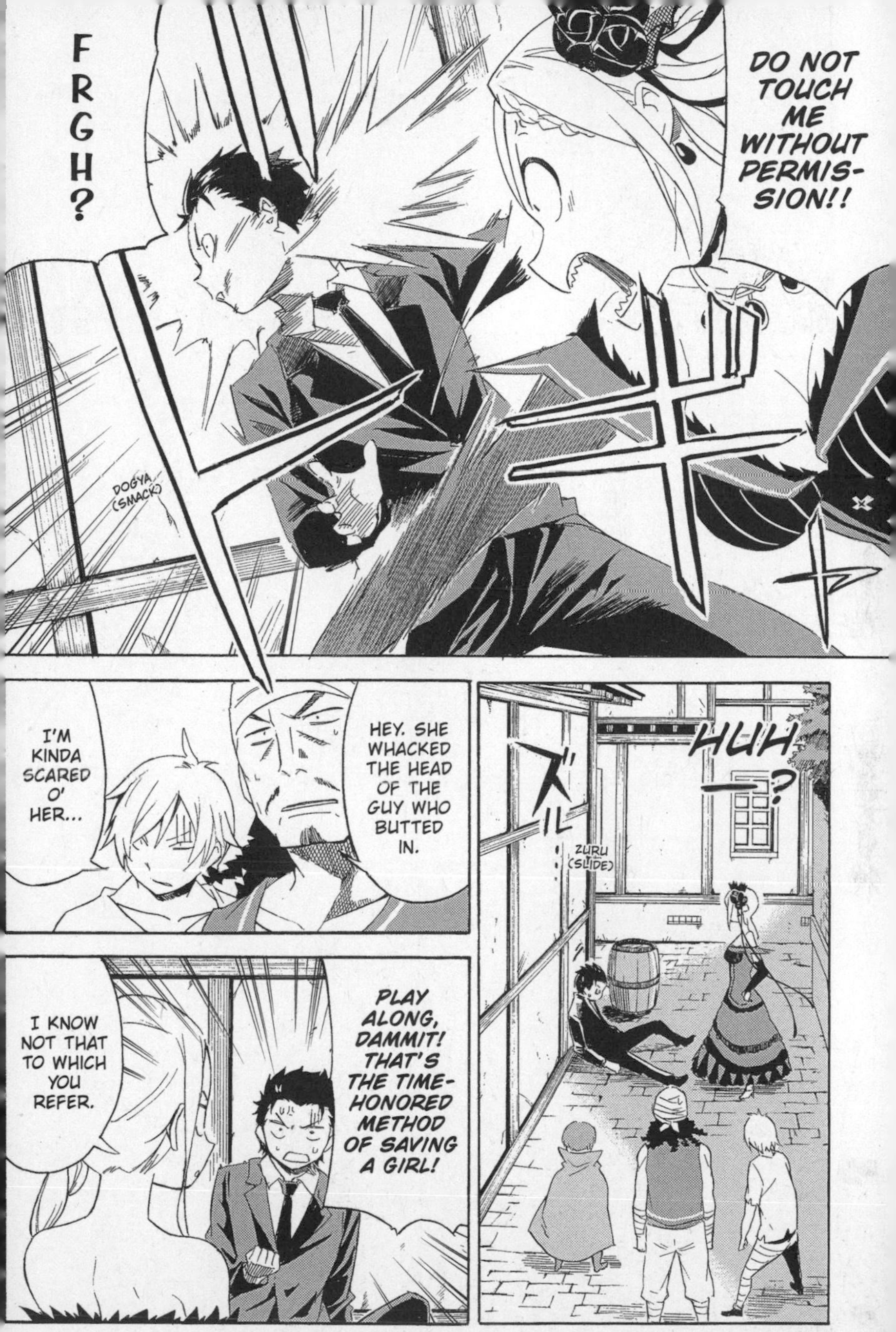
DO NOT TOUCH ME WITHOUT PERMIS-SION!!
FRGH?
DOGYA (SMACK)
HUH—?
ズル
ZURU (SLIDE)
HEY. SHE WHACKED THE HEAD OF THE GUY WHO BUTTED IN.
I'M KINDA SCARED O' HER...
PLAY ALONG, DAMMIT! THAT'S THE TIME-HONORED METHOD OF SAVING A GIRL!
I KNOW NOT THAT TO WHICH YOU REFER.

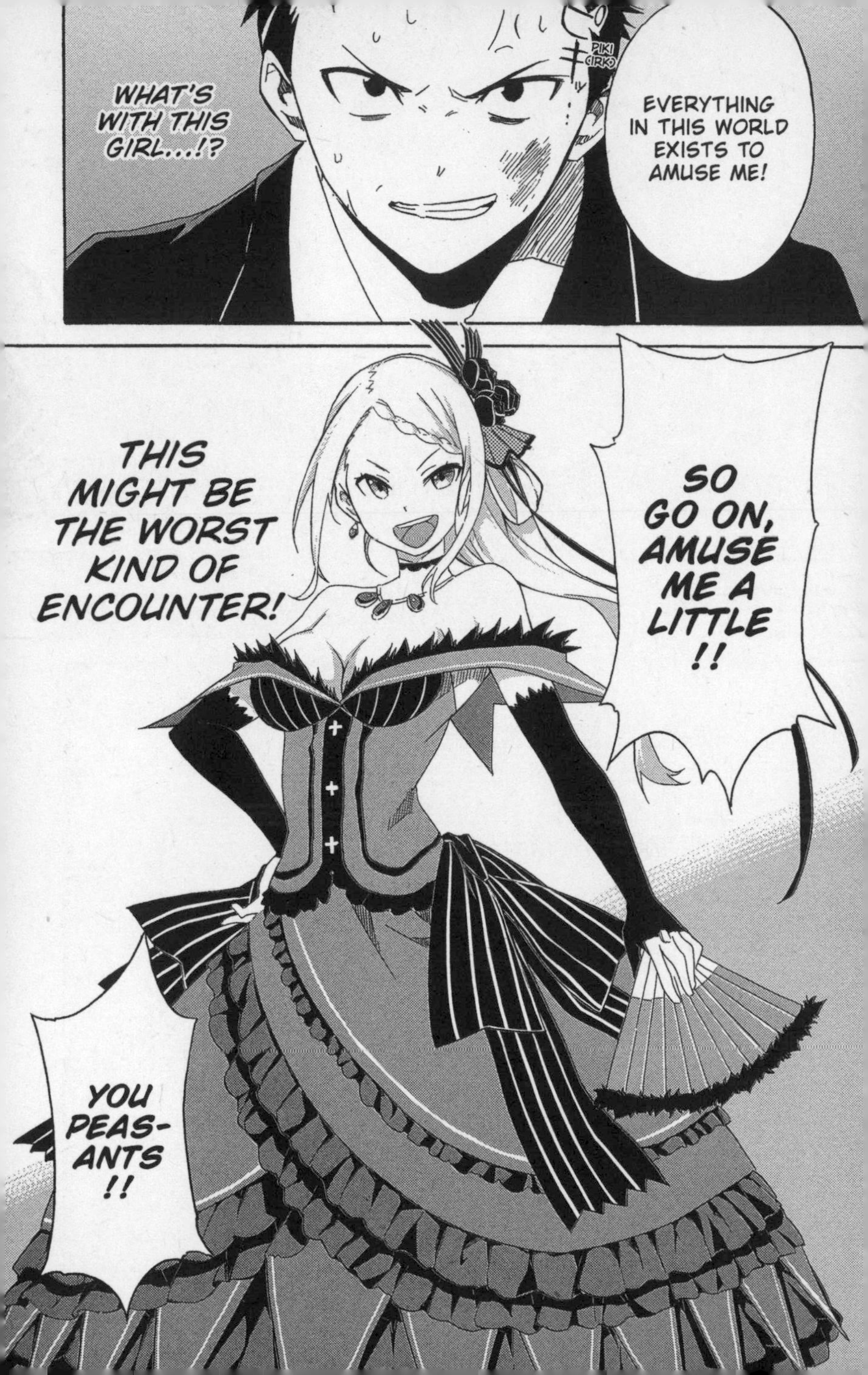
EVERYTHING IN THIS WORLD EXISTS TO AMUSE ME!
PIKI (IRK)
WHAT'S WITH THIS GIRL...!?
SO GO ON, AMUSE ME A LITTLE!!
THIS MIGHT BE THE WORST KIND OF ENCOUNTER!
YOU PEASANTS!!

The only ability Subaru Natsuki gets when
he's summoned to another world is time
travel via his own death. But to save her,
he'll die as many times as it takes.

Truth of Zero

Re:ZERO -Starting Life in Another World-

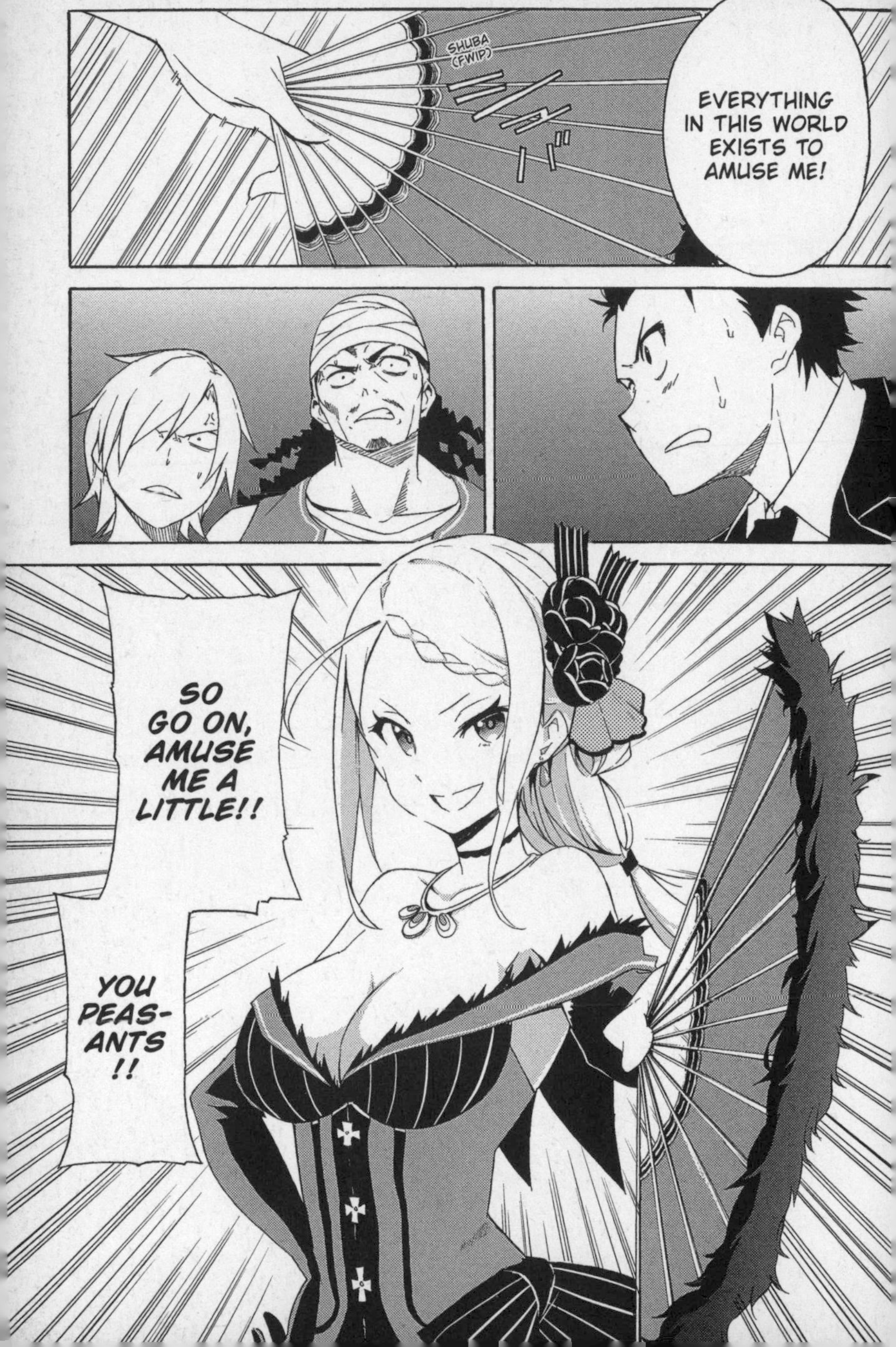
EVERYTHING IN THIS WORLD EXISTS TO AMUSE ME!
SHUBA (FWIP)
SO GO ON, AMUSE ME A LITTLE!!
YOU PEAS-ANTS!!

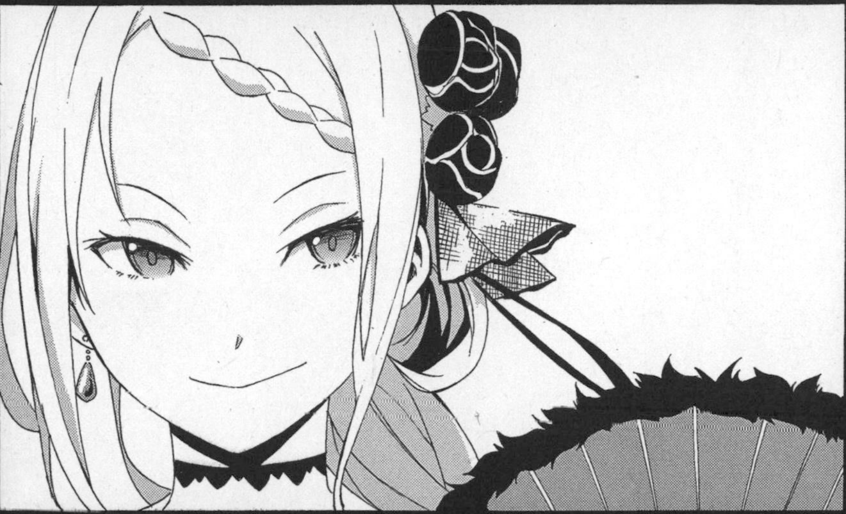

EPISODE 2

The Orange Girl

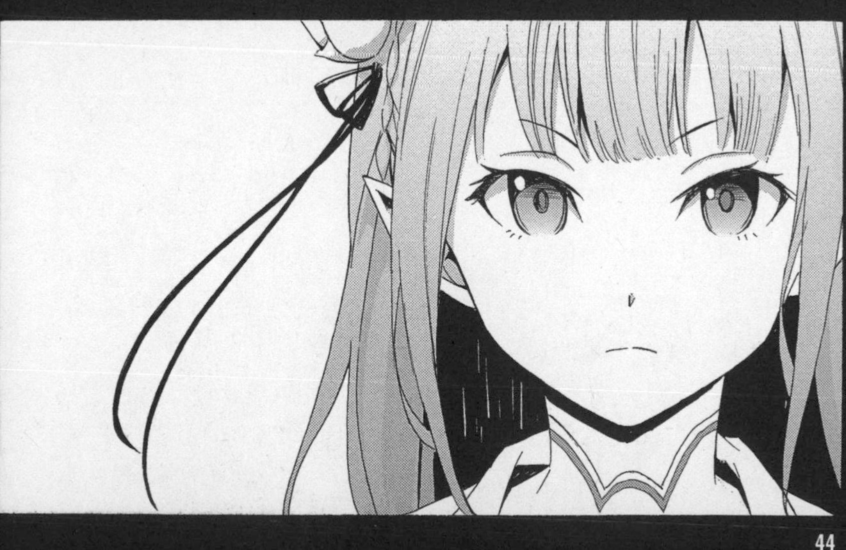

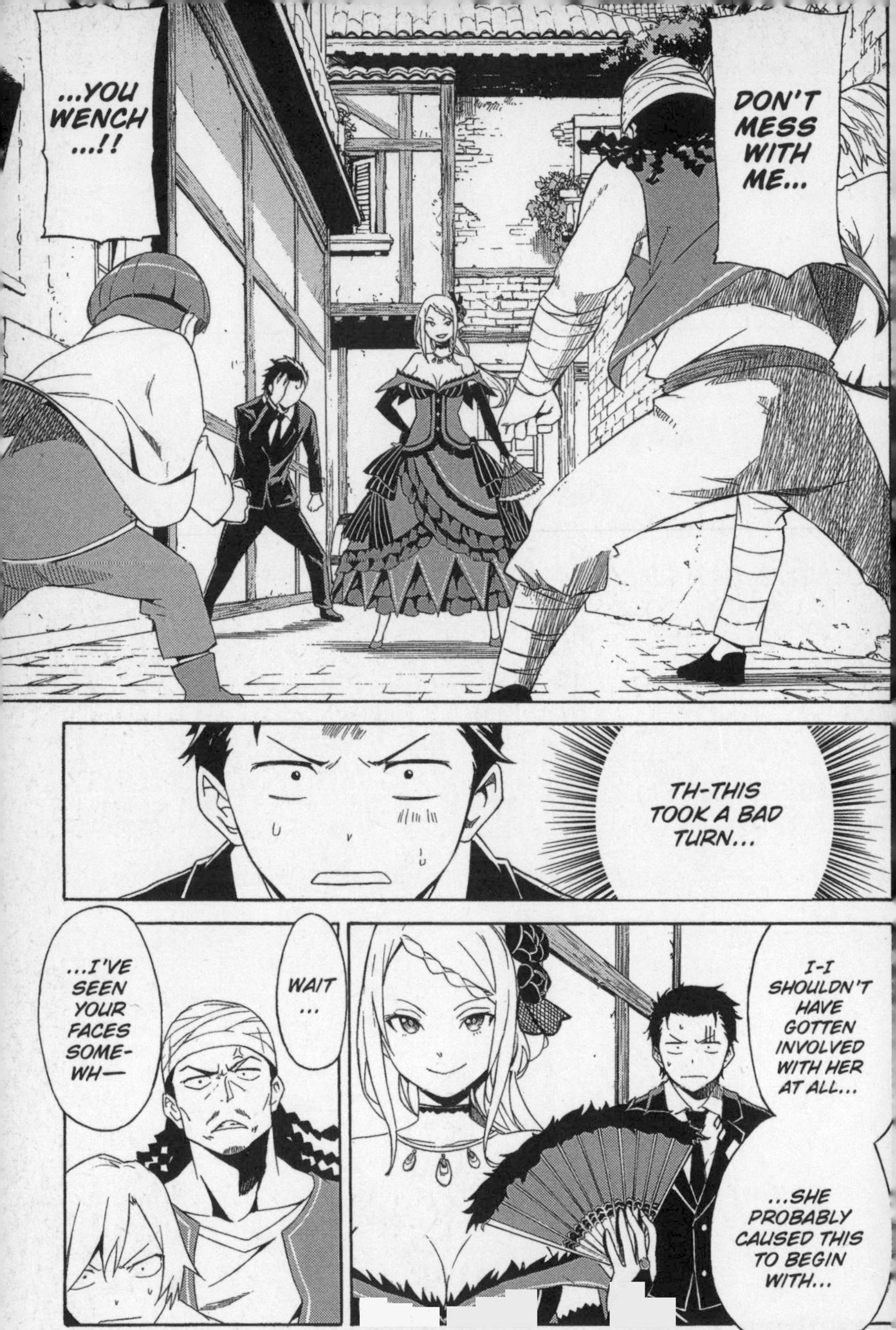
DON'T MESS WITH ME...
...YOU WENCH ...!!
TH-THIS TOOK A BAD TURN...
I-I SHOULDN'T HAVE GOTTEN INVOLVED WITH HER AT ALL...
...SHE PROBABLY CAUSED THIS TO BEGIN WITH...
WAIT ...
...I'VE SEEN YOUR FACES SOME-WH—

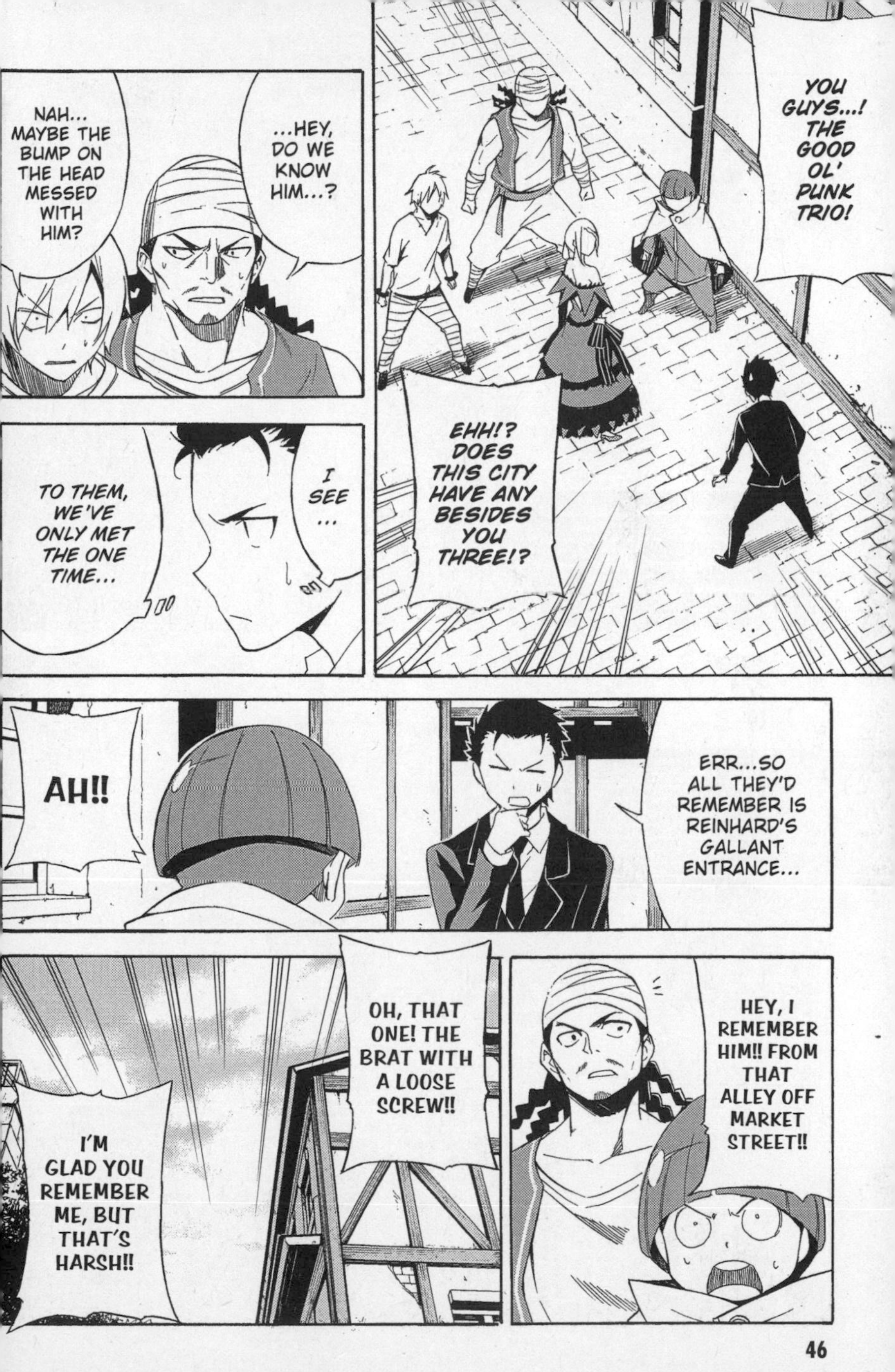
YOU GUYS...! THE GOOD OL' PUNK TRIO!
EHH!? DOES THIS CITY HAVE ANY BESIDES YOU THREE!?
...HEY, DO WE KNOW HIM...?
NAH... MAYBE THE BUMP ON THE HEAD MESSED WITH HIM?
I SEE...
TO THEM, WE'VE ONLY MET THE ONE TIME...
ERR...SO ALL THEY'D REMEMBER IS REINHARD'S GALLANT ENTRANCE...
AH!!
HEY, I REMEMBER HIM!! FROM THAT ALLEY OFF MARKET STREET!!
OH, THAT ONE! THE BRAT WITH A LOOSE SCREW!!
I'M GLAD YOU REMEMBER ME, BUT THAT'S HARSH!!

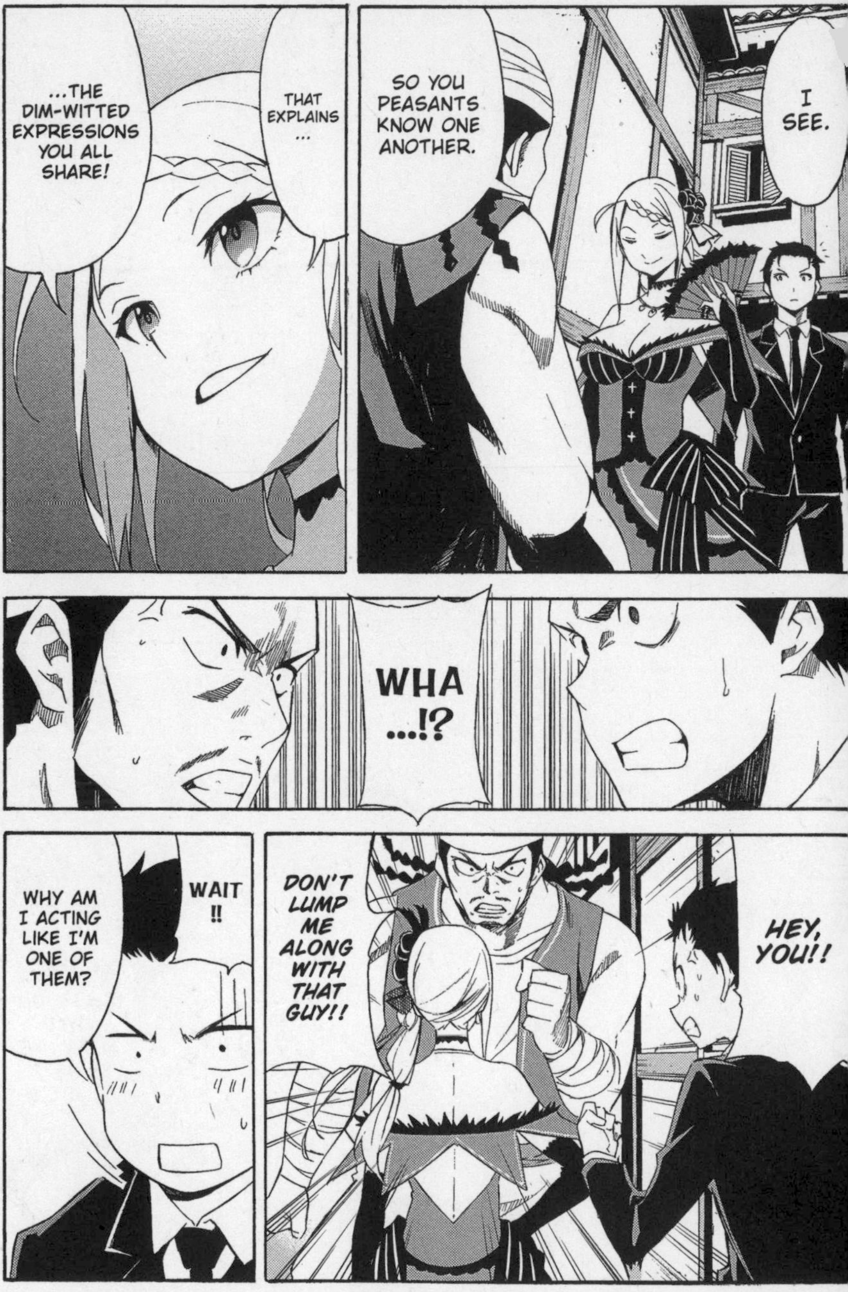
I SEE.
SO YOU PEASANTS KNOW ONE ANOTHER.
THAT EXPLAINS ...
...THE DIM-WITTED EXPRESSIONS YOU ALL SHARE!
WHA ...!?
HEY, YOU!!
DON'T LUMP ME ALONG WITH THAT GUY!!
WAIT !!
WHY AM I ACTING LIKE I'M ONE OF THEM?

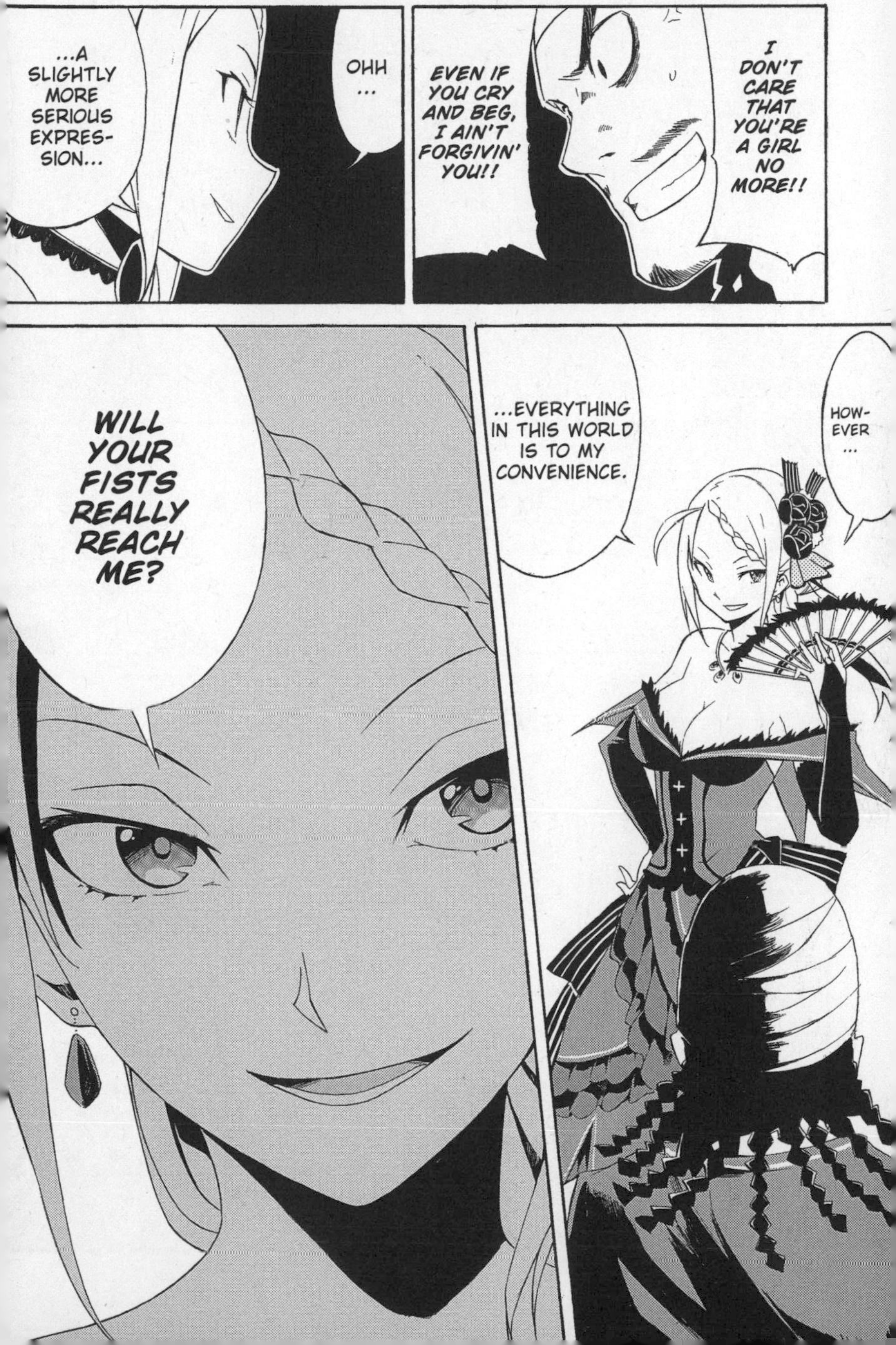
I DON'T CARE THAT YOU'RE A GIRL NO MORE!!
EVEN IF YOU CRY AND BEG, I AIN'T FORGIVIN' YOU!!
OHH...
...A SLIGHTLY MORE SERIOUS EXPRESSION...
HOWEVER...
...EVERYTHING IN THIS WORLD IS TO MY CONVENIENCE.
WILL YOUR FISTS REALLY REACH ME?

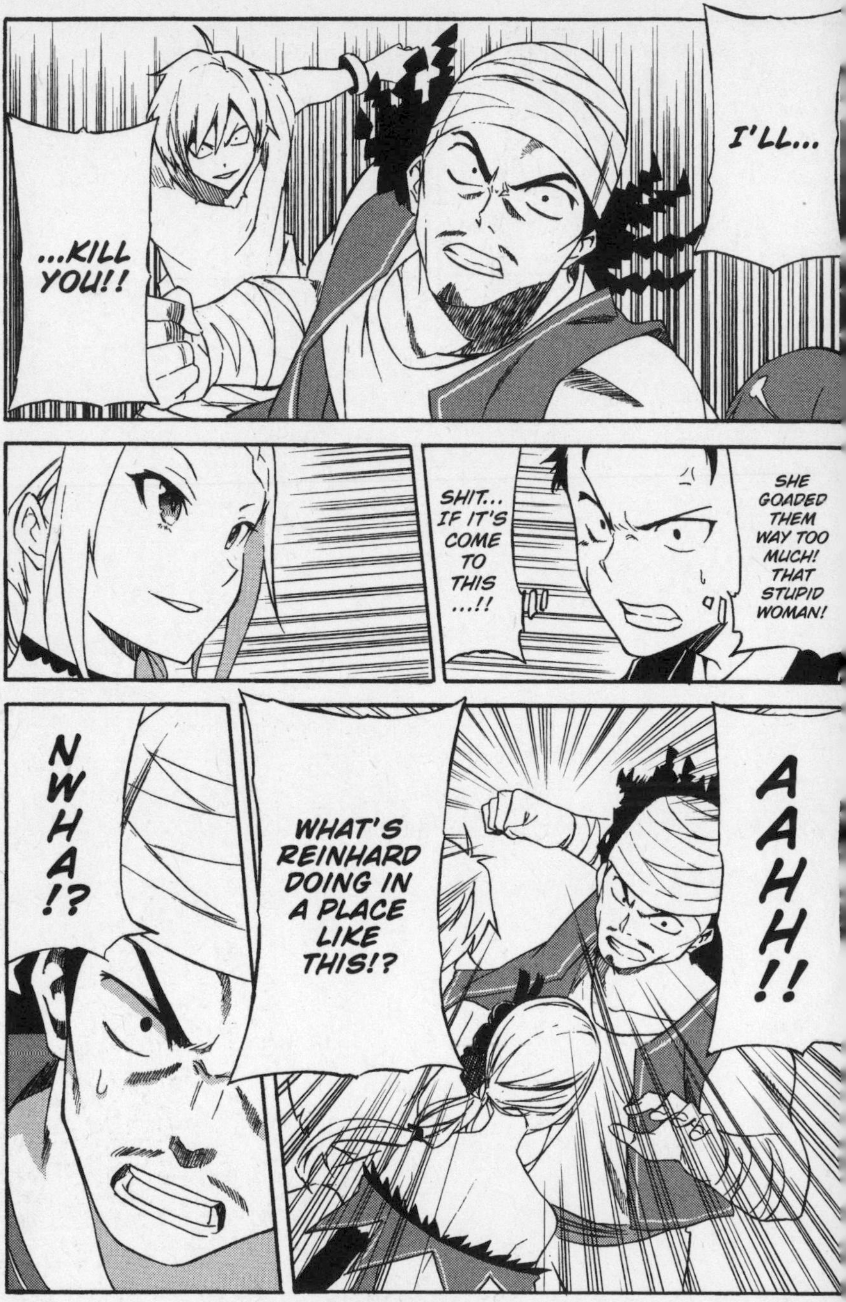
I'LL...
...KILL YOU!!
SHE GOADED THEM WAY TOO MUCH! THAT STUPID WOMAN!
SHIT... IF IT'S COME TO THIS ...!!
AAHH!!
WHAT'S REINHARD DOING IN A PLACE LIKE THIS!?
NWHA!?

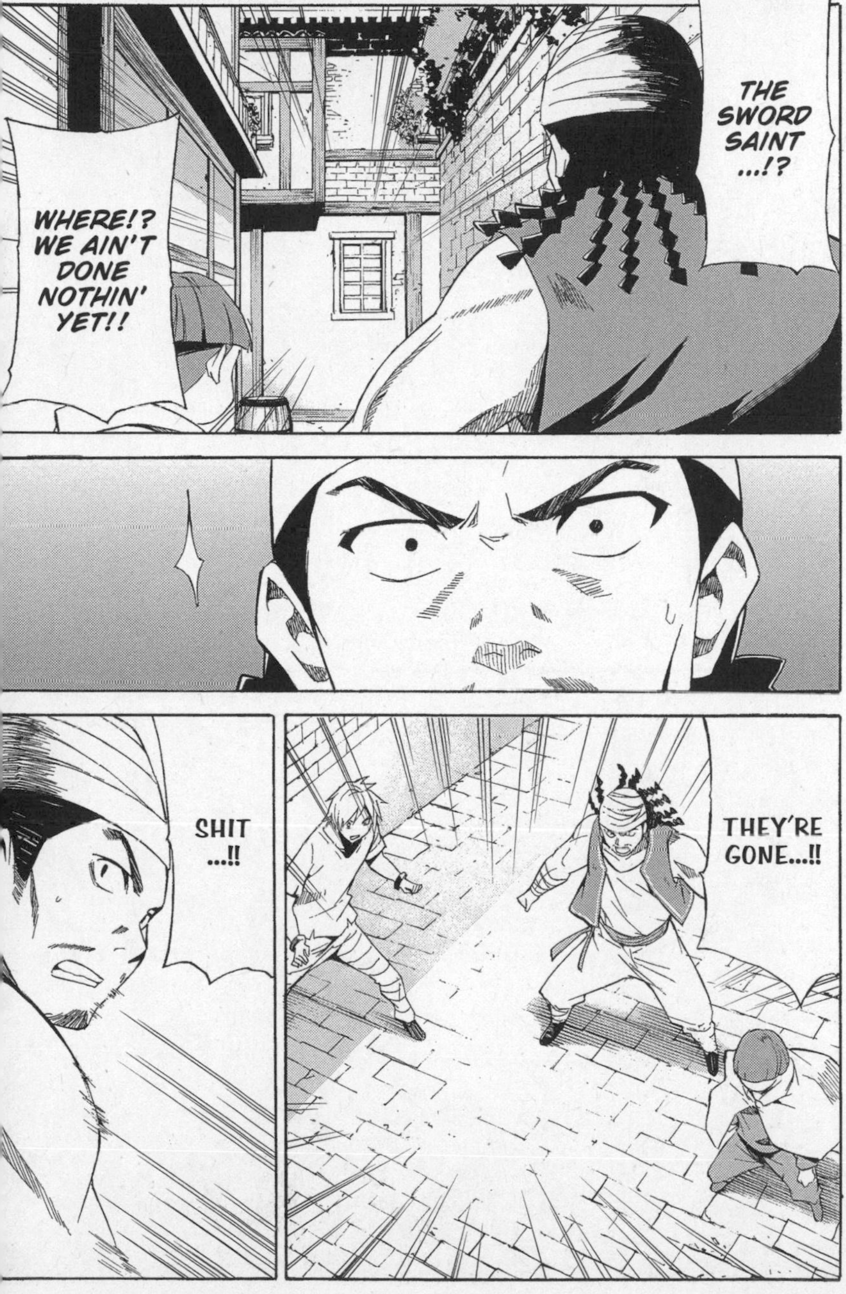
THE SWORD SAINT ...!?
WHERE!? WE AIN'T DONE NOTHIN' YET!!
THEY'RE GONE...!!
SHIT ...!!

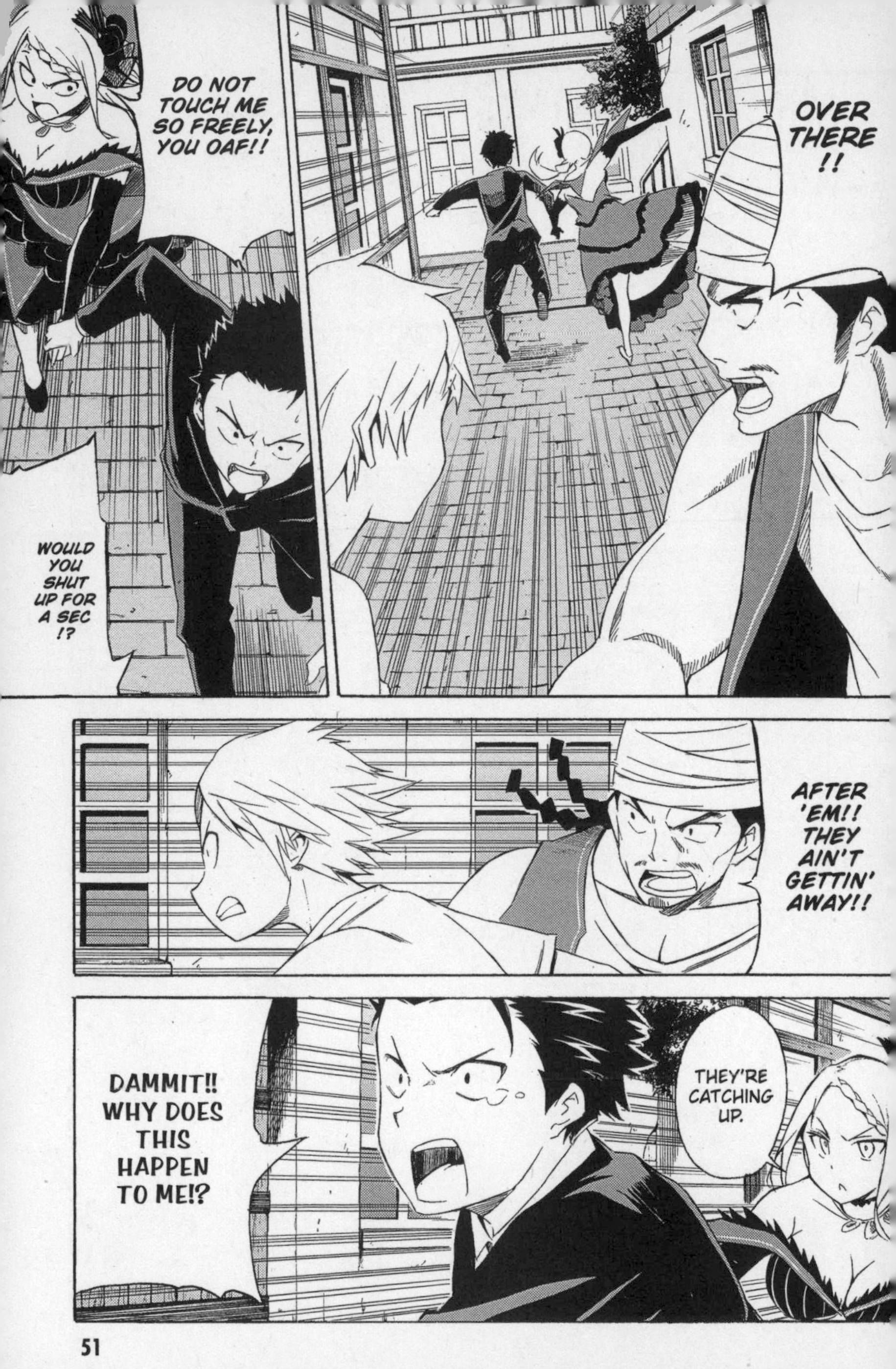
OVER THERE!!
DO NOT TOUCH ME SO FREELY, YOU OAF!!
WOULD YOU SHUT UP FOR A SEC!?
AFTER 'EM!! THEY AIN'T GETTIN' AWAY!!
THEY'RE CATCHING UP.
DAMMIT!! WHY DOES THIS HAPPEN TO ME!?

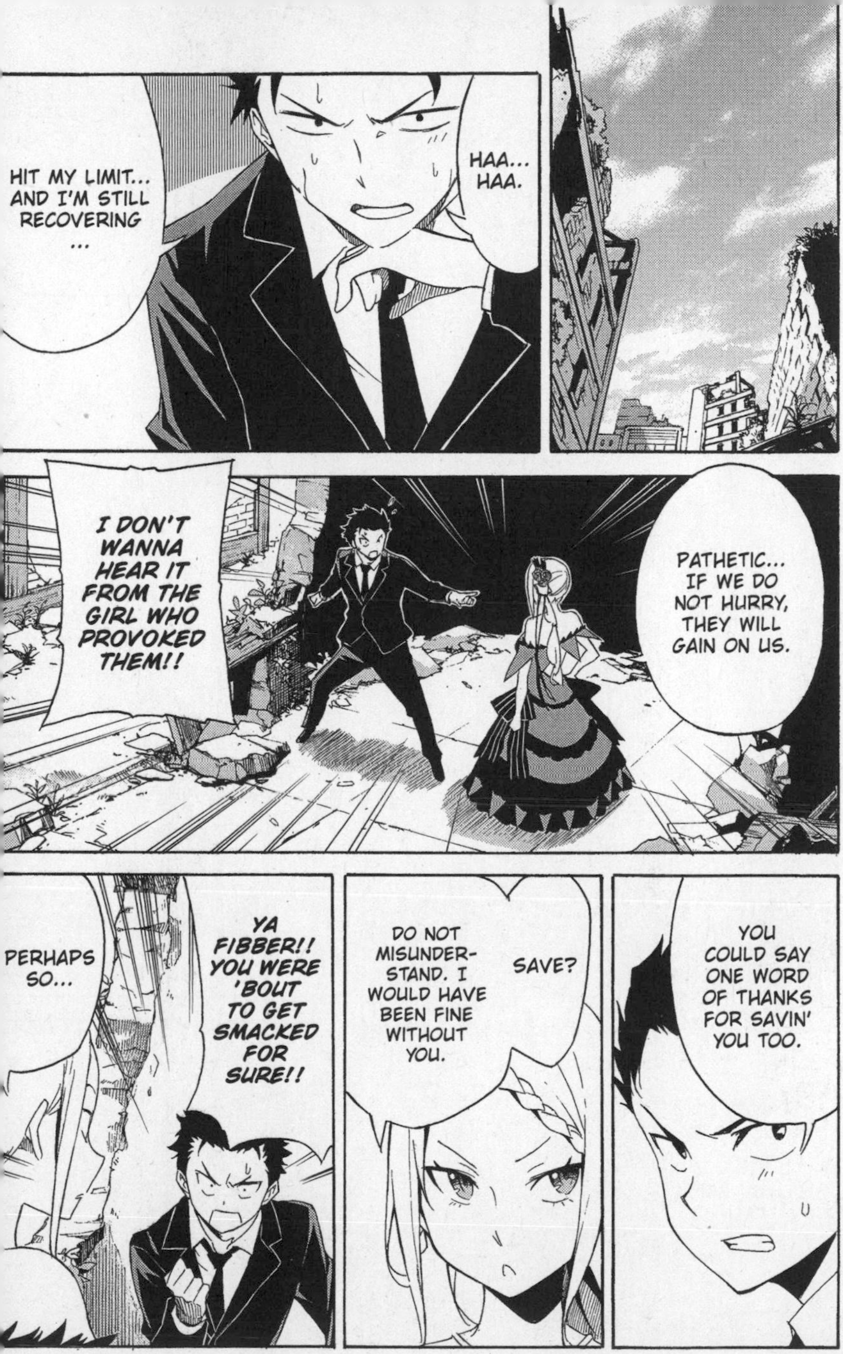
HAA... HAA.
HIT MY LIMIT... AND I'M STILL RECOVERING ...
PATHETIC... IF WE DO NOT HURRY, THEY WILL GAIN ON US.
I DON'T WANNA HEAR IT FROM THE GIRL WHO PROVOKED THEM!!
YOU COULD SAY ONE WORD OF THANKS FOR SAVIN' YOU TOO.
SAVE?
DO NOT MISUNDER-STAND. I WOULD HAVE BEEN FINE WITHOUT YOU.
YA FIBBER!! YOU WERE 'BOUT TO GET SMACKED FOR SURE!!
PERHAPS SO...

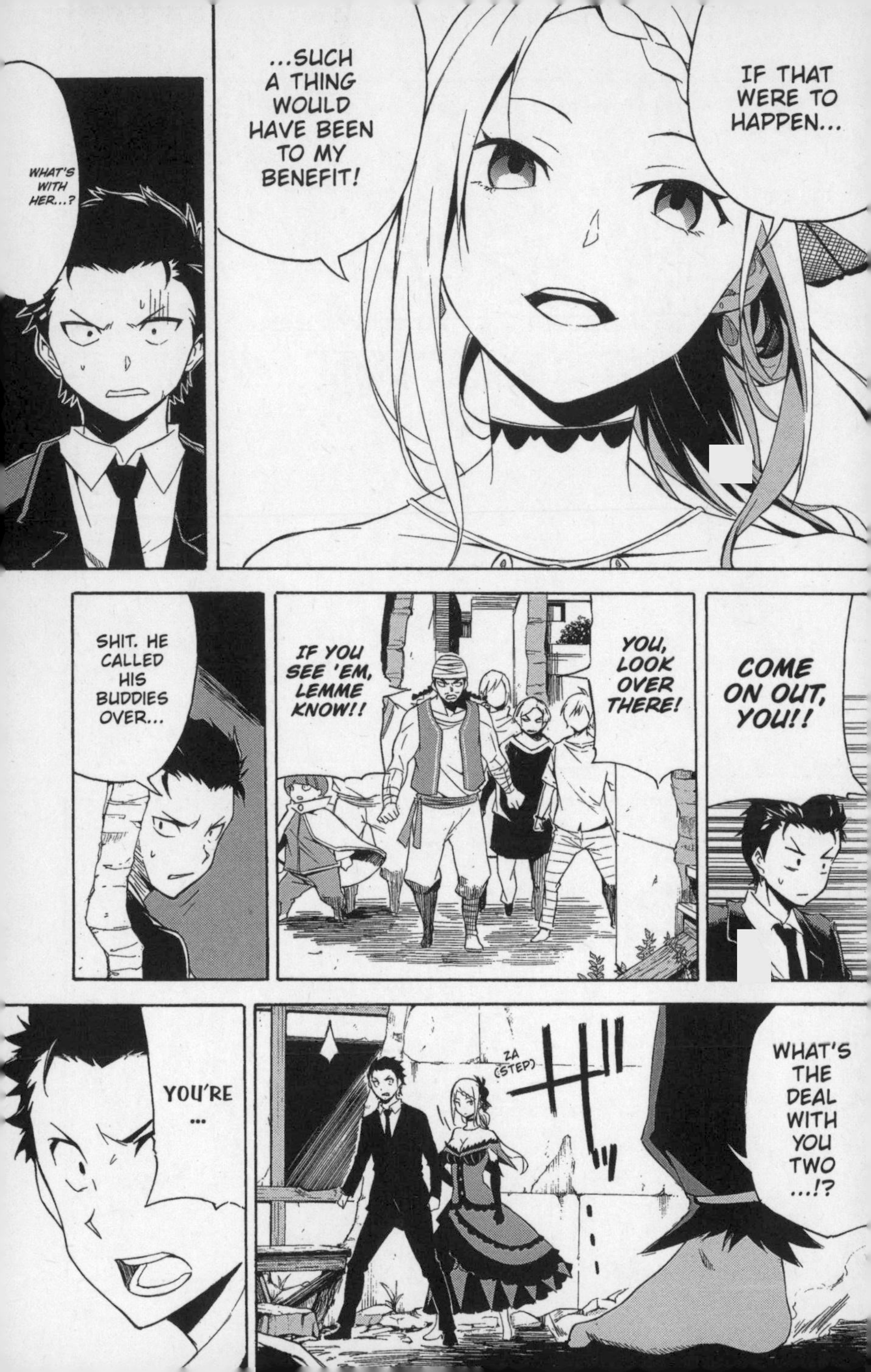
IF THAT WERE TO HAPPEN...
...SUCH A THING WOULD HAVE BEEN TO MY BENEFIT!
WHAT'S WITH HER...?
COME ON OUT, YOU!!
YOU, LOOK OVER THERE!
IF YOU SEE 'EM, LEMME KNOW!!
SHIT. HE CALLED HIS BUDDIES OVER...
WHAT'S THE DEAL WITH YOU TWO ...!?
ZA (STEP)
YOU'RE ...

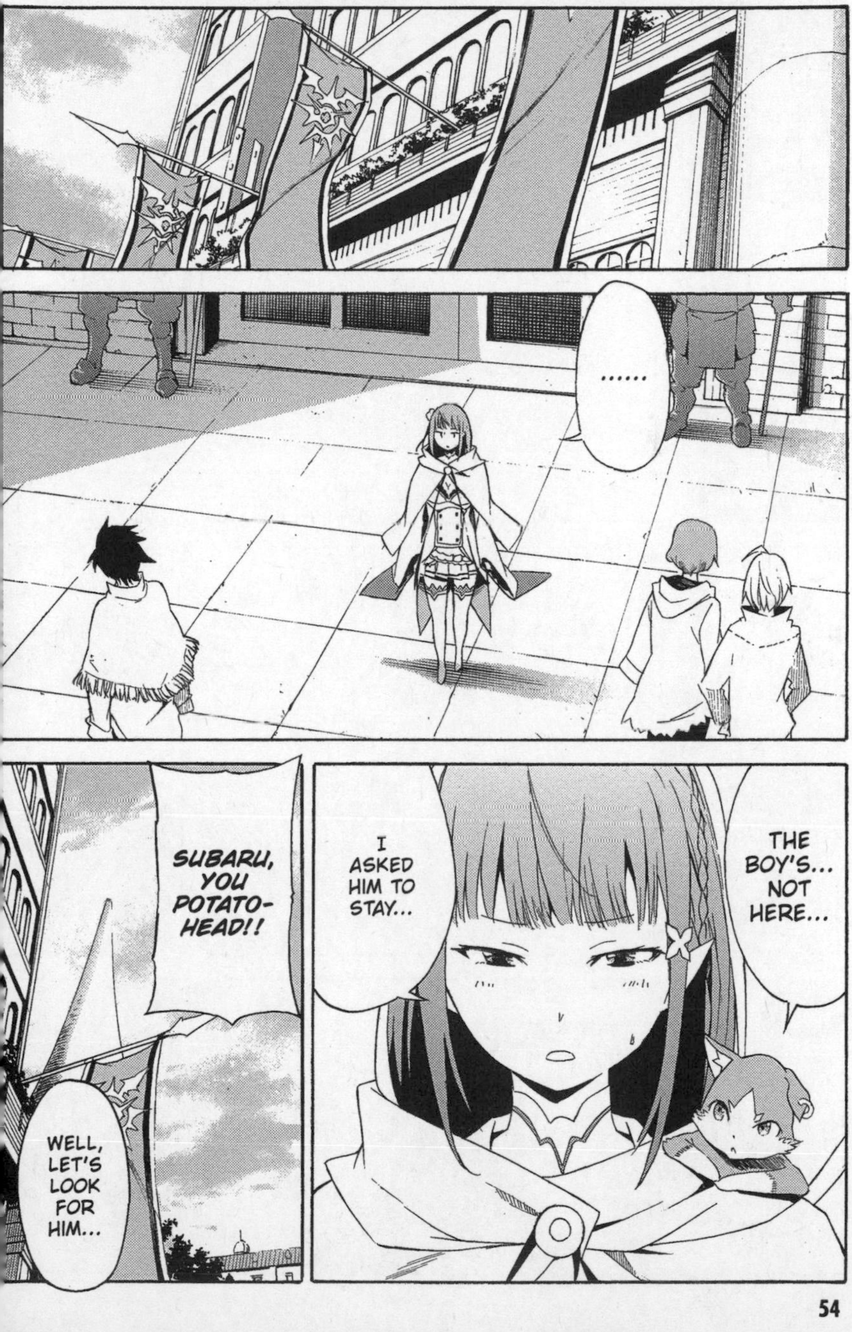
......
THE BOY'S... NOT HERE...
I ASKED HIM TO STAY...
SUBARU, YOU POTATO-HEAD!!
WELL, LET'S LOOK FOR HIM...

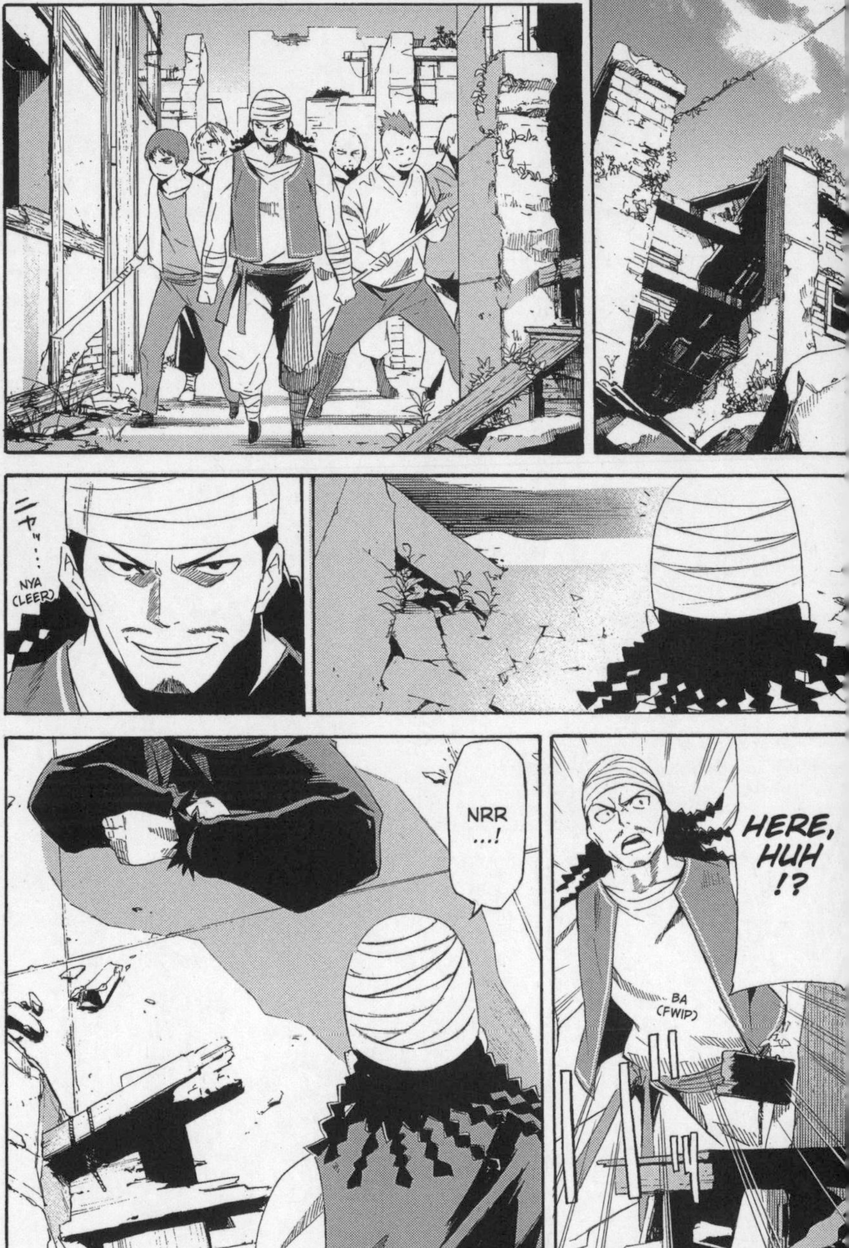
ニヤッ…
NYA (LEER)
HERE, HUH!?
BA (FWIP)
NRR ...!

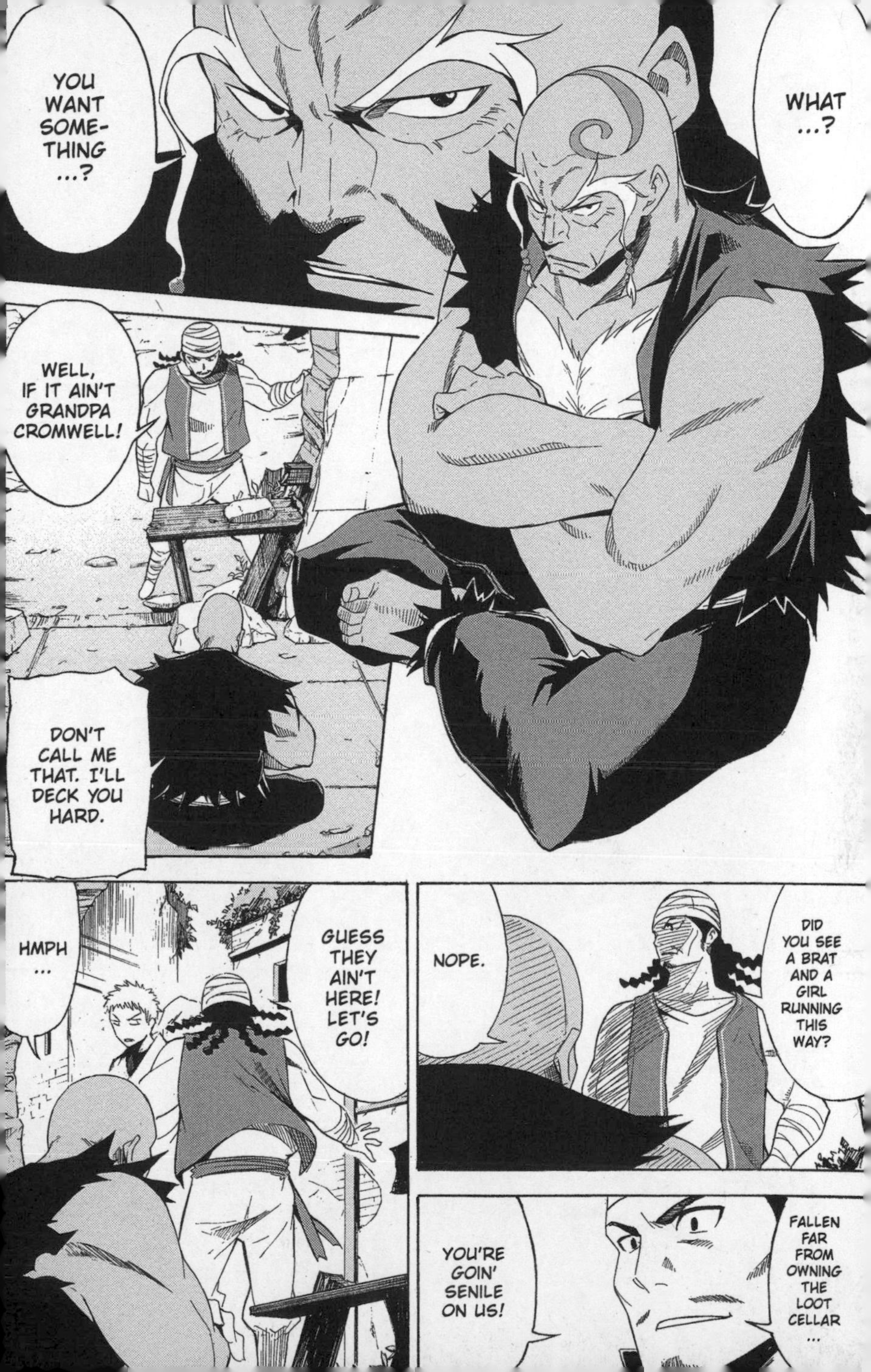
WHAT ...?
YOU WANT SOME-THING ...?
WELL, IF IT AIN'T GRANDPA CROMWELL!
DON'T CALL ME THAT. I'LL DECK YOU HARD.
DID YOU SEE A BRAT AND A GIRL RUNNING THIS WAY?
NOPE.
FALLEN FAR FROM OWNING THE LOOT CELLAR ...
YOU'RE GOIN' SENILE ON US!
GUESS THEY AIN'T HERE! LET'S GO!
HMPH ...

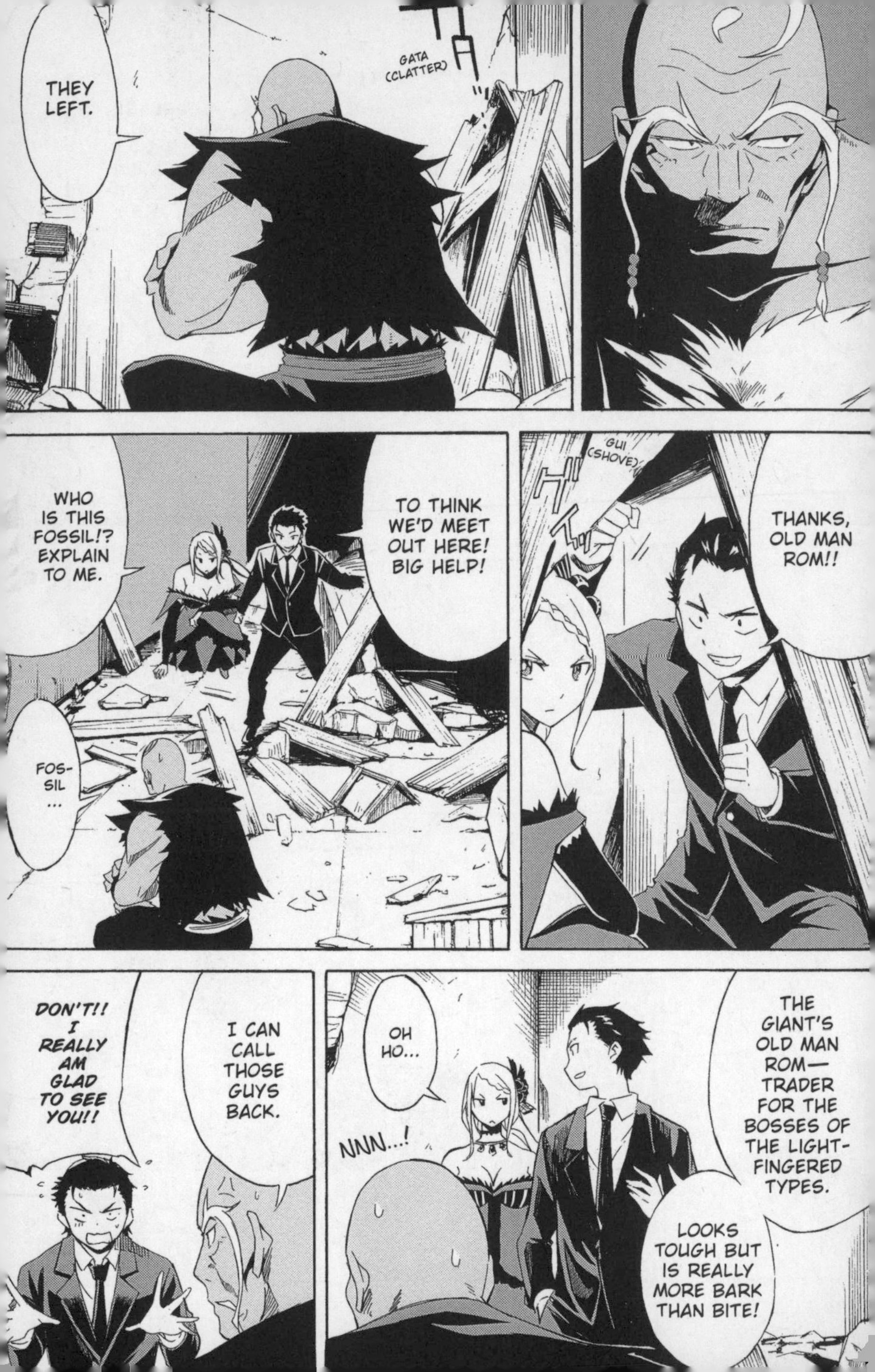
GATA (CLATTER)
THEY LEFT.
GUI (SHOVE)
THANKS, OLD MAN ROM!!
TO THINK WE'D MEET OUT HERE! BIG HELP!
WHO IS THIS FOSSIL!? EXPLAIN TO ME.
FOS-SIL...
THE GIANT'S OLD MAN ROM—TRADER FOR THE BOSSES OF THE LIGHT-FINGERED TYPES.
OH HO...
NNN...!
LOOKS TOUGH BUT IS REALLY MORE BARK THAN BITE!
I CAN CALL THOSE GUYS BACK.
DON'T!! I REALLY AM GLAD TO SEE YOU!!

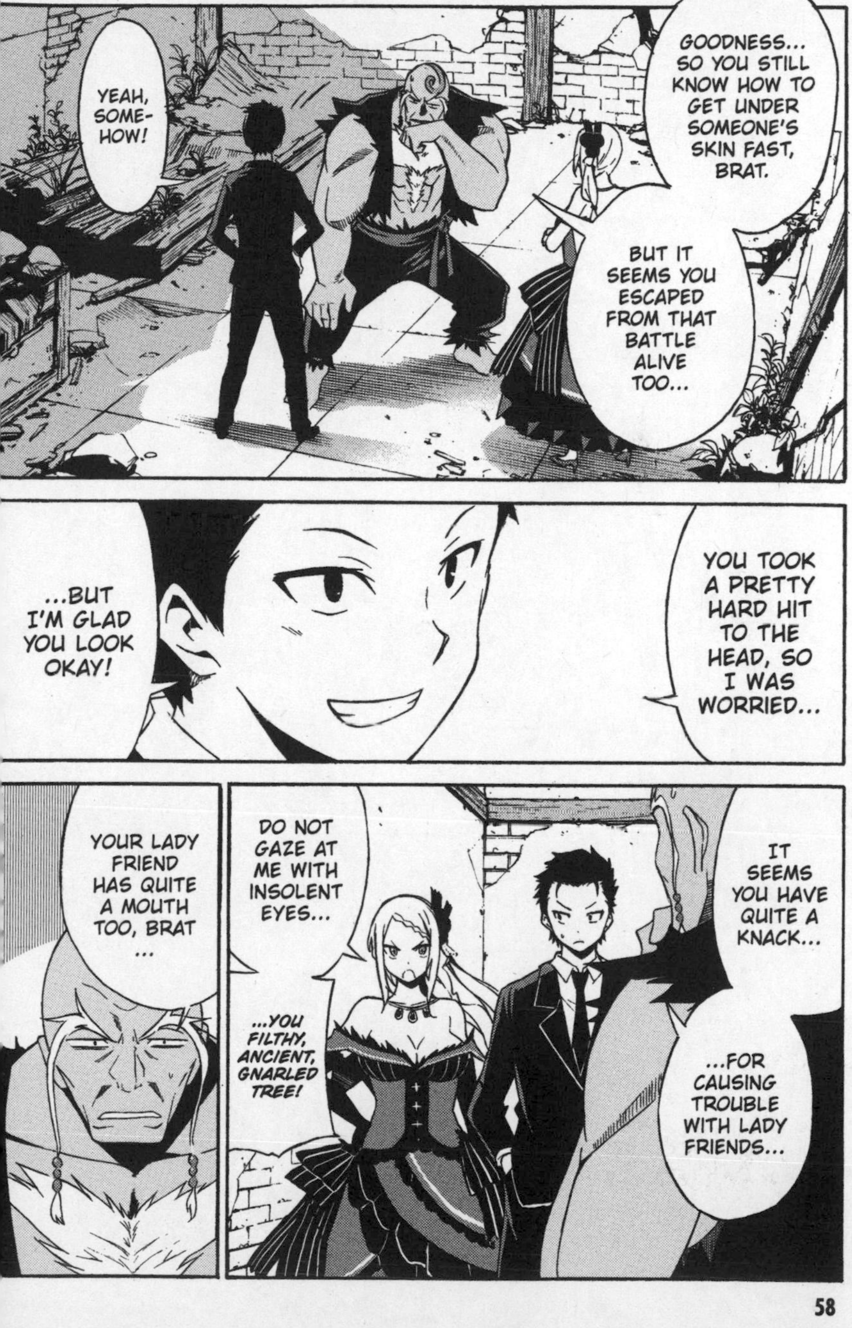
GOODNESS... SO YOU STILL KNOW HOW TO GET UNDER SOMEONE'S SKIN FAST, BRAT.
BUT IT SEEMS YOU ESCAPED FROM THAT BATTLE ALIVE TOO...
YEAH, SOME-HOW!
YOU TOOK A PRETTY HARD HIT TO THE HEAD, SO I WAS WORRIED...
...BUT I'M GLAD YOU LOOK OKAY!
IT SEEMS YOU HAVE QUITE A KNACK...
...FOR CAUSING TROUBLE WITH LADY FRIENDS...
DO NOT GAZE AT ME WITH INSOLENT EYES...
...YOU FILTHY, ANCIENT, GNARLED TREE!
YOUR LADY FRIEND HAS QUITE A MOUTH TOO, BRAT ...

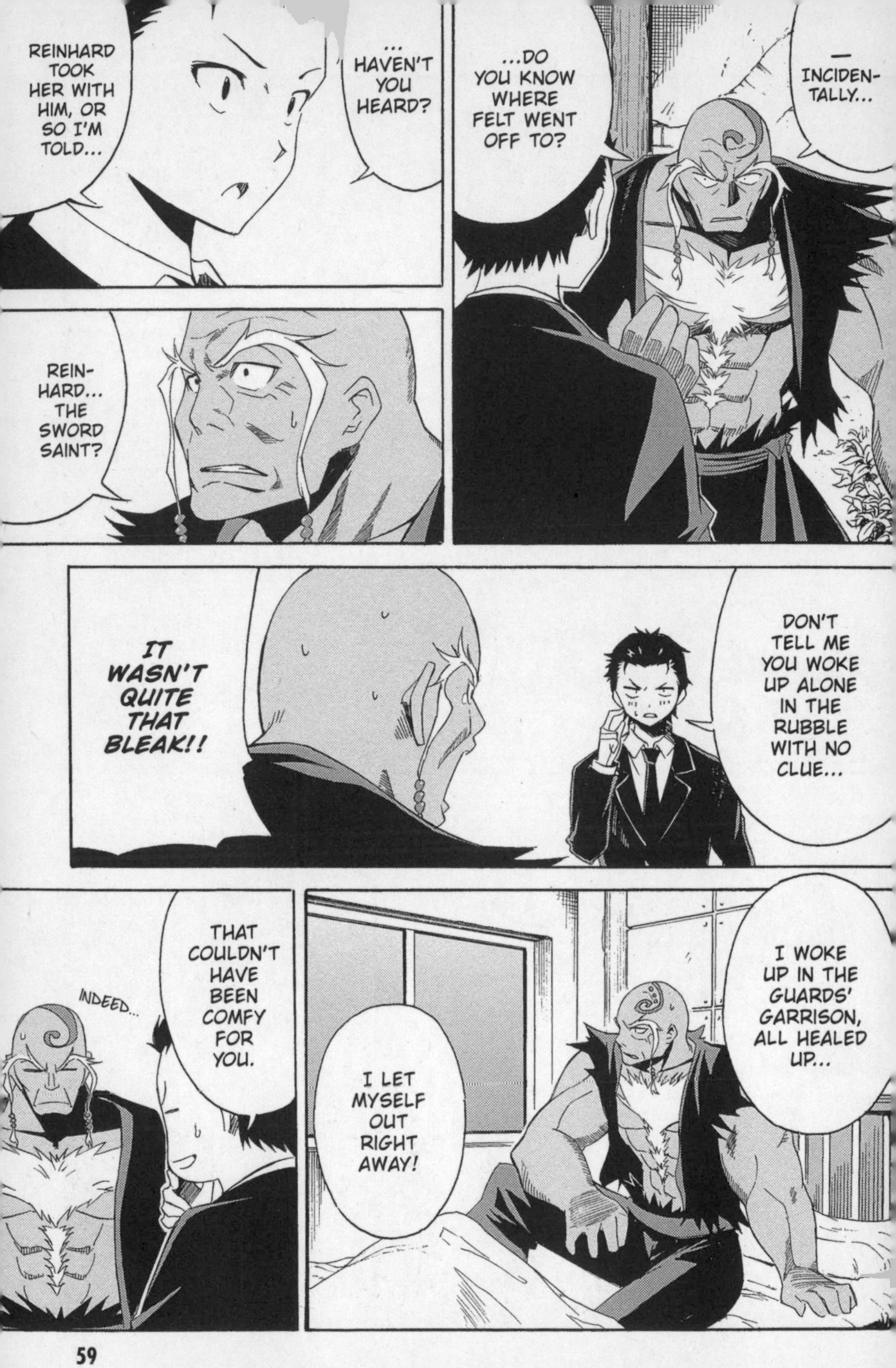
—INCIDENTALLY...
...DO YOU KNOW WHERE FELT WENT OFF TO?
...HAVEN'T YOU HEARD?
REINHARD TOOK HER WITH HIM, OR SO I'M TOLD...
REINHARD... THE SWORD SAINT?
DON'T TELL ME YOU WOKE UP ALONE IN THE RUBBLE WITH NO CLUE...
IT WASN'T QUITE THAT BLEAK!!
I WOKE UP IN THE GUARDS' GARRISON, ALL HEALED UP...
I LET MYSELF OUT RIGHT AWAY!
THAT COULDN'T HAVE BEEN COMFY FOR YOU.
INDEED...

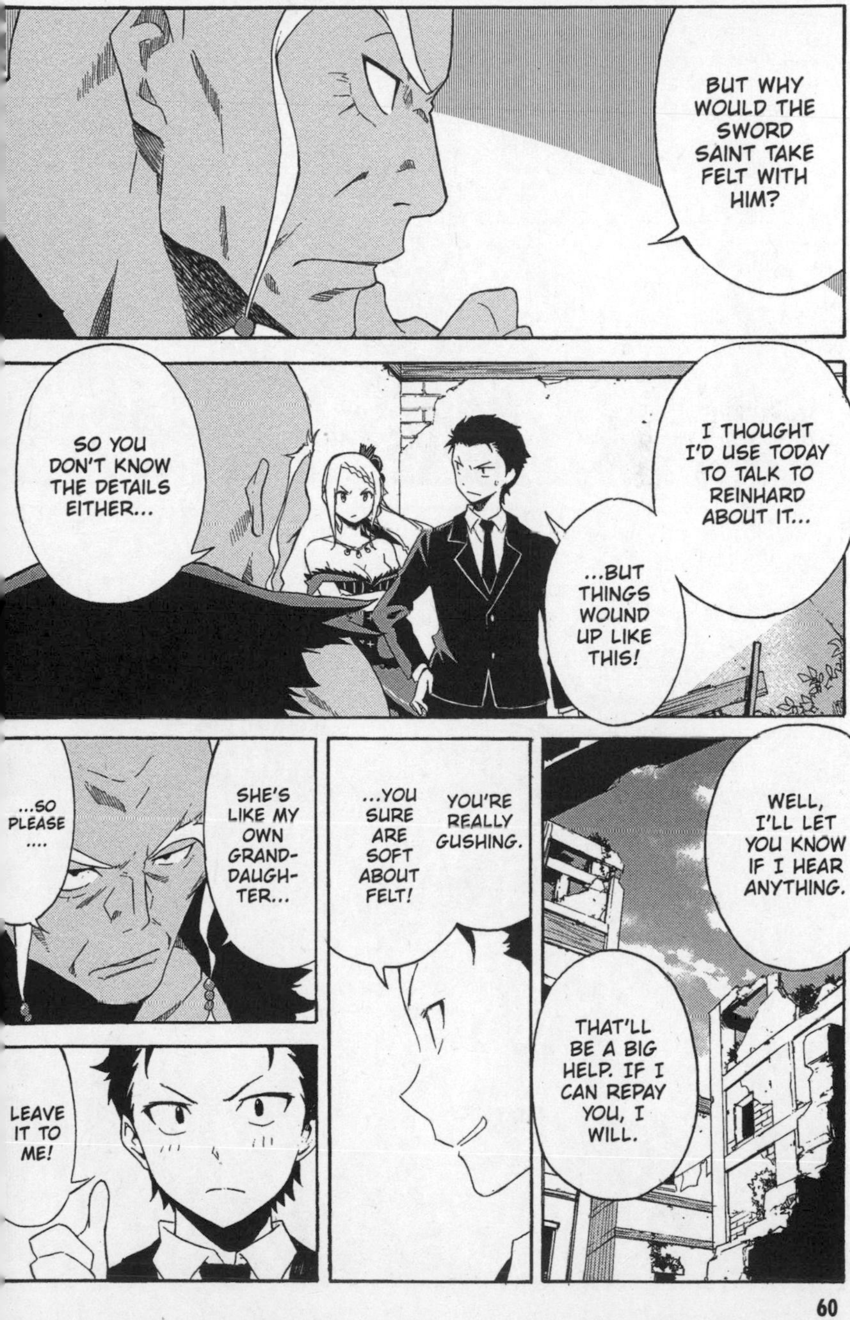
BUT WHY WOULD THE SWORD SAINT TAKE FELT WITH HIM?
I THOUGHT I'D USE TODAY TO TALK TO REINHARD ABOUT IT...
...BUT THINGS WOUND UP LIKE THIS!
SO YOU DON'T KNOW THE DETAILS EITHER...
WELL, I'LL LET YOU KNOW IF I HEAR ANYTHING.
THAT'LL BE A BIG HELP. IF I CAN REPAY YOU, I WILL.
YOU'RE REALLY GUSHING.
...YOU SURE ARE SOFT ABOUT FELT!
SHE'S LIKE MY OWN GRAND-DAUGH-TER...
...SO PLEASE ....
LEAVE IT TO ME!

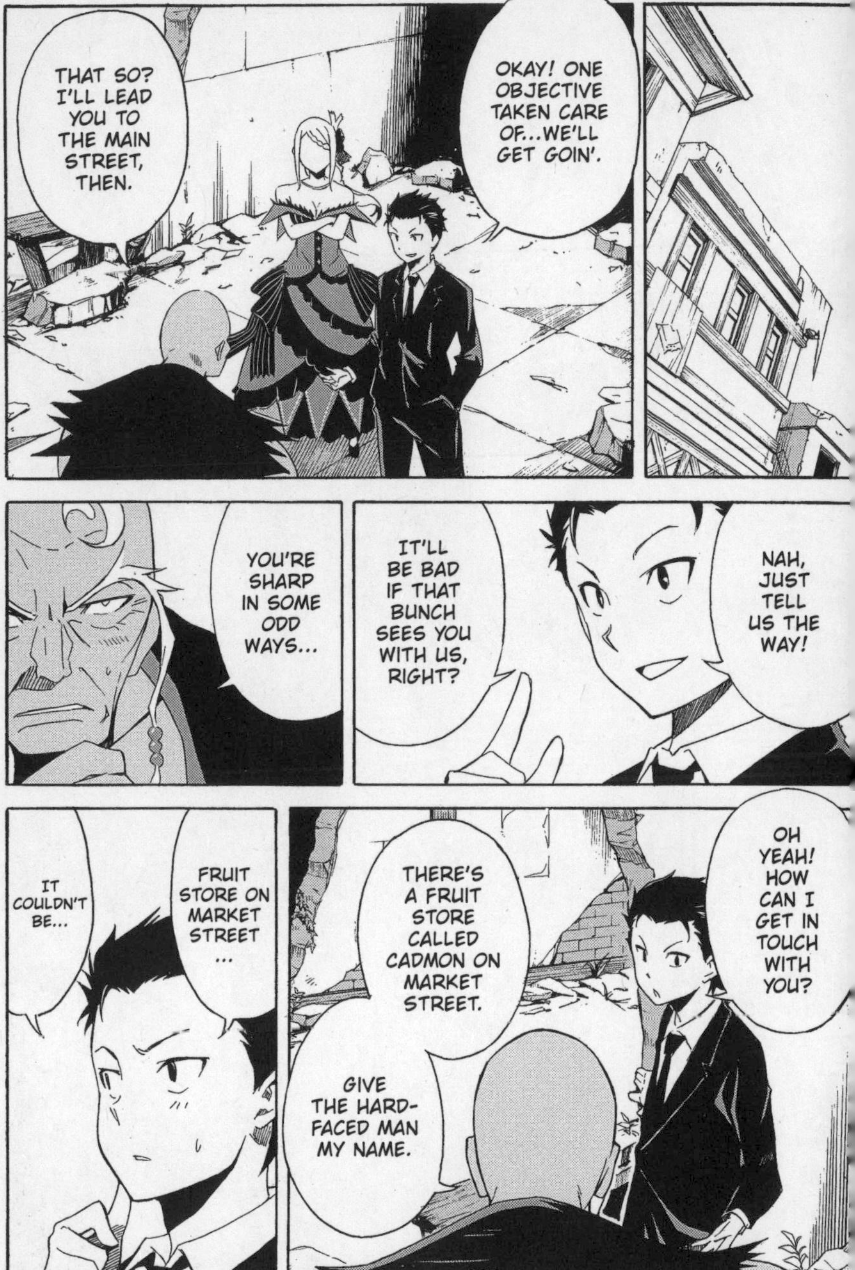
OKAY! ONE OBJECTIVE TAKEN CARE OF...WE'LL GET GOIN'.
THAT SO? I'LL LEAD YOU TO THE MAIN STREET, THEN.
NAH, JUST TELL US THE WAY!
IT'LL BE BAD IF THAT BUNCH SEES YOU WITH US, RIGHT?
YOU'RE SHARP IN SOME ODD WAYS...
OH YEAH! HOW CAN I GET IN TOUCH WITH YOU?
THERE'S A FRUIT STORE CALLED CADMON ON MARKET STREET.
GIVE THE HARD-FACED MAN MY NAME.
FRUIT STORE ON MARKET STREET...
IT COULDN'T BE...

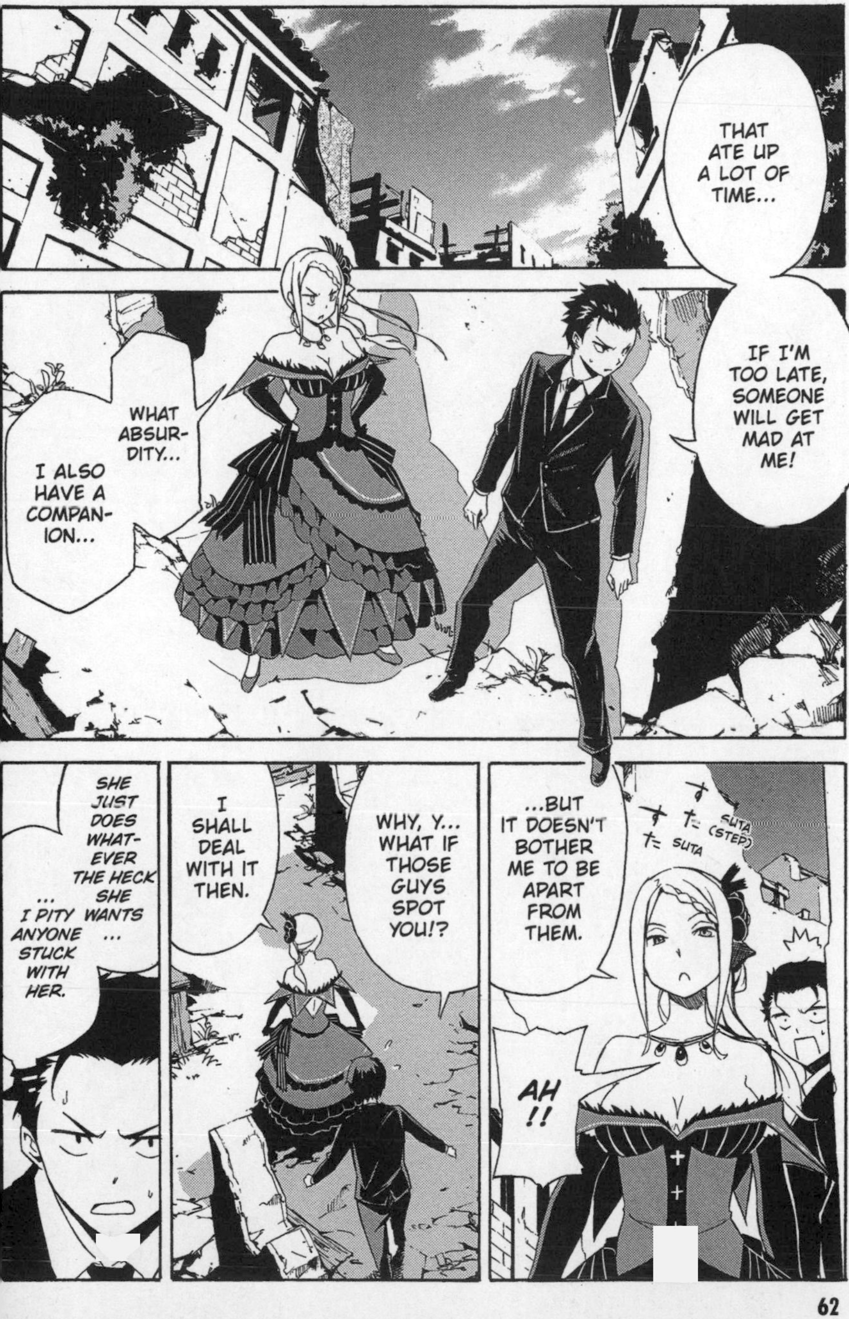
THAT ATE UP A LOT OF TIME...
IF I'M TOO LATE, SOMEONE WILL GET MAD AT ME!
WHAT ABSURDITY...
I ALSO HAVE A COMPANION...
すた すた SUTA SUTA (STEP)
...BUT IT DOESN'T BOTHER ME TO BE APART FROM THEM.
AH!!
WHY, Y... WHAT IF THOSE GUYS SPOT YOU!?
I SHALL DEAL WITH IT THEN.
SHE JUST DOES WHATEVER THE HECK SHE WANTS...
...I PITY ANYONE STUCK WITH HER.

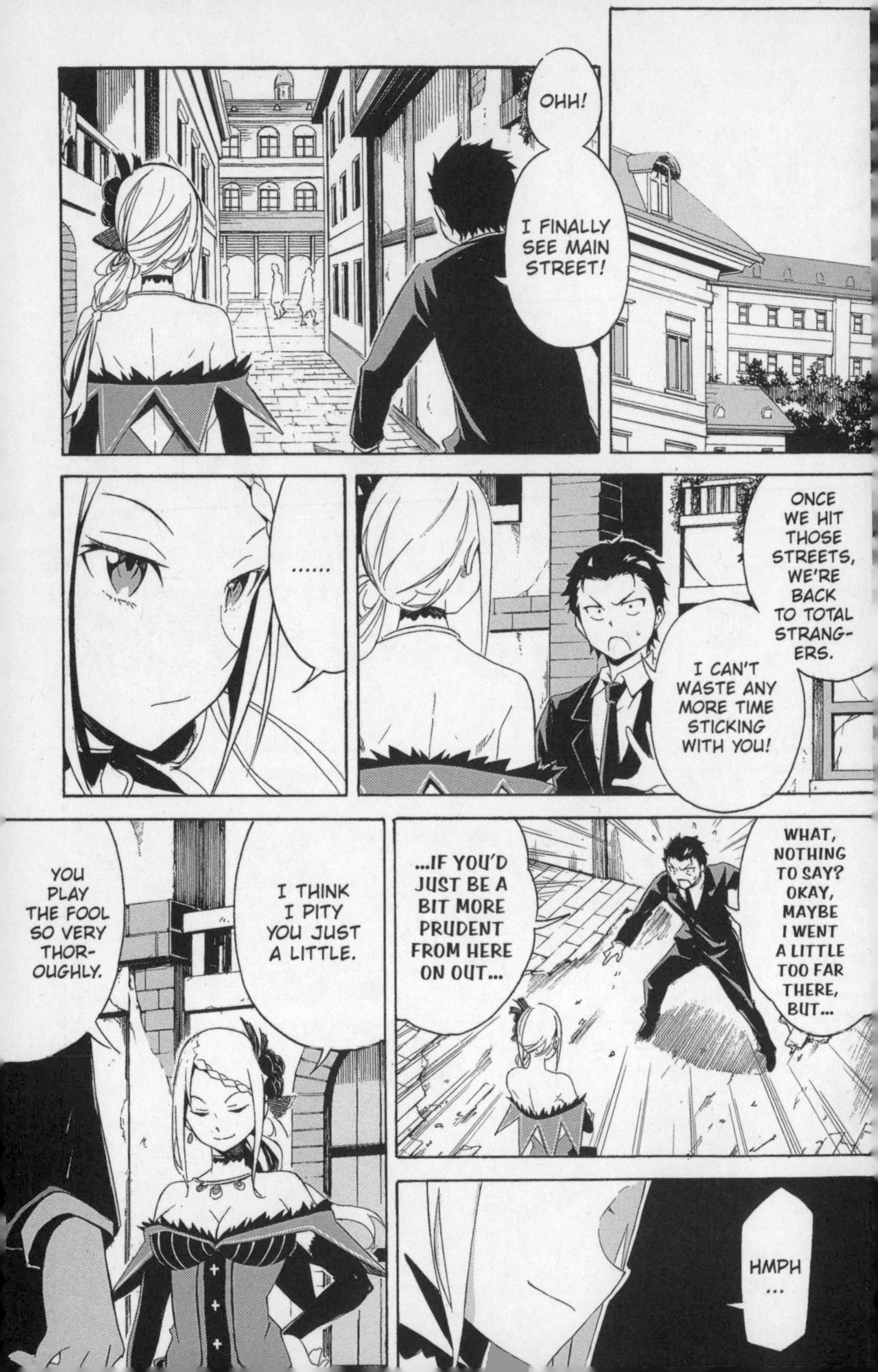
OHH!
I FINALLY SEE MAIN STREET!
ONCE WE HIT THOSE STREETS, WE'RE BACK TO TOTAL STRANGERS.
I CAN'T WASTE ANY MORE TIME STICKING WITH YOU!
......
WHAT, NOTHING TO SAY? OKAY, MAYBE I WENT A LITTLE TOO FAR THERE, BUT...
...IF YOU'D JUST BE A BIT MORE PRUDENT FROM HERE ON OUT...
HMPH ...
I THINK I PITY YOU JUST A LITTLE.
YOU PLAY THE FOOL SO VERY THOROUGHLY.

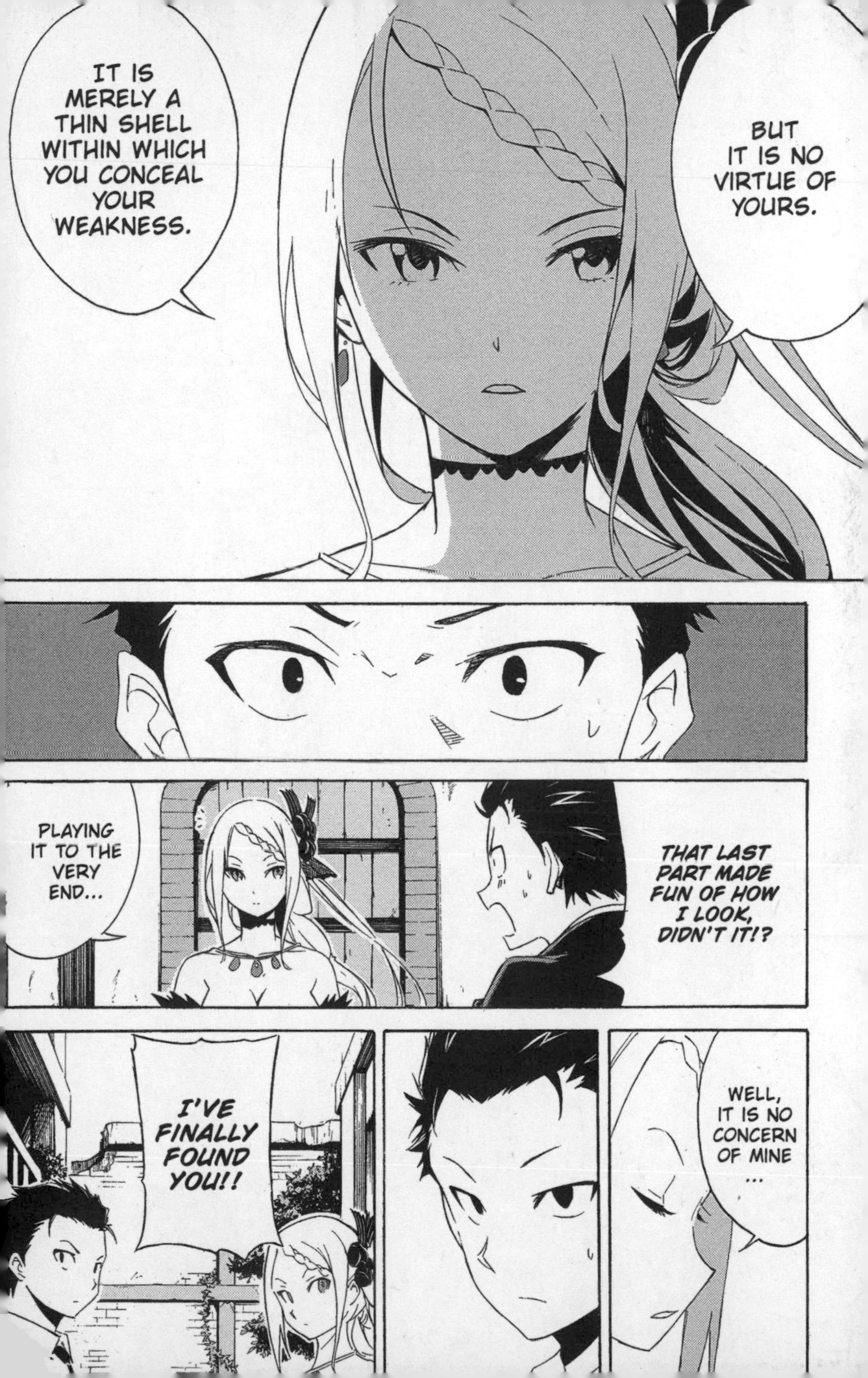
BUT IT IS NO VIRTUE OF YOURS.
IT IS MERELY A THIN SHELL WITHIN WHICH YOU CONCEAL YOUR WEAKNESS.
THAT LAST PART MADE FUN OF HOW I LOOK, DIDN'T IT!?
PLAYING IT TO THE VERY END...
WELL, IT IS NO CONCERN OF MINE...
I'VE FINALLY FOUND YOU!!

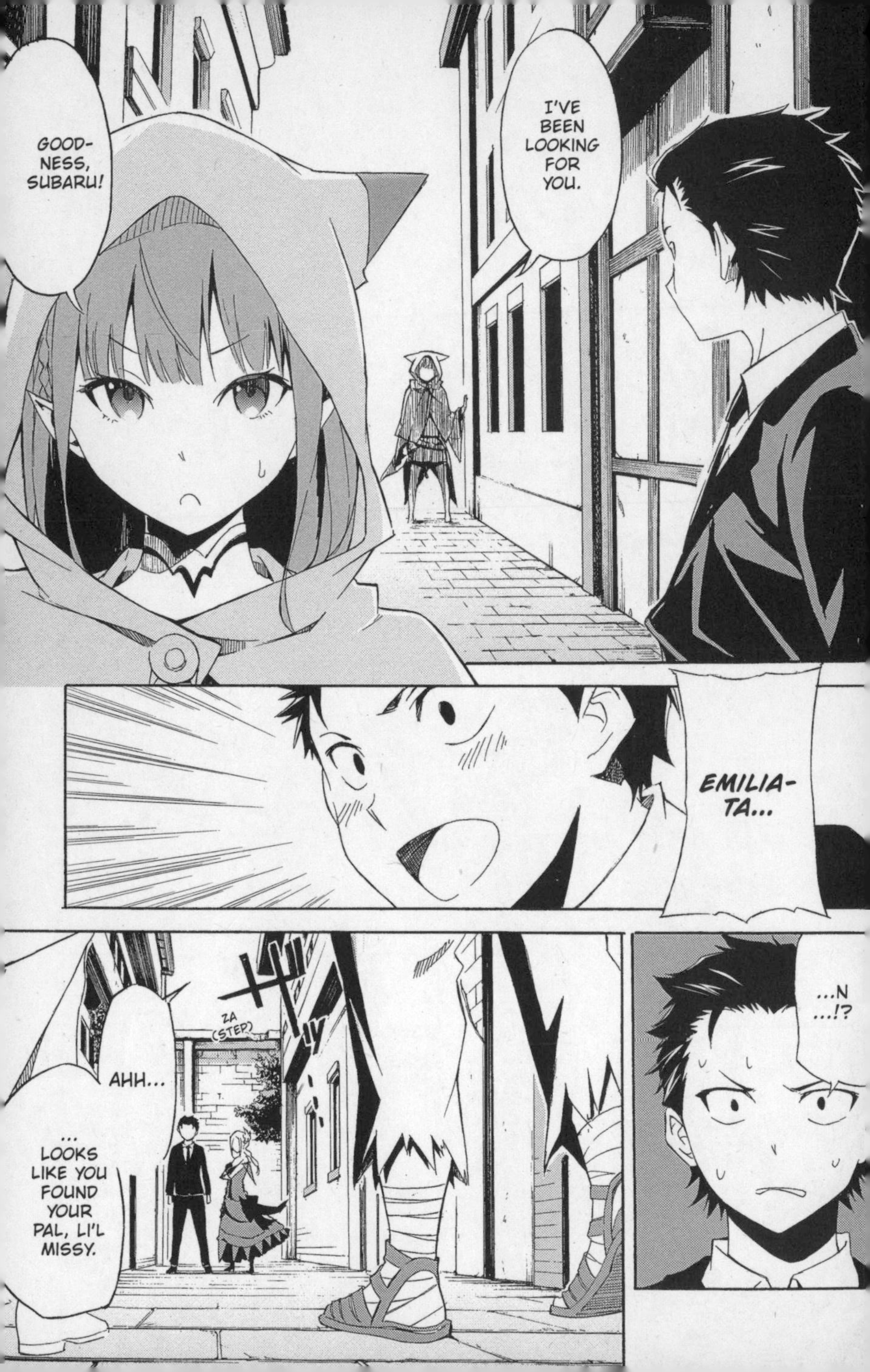
I'VE BEEN LOOKING FOR YOU.
GOOD-NESS, SUBARU!
EMILIA-TA...
...N ...!?
ZA (STEP)
AHH...
... LOOKS LIKE YOU FOUND YOUR PAL, LI'L MISSY.

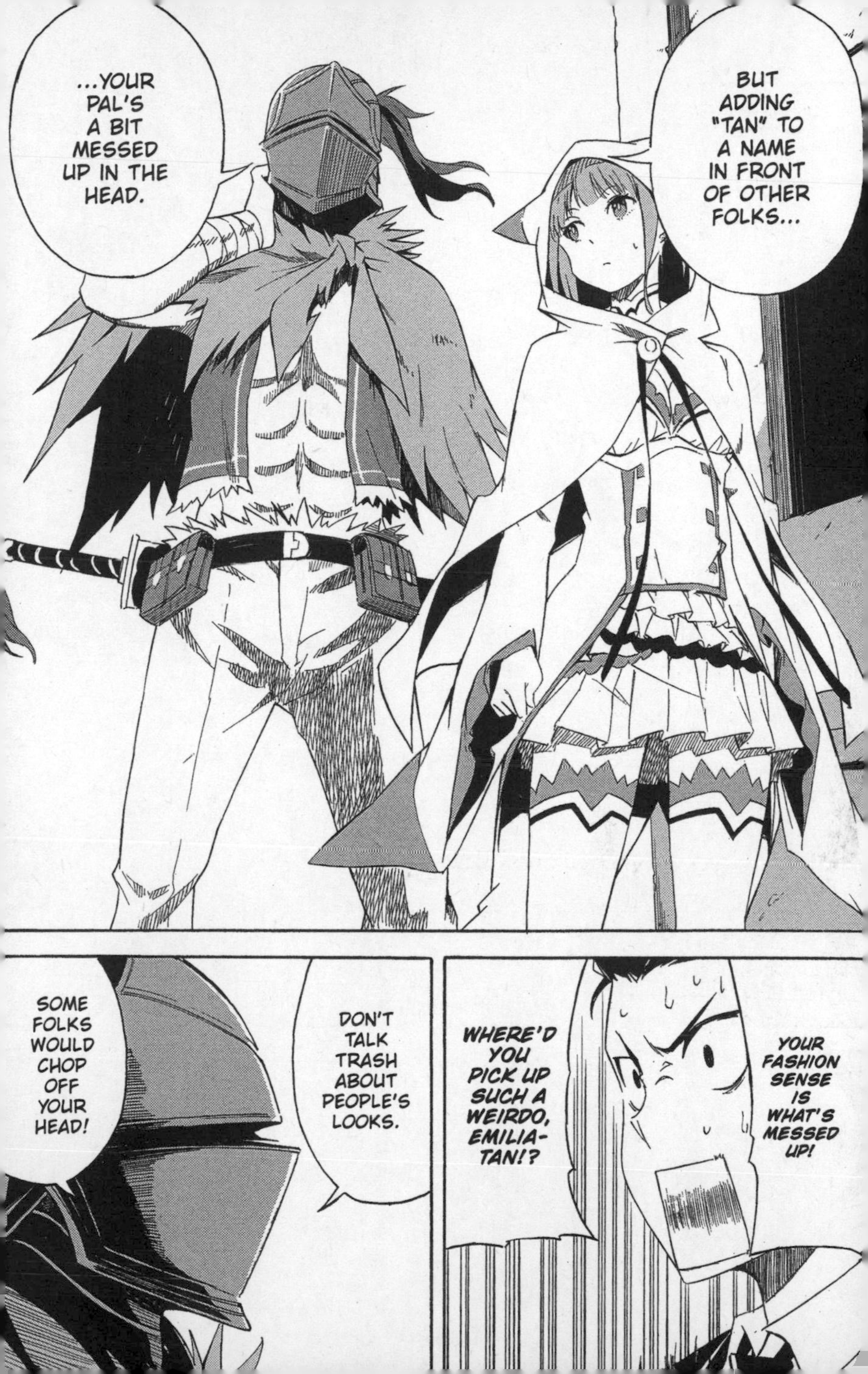
BUT ADDING "TAN" TO A NAME IN FRONT OF OTHER FOLKS...
...YOUR PAL'S A BIT MESSED UP IN THE HEAD.
YOUR FASHION SENSE IS WHAT'S MESSED UP!
WHERE'D YOU PICK UP SUCH A WEIRDO, EMILIA-TAN!?
DON'T TALK TRASH ABOUT PEOPLE'S LOOKS.
SOME FOLKS WOULD CHOP OFF YOUR HEAD!

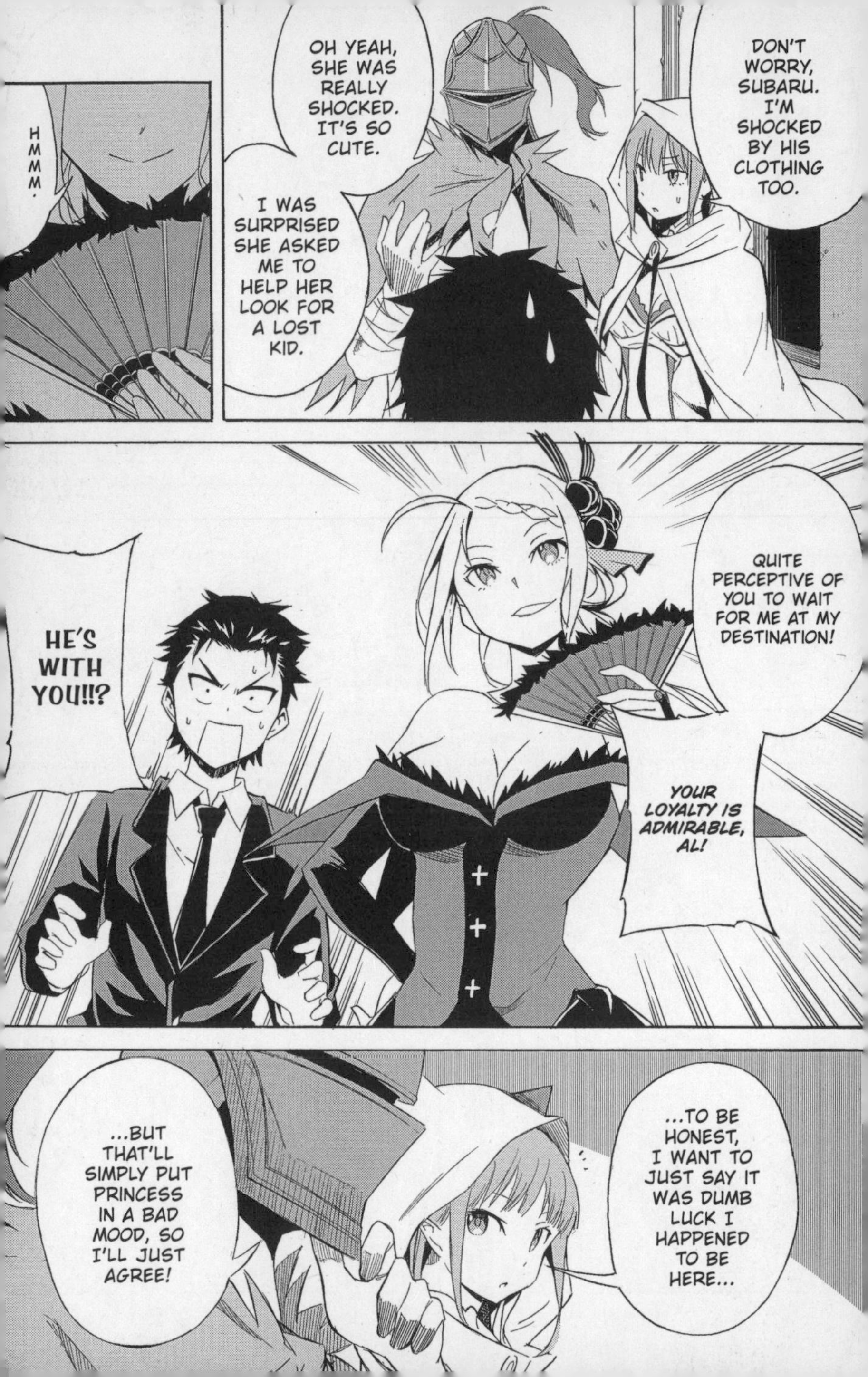
DON'T WORRY, SUBARU. I'M SHOCKED BY HIS CLOTHING TOO.
OH YEAH, SHE WAS REALLY SHOCKED. IT'S SO CUTE.
I WAS SURPRISED SHE ASKED ME TO HELP HER LOOK FOR A LOST KID.
HMMM.
QUITE PERCEPTIVE OF YOU TO WAIT FOR ME AT MY DESTINATION!
YOUR LOYALTY IS ADMIRABLE, AL!
HE'S WITH YOU!!?
...TO BE HONEST, I WANT TO JUST SAY IT WAS DUMB LUCK I HAPPENED TO BE HERE...
...BUT THAT'LL SIMPLY PUT PRINCESS IN A BAD MOOD, SO I'LL JUST AGREE!

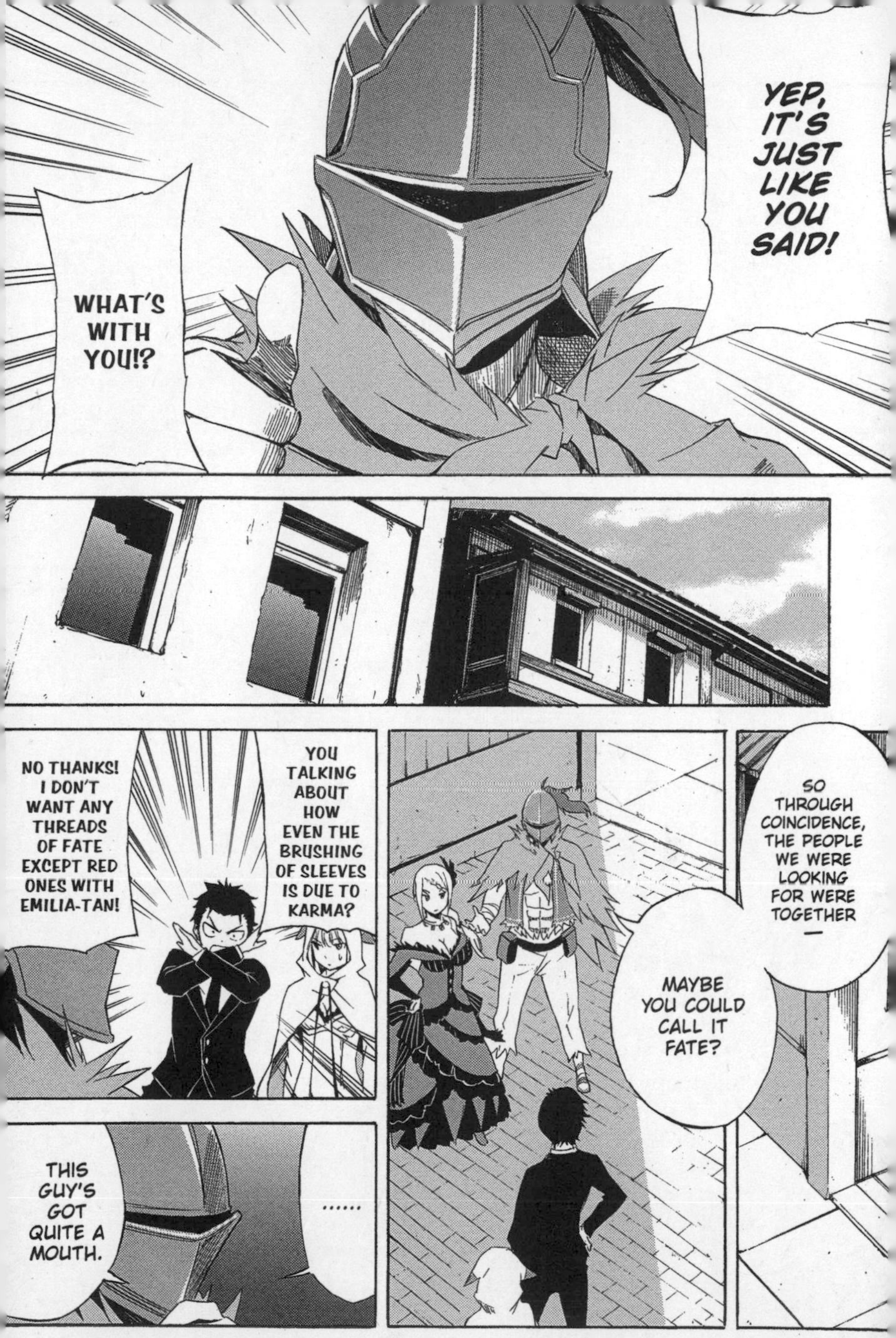
YEP, IT'S JUST LIKE YOU SAID!
WHAT'S WITH YOU!?
SO THROUGH COINCIDENCE, THE PEOPLE WE WERE LOOKING FOR WERE TOGETHER —
MAYBE YOU COULD CALL IT FATE?
YOU TALKING ABOUT HOW EVEN THE BRUSHING OF SLEEVES IS DUE TO KARMA?
NO THANKS! I DON'T WANT ANY THREADS OF FATE EXCEPT RED ONES WITH EMILIA-TAN!
......
THIS GUY'S GOT QUITE A MOUTH.

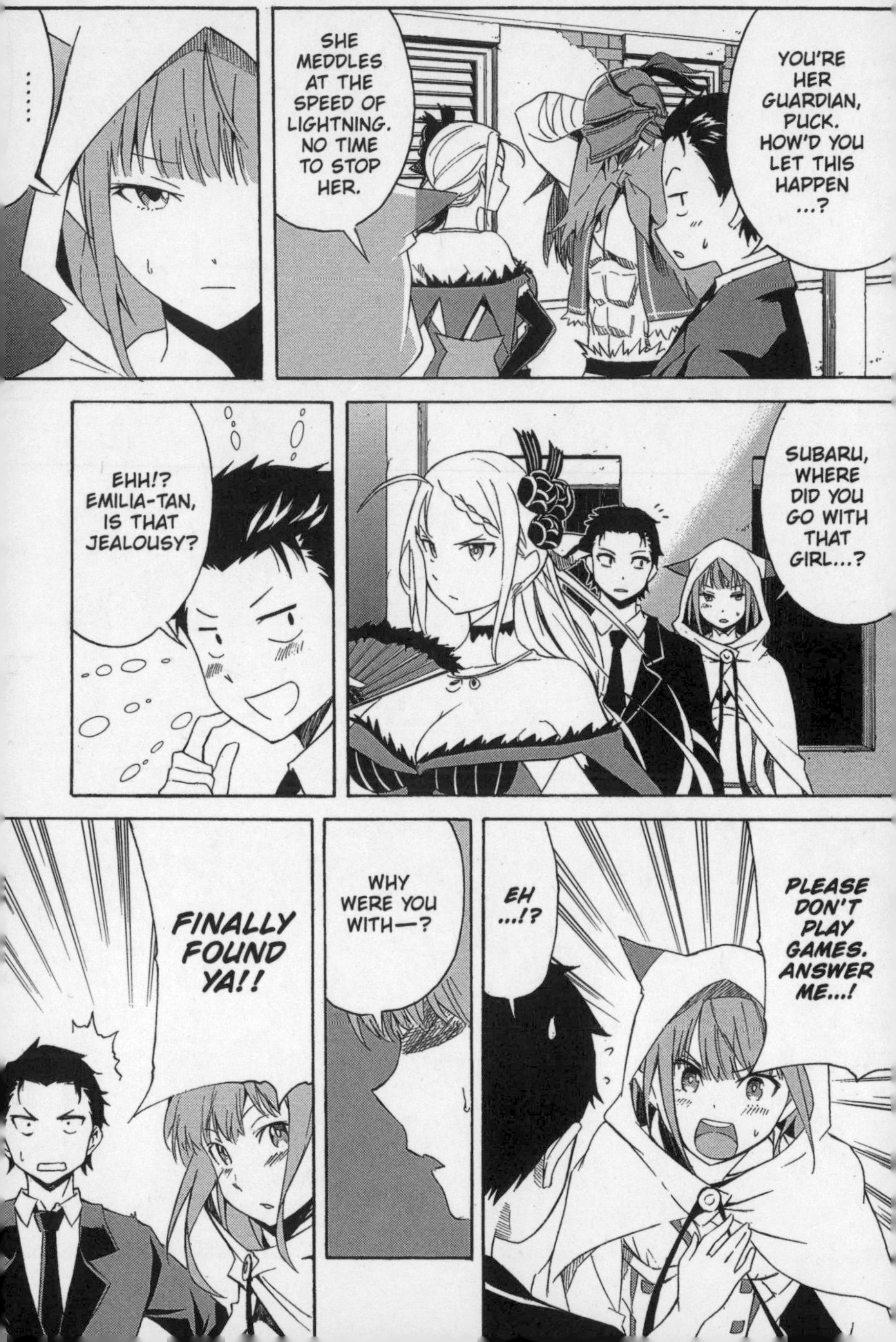
YOU'RE HER GUARDIAN, PUCK. HOW'D YOU LET THIS HAPPEN ...?
SHE MEDDLES AT THE SPEED OF LIGHTNING. NO TIME TO STOP HER.
......
SUBARU, WHERE DID YOU GO WITH THAT GIRL...?
EHH!? EMILIA-TAN, IS THAT JEALOUSY?
PLEASE DON'T PLAY GAMES. ANSWER ME...!
EH ...!?
WHY WERE YOU WITH—?
FINALLY FOUND YA!!

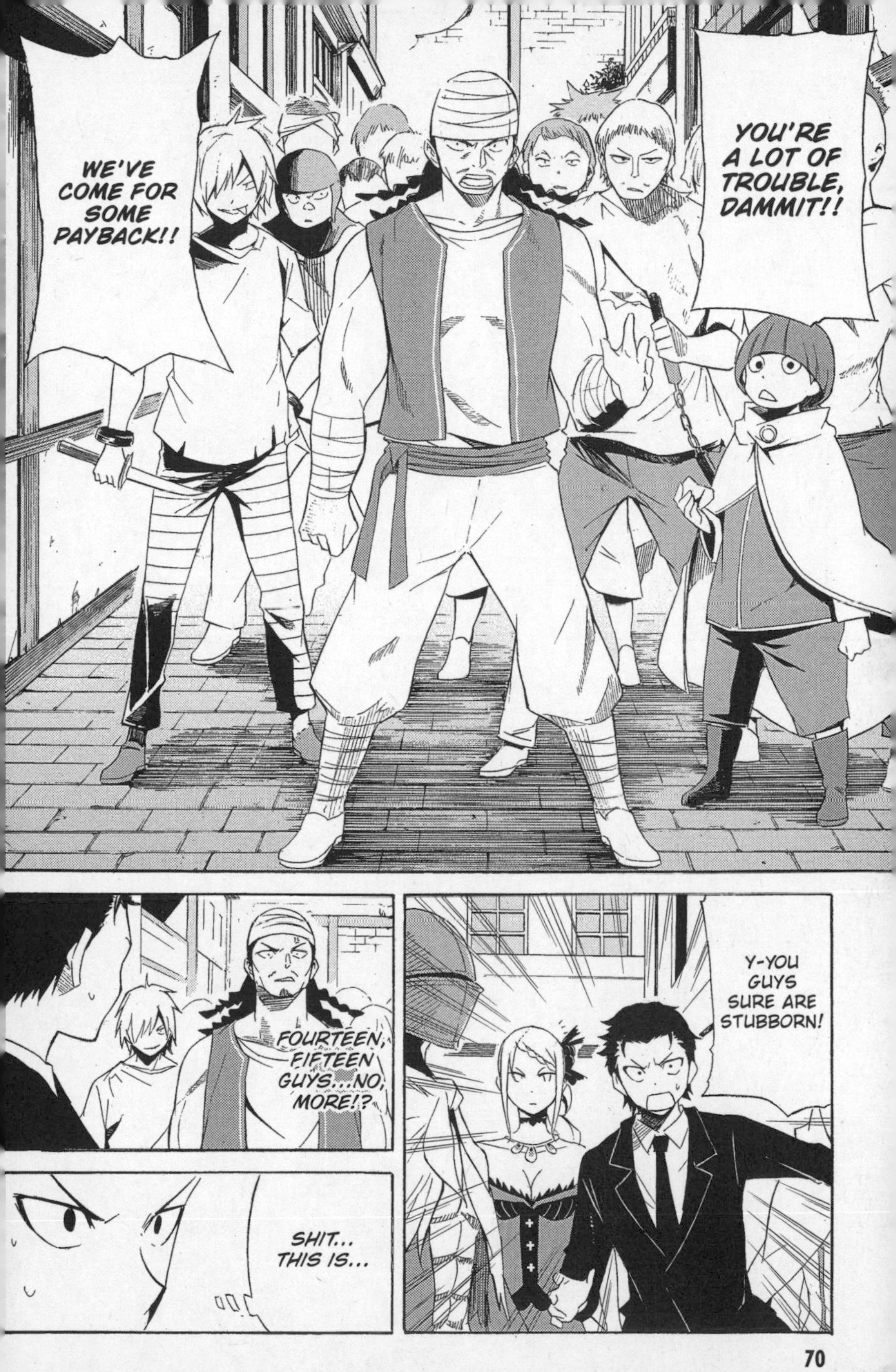
YOU'RE A LOT OF TROUBLE, DAMMIT!!
WE'VE COME FOR SOME PAYBACK!!
Y-YOU GUYS SURE ARE STUBBORN!
FOURTEEN, FIFTEEN GUYS...NO, MORE!?
SHIT... THIS IS...

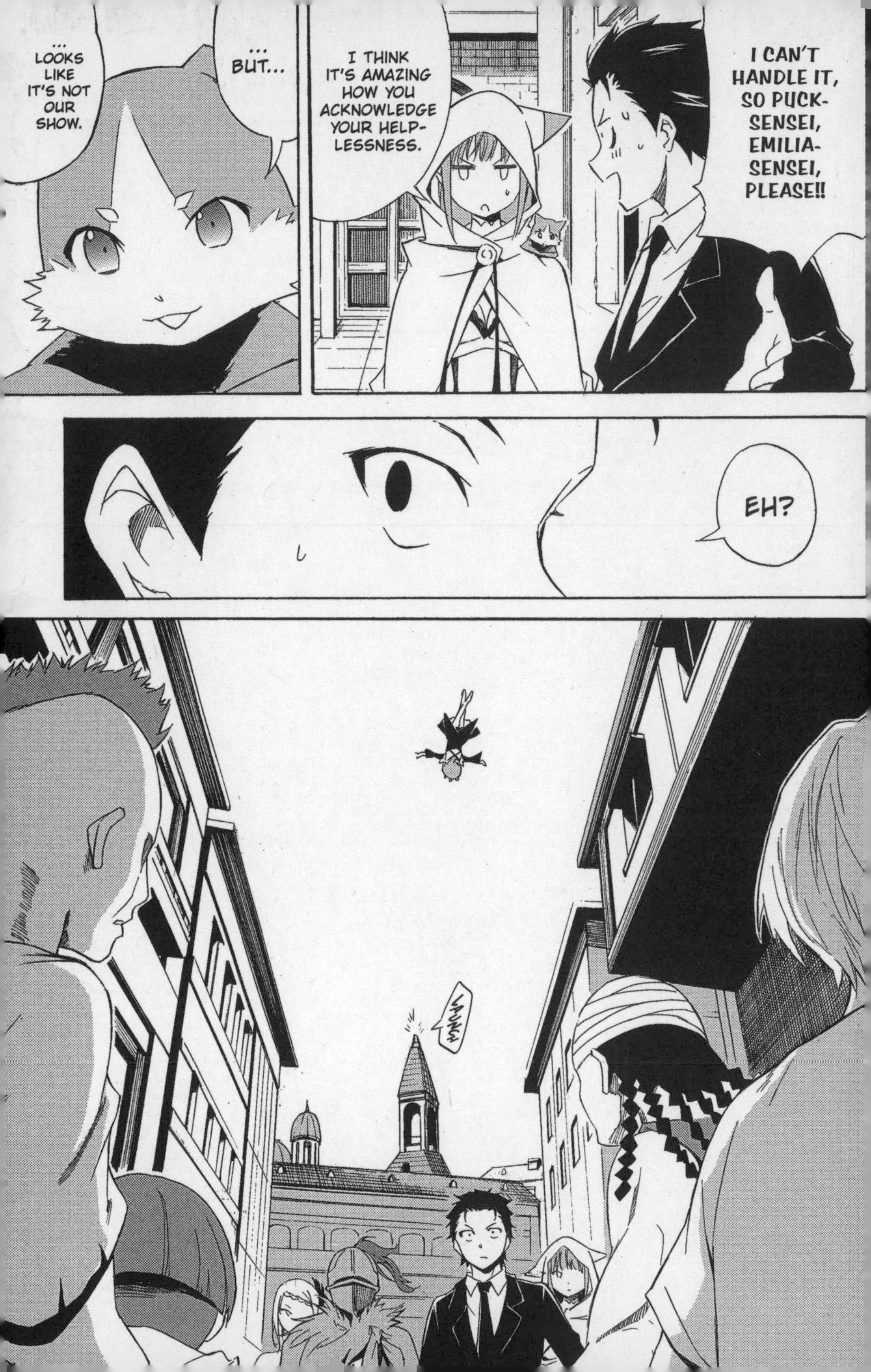
I CAN'T HANDLE IT, SO PUCK-SENSEI, EMILIA-SENSEI, PLEASE!!
I THINK IT'S AMAZING HOW YOU ACKNOWLEDGE YOUR HELP-LESSNESS.
... BUT...
... LOOKS LIKE IT'S NOT OUR SHOW.
EH?
LAUNCH

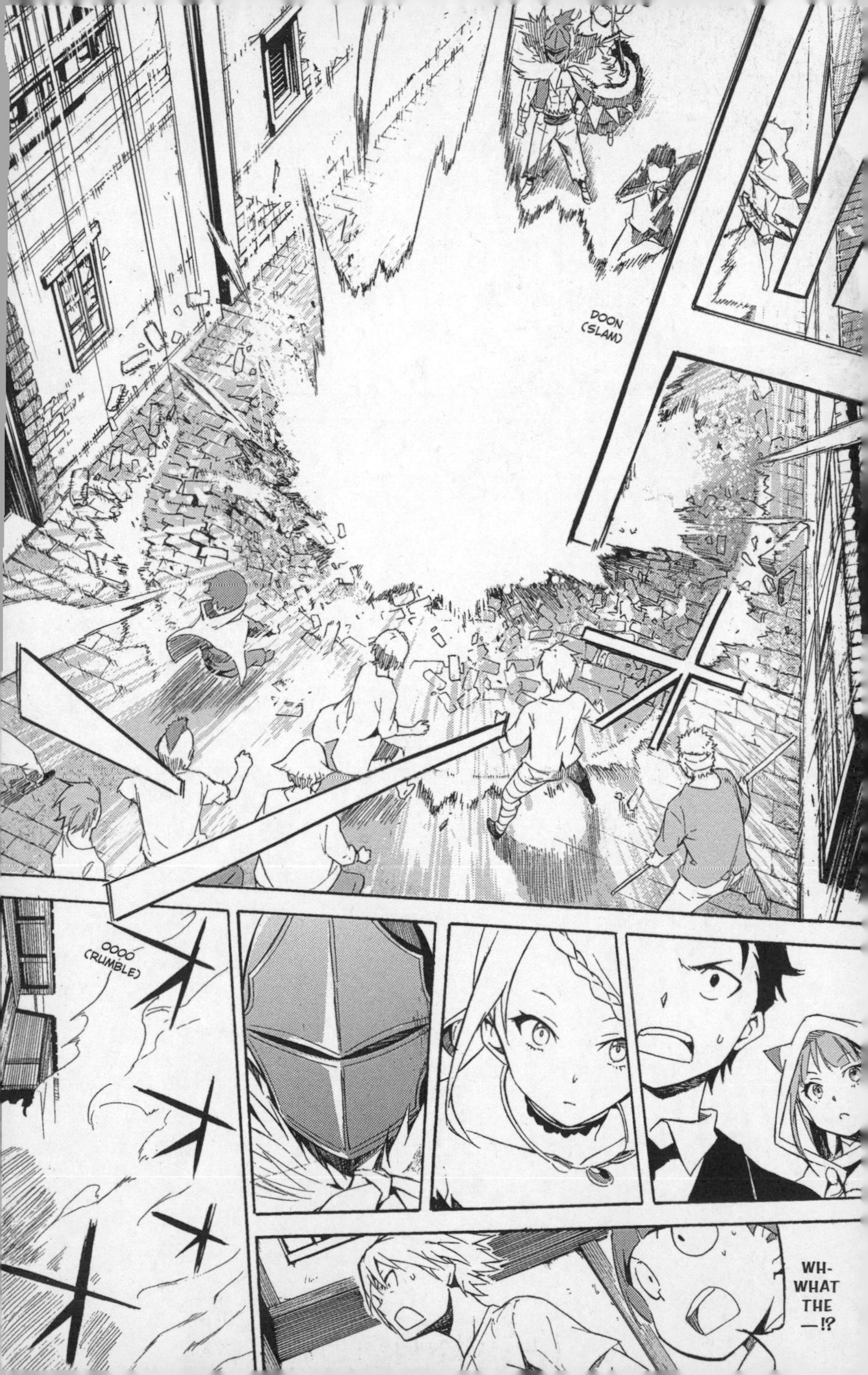
DOON
(SLAM)
OOOO
(RUMBLE)
WH-
WHAT
THE
—!?

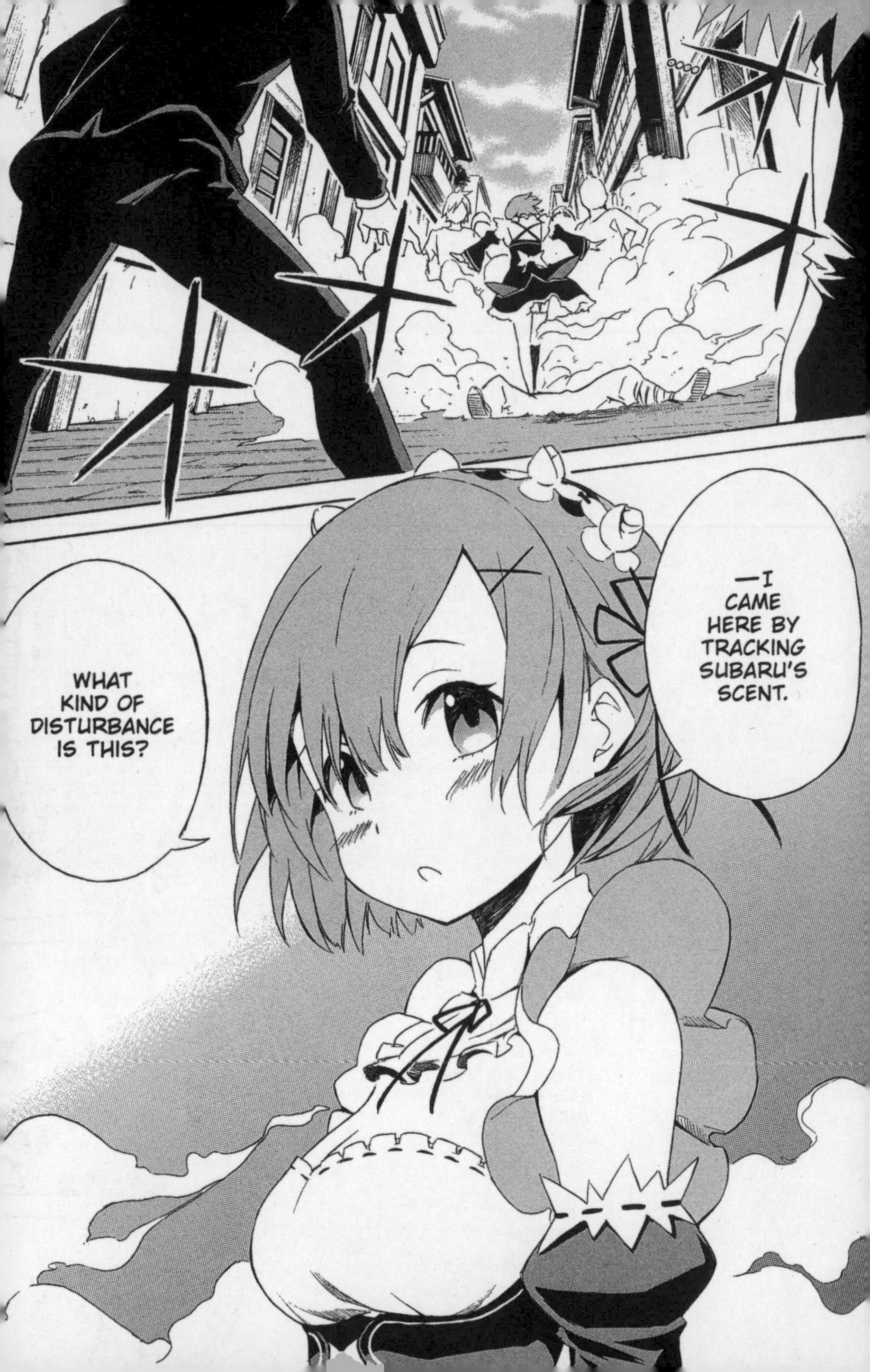
—I CAME HERE BY TRACKING SUBARU'S SCENT.
WHAT KIND OF DISTURBANCE IS THIS?

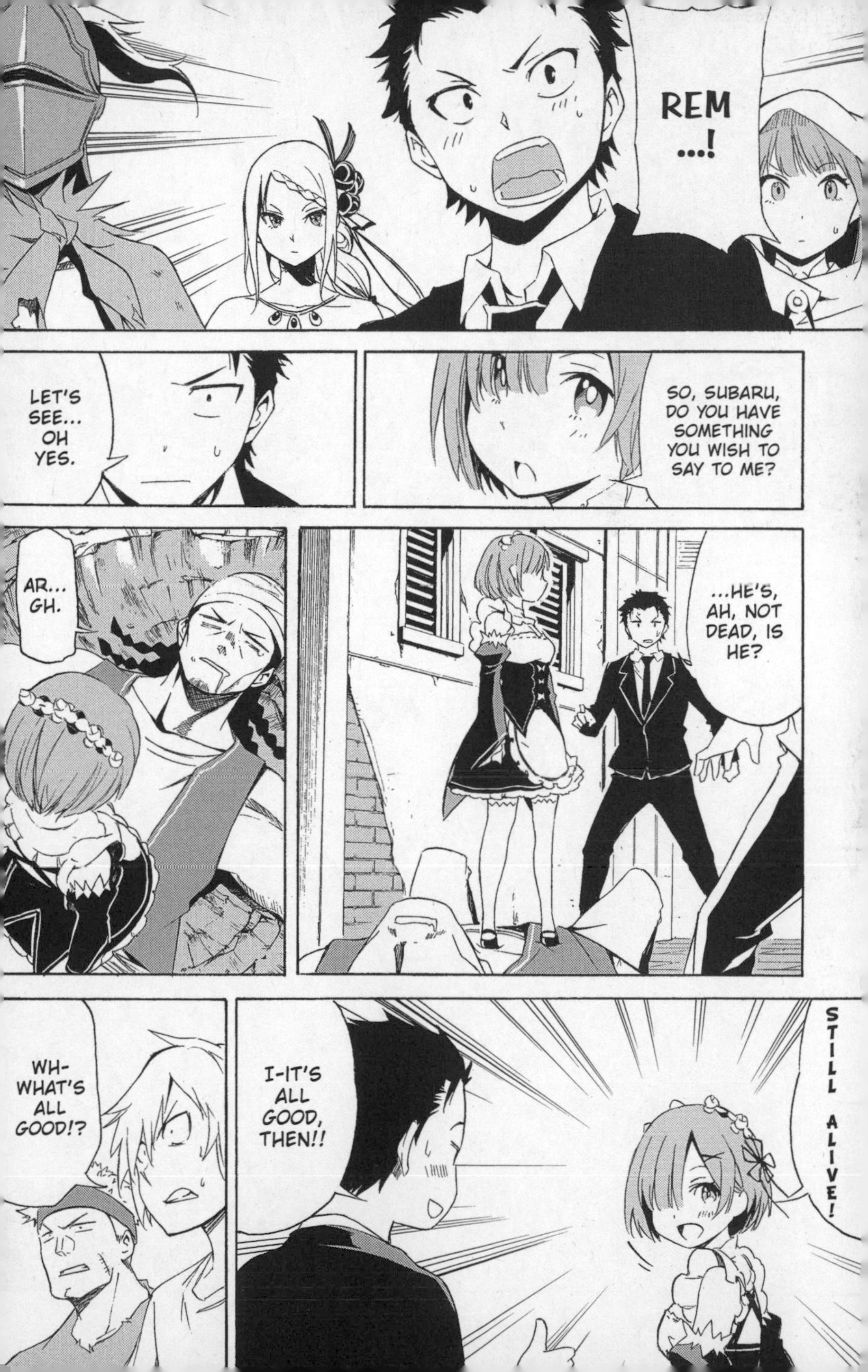
REM ...!
SO, SUBARU, DO YOU HAVE SOMETHING YOU WISH TO SAY TO ME?
LET'S SEE... OH YES.
...HE'S, AH, NOT DEAD, IS HE?
AR... GH.
STILL ALIVE!
I-IT'S ALL GOOD, THEN!!
WH-WHAT'S ALL GOOD!?

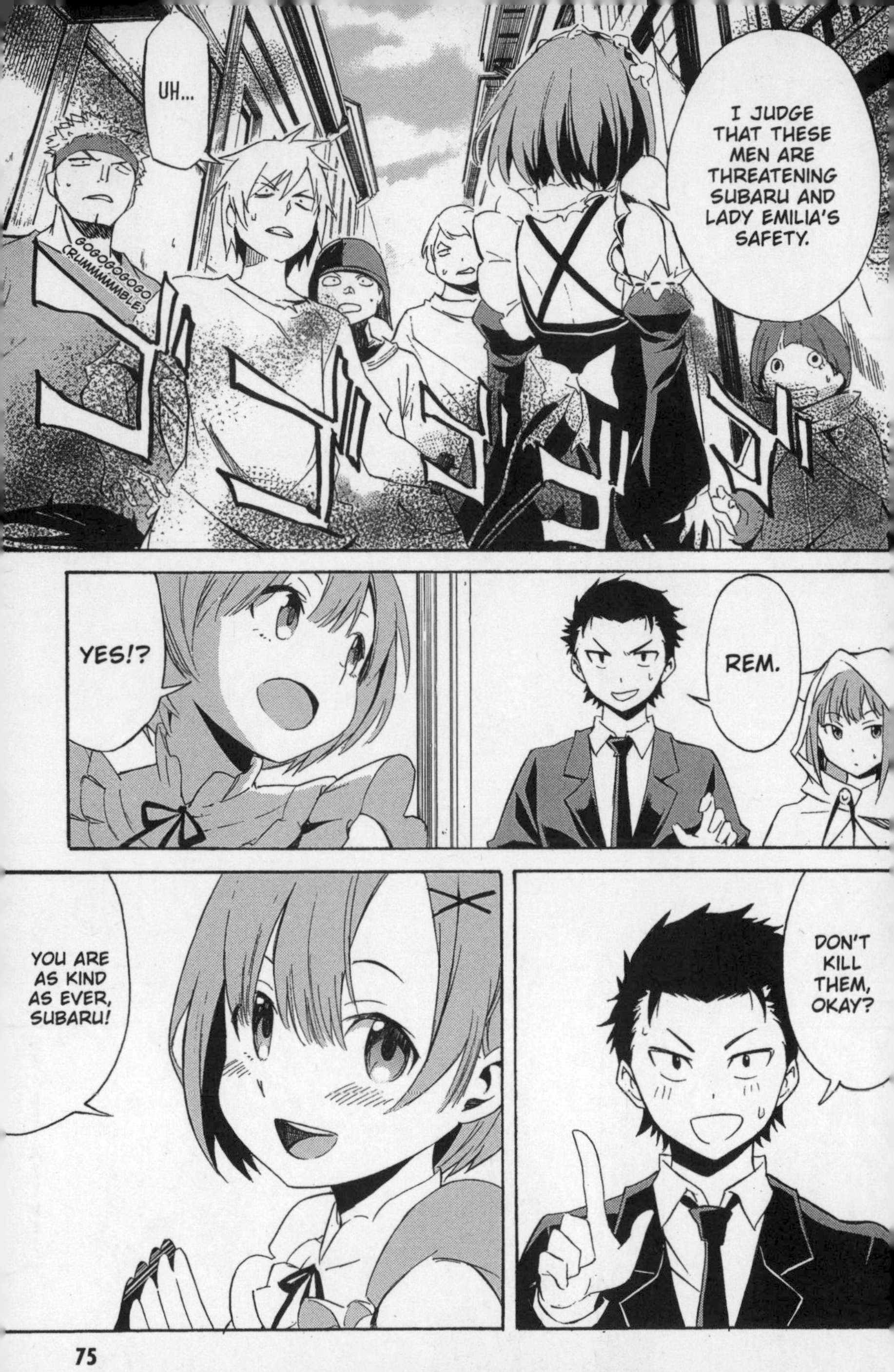
I JUDGE THAT THESE MEN ARE THREATENING SUBARU AND LADY EMILIA'S SAFETY.
UH...
GOGOGOGOGO (RUMMMMMMBLE)
REM.
YES!?
DON'T KILL THEM, OKAY?
YOU ARE AS KIND AS EVER, SUBARU!

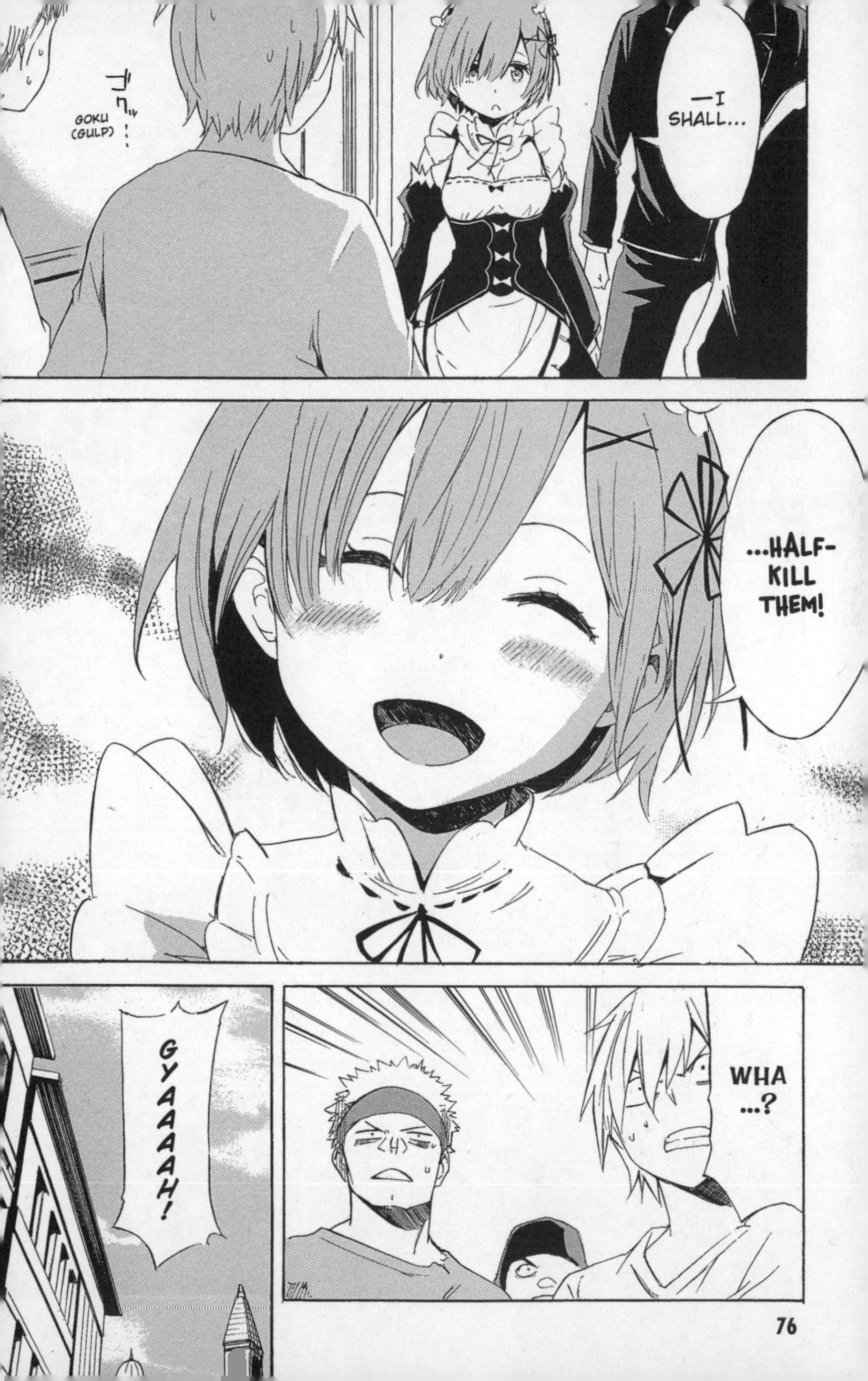
—I SHALL...
ゴクッ
GOKU (GULP)
...HALF-KILL THEM!
WHA ...?
GYAAAAAH!

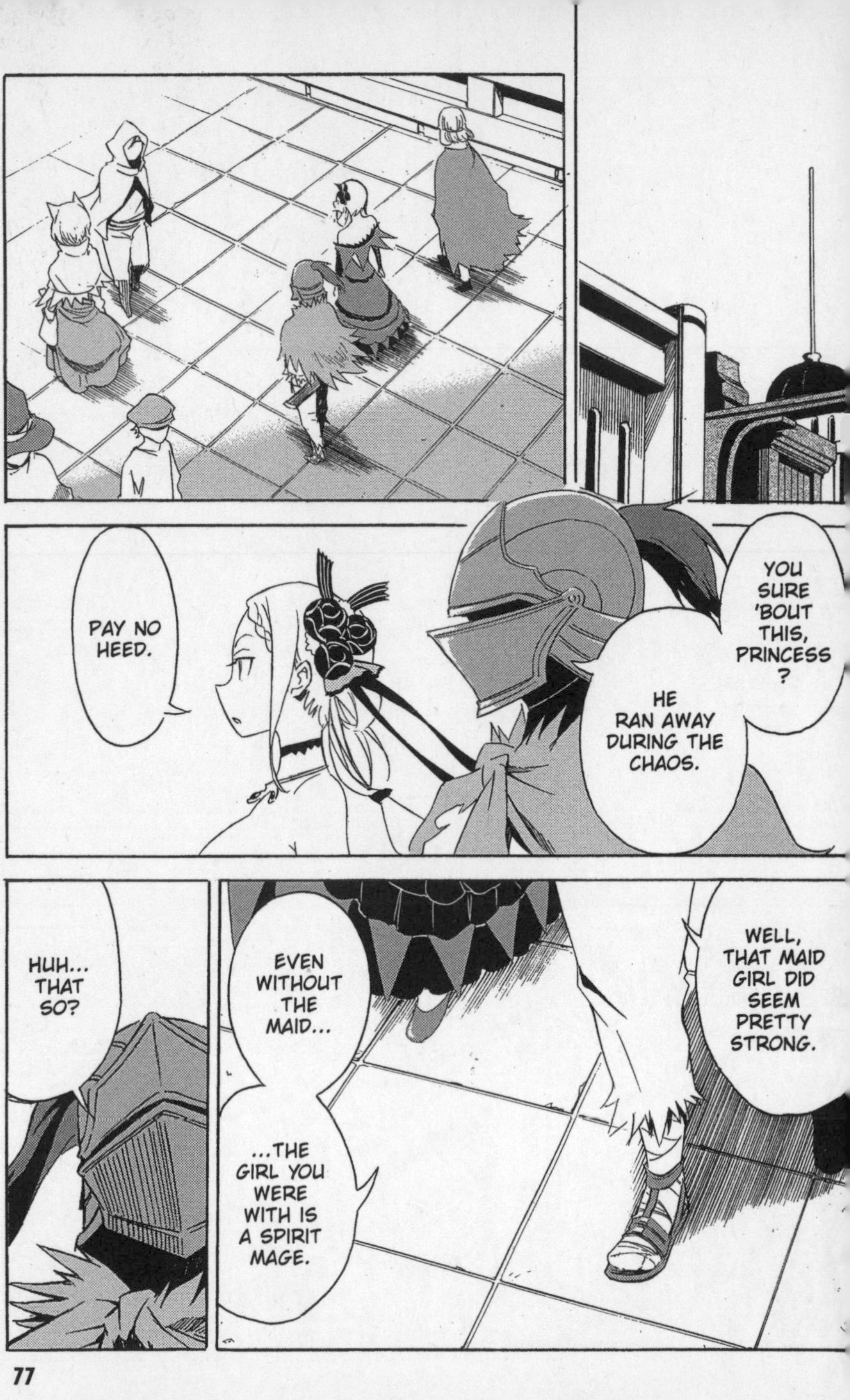
YOU SURE 'BOUT THIS, PRINCESS?
HE RAN AWAY DURING THE CHAOS.
PAY NO HEED.
WELL, THAT MAID GIRL DID SEEM PRETTY STRONG.
EVEN WITHOUT THE MAID...
...THE GIRL YOU WERE WITH IS A SPIRIT MAGE.
HUH... THAT SO?

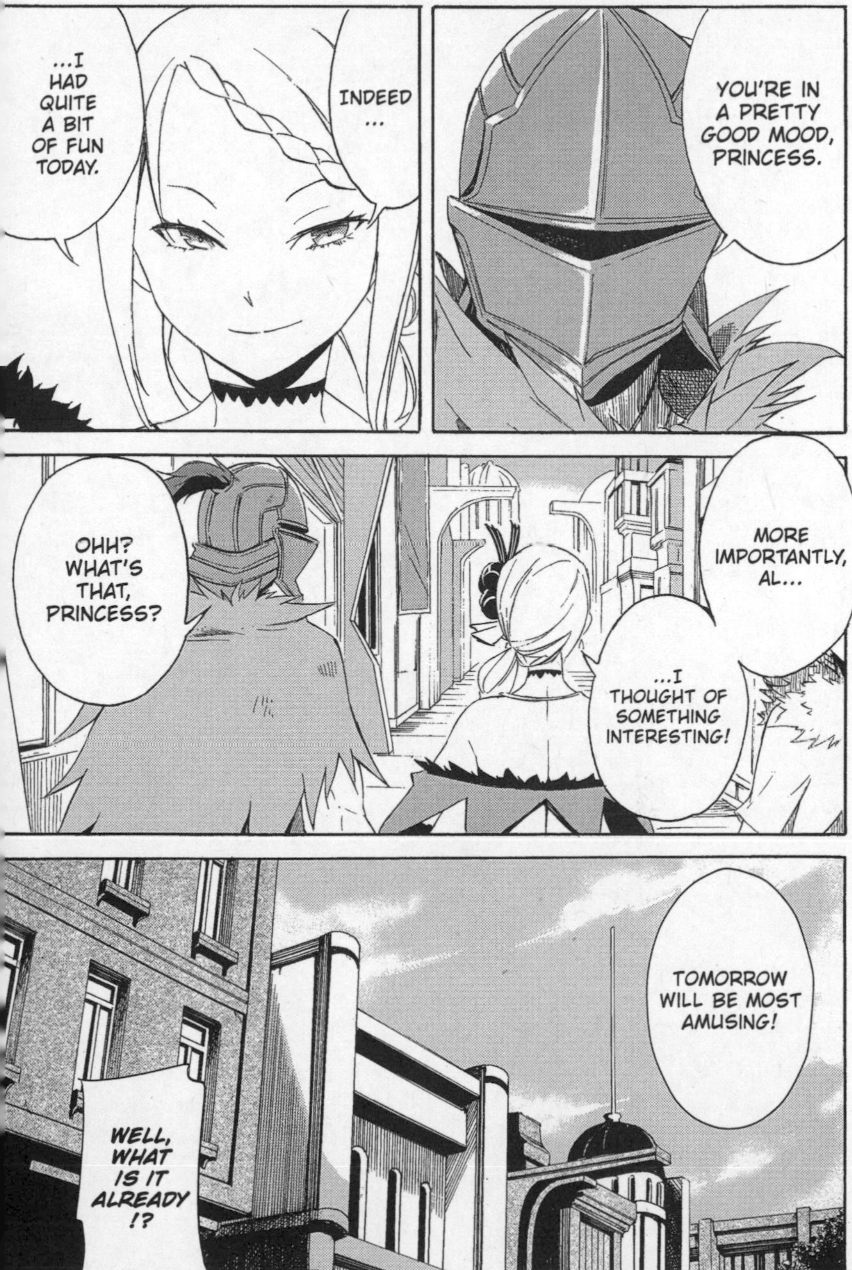
YOU'RE IN A PRETTY GOOD MOOD, PRINCESS.
INDEED...
...I HAD QUITE A BIT OF FUN TODAY.
MORE IMPORTANTLY, AL...
...I THOUGHT OF SOMETHING INTERESTING!
OHH? WHAT'S THAT, PRINCESS?
TOMORROW WILL BE MOST AMUSING!
WELL, WHAT IS IT ALREADY!?

Episode 3
Shared Homeland

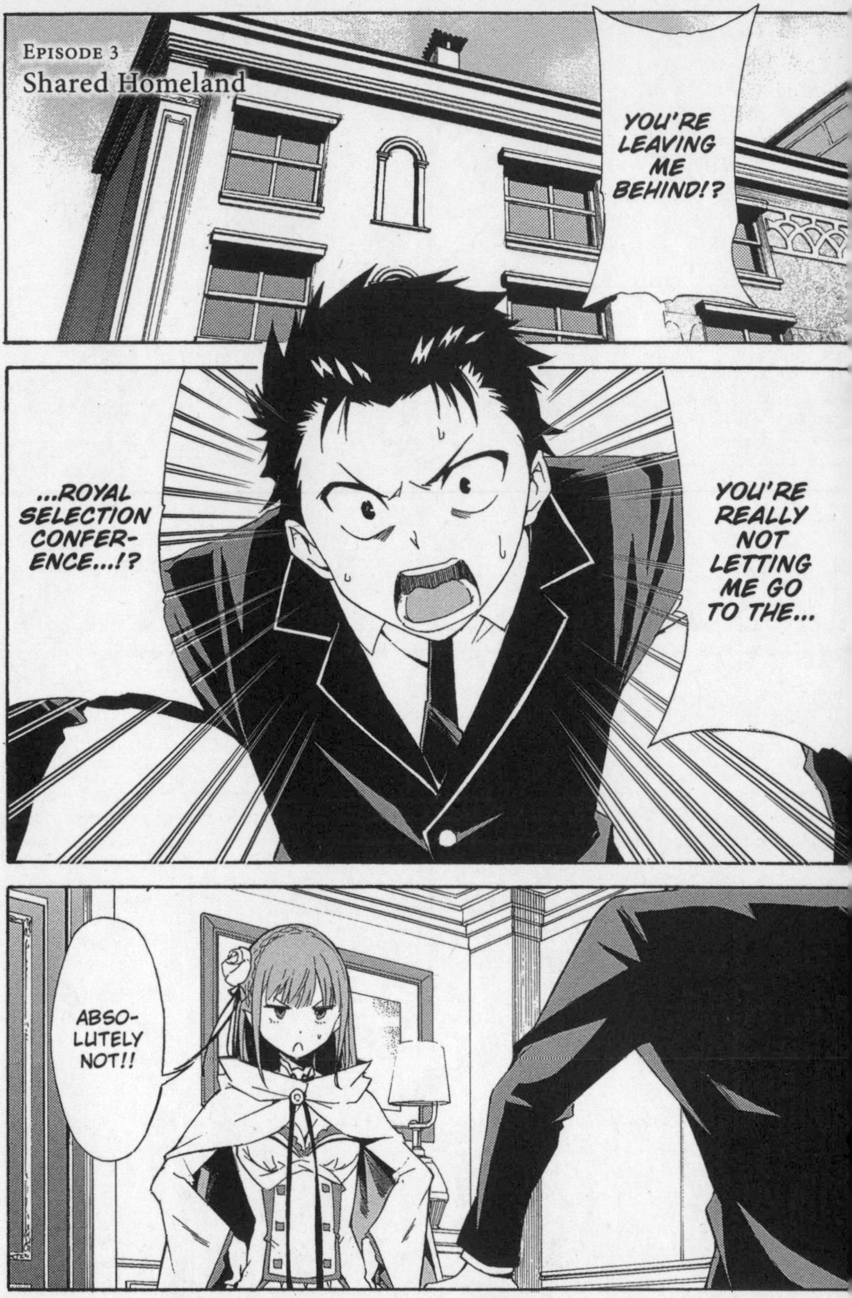
YOU'RE LEAVING ME BEHIND!?
YOU'RE REALLY NOT LETTING ME GO TO THE...
...ROYAL SELECTION CONFER-ENCE...!?
ABSO-LUTELY NOT!!

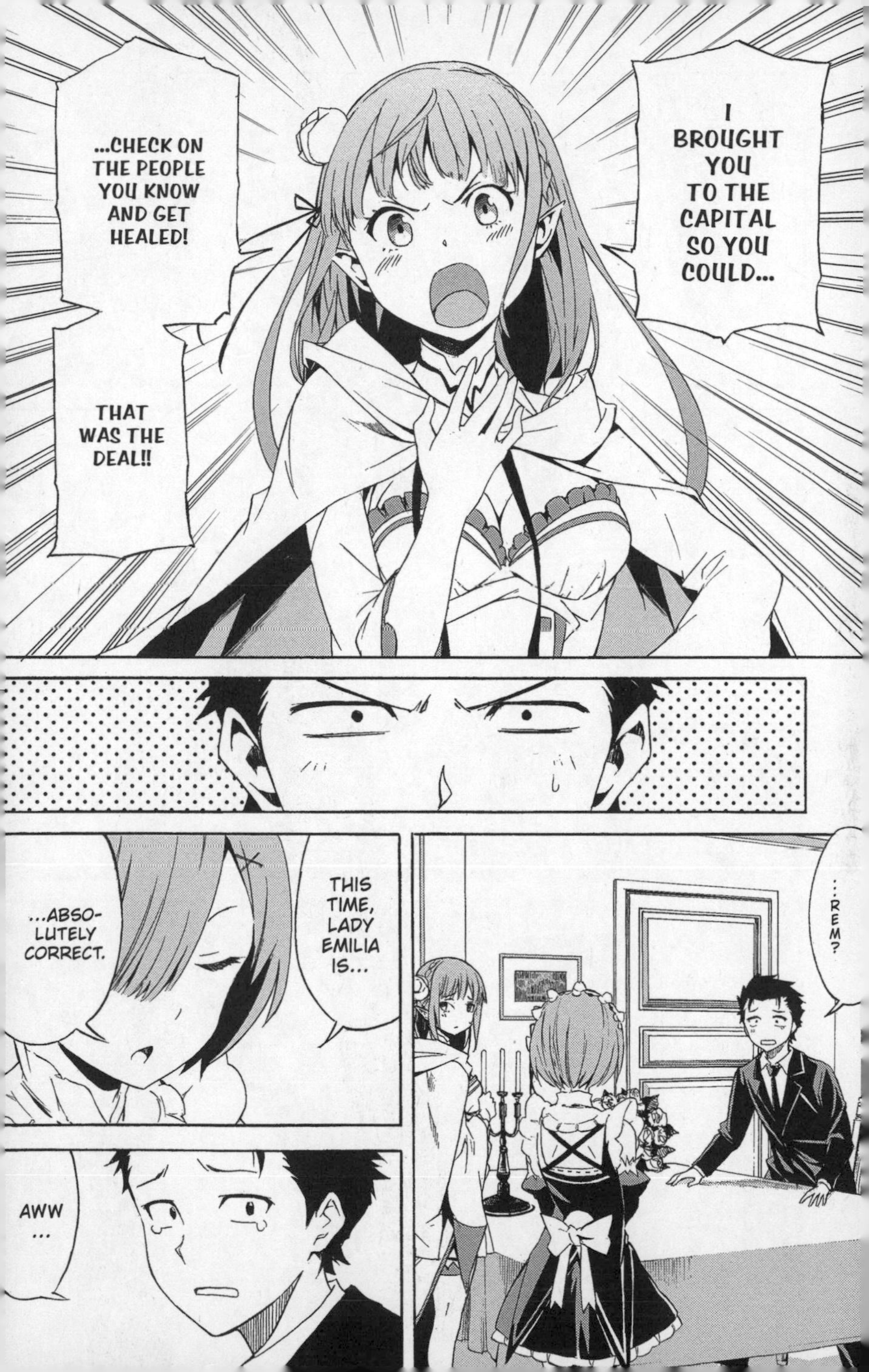
I BROUGHT YOU TO THE CAPITAL SO YOU COULD...
...CHECK ON THE PEOPLE YOU KNOW AND GET HEALED!
THAT WAS THE DEAL!!
...REM?
THIS TIME, LADY EMILIA IS...
...ABSO-LUTELY CORRECT.
AWW ...

Episode 3 Shared Homeland

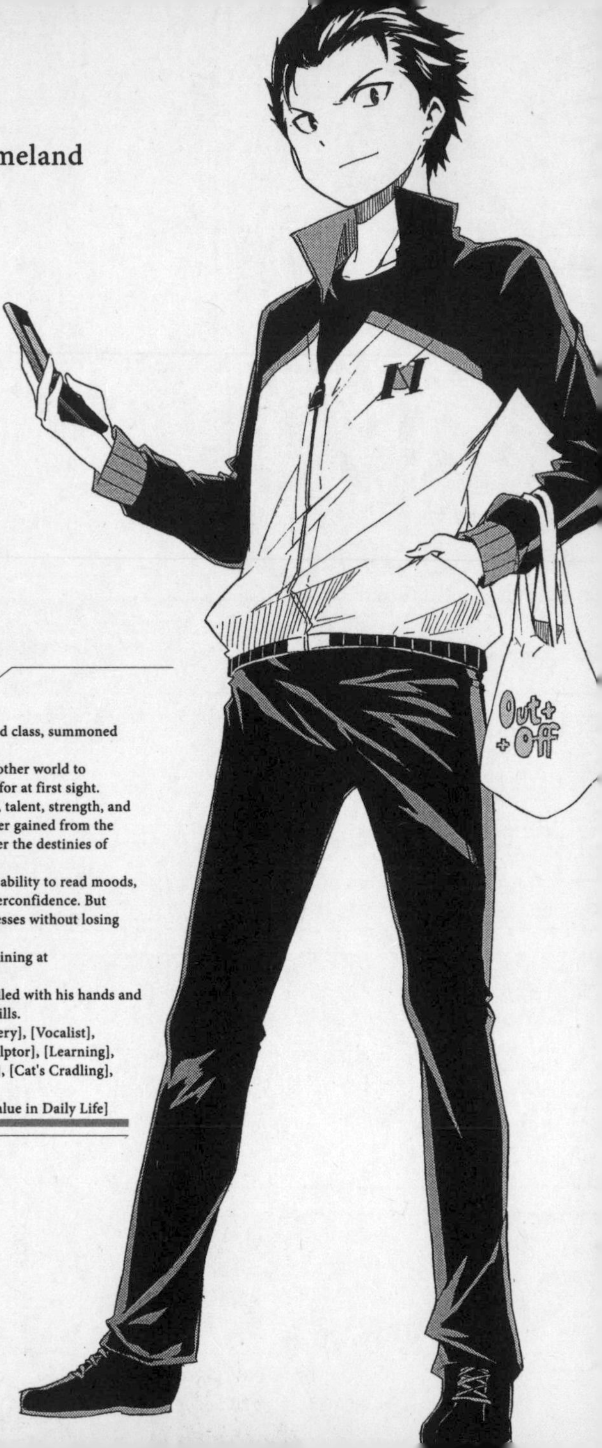
Out+
+Off

SUBARU NATSUKI

- Former shut-in who never attended class, summoned from Earth to another world.
- Scrambling without a clue in this other world to repay his debt to Emilia, who he fell for at first sight.
- A main character lacking intellect, talent, strength, and good sense, but he uses the sole power gained from the summoning, Return by Death, to alter the destinies of those around him.
- His personality lacks delicacy, the ability to read moods, and is prone to frivolousness and overconfidence. But he is able to act despite these weaknesses without losing optimism.
- Currently receiving on-the-job training at Roswaal Manor.
- No combat ability but is oddly skilled with his hands and has a number of worthless special skills.
- Special skills: [Sewing], [Embroidery], [Vocalist], [Portraits], [Bed-Making], [Clay Sculptor], [Learning], [Day Laborer], [Juggling], [Origami], [Cat's Cradling], [Othello], [Puzzles], [IQ Tests], etc.
- Hobbies: [Learning Skills of No Value in Daily Life]

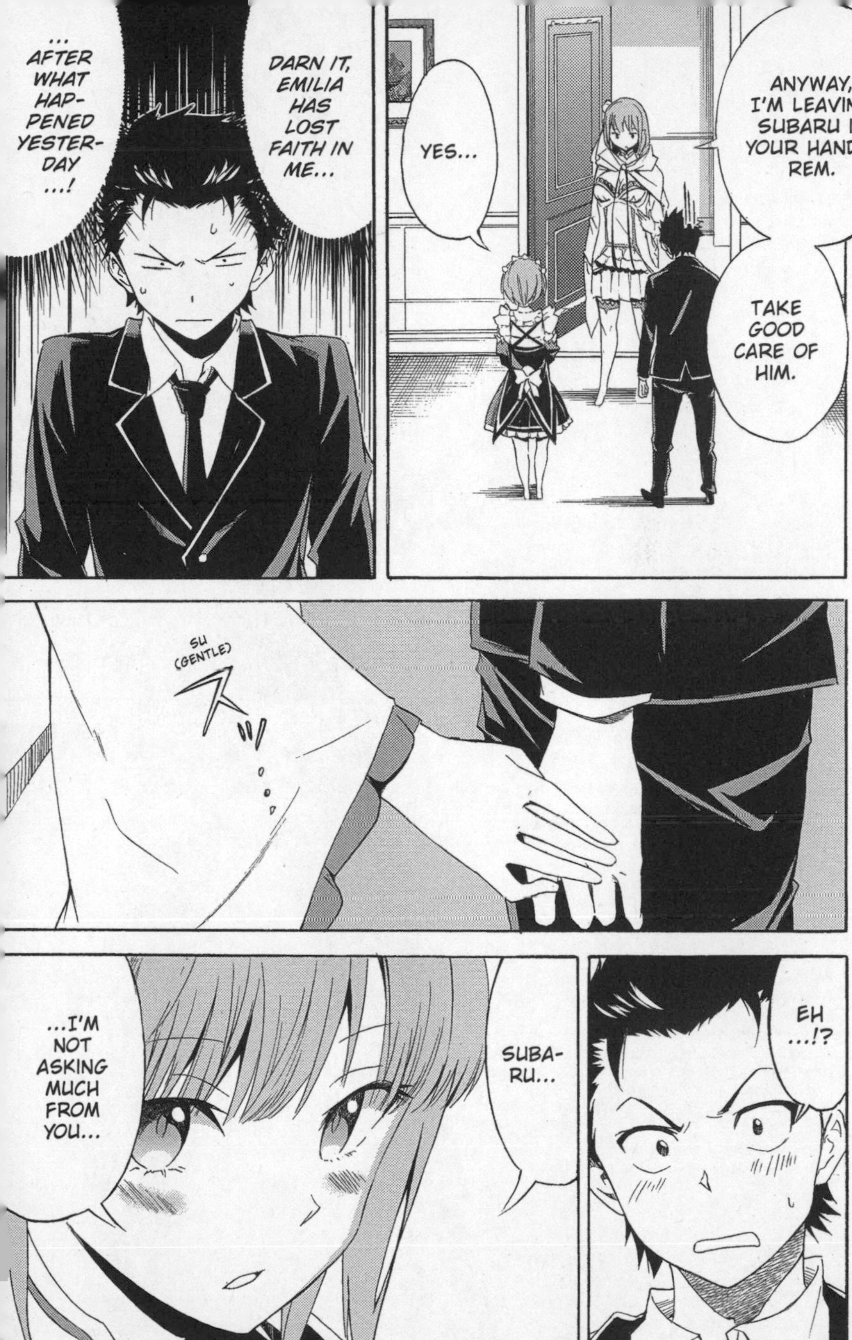
ANYWAY, I'M LEAVING SUBARU IN YOUR HANDS, REM.
TAKE GOOD CARE OF HIM.
YES...
DARN IT, EMILIA HAS LOST FAITH IN ME...
...AFTER WHAT HAP-PENED YESTER-DAY...!
SU (GENTLE)
EH ...!?
SUBA-RU...
...I'M NOT ASKING MUCH FROM YOU...

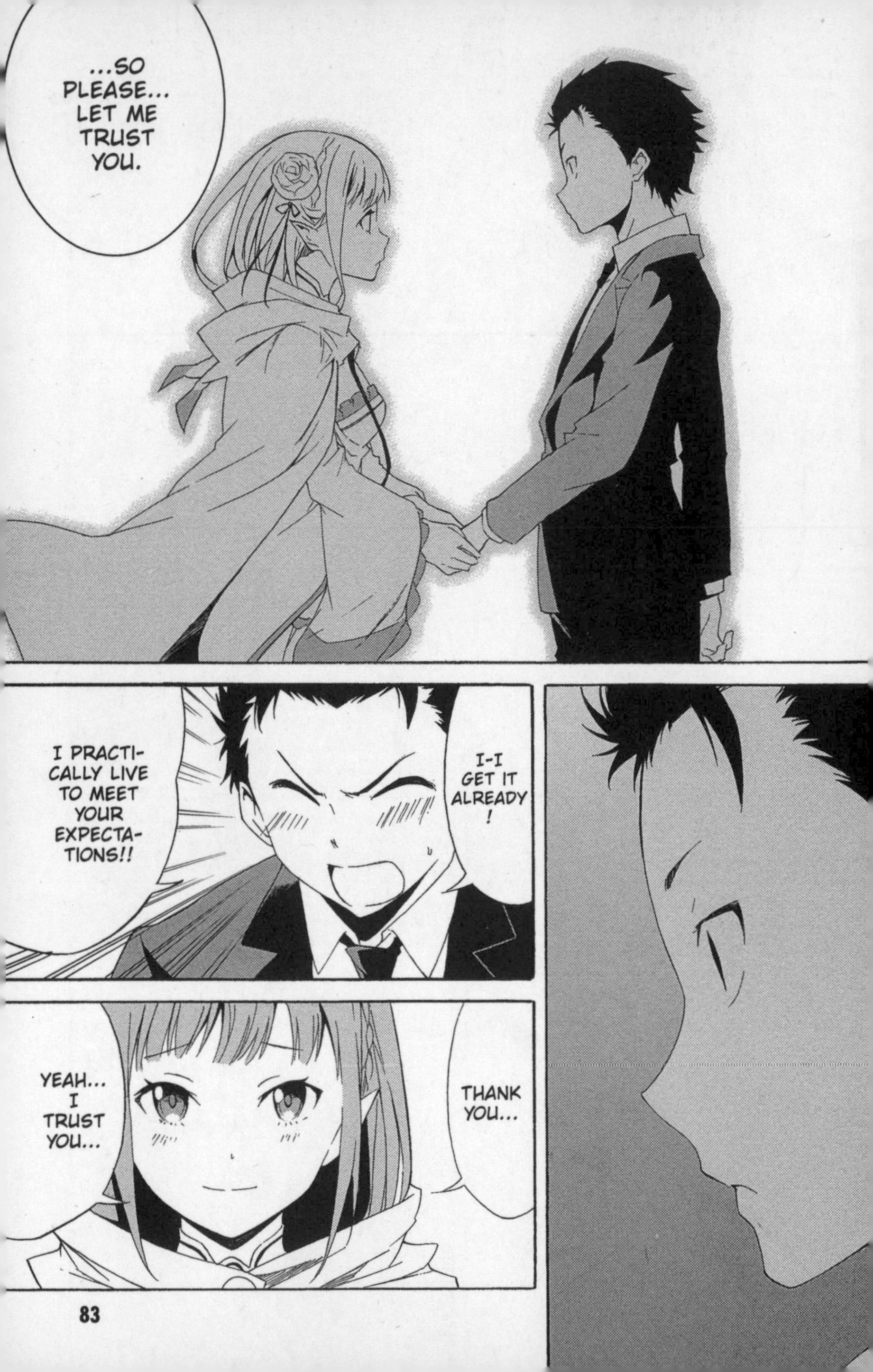
...SO PLEASE... LET ME TRUST YOU.
I-I GET IT ALREADY!
I PRACTICALLY LIVE TO MEET YOUR EXPECTATIONS!!
THANK YOU...
YEAH... I TRUST YOU...

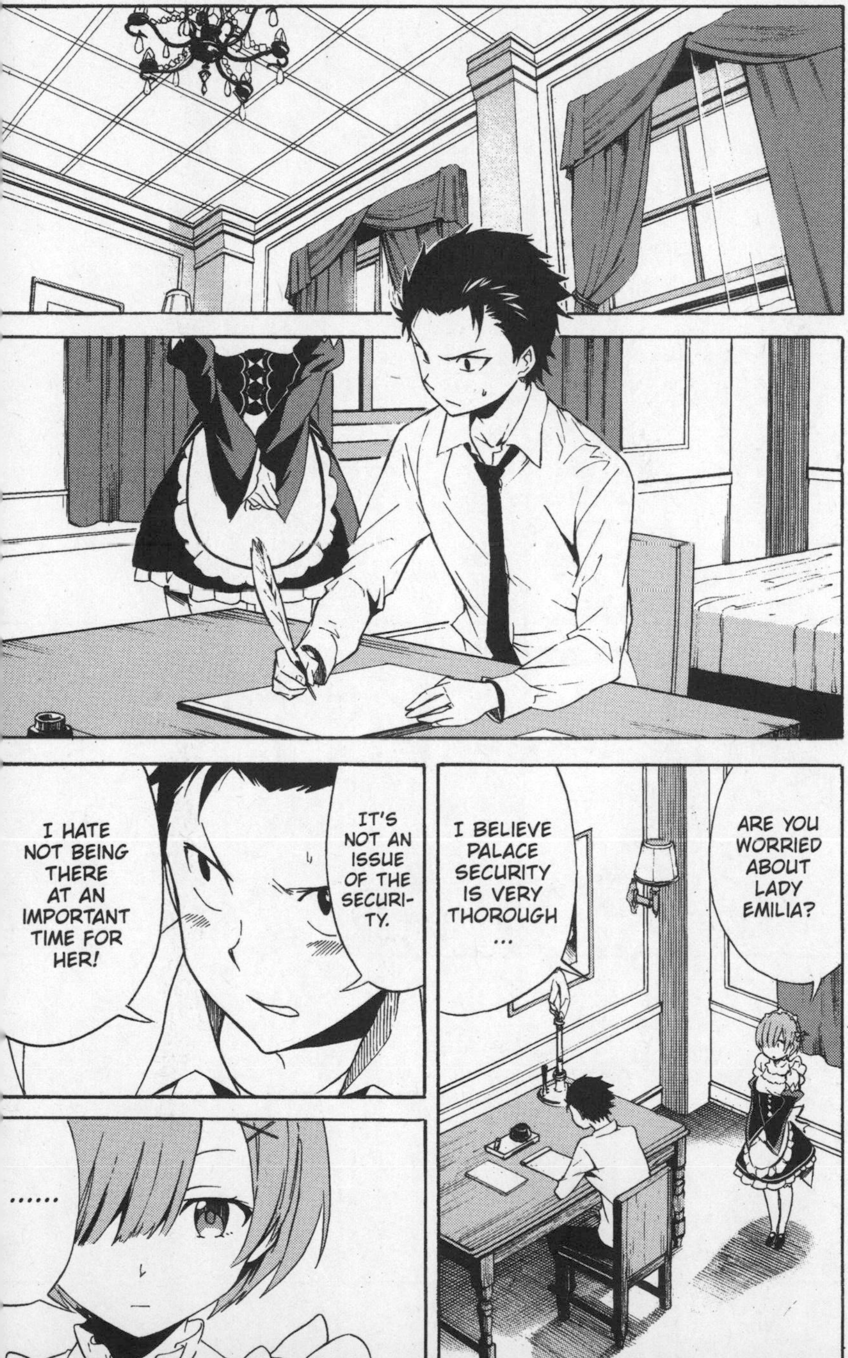
ARE YOU WORRIED ABOUT LADY EMILIA?
I BELIEVE PALACE SECURITY IS VERY THOROUGH...
IT'S NOT AN ISSUE OF THE SECURITY.
I HATE NOT BEING THERE AT AN IMPORTANT TIME FOR HER!
......

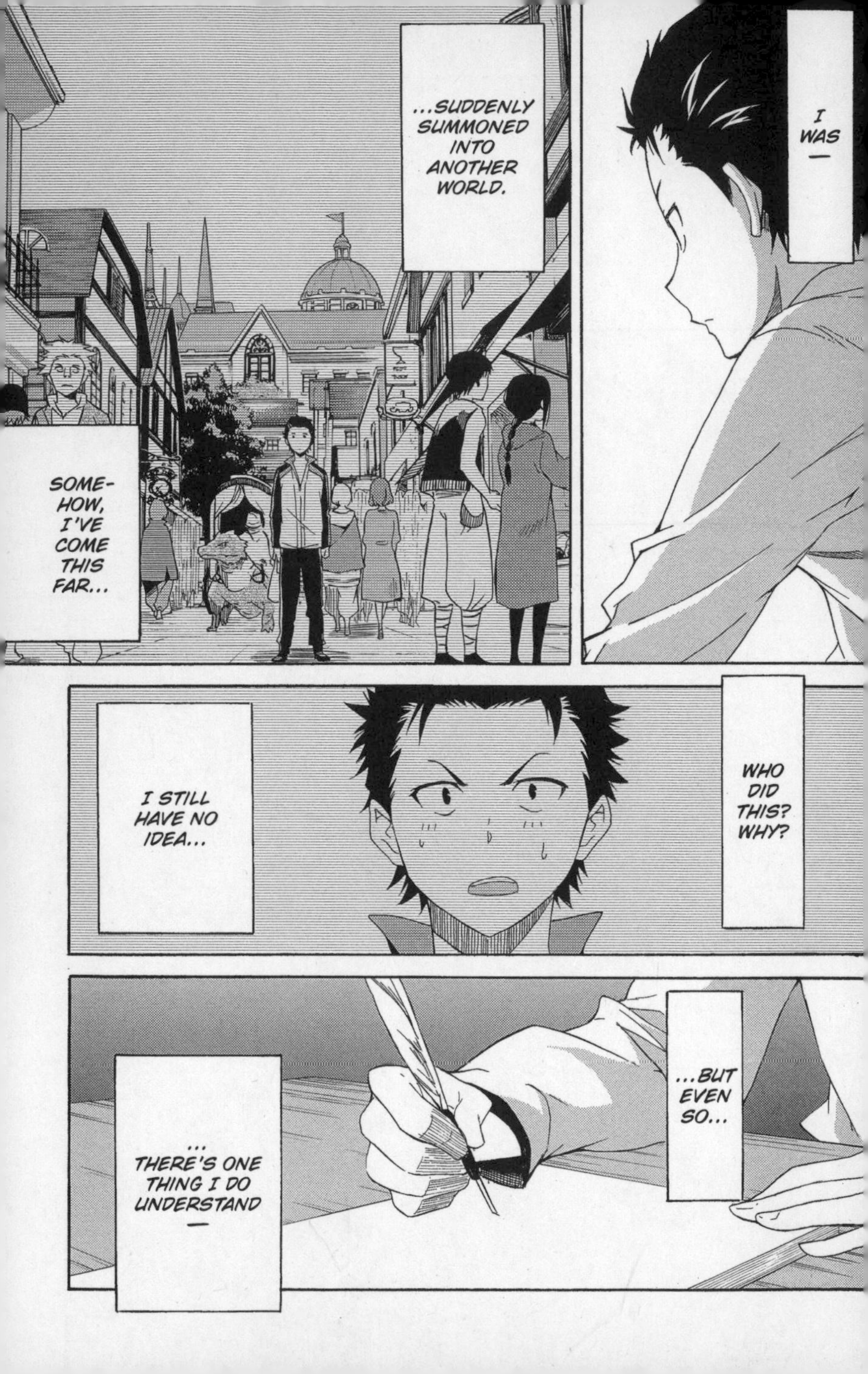
I WAS —
...SUDDENLY SUMMONED INTO ANOTHER WORLD.
SOME-HOW, I'VE COME THIS FAR...
WHO DID THIS? WHY?
I STILL HAVE NO IDEA...
...BUT EVEN SO...
... THERE'S ONE THING I DO UNDERSTAND —

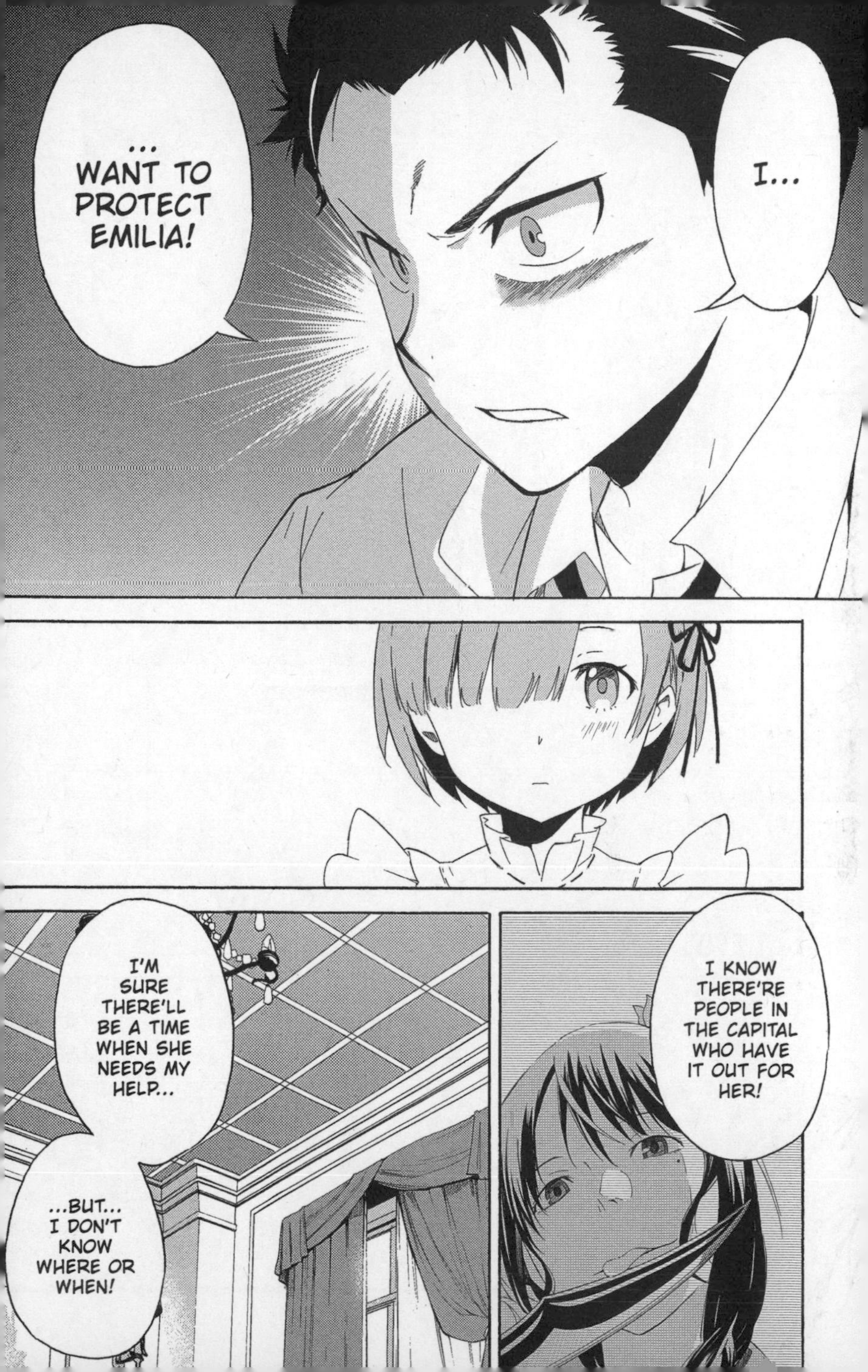
I...
...WANT TO PROTECT EMILIA!
I KNOW THERE'RE PEOPLE IN THE CAPITAL WHO HAVE IT OUT FOR HER!
I'M SURE THERE'LL BE A TIME WHEN SHE NEEDS MY HELP...
...BUT... I DON'T KNOW WHERE OR WHEN!

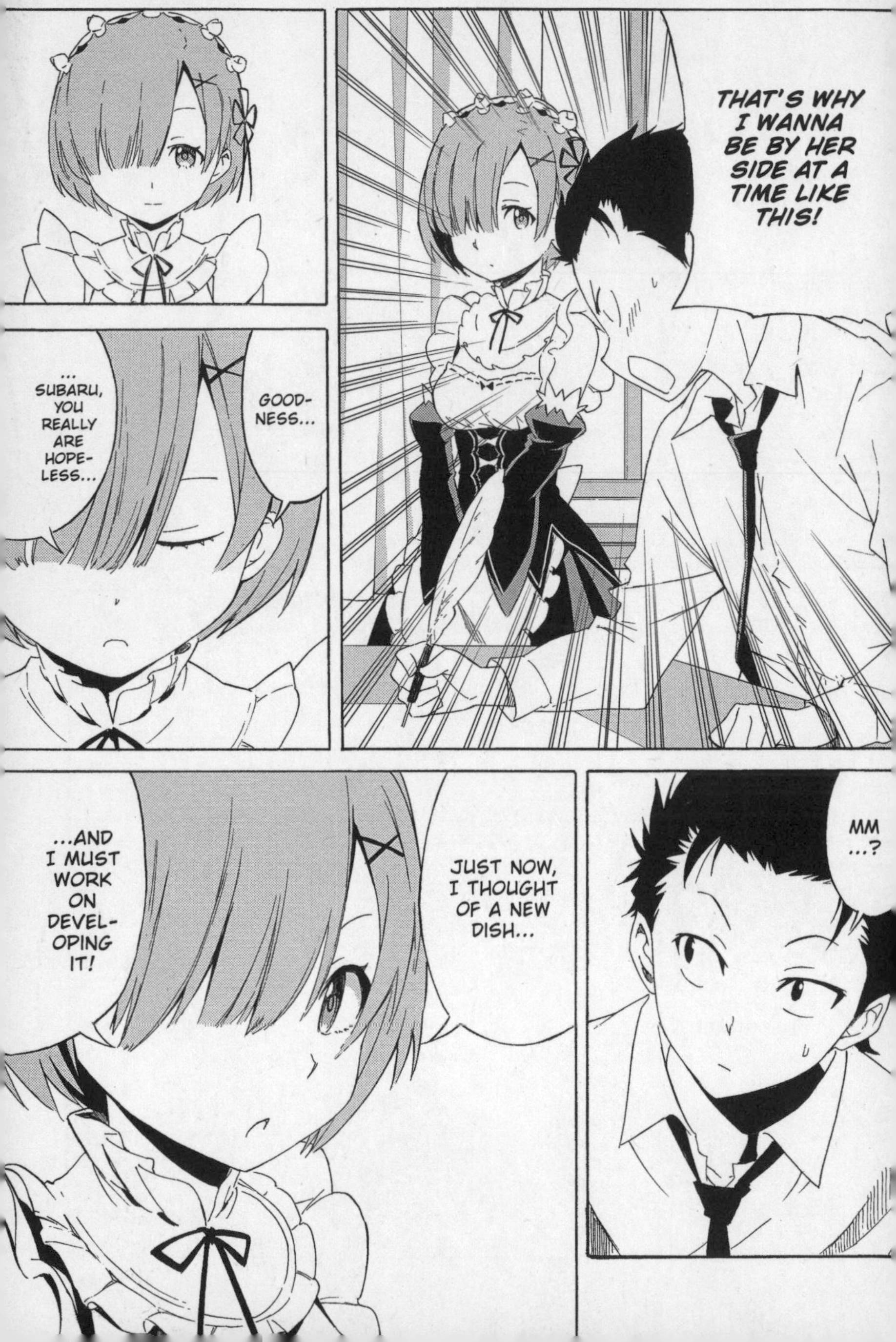
THAT'S WHY I WANNA BE BY HER SIDE AT A TIME LIKE THIS!
GOOD-NESS...
...SUBARU, YOU REALLY ARE HOPE-LESS...
MM ...?
JUST NOW, I THOUGHT OF A NEW DISH...
...AND I MUST WORK ON DEVEL-OPING IT!

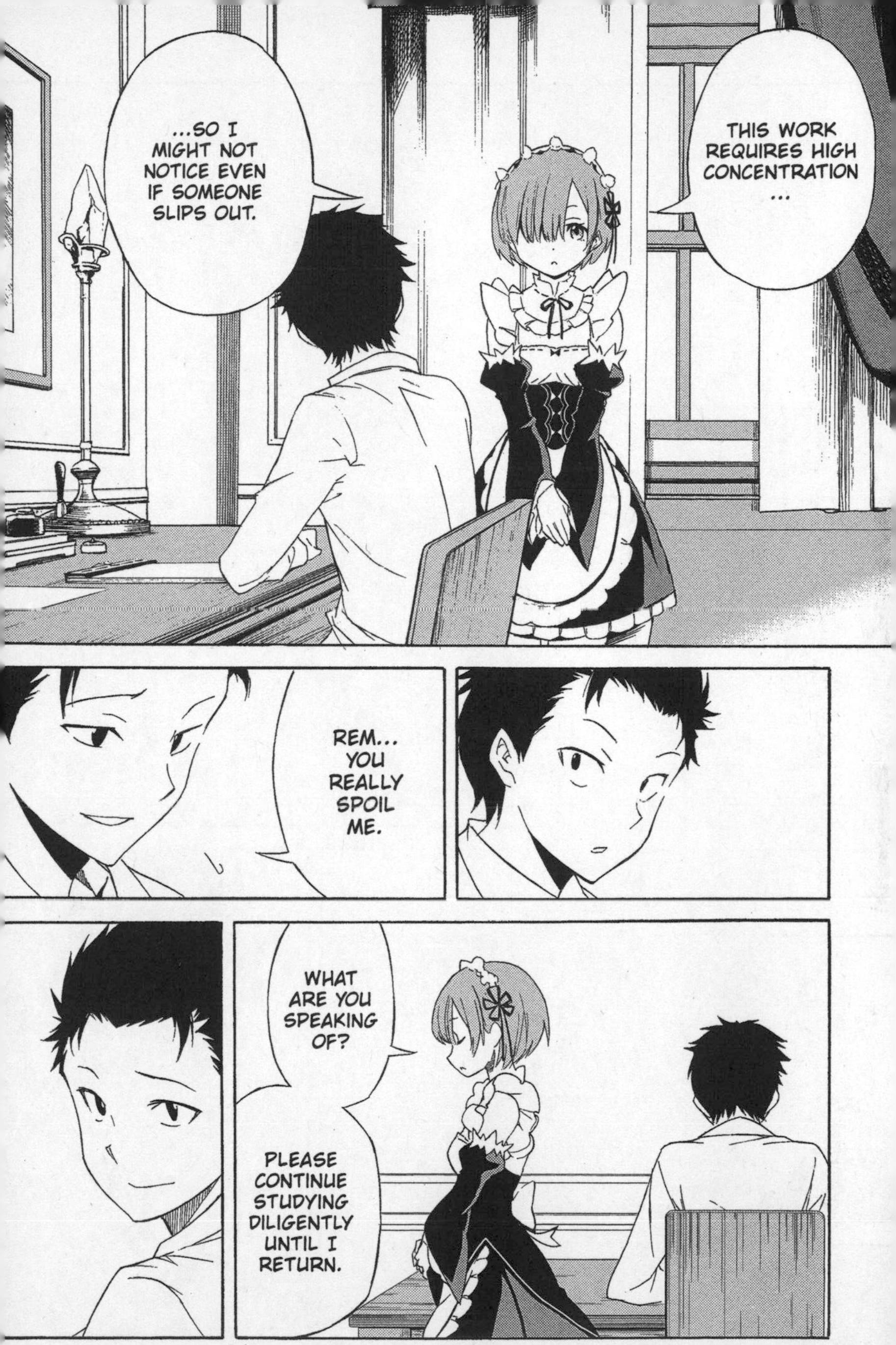
THIS WORK REQUIRES HIGH CONCENTRATION ...
...SO I MIGHT NOT NOTICE EVEN IF SOMEONE SLIPS OUT.
REM... YOU REALLY SPOIL ME.
WHAT ARE YOU SPEAKING OF?
PLEASE CONTINUE STUDYING DILIGENTLY UNTIL I RETURN.

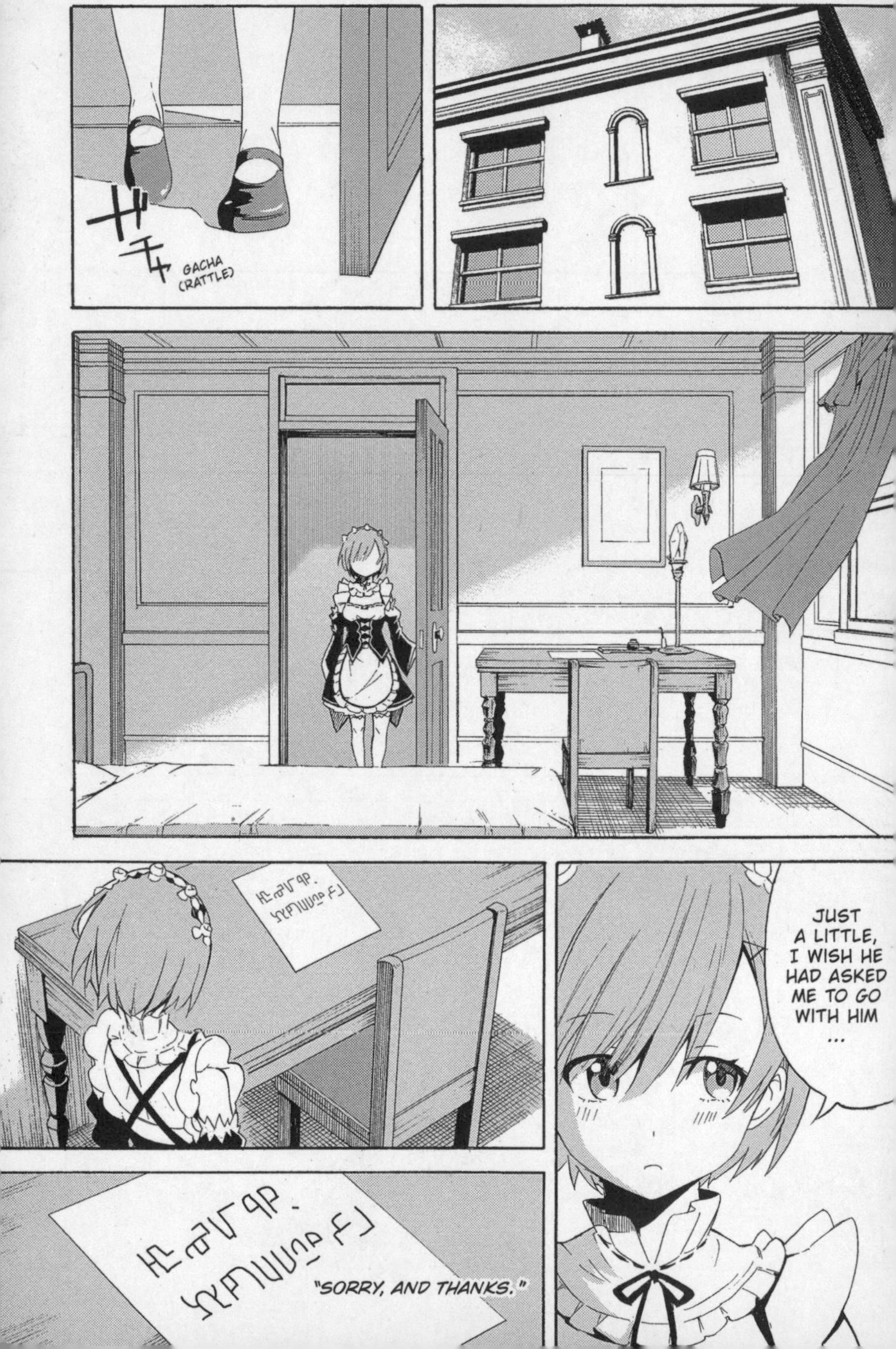
ガチャ
GACHA (RATTLE)
JUST A LITTLE, I WISH HE HAD ASKED ME TO GO WITH HIM ...
"SORRY, AND THANKS."

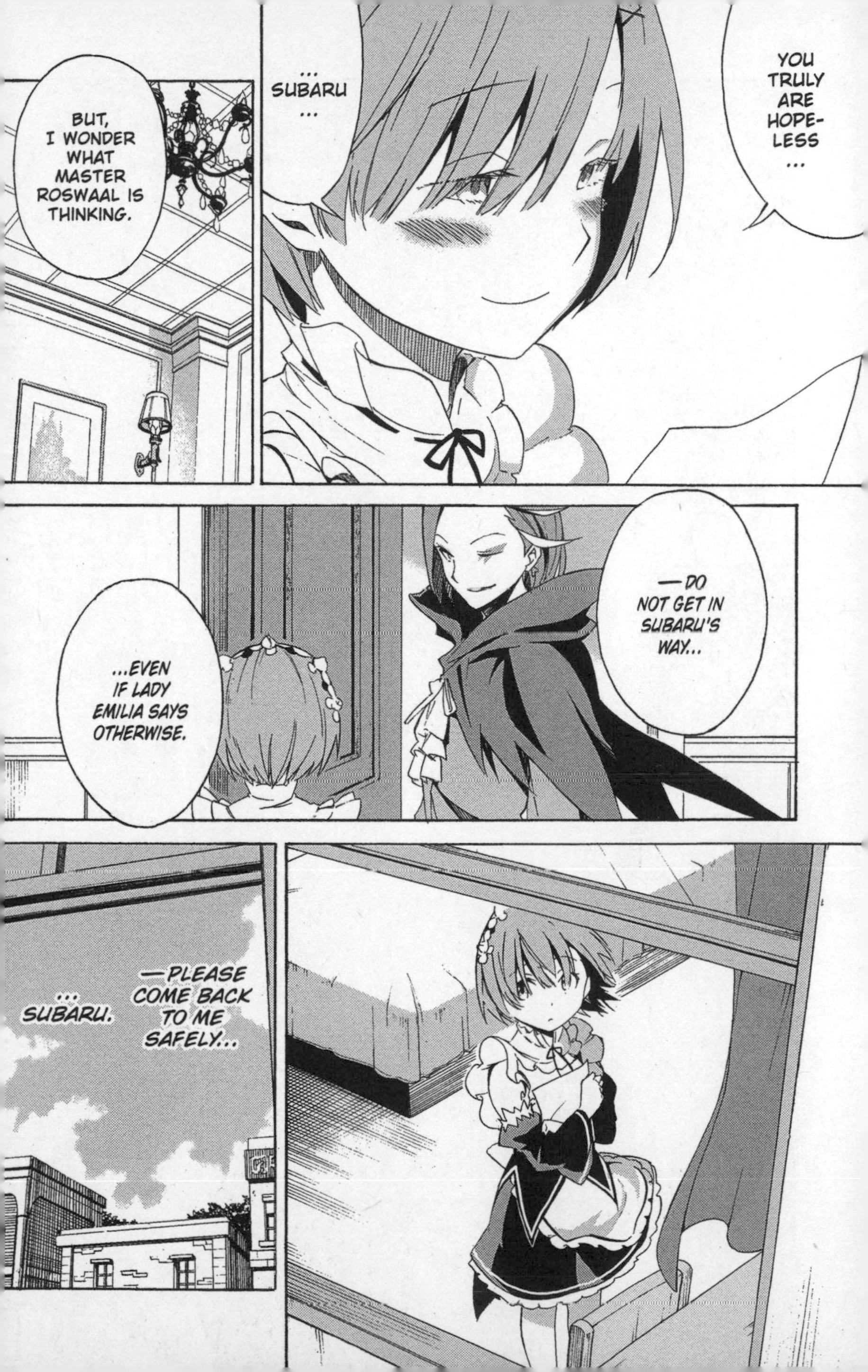
YOU TRULY ARE HOPELESS...
...SUBARU...
BUT, I WONDER WHAT MASTER ROSWAAL IS THINKING.
—DO NOT GET IN SUBARU'S WAY...
...EVEN IF LADY EMILIA SAYS OTHERWISE.
—PLEASE COME BACK TO ME SAFELY...
...SUBARU.

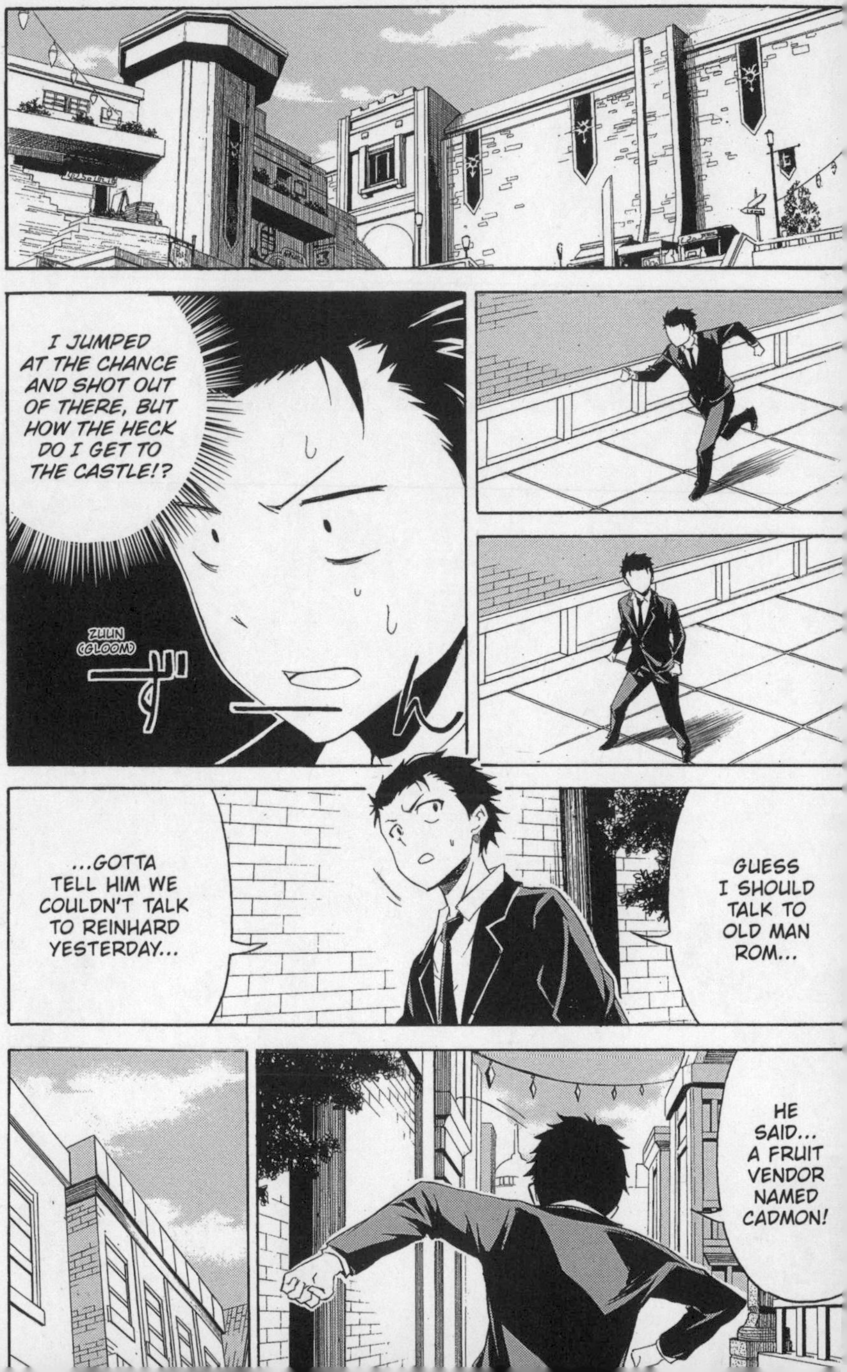
I JUMPED AT THE CHANCE AND SHOT OUT OF THERE, BUT HOW THE HECK DO I GET TO THE CASTLE!?
ZUUN (GLOOM)
GUESS I SHOULD TALK TO OLD MAN ROM...
...GOTTA TELL HIM WE COULDN'T TALK TO REINHARD YESTERDAY...
HE SAID... A FRUIT VENDOR NAMED CADMON!

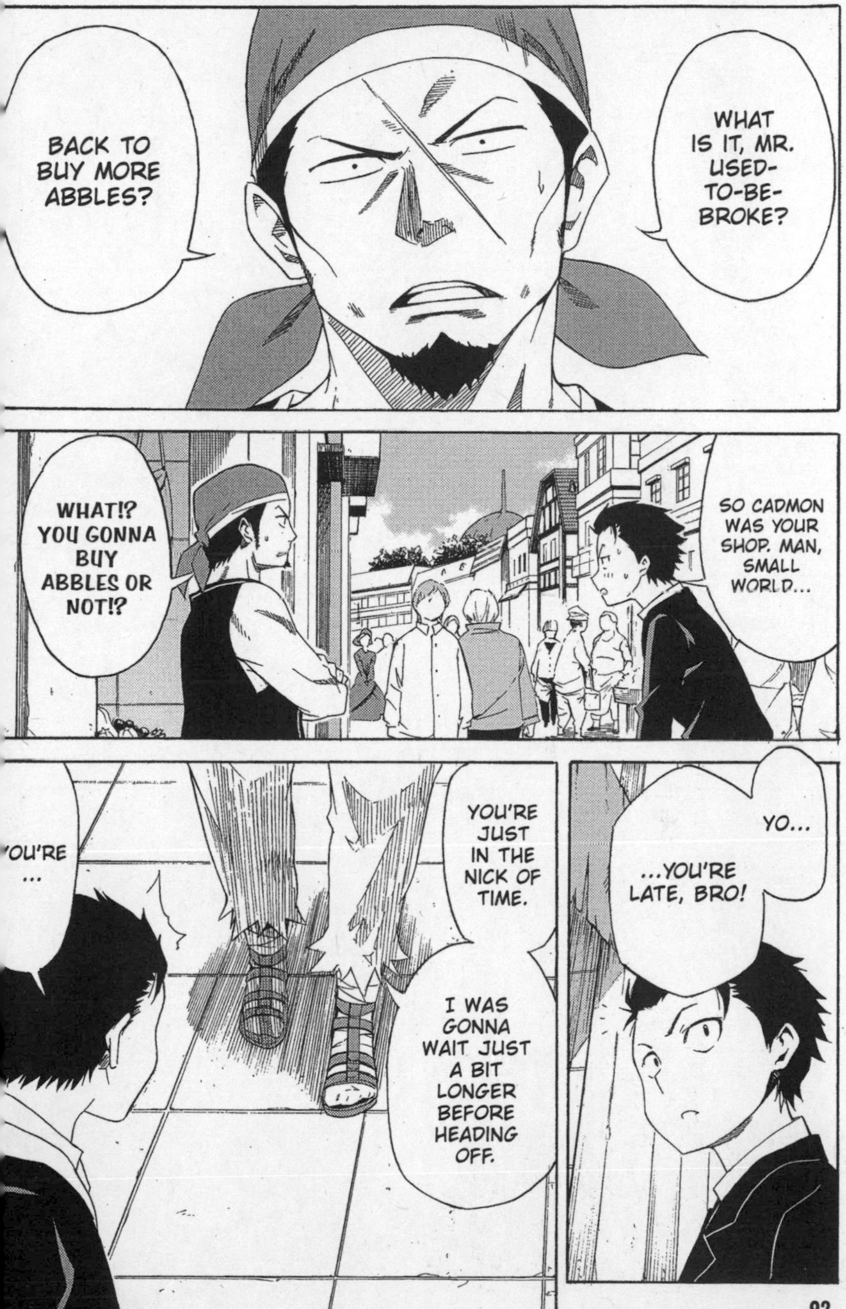
WHAT IS IT, MR. USED-TO-BE-BROKE?
BACK TO BUY MORE ABBLES?
SO CADMON WAS YOUR SHOP. MAN, SMALL WORLD...
WHAT!? YOU GONNA BUY ABBLES OR NOT!?
YO...
...YOU'RE LATE, BRO!
YOU'RE JUST IN THE NICK OF TIME.
I WAS GONNA WAIT JUST A BIT LONGER BEFORE HEADING OFF.
'OU'RE ...

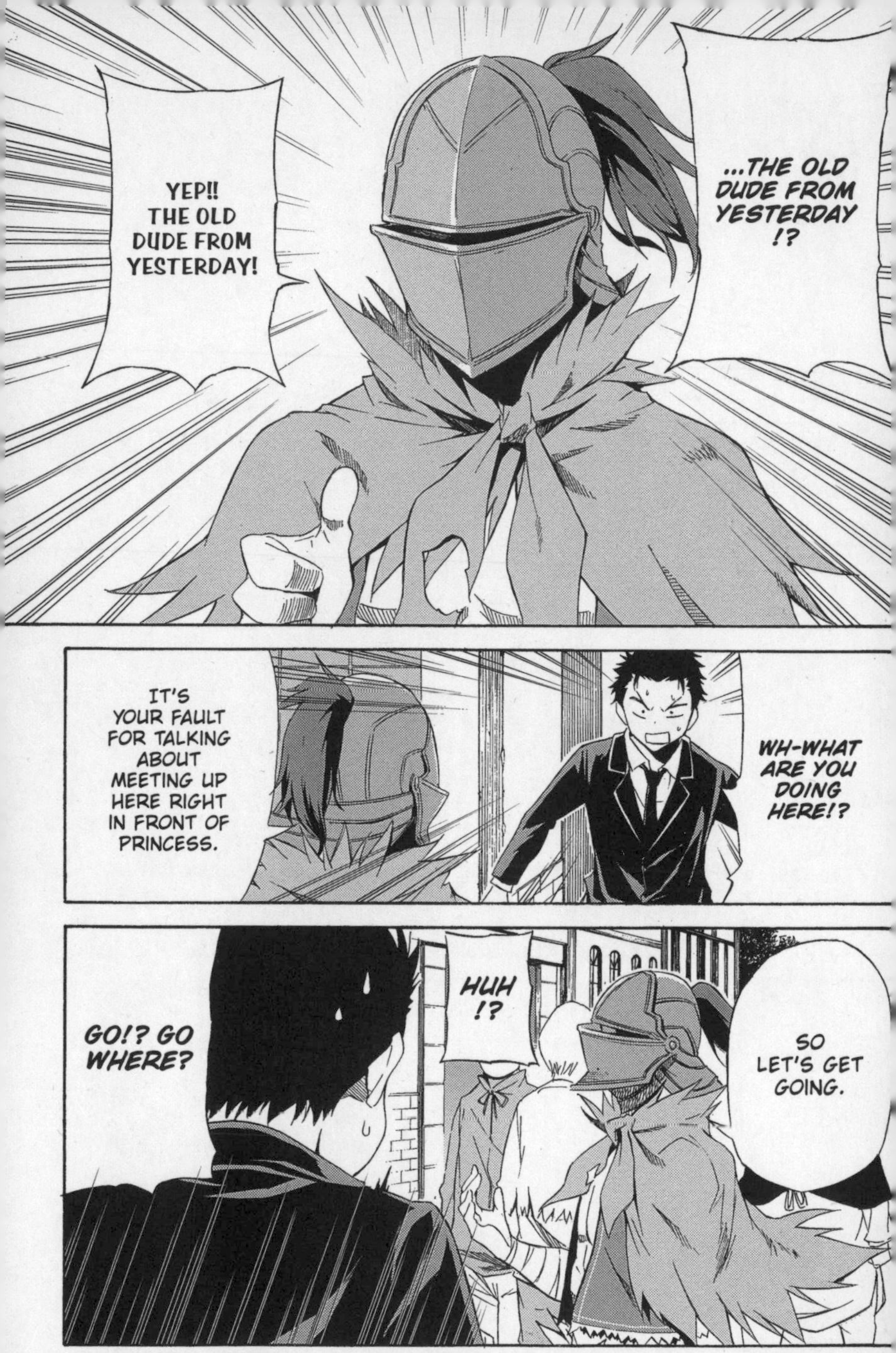
...THE OLD DUDE FROM YESTERDAY !?
YEP!! THE OLD DUDE FROM YESTERDAY!
WH-WHAT ARE YOU DOING HERE!?
IT'S YOUR FAULT FOR TALKING ABOUT MEETING UP HERE RIGHT IN FRONT OF PRINCESS.
SO LET'S GET GOING.
HUH !?
GO!? GO WHERE?

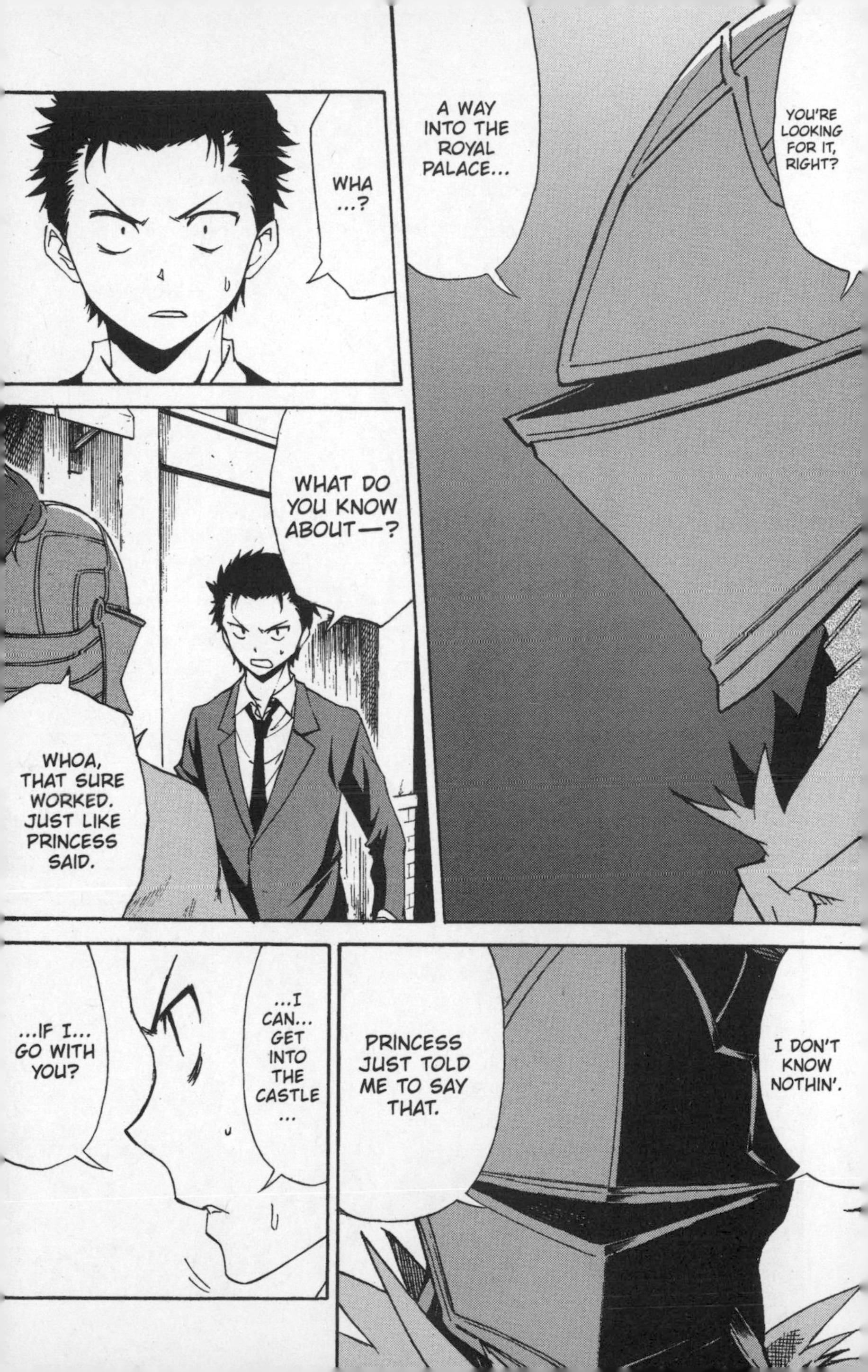
A WAY INTO THE ROYAL PALACE...
YOU'RE LOOKING FOR IT, RIGHT?
WHA ...?
WHAT DO YOU KNOW ABOUT—?
WHOA, THAT SURE WORKED. JUST LIKE PRINCESS SAID.
I DON'T KNOW NOTHIN'.
PRINCESS JUST TOLD ME TO SAY THAT.
...I CAN... GET INTO THE CASTLE ...
...IF I... GO WITH YOU?

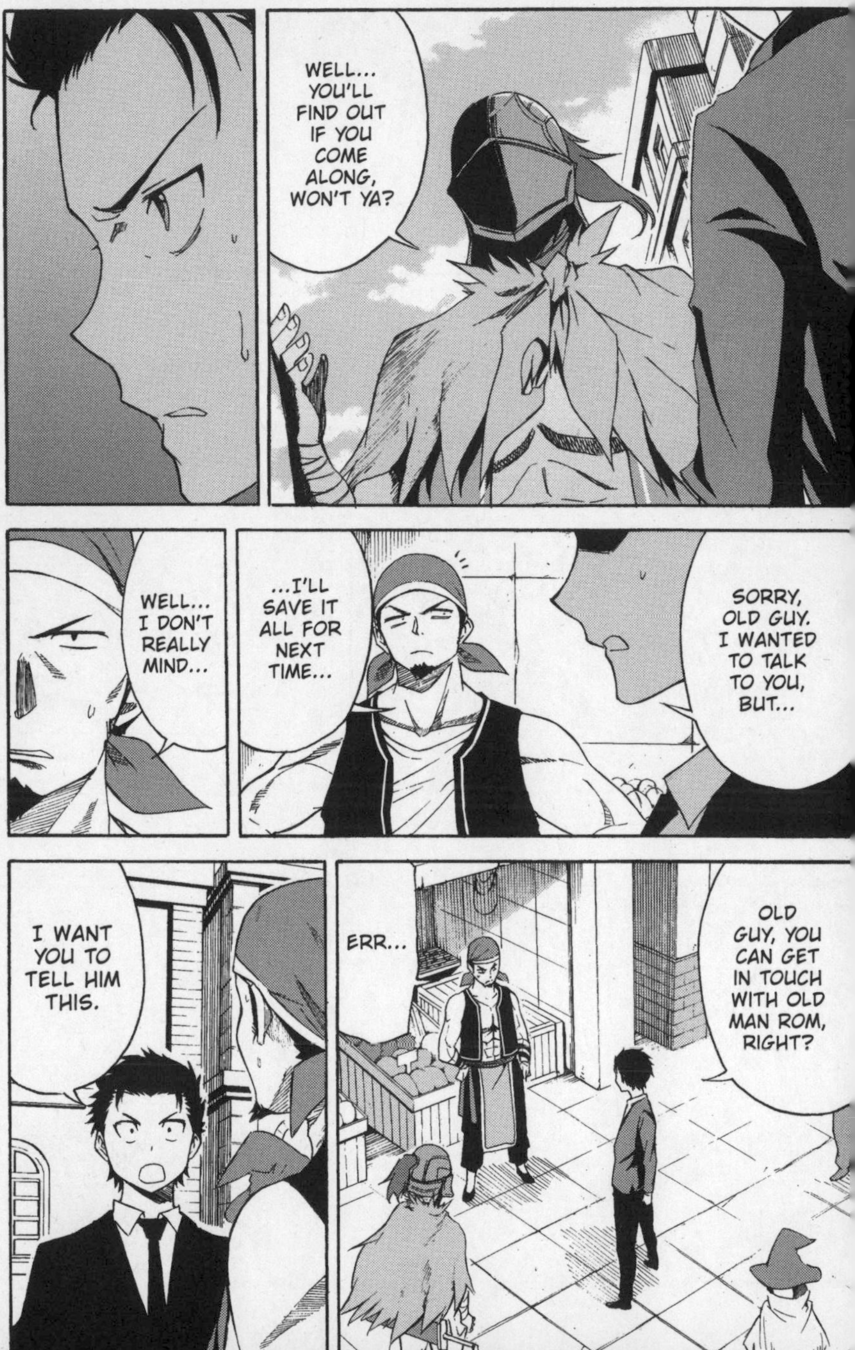
WELL... YOU'LL FIND OUT IF YOU COME ALONG, WON'T YA?
SORRY, OLD GUY. I WANTED TO TALK TO YOU, BUT...
...I'LL SAVE IT ALL FOR NEXT TIME...
WELL... I DON'T REALLY MIND...
OLD GUY, YOU CAN GET IN TOUCH WITH OLD MAN ROM, RIGHT?
ERR...
I WANT YOU TO TELL HIM THIS.

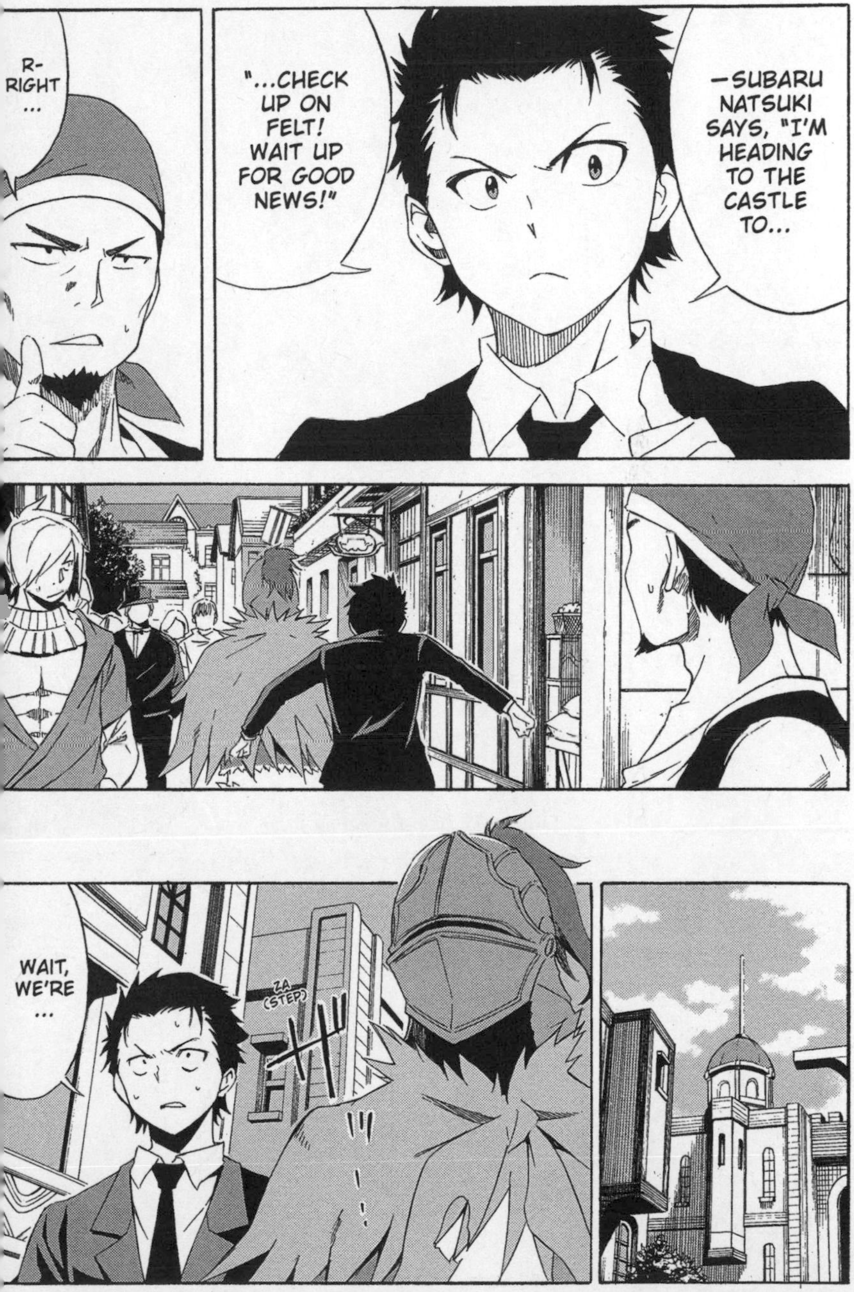
—SUBARU NATSUKI SAYS, "I'M HEADING TO THE CASTLE TO...
"...CHECK UP ON FELT! WAIT UP FOR GOOD NEWS!"
R-RIGHT ...
ZA (STEP)
WAIT, WE'RE ...

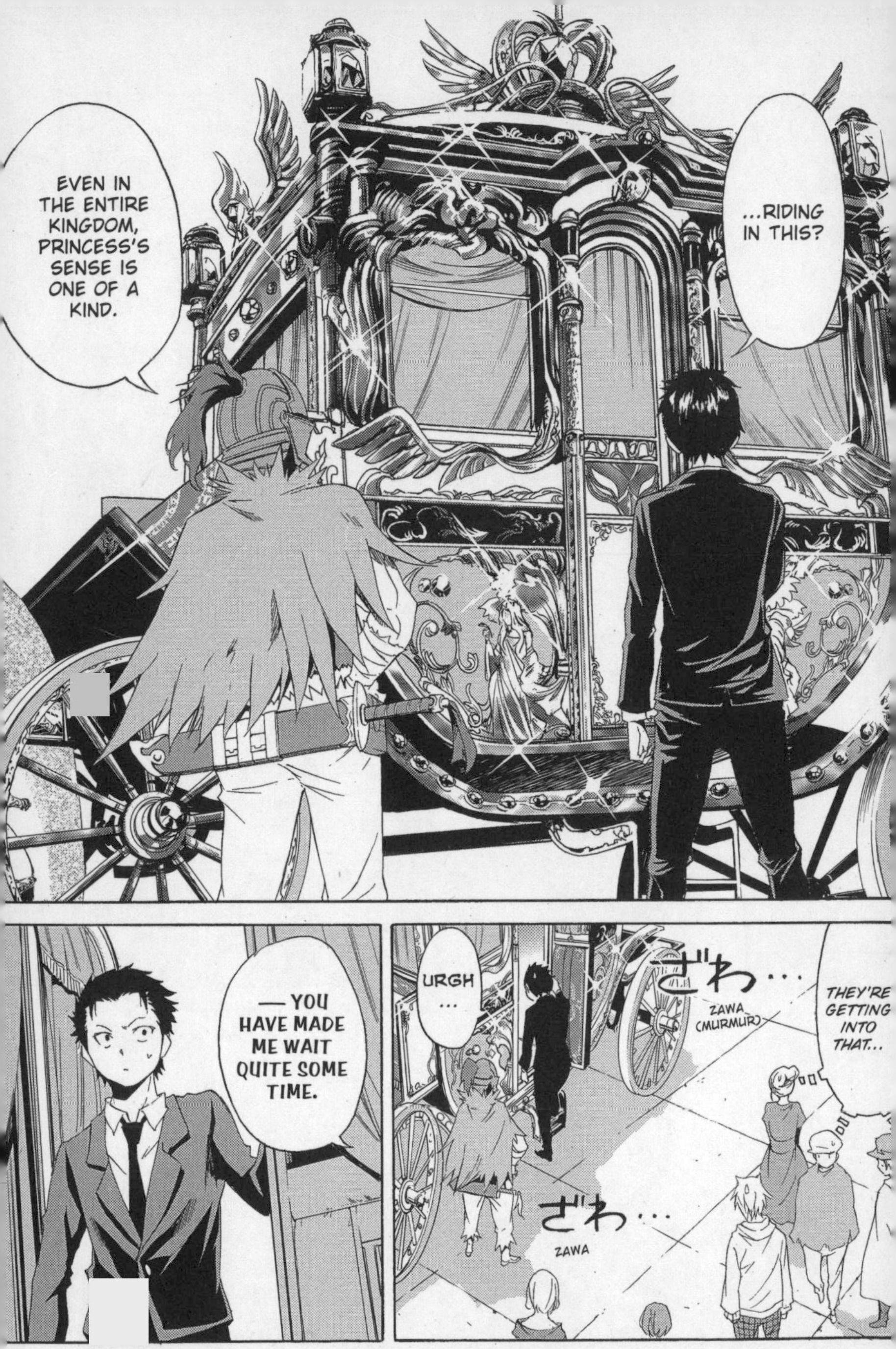
...RIDING IN THIS?
EVEN IN THE ENTIRE KINGDOM, PRINCESS'S SENSE IS ONE OF A KIND.
THEY'RE GETTING INTO THAT...
ざわ…
ZAWA (MURMUR)
URGH ...
ざわ…
ZAWA
— YOU HAVE MADE ME WAIT QUITE SOME TIME.

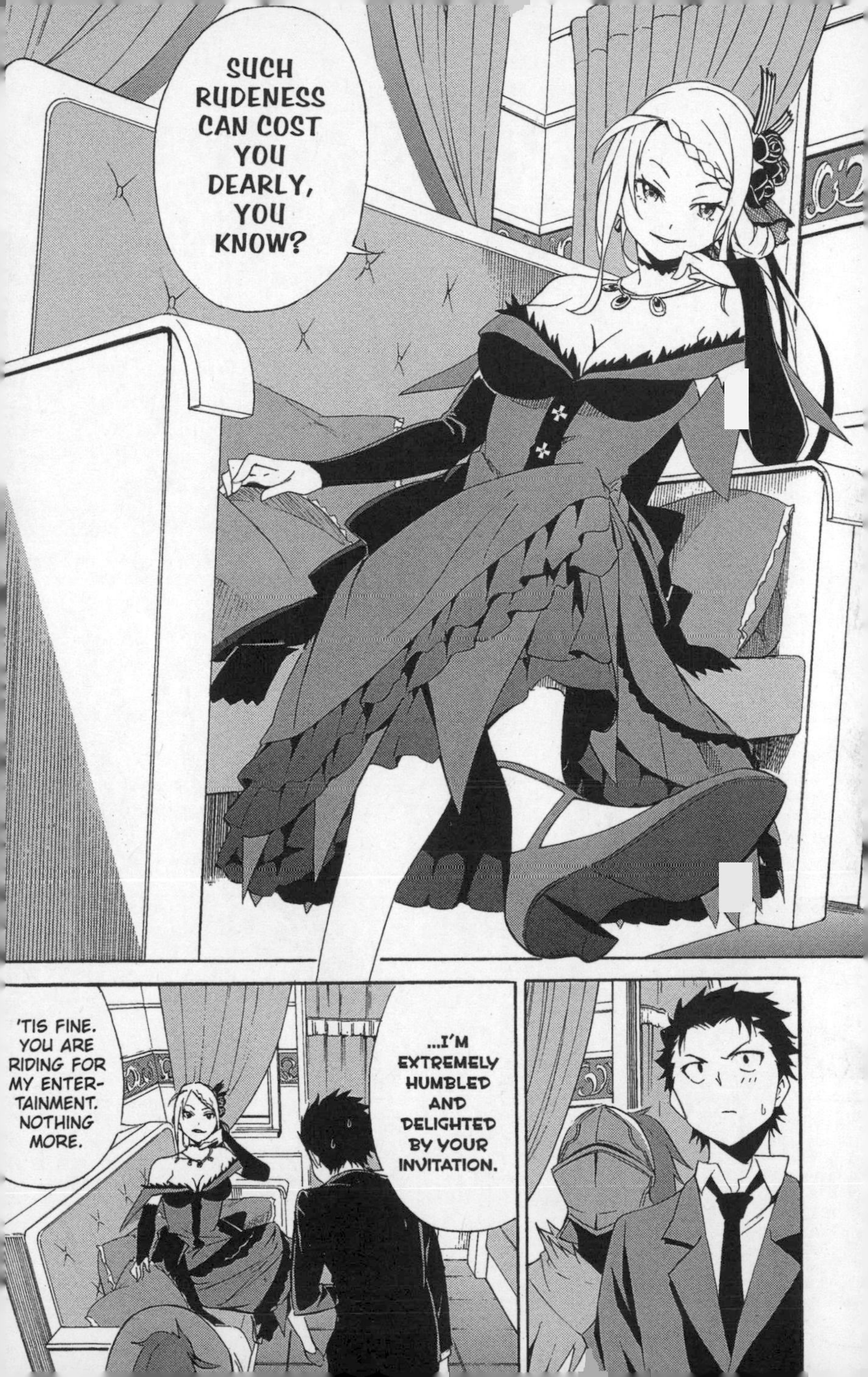
SUCH RUDENESS CAN COST YOU DEARLY, YOU KNOW?
...I'M EXTREMELY HUMBLED AND DELIGHTED BY YOUR INVITATION.
'TIS FINE. YOU ARE RIDING FOR MY ENTER-TAINMENT. NOTHING MORE.

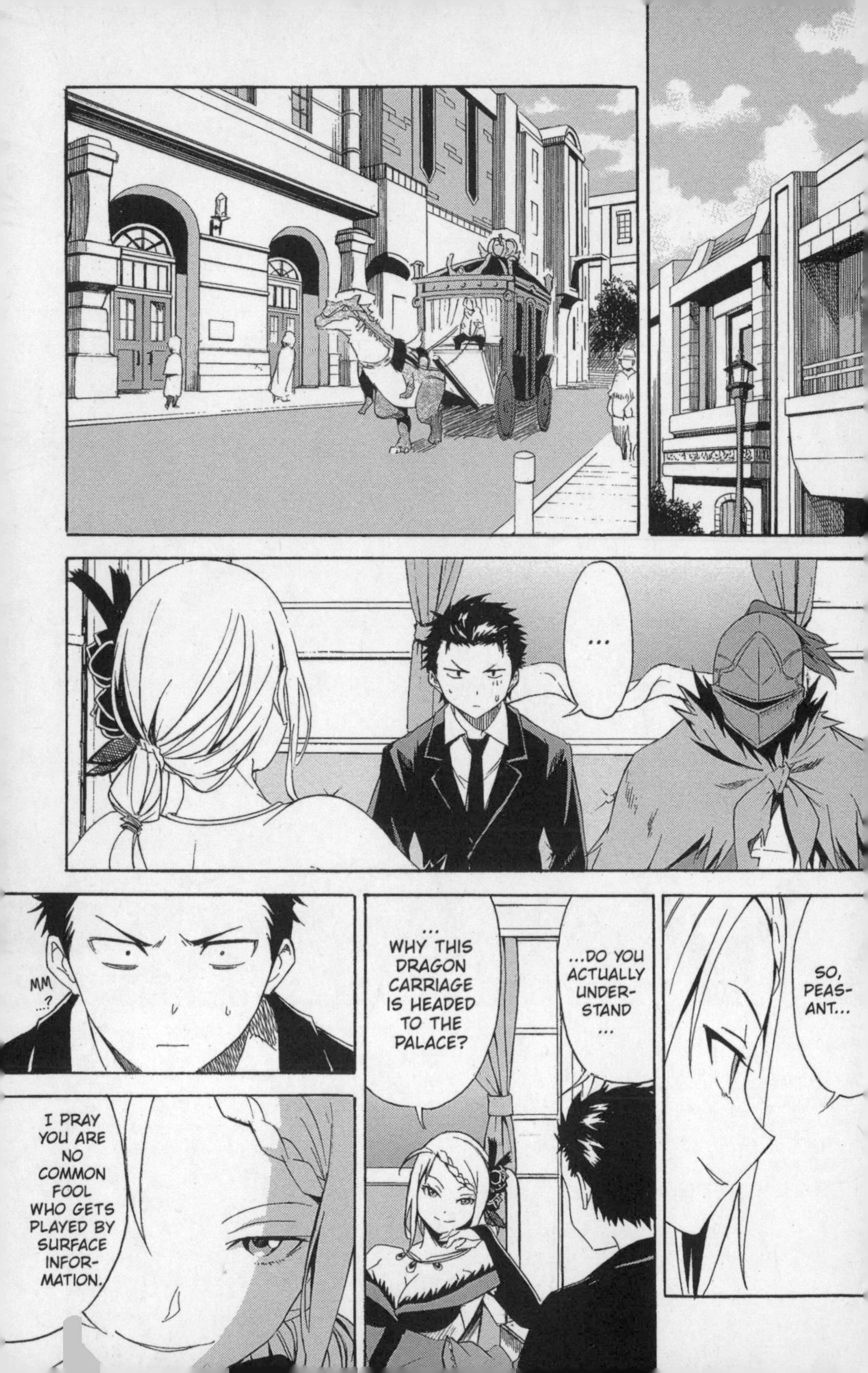
...
SO, PEASANT...
...DO YOU ACTUALLY UNDERSTAND ...
... WHY THIS DRAGON CARRIAGE IS HEADED TO THE PALACE?
MM ...?
I PRAY YOU ARE NO COMMON FOOL WHO GETS PLAYED BY SURFACE INFORMATION.

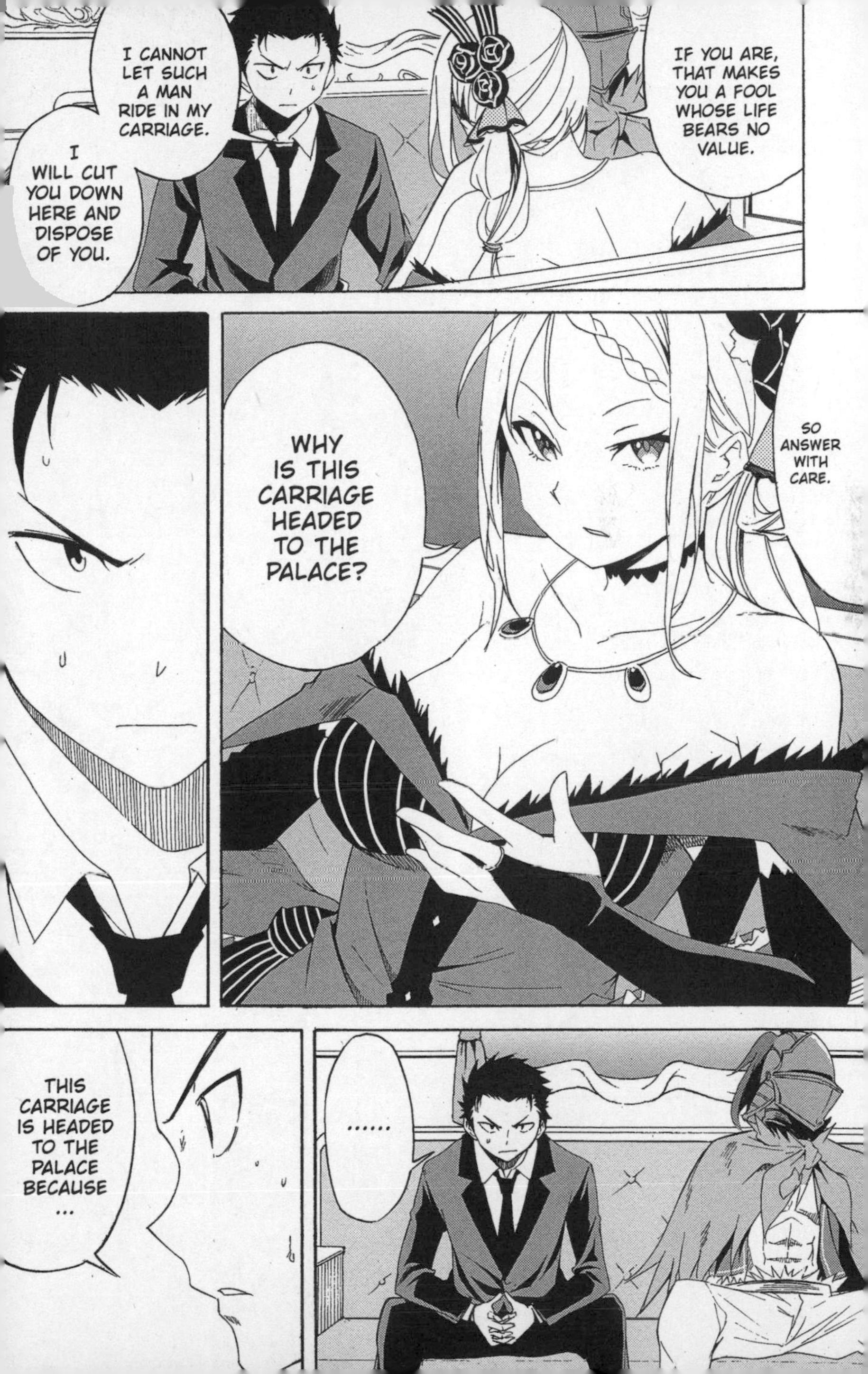
IF YOU ARE, THAT MAKES YOU A FOOL WHOSE LIFE BEARS NO VALUE.
I CANNOT LET SUCH A MAN RIDE IN MY CARRIAGE.
I WILL CUT YOU DOWN HERE AND DISPOSE OF YOU.
WHY IS THIS CARRIAGE HEADED TO THE PALACE?
SO ANSWER WITH CARE.
......
THIS CARRIAGE IS HEADED TO THE PALACE BECAUSE ...

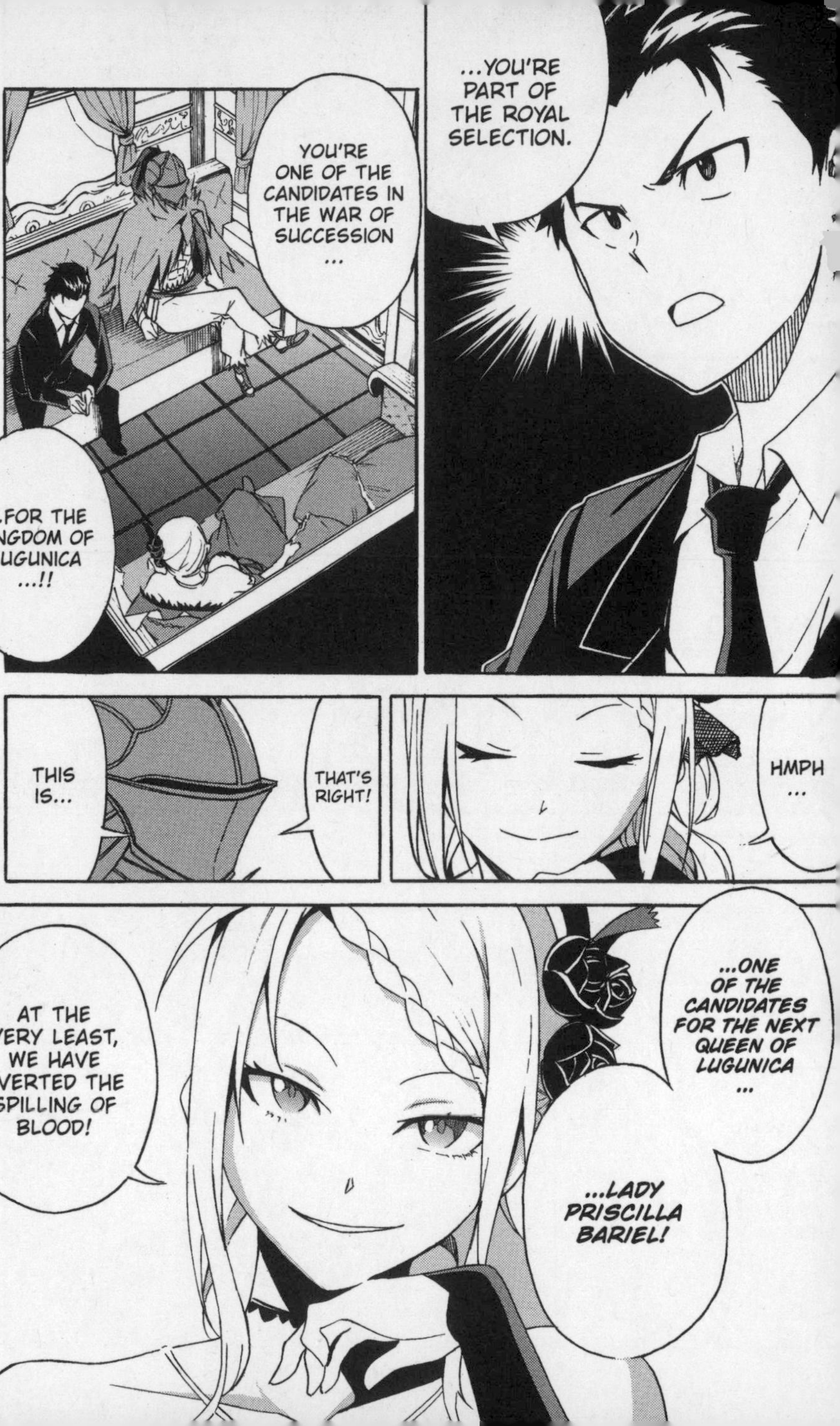
...YOU'RE PART OF THE ROYAL SELECTION.
YOU'RE ONE OF THE CANDIDATES IN THE WAR OF SUCCESSION ...
...FOR THE KINGDOM OF LUGUNICA ...!!
HMPH ...
THAT'S RIGHT!
THIS IS...
...ONE OF THE CANDIDATES FOR THE NEXT QUEEN OF LUGUNICA ...
...LADY PRISCILLA BARIEL!
AT THE VERY LEAST, WE HAVE AVERTED THE SPILLING OF BLOOD!

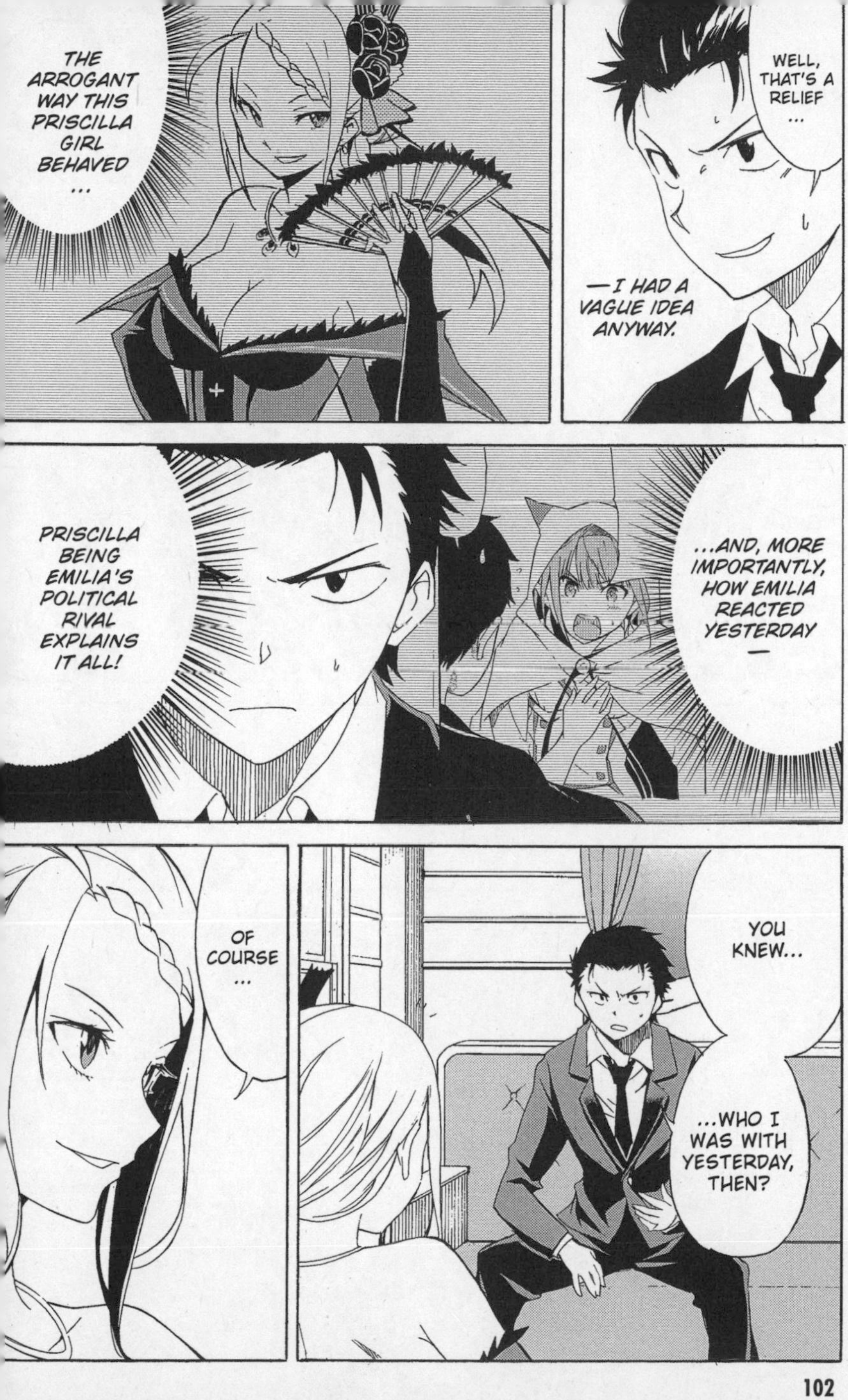
WELL, THAT'S A RELIEF ...
—I HAD A VAGUE IDEA ANYWAY.
THE ARROGANT WAY THIS PRISCILLA GIRL BEHAVED ...
...AND, MORE IMPORTANTLY, HOW EMILIA REACTED YESTERDAY —
PRISCILLA BEING EMILIA'S POLITICAL RIVAL EXPLAINS IT ALL!
YOU KNEW...
...WHO I WAS WITH YESTERDAY, THEN?
OF COURSE ...

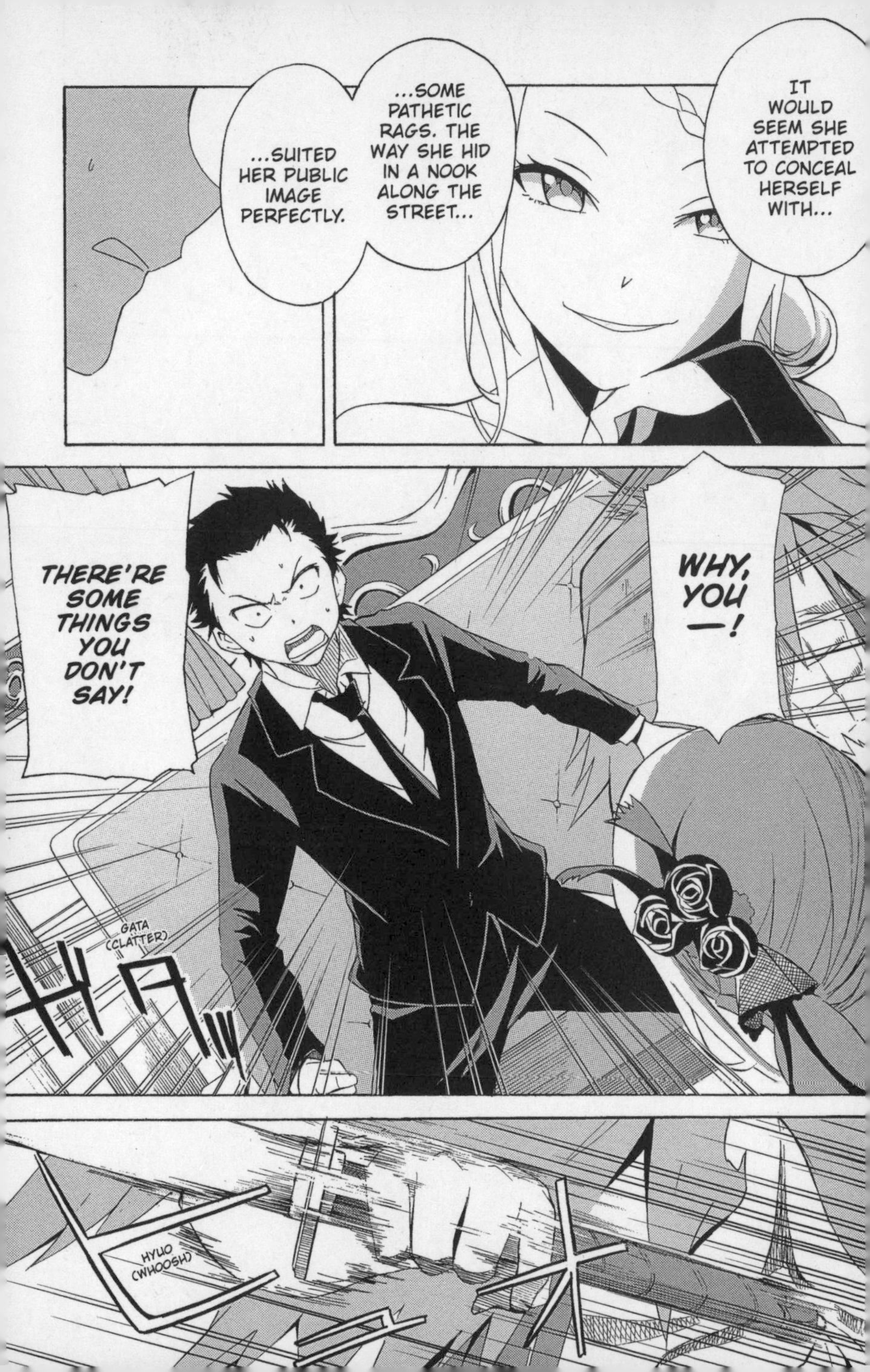
IT WOULD SEEM SHE ATTEMPTED TO CONCEAL HERSELF WITH...
...SOME PATHETIC RAGS. THE WAY SHE HID IN A NOOK ALONG THE STREET...
...SUITED HER PUBLIC IMAGE PERFECTLY.
WHY, YOU—!
THERE'RE SOME THINGS YOU DON'T SAY!
GATA (CLATTER)
HYUO (WHOOSH)

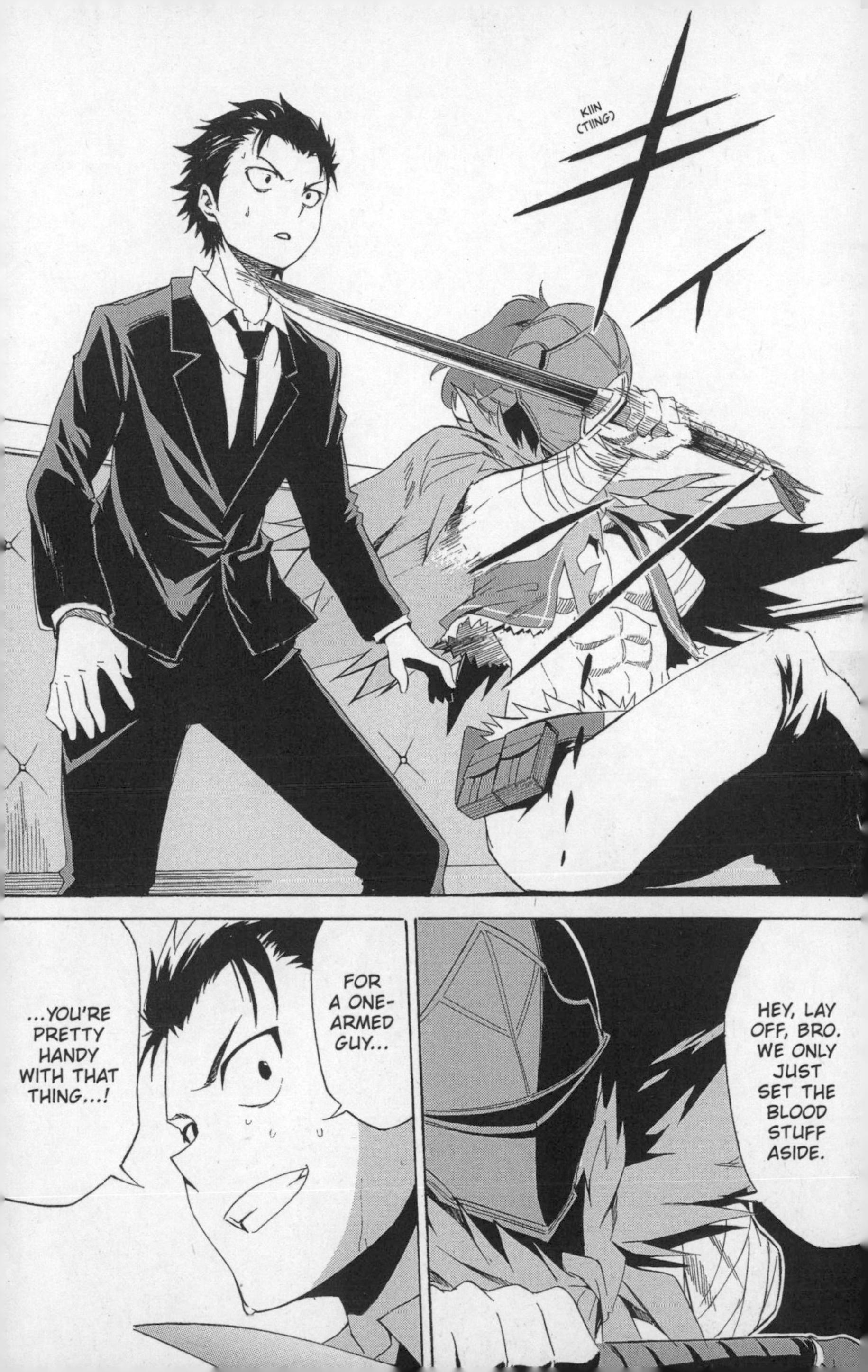
KIIN (TIING)
HEY, LAY OFF, BRO. WE ONLY JUST SET THE BLOOD STUFF ASIDE.
FOR A ONE-ARMED GUY...
...YOU'RE PRETTY HANDY WITH THAT THING...!

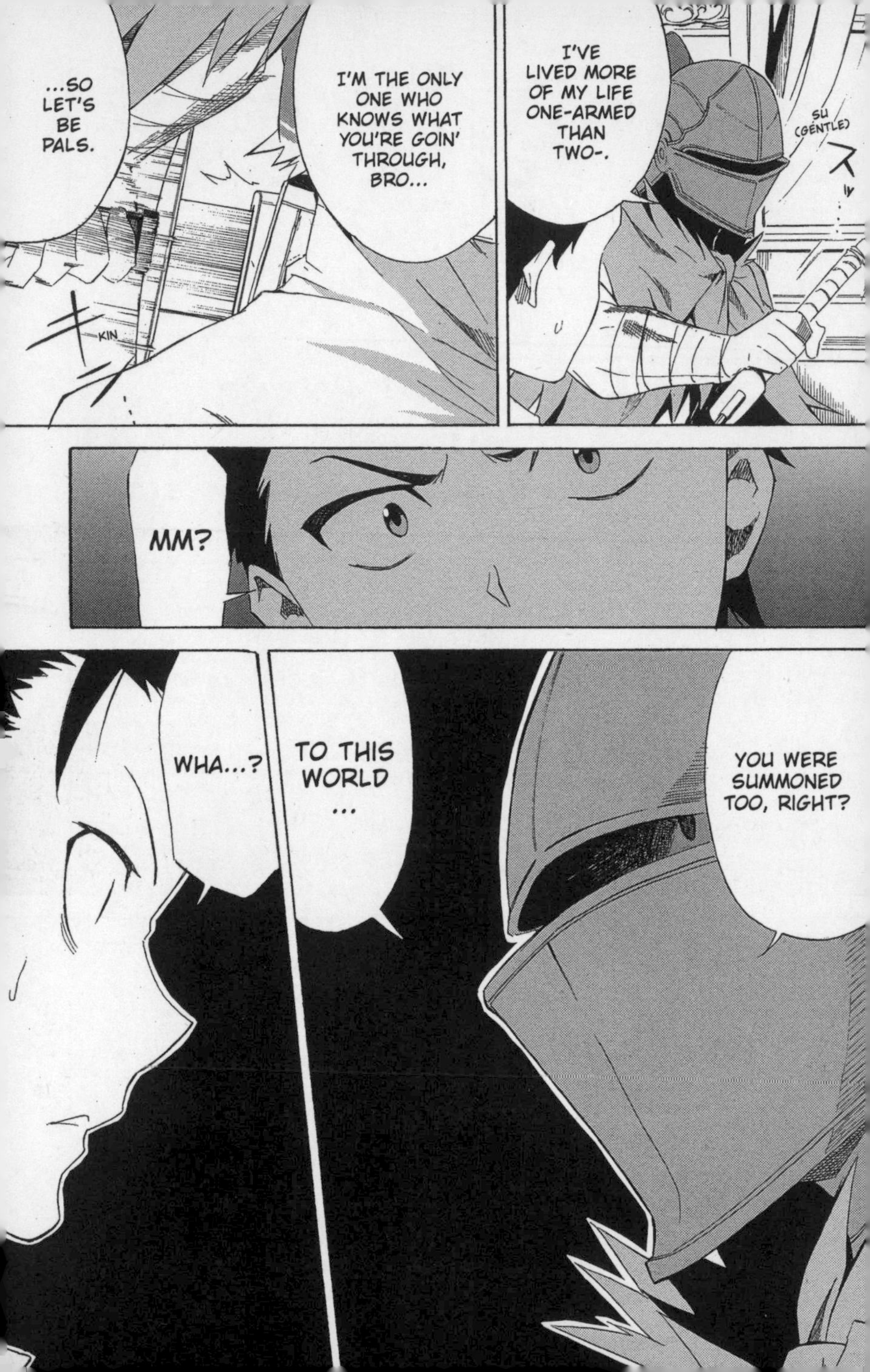
I'VE LIVED MORE OF MY LIFE ONE-ARMED THAN TWO-.
SU (GENTLE)
I'M THE ONLY ONE WHO KNOWS WHAT YOU'RE GOIN' THROUGH, BRO...
...SO LET'S BE PALS.
KIN
MM?
YOU WERE SUMMONED TOO, RIGHT?
TO THIS WORLD ...
WHA...?

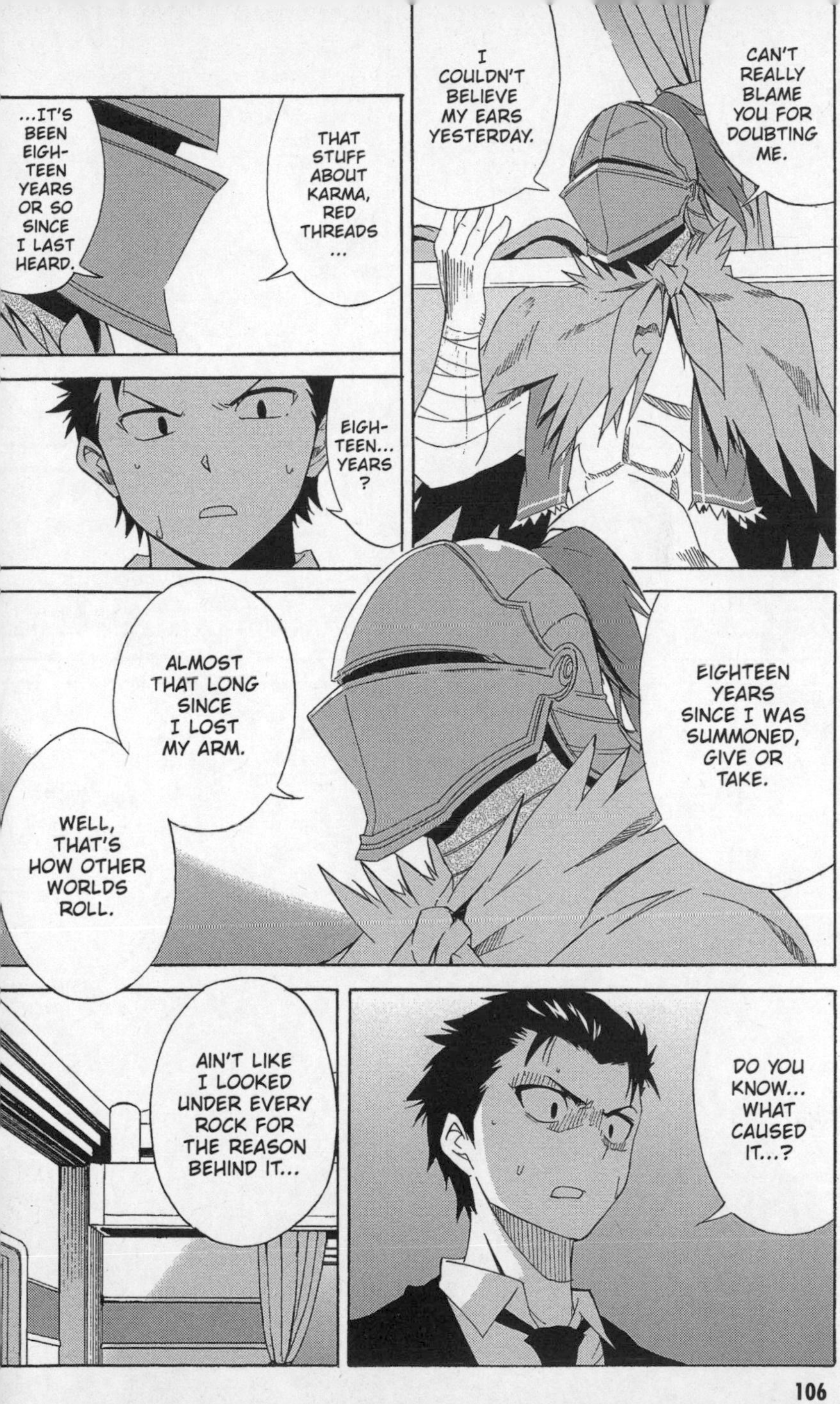
CAN'T REALLY BLAME YOU FOR DOUBTING ME.
I COULDN'T BELIEVE MY EARS YESTERDAY.
THAT STUFF ABOUT KARMA, RED THREADS...
...IT'S BEEN EIGHTEEN YEARS OR SO SINCE I LAST HEARD.
EIGHTEEN... YEARS?
EIGHTEEN YEARS SINCE I WAS SUMMONED, GIVE OR TAKE.
ALMOST THAT LONG SINCE I LOST MY ARM.
WELL, THAT'S HOW OTHER WORLDS ROLL.
DO YOU KNOW... WHAT CAUSED IT...?
AIN'T LIKE I LOOKED UNDER EVERY ROCK FOR THE REASON BEHIND IT...

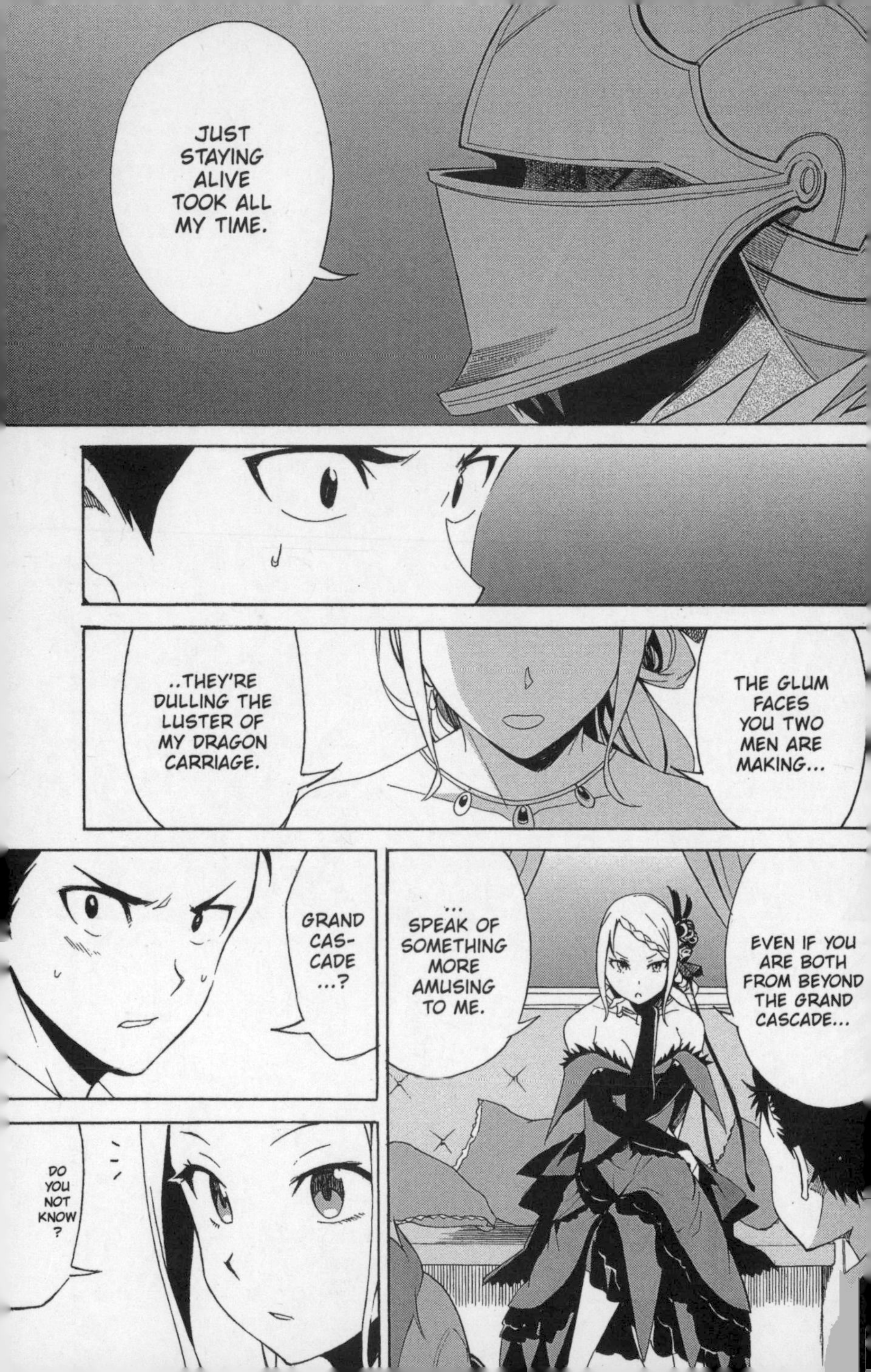
JUST STAYING ALIVE TOOK ALL MY TIME.
THE GLUM FACES YOU TWO MEN ARE MAKING...
..THEY'RE DULLING THE LUSTER OF MY DRAGON CARRIAGE.
EVEN IF YOU ARE BOTH FROM BEYOND THE GRAND CASCADE...
... SPEAK OF SOMETHING MORE AMUSING TO ME.
GRAND CAS-CADE ...?
DO YOU NOT KNOW ?

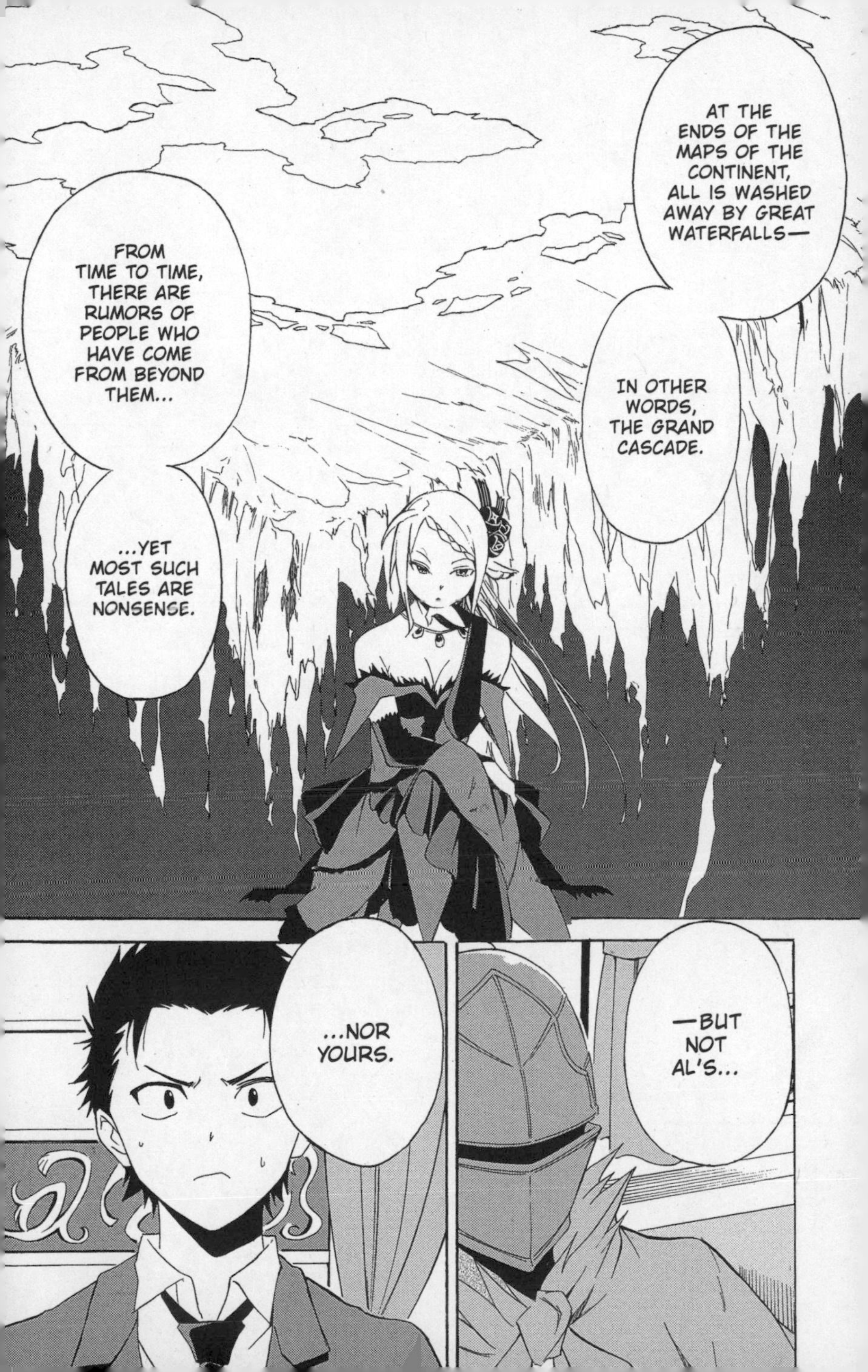
AT THE ENDS OF THE MAPS OF THE CONTINENT, ALL IS WASHED AWAY BY GREAT WATERFALLS—
IN OTHER WORDS, THE GRAND CASCADE.
FROM TIME TO TIME, THERE ARE RUMORS OF PEOPLE WHO HAVE COME FROM BEYOND THEM...
...YET MOST SUCH TALES ARE NONSENSE.
—BUT NOT AL'S...
...NOR YOURS.

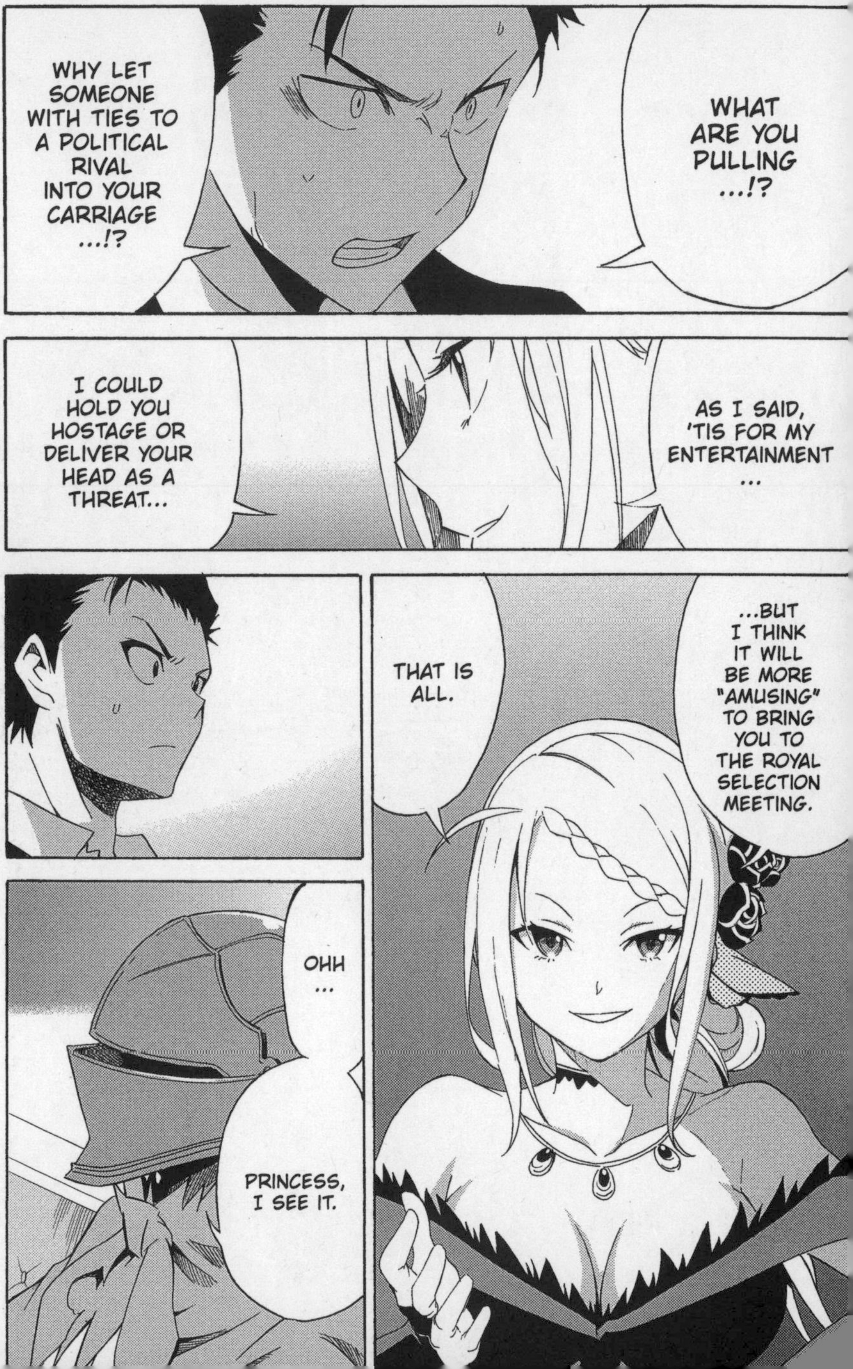
WHAT ARE YOU PULLING ...!?
WHY LET SOMEONE WITH TIES TO A POLITICAL RIVAL INTO YOUR CARRIAGE ...!?
AS I SAID, 'TIS FOR MY ENTERTAINMENT ...
I COULD HOLD YOU HOSTAGE OR DELIVER YOUR HEAD AS A THREAT...
...BUT I THINK IT WILL BE MORE "AMUSING" TO BRING YOU TO THE ROYAL SELECTION MEETING.
THAT IS ALL.
OHH ...
PRINCESS, I SEE IT.

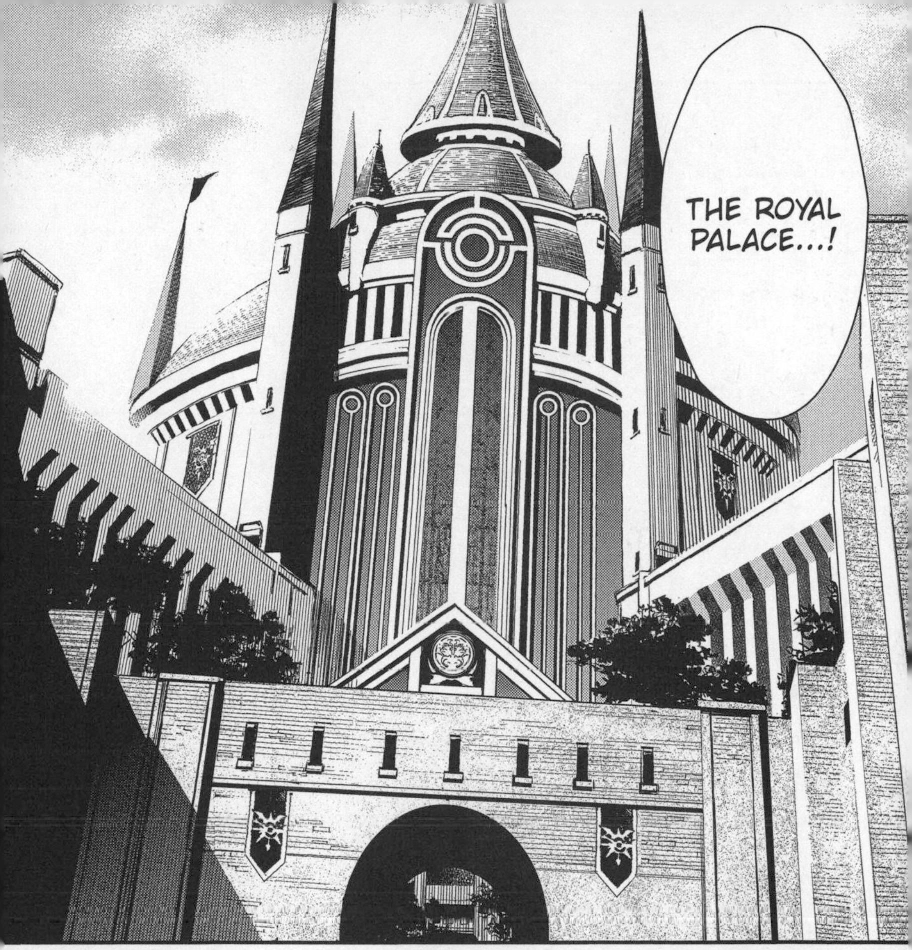
THE ROYAL PALACE...!

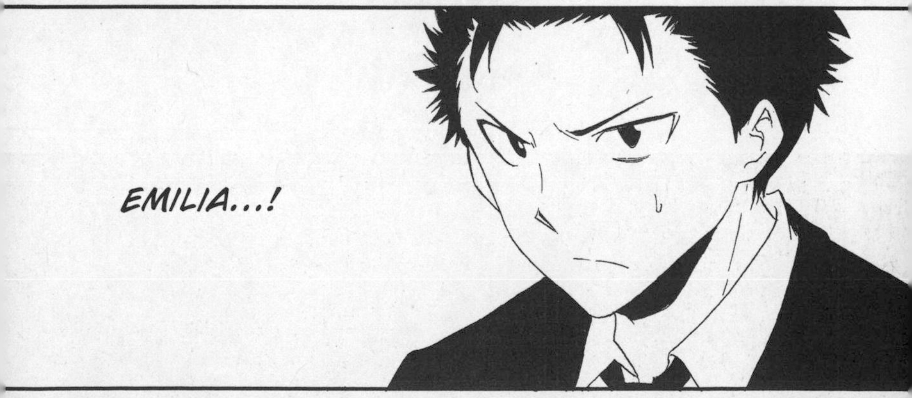
EMILIA...!

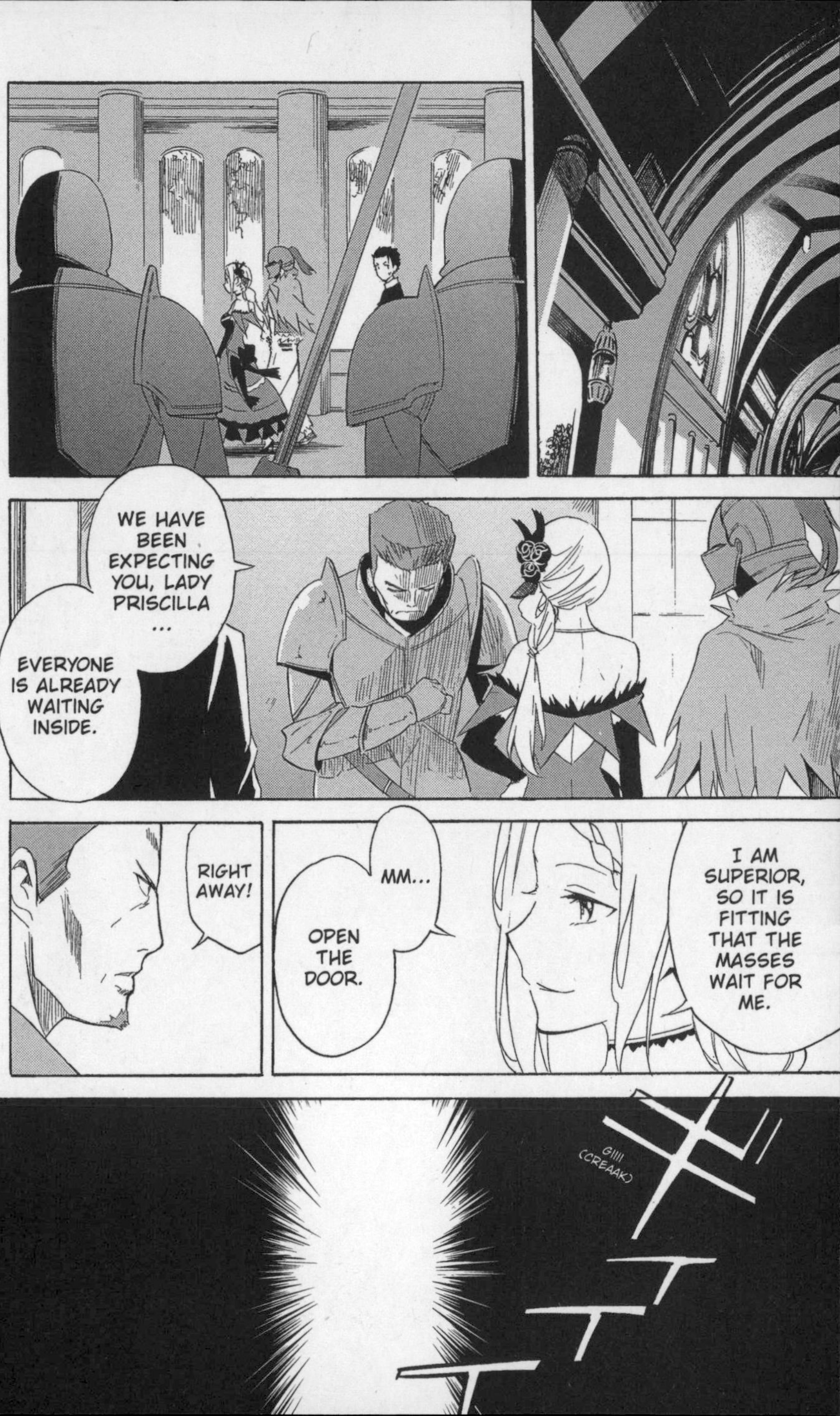
I AM SUPERIOR, SO IT IS FITTING THAT THE MASSES WAIT FOR ME.
MM...
OPEN THE DOOR.
RIGHT AWAY!
WE HAVE BEEN EXPECTING YOU, LADY PRISCILLA...
EVERYONE IS ALREADY WAITING INSIDE.
GIIII (CREAAK)

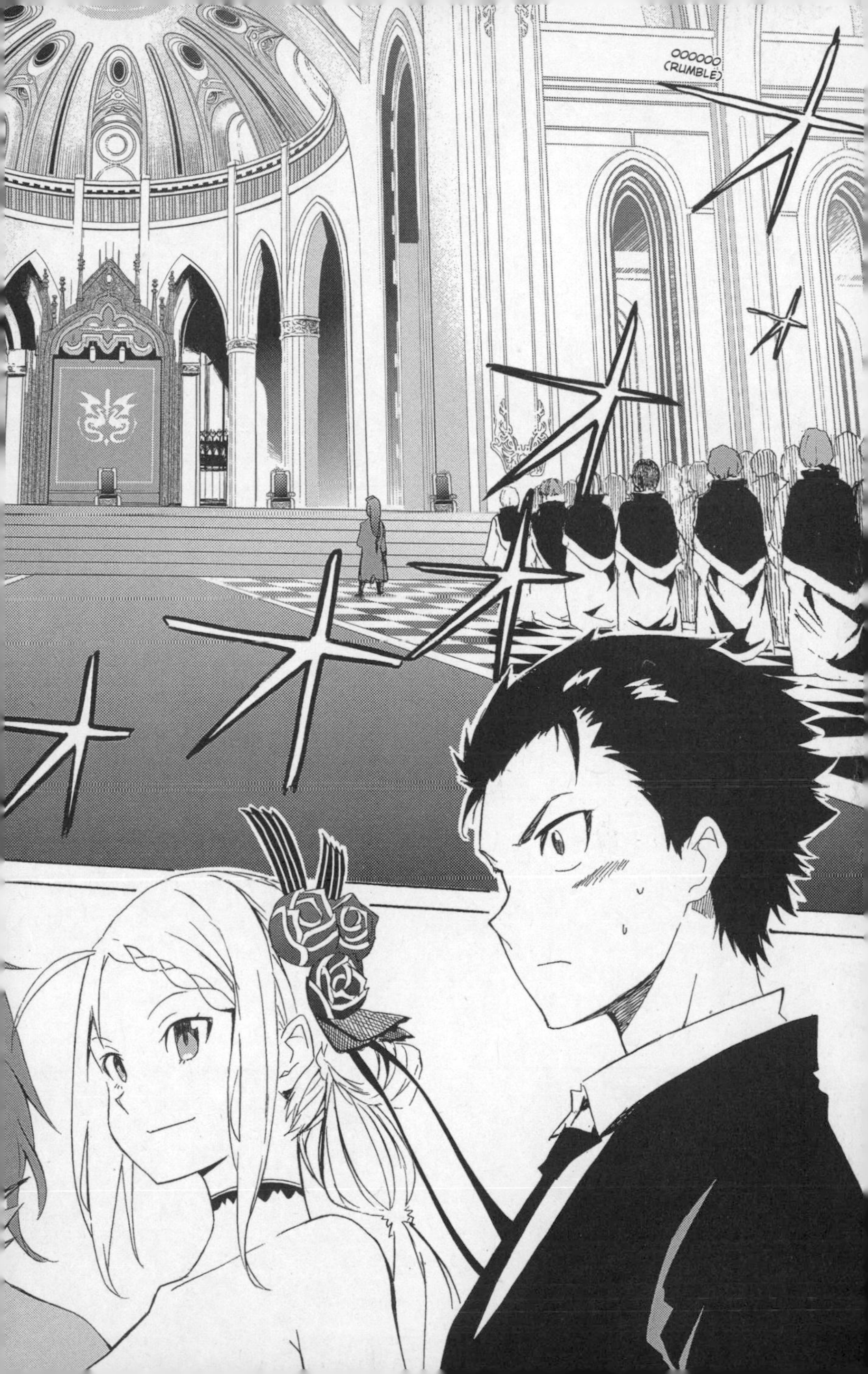
OOOOOO
(RUMBLE)

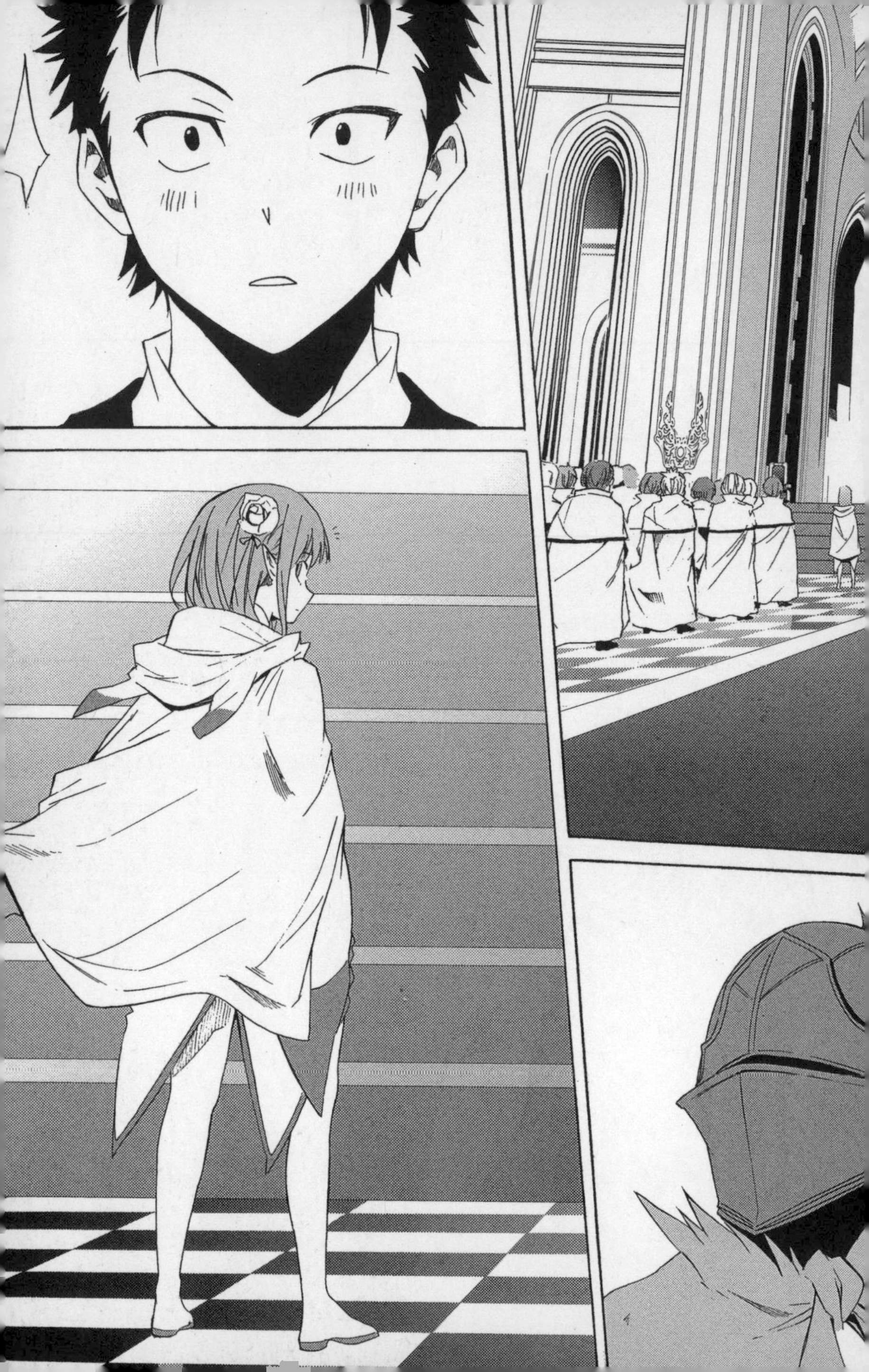

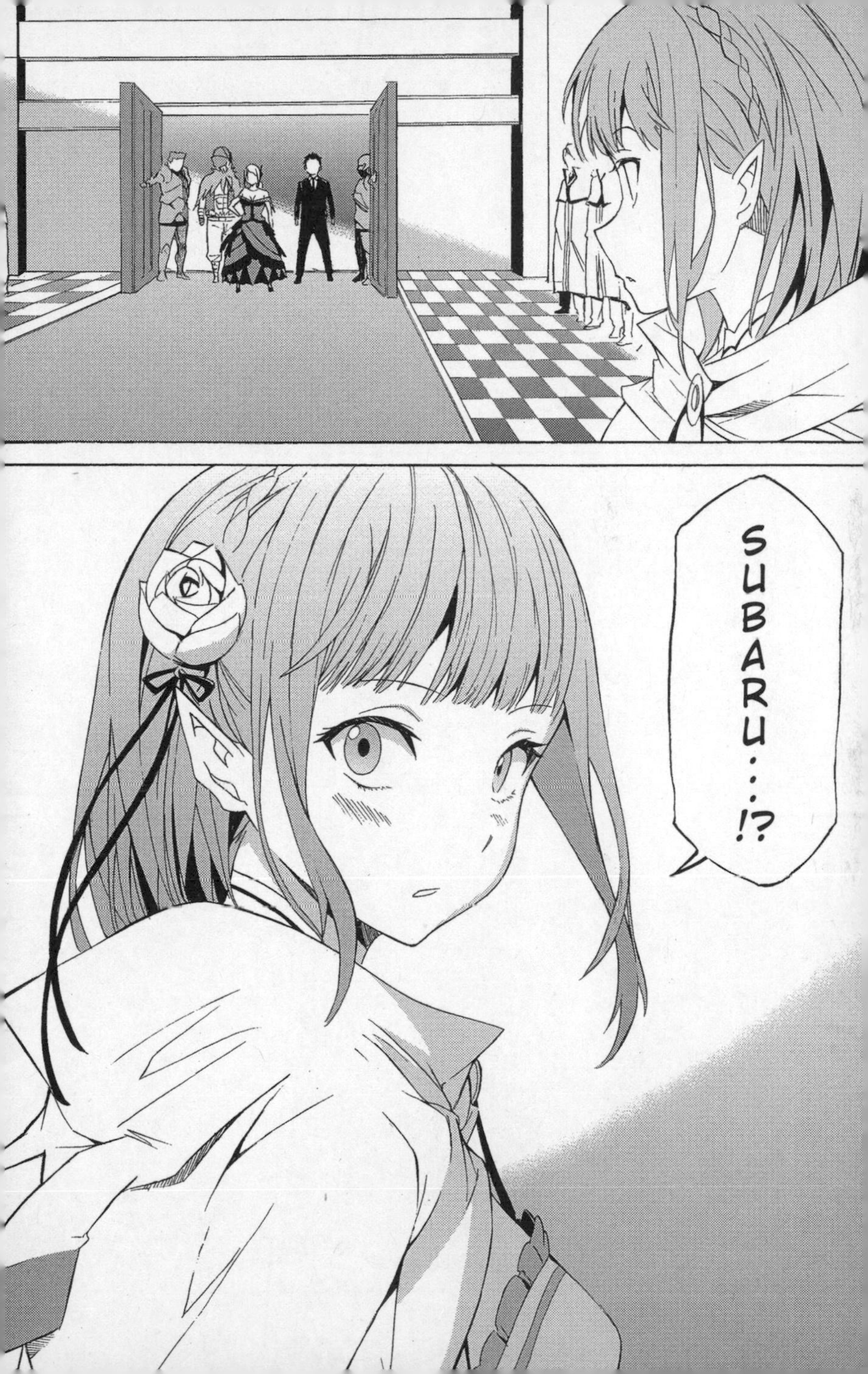
SUBARU...!?

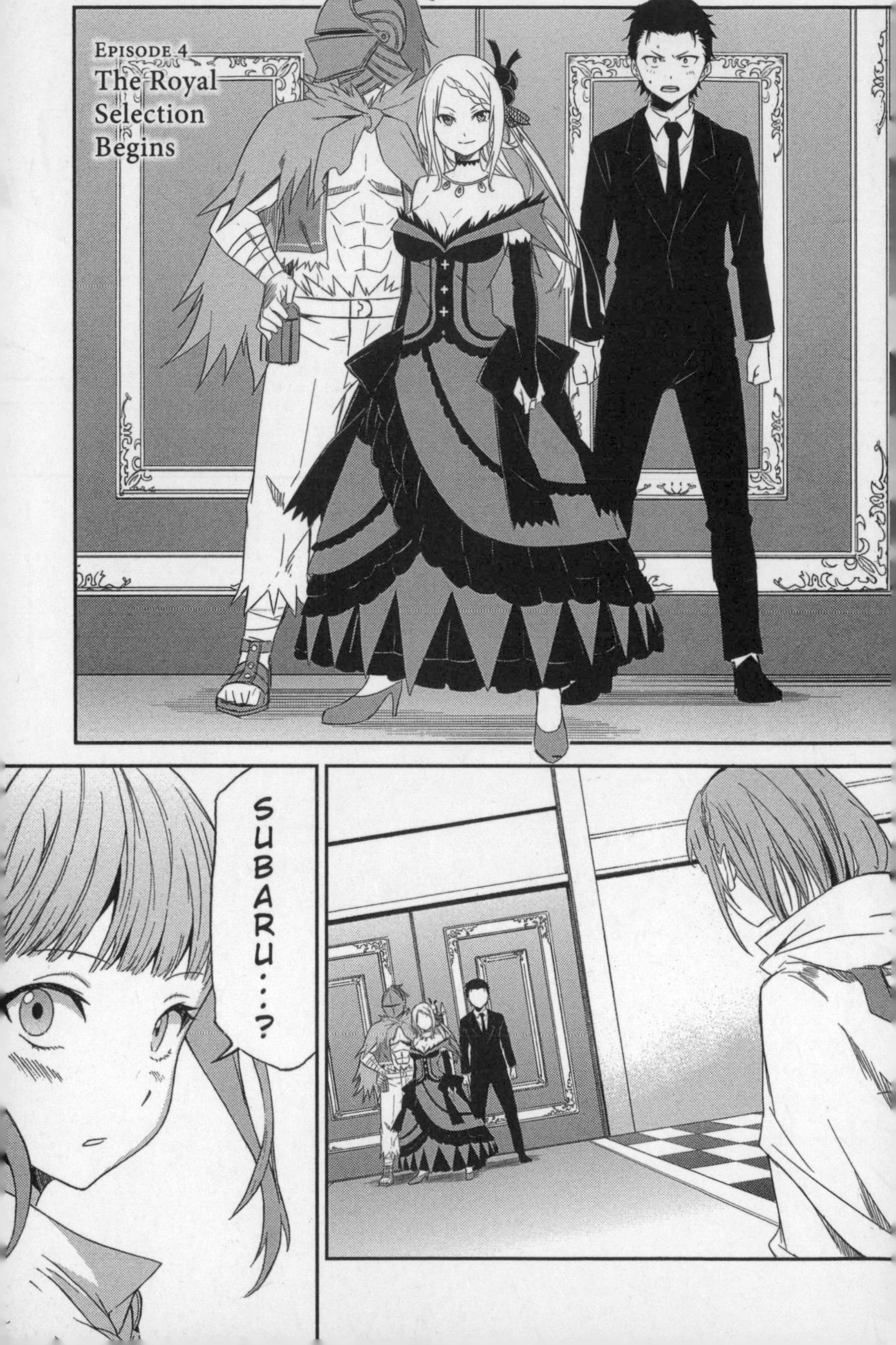
Episode 4
The Royal Selection Begins
SUBARU...?

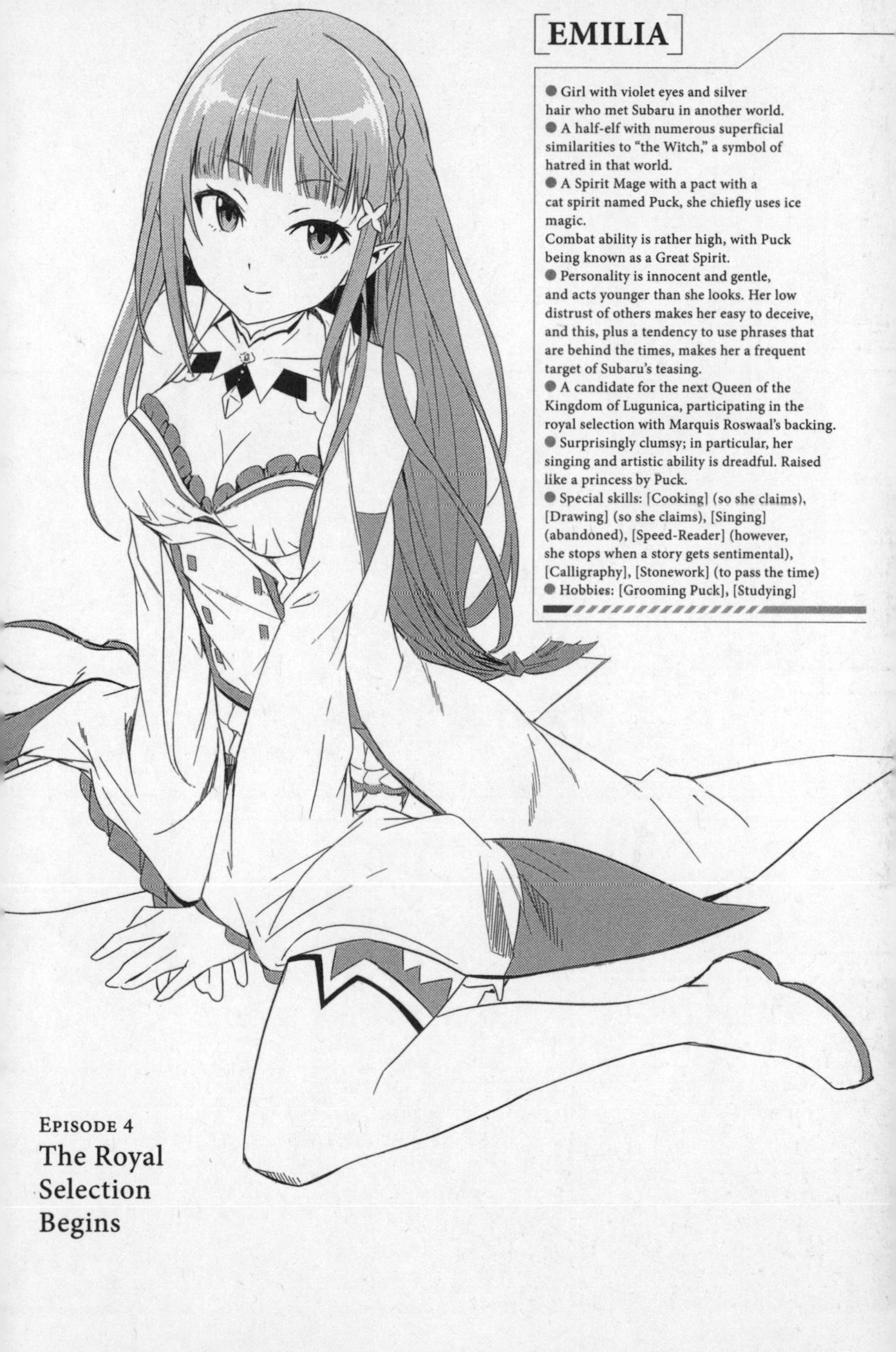

EMILIA

- Girl with violet eyes and silver hair who met Subaru in another world.
- A half-elf with numerous superficial similarities to "the Witch," a symbol of hatred in that world.
- A Spirit Mage with a pact with a cat spirit named Puck, she chiefly uses ice magic.
Combat ability is rather high, with Puck being known as a Great Spirit.
- Personality is innocent and gentle, and acts younger than she looks. Her low distrust of others makes her easy to deceive, and this, plus a tendency to use phrases that are behind the times, makes her a frequent target of Subaru's teasing.
- A candidate for the next Queen of the Kingdom of Lugunica, participating in the royal selection with Marquis Roswaal's backing.
- Surprisingly clumsy; in particular, her singing and artistic ability is dreadful. Raised like a princess by Puck.
- Special skills: [Cooking] (so she claims), [Drawing] (so she claims), [Singing] (abandoned), [Speed-Reader] (however, she stops when a story gets sentimental), [Calligraphy], [Stonework] (to pass the time)
- Hobbies: [Grooming Puck], [Studying]

EPISODE 4

The Royal Selection Begins

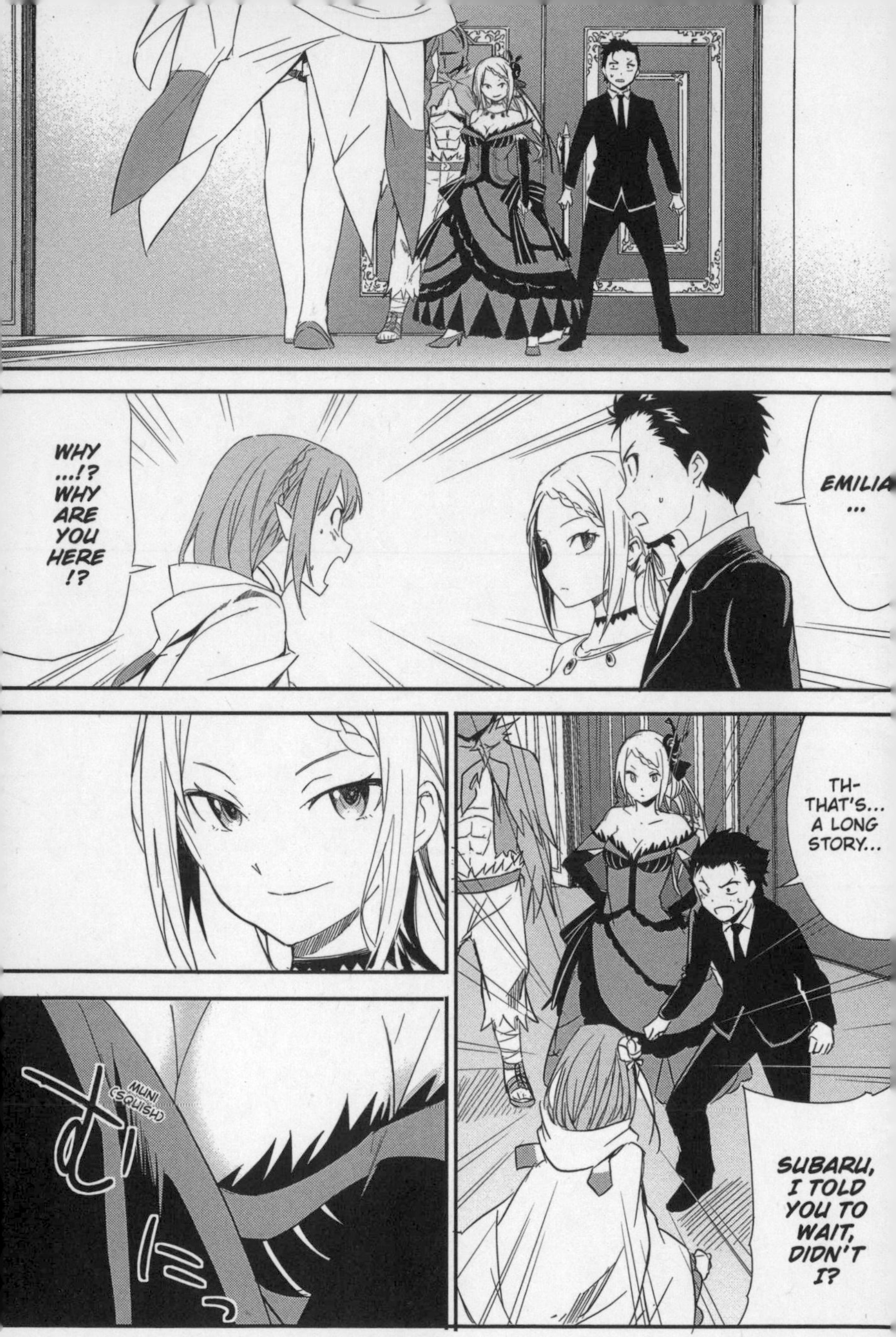
EMILIA...
WHY...!? WHY ARE YOU HERE!?
TH-THAT'S... A LONG STORY...
SUBARU, I TOLD YOU TO WAIT, DIDN'T I?
MUNI (SQUISH)

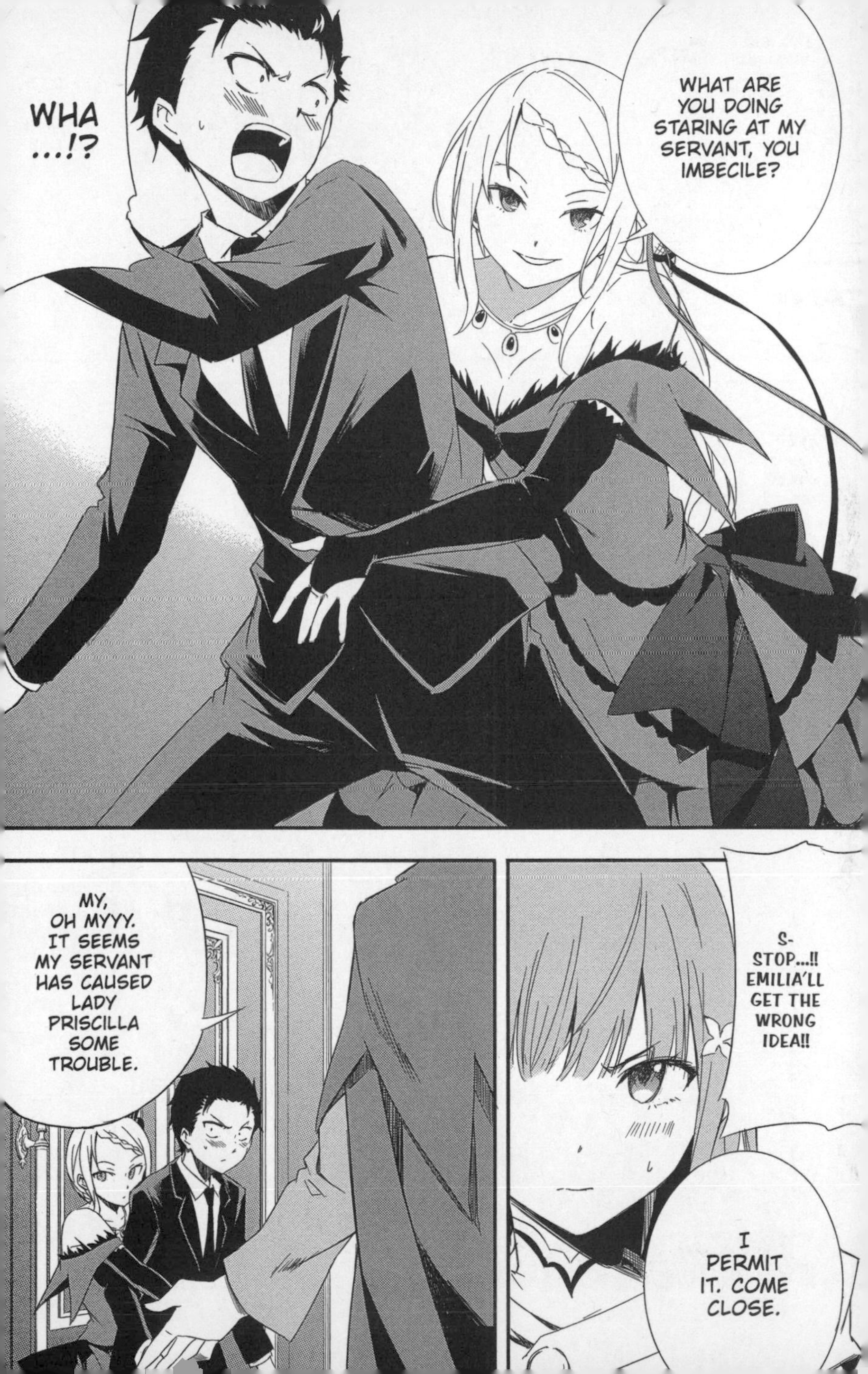
WHAT ARE YOU DOING STARING AT MY SERVANT, YOU IMBECILE?
WHA ...!?
S- STOP...!! EMILIA'LL GET THE WRONG IDEA!!
I PERMIT IT. COME CLOSE.
MY, OH MYYY. IT SEEMS MY SERVANT HAS CAUSED LADY PRISCILLA SOME TROUBLE.

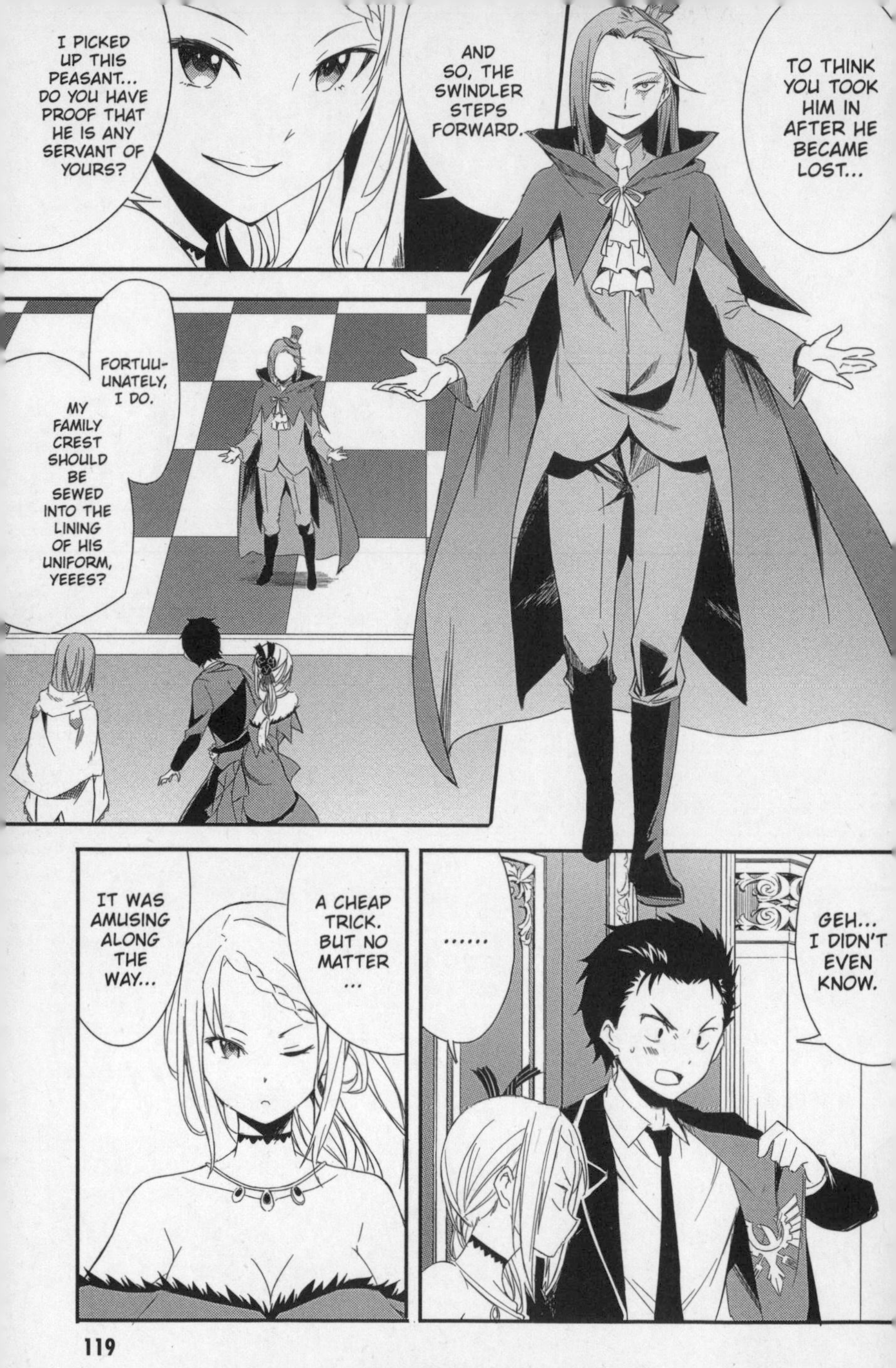
TO THINK YOU TOOK HIM IN AFTER HE BECAME LOST...
AND SO, THE SWINDLER STEPS FORWARD.
I PICKED UP THIS PEASANT... DO YOU HAVE PROOF THAT HE IS ANY SERVANT OF YOURS?
FORTUU-UNATELY, I DO.
MY FAMILY CREST SHOULD BE SEWED INTO THE LINING OF HIS UNIFORM, YEEES?
GEH... I DIDN'T EVEN KNOW.
......
A CHEAP TRICK. BUT NO MATTER ...
IT WAS AMUSING ALONG THE WAY...

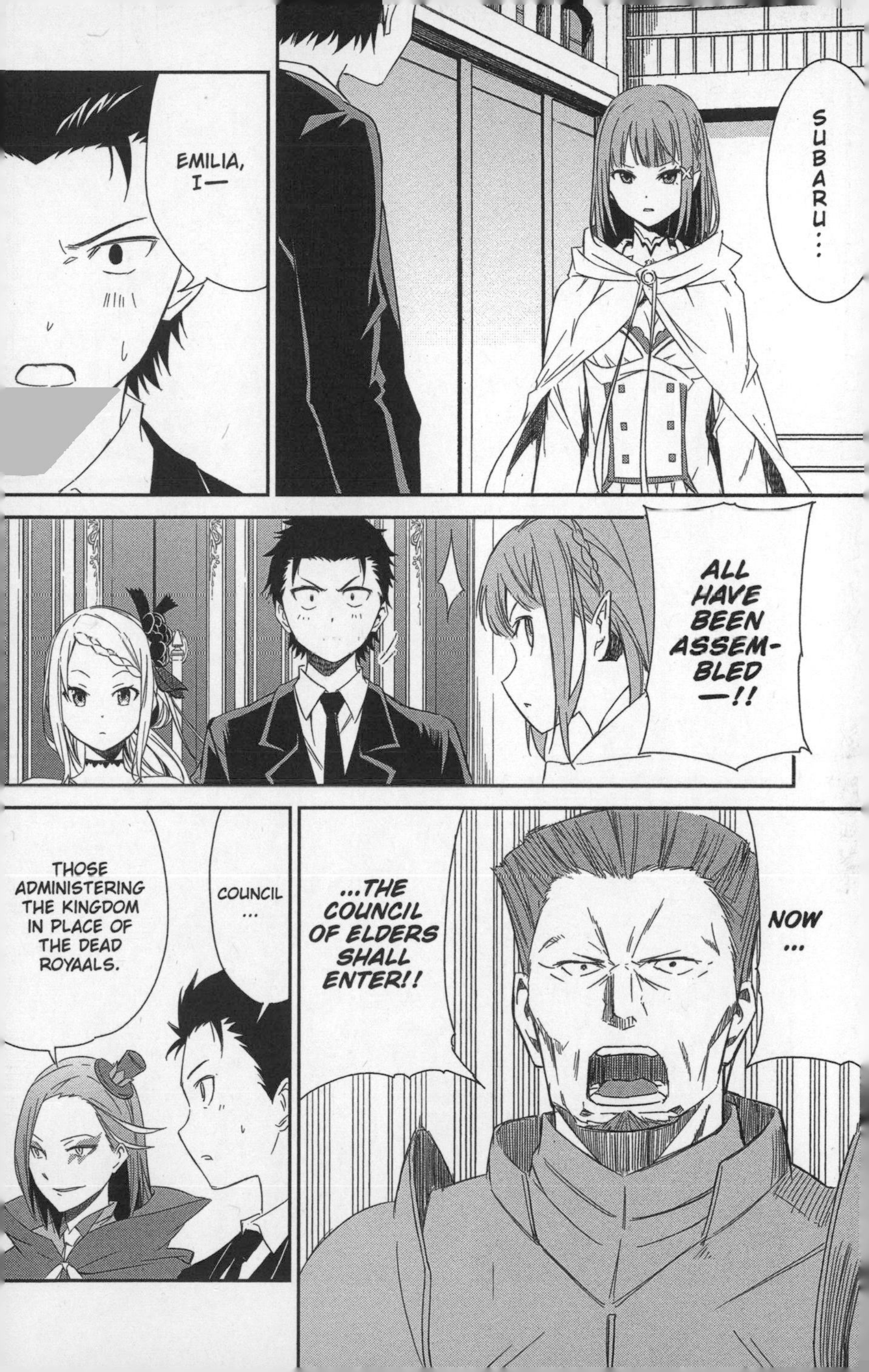
SUBARU...
EMILIA, I—
ALL HAVE BEEN ASSEMBLED—!!
NOW...
...THE COUNCIL OF ELDERS SHALL ENTER!!
COUNCIL...
THOSE ADMINISTERING THE KINGDOM IN PLACE OF THE DEAD ROYAALS.

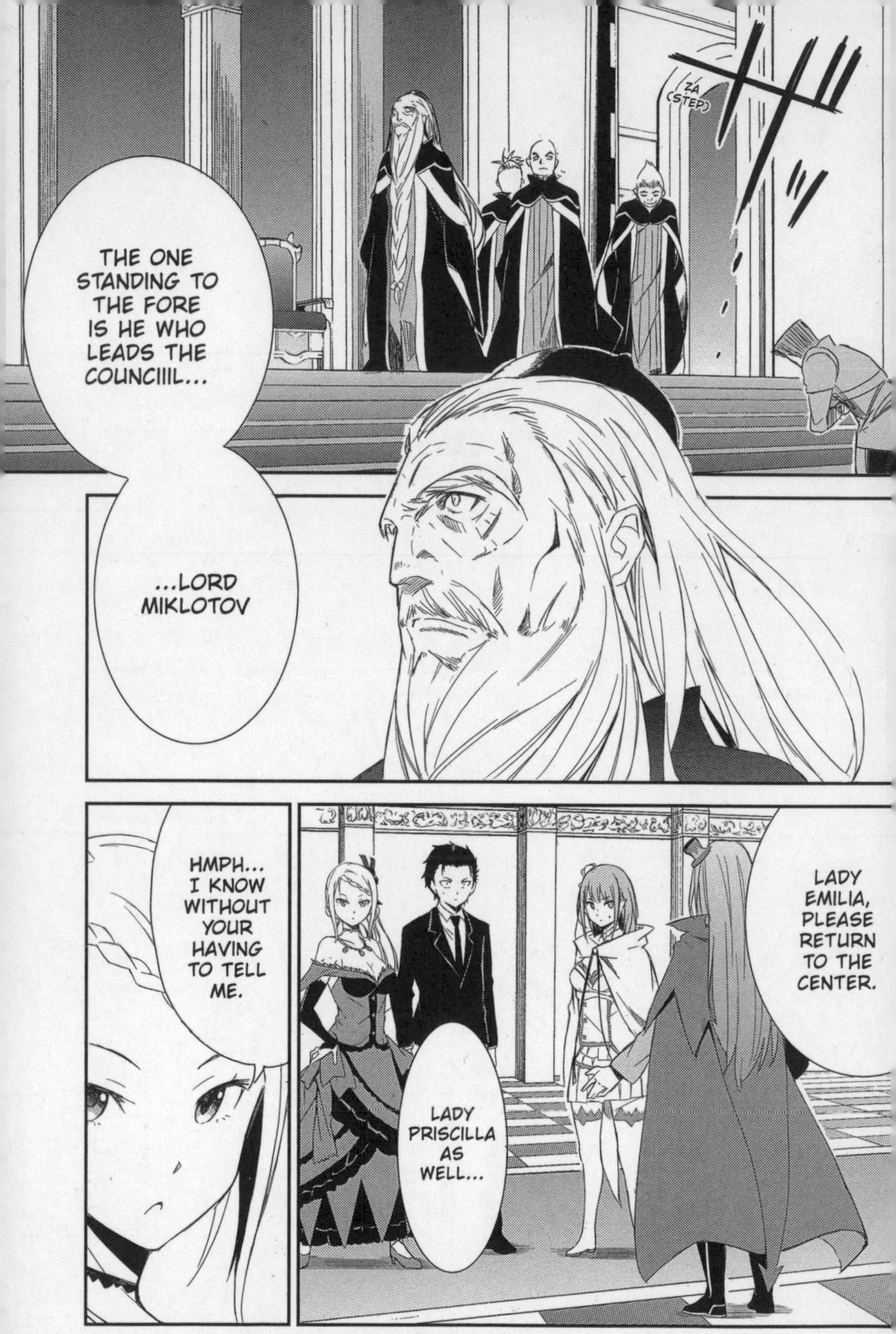
ZA (STEP)
THE ONE STANDING TO THE FORE IS HE WHO LEADS THE COUNCIIIL...
...LORD MIKLOTOV
LADY EMILIA, PLEASE RETURN TO THE CENTER.
LADY PRISCILLA AS WELL...
HMPH... I KNOW WITHOUT YOUR HAVING TO TELL ME.

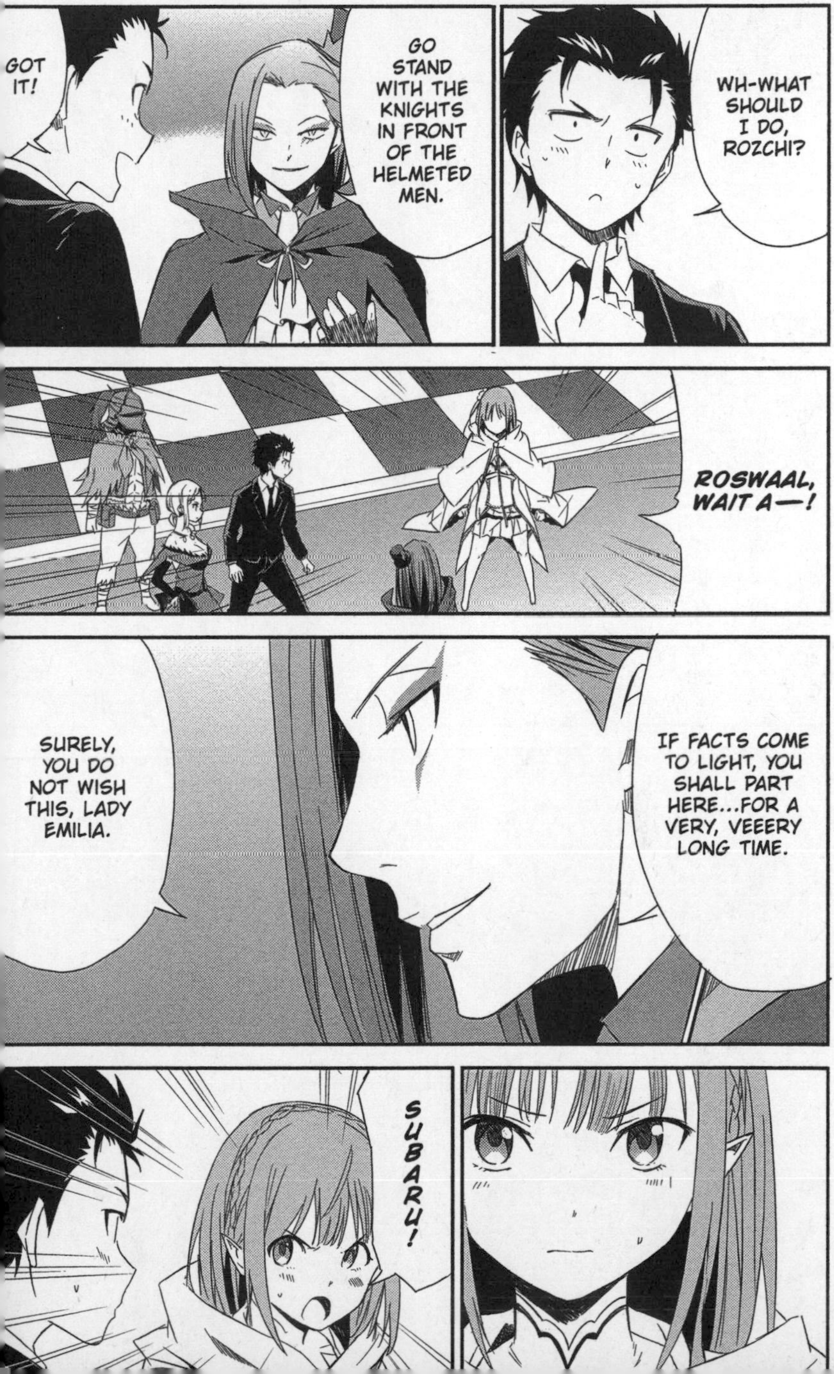
WH-WHAT SHOULD I DO, ROZCHI?
GO STAND WITH THE KNIGHTS IN FRONT OF THE HELMETED MEN.
GOT IT!
ROSWAAL, WAIT A—!
IF FACTS COME TO LIGHT, YOU SHALL PART HERE...FOR A VERY, VEEERY LONG TIME.
SURELY, YOU DO NOT WISH THIS, LADY EMILIA.
SUBARU!

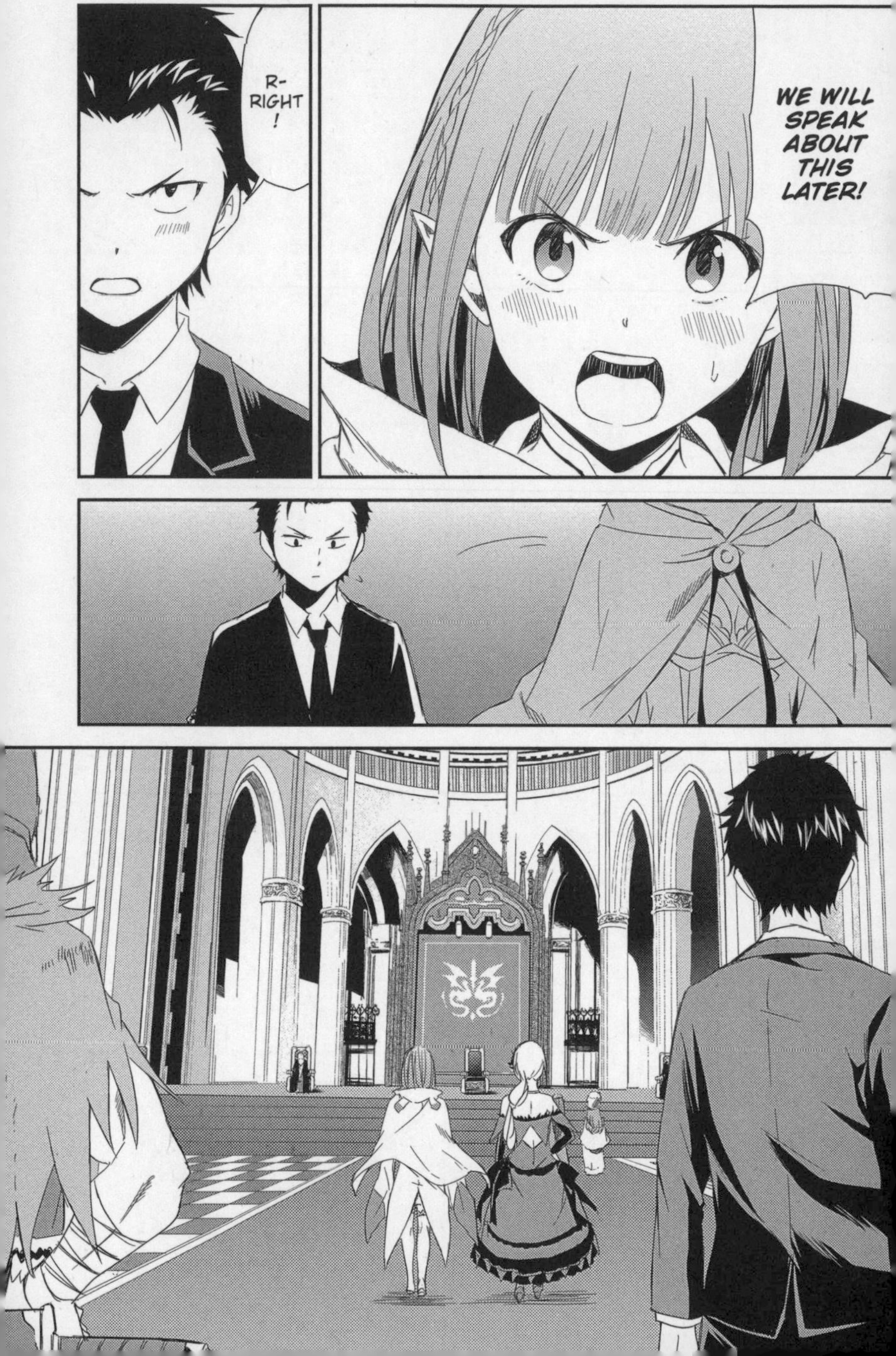
WE WILL SPEAK ABOUT THIS LATER!
R-RIGHT!

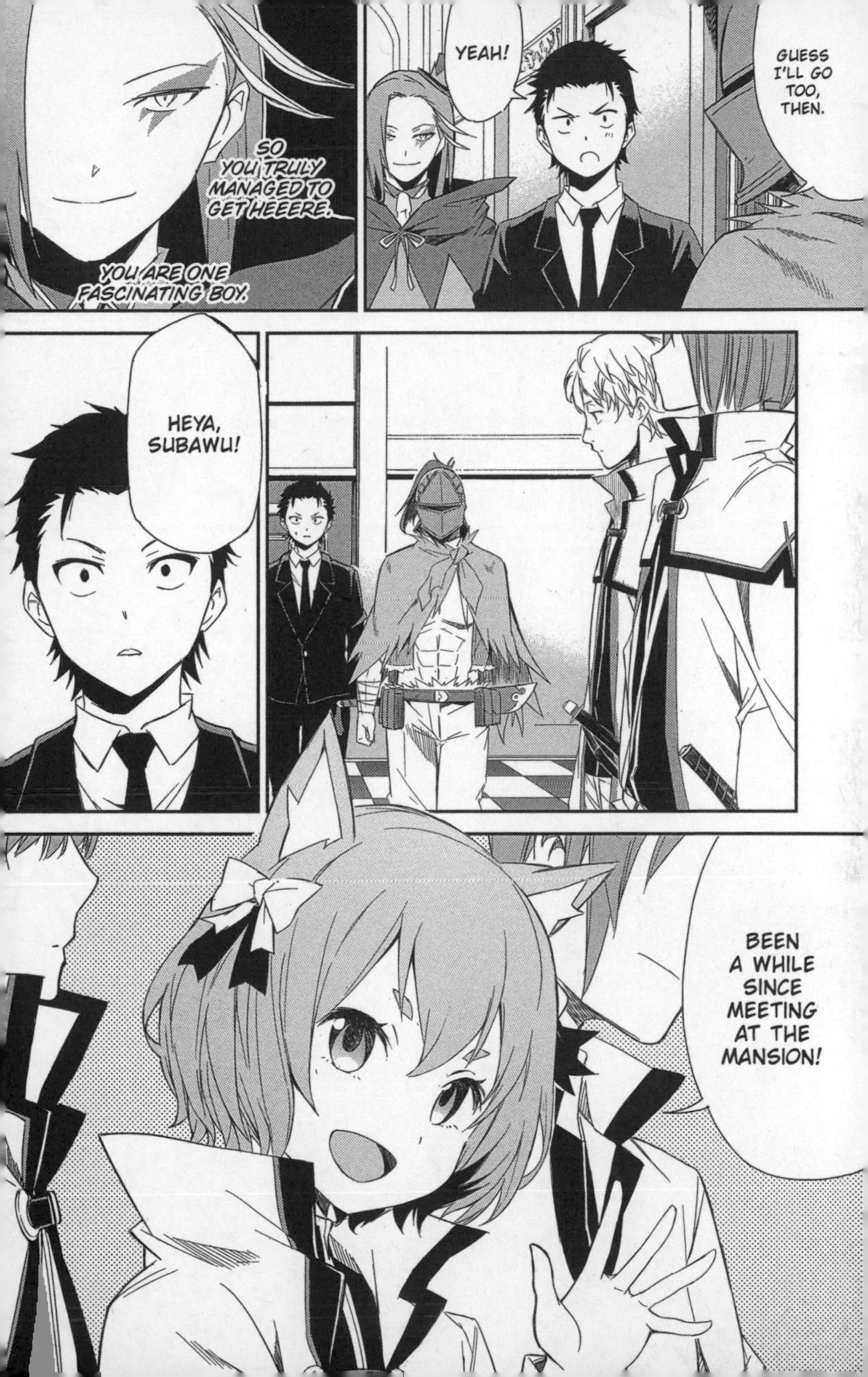
GUESS I'LL GO TOO, THEN.
YEAH!
SO YOU TRULY MANAGED TO GET HEEERE.
YOU ARE ONE FASCINATING BOY.
HEYA, SUBAWU!
BEEN A WHILE SINCE MEETING AT THE MANSION!

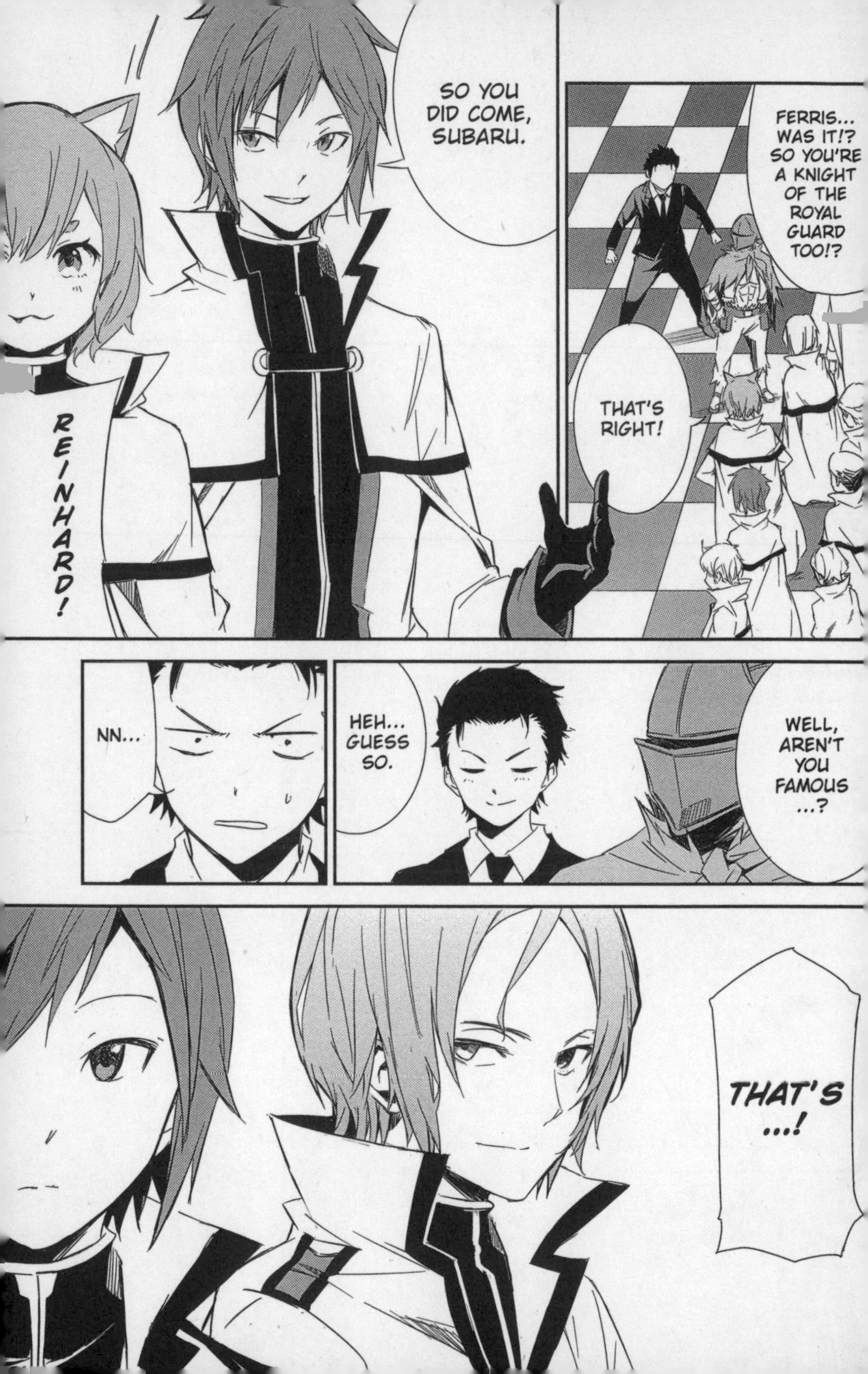
FERRIS... WAS IT!? SO YOU'RE A KNIGHT OF THE ROYAL GUARD TOO!?
THAT'S RIGHT!
SO YOU DID COME, SUBARU.
REINHARD!
WELL, AREN'T YOU FAMOUS ...?
HEH... GUESS SO.
NN...
THAT'S ...!

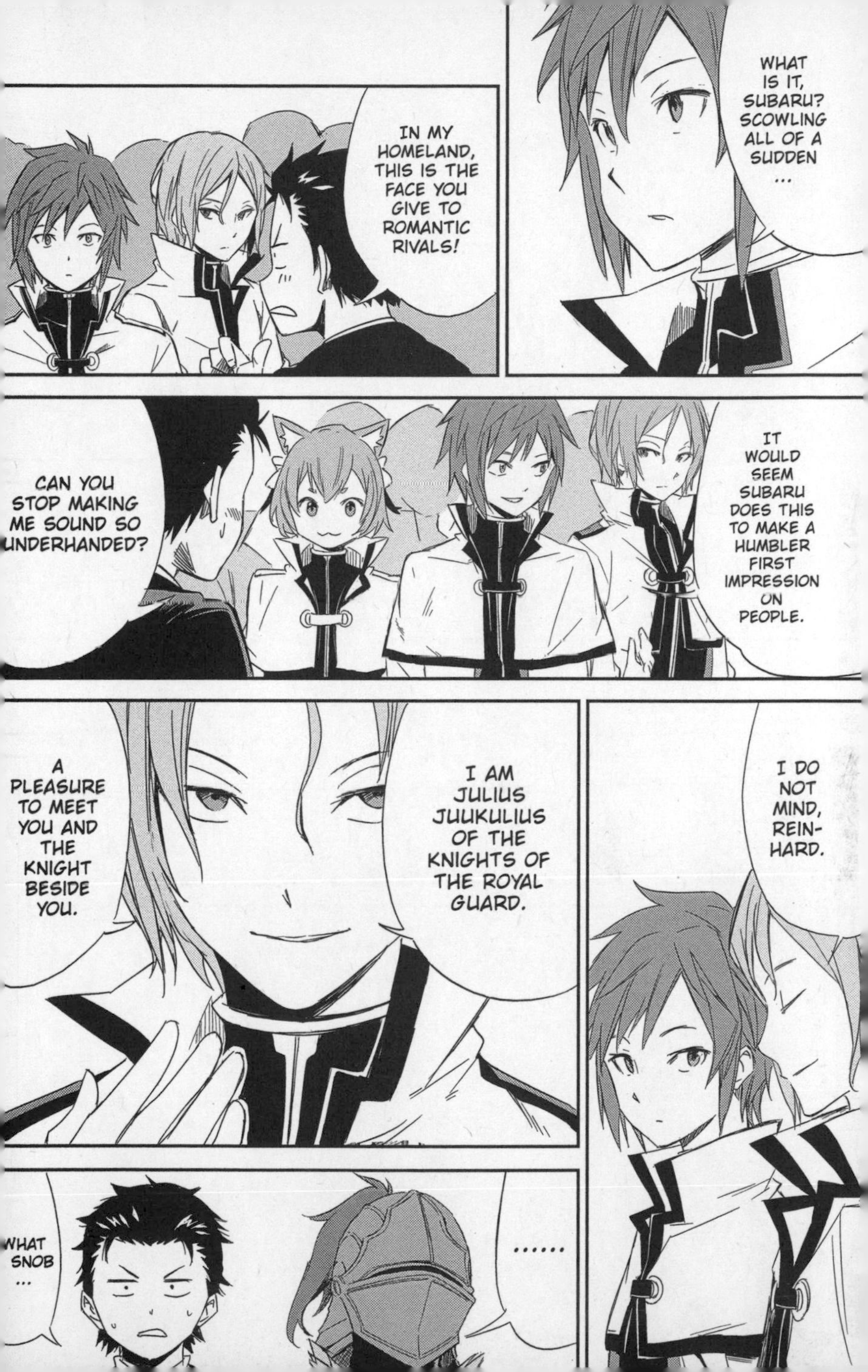
WHAT IS IT, SUBARU? SCOWLING ALL OF A SUDDEN ...
IN MY HOMELAND, THIS IS THE FACE YOU GIVE TO ROMANTIC RIVALS!
IT WOULD SEEM SUBARU DOES THIS TO MAKE A HUMBLER FIRST IMPRESSION ON PEOPLE.
CAN YOU STOP MAKING ME SOUND SO UNDERHANDED?
I DO NOT MIND, REIN-HARD.
I AM JULIUS JUUKULIUS OF THE KNIGHTS OF THE ROYAL GUARD.
A PLEASURE TO MEET YOU AND THE KNIGHT BESIDE YOU.
......
WHAT SNOB ...

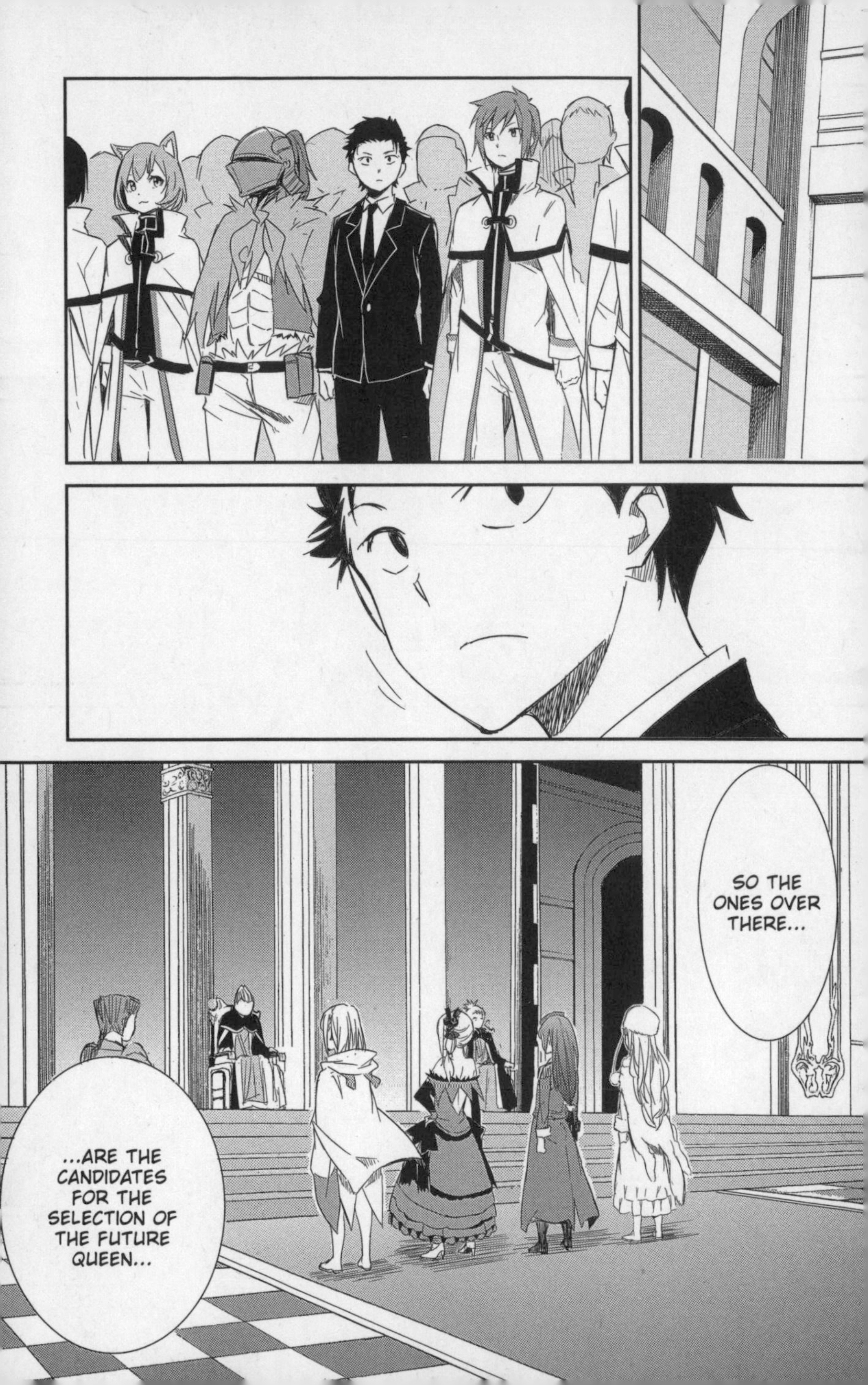
SO THE ONES OVER THERE...
...ARE THE CANDIDATES FOR THE SELECTION OF THE FUTURE QUEEN...

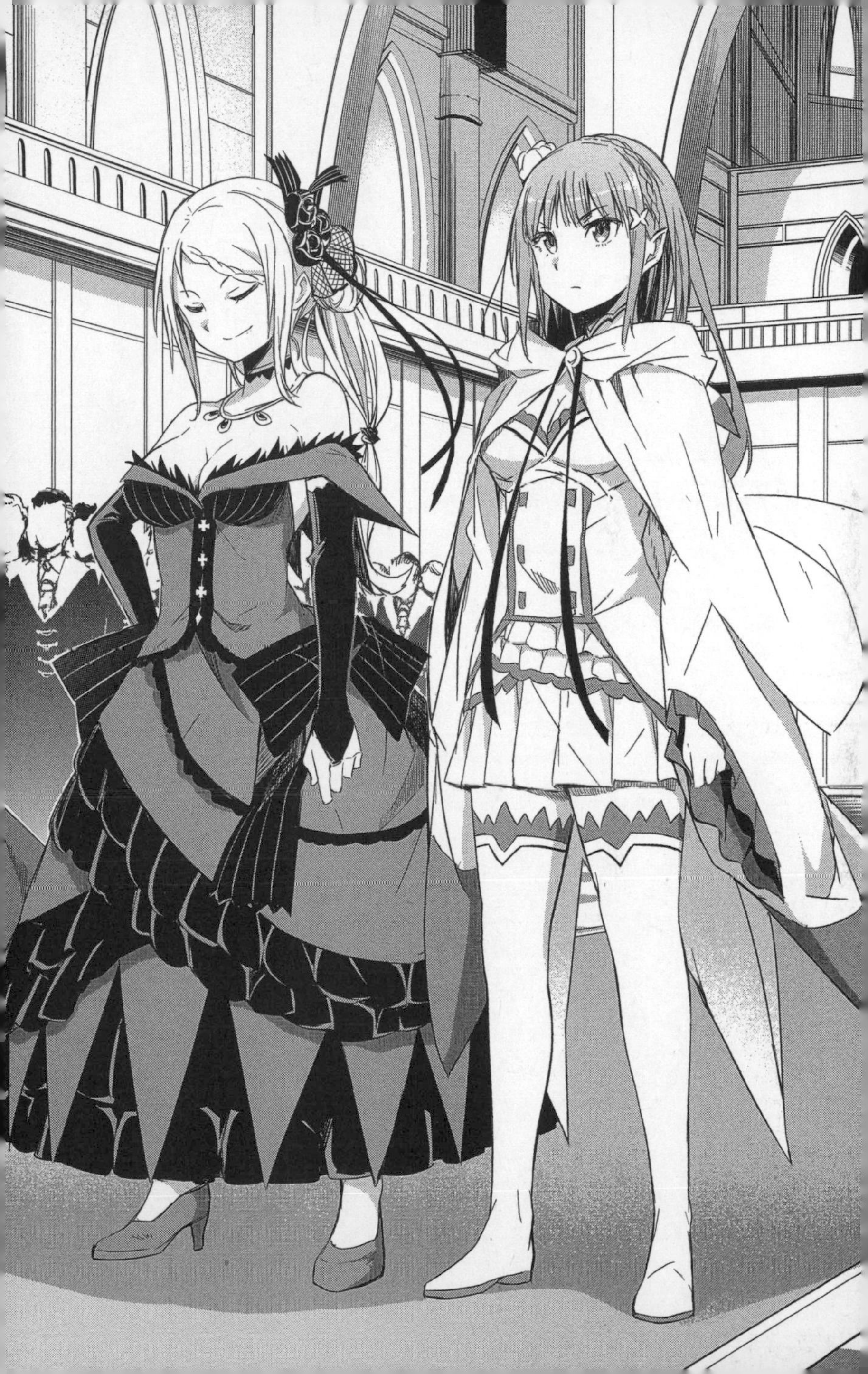

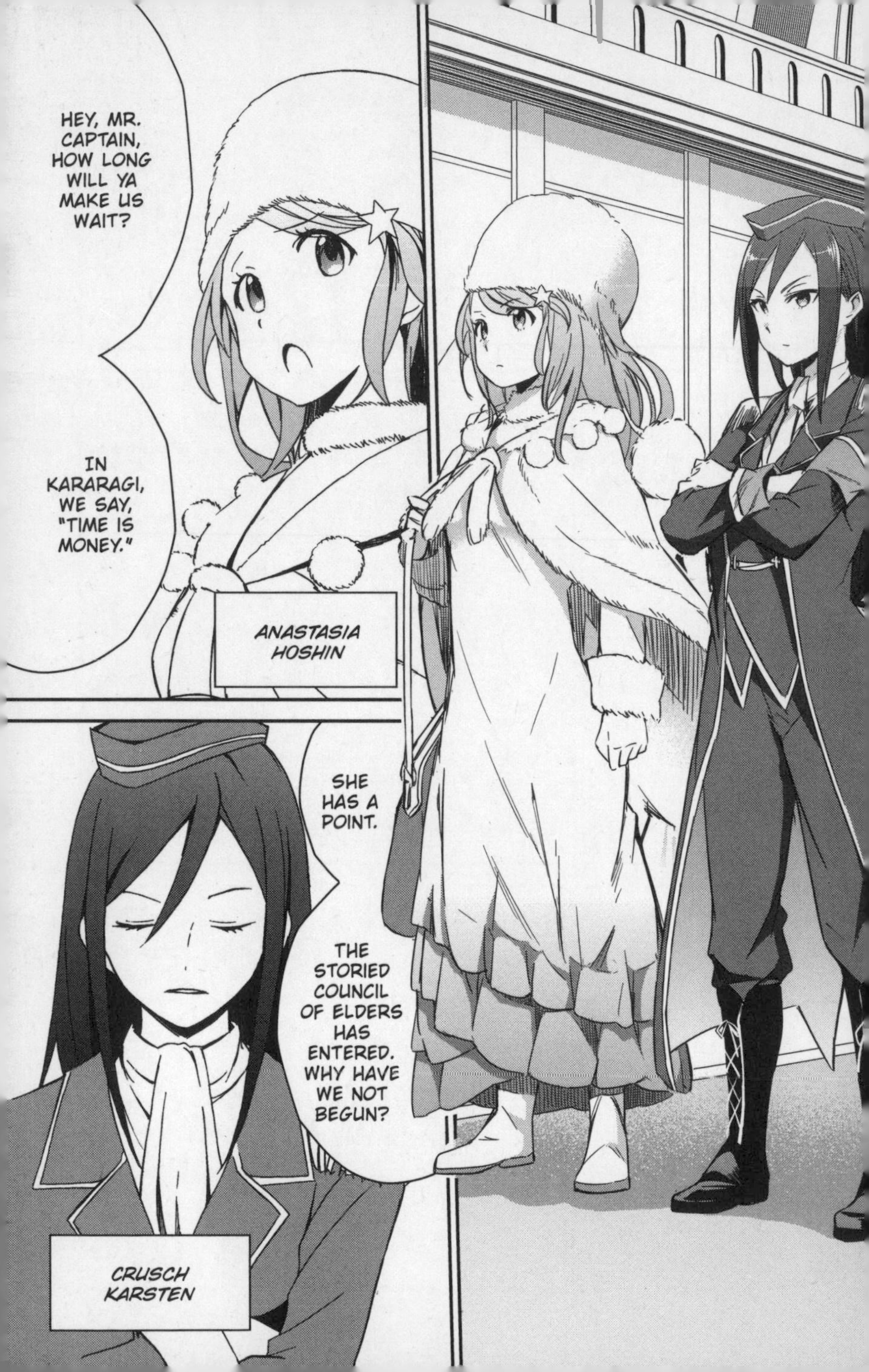
HEY, MR. CAPTAIN, HOW LONG WILL YA MAKE US WAIT?
IN KARARAGI, WE SAY, "TIME IS MONEY."
ANASTASIA HOSHIN
SHE HAS A POINT.
THE STORIED COUNCIL OF ELDERS HAS ENTERED. WHY HAVE WE NOT BEGUN?
CRUSCH KARSTEN

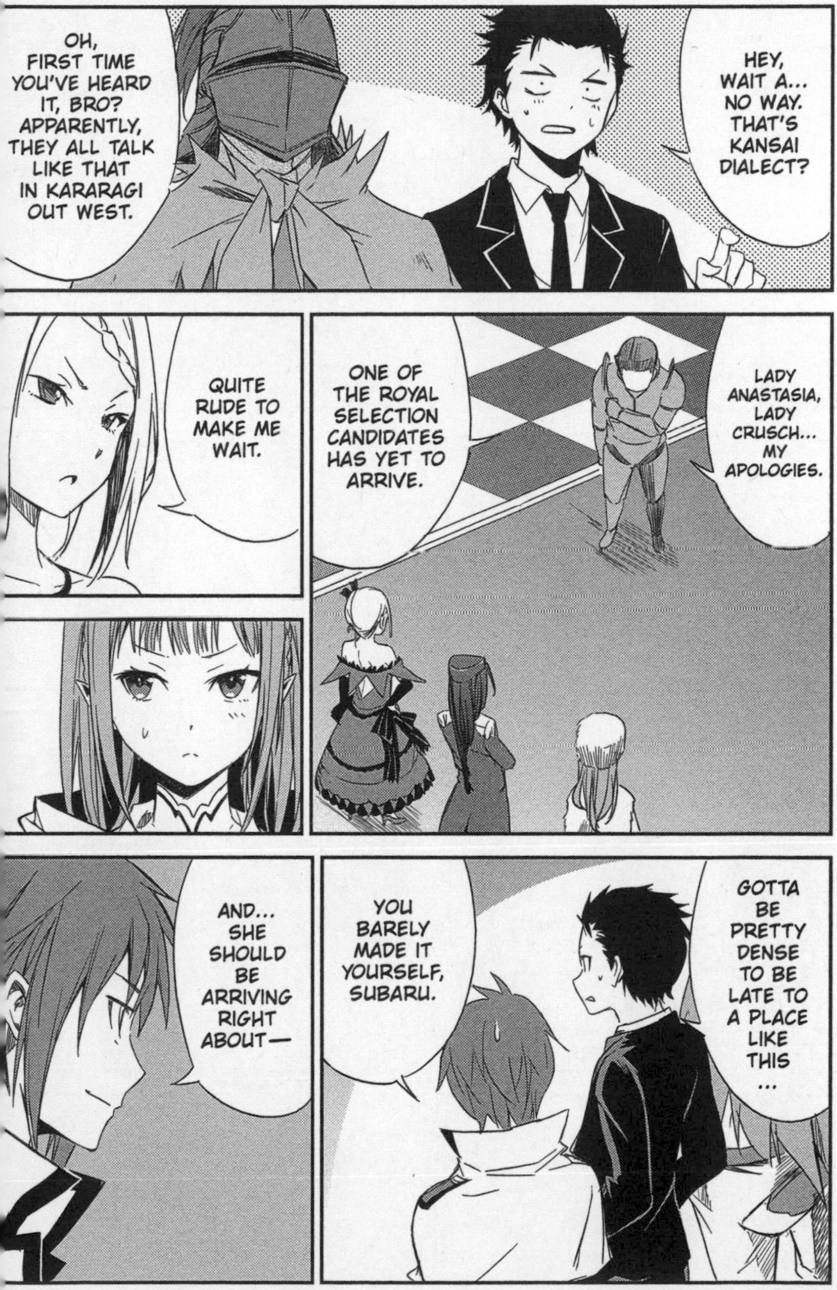
HEY, WAIT A... NO WAY. THAT'S KANSAI DIALECT?
OH, FIRST TIME YOU'VE HEARD IT, BRO? APPARENTLY, THEY ALL TALK LIKE THAT IN KARARAGI OUT WEST.
LADY ANASTASIA, LADY CRUSCH... MY APOLOGIES.
ONE OF THE ROYAL SELECTION CANDIDATES HAS YET TO ARRIVE.
QUITE RUDE TO MAKE ME WAIT.
GOTTA BE PRETTY DENSE TO BE LATE TO A PLACE LIKE THIS ...
YOU BARELY MADE IT YOURSELF, SUBARU.
AND... SHE SHOULD BE ARRIVING RIGHT ABOUT—

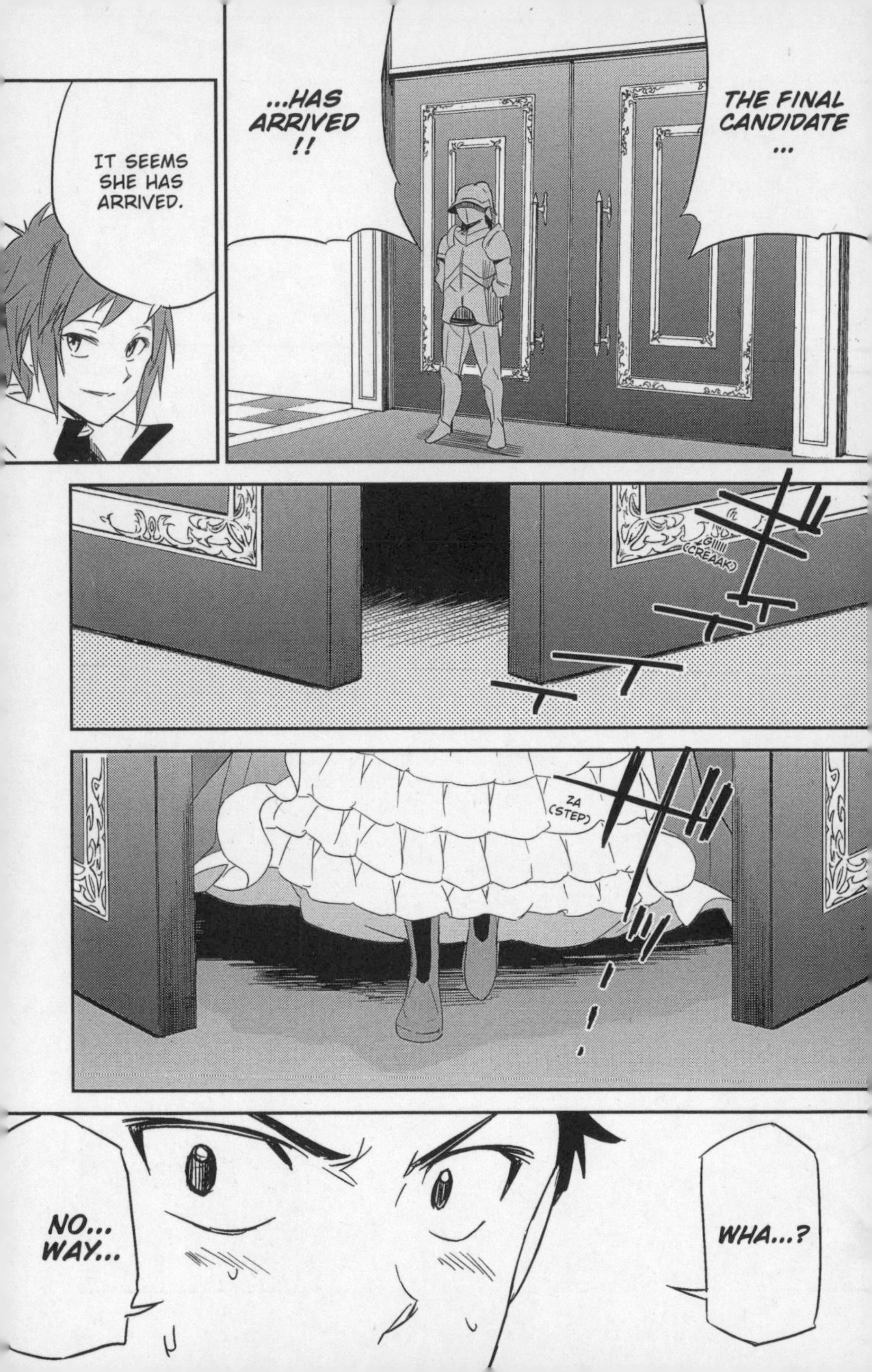
THE FINAL CANDIDATE ...
...HAS ARRIVED !!
IT SEEMS SHE HAS ARRIVED.
GIIIII (CREAAK)
ZA (STEP)
WHA...?
NO... WAY...

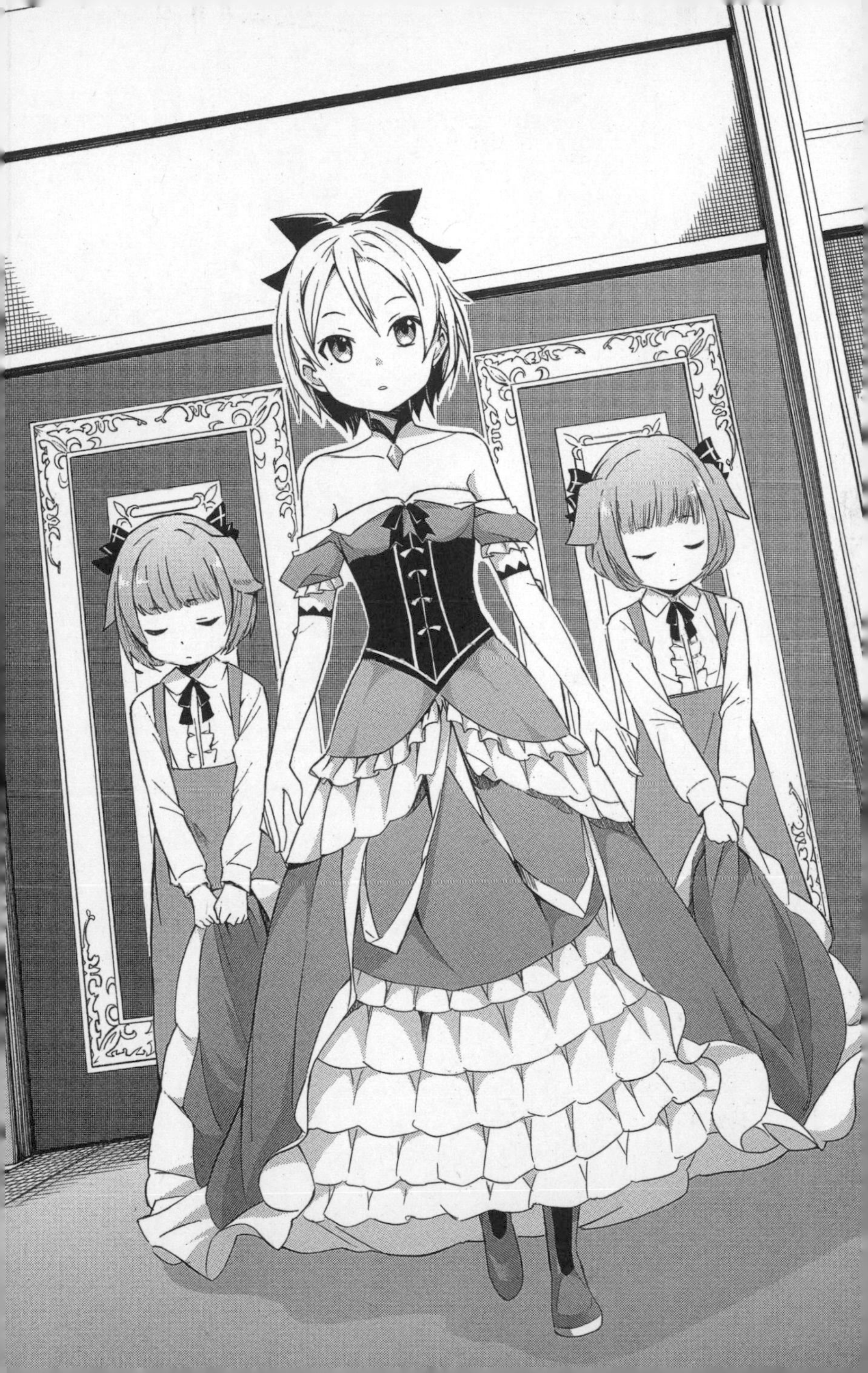

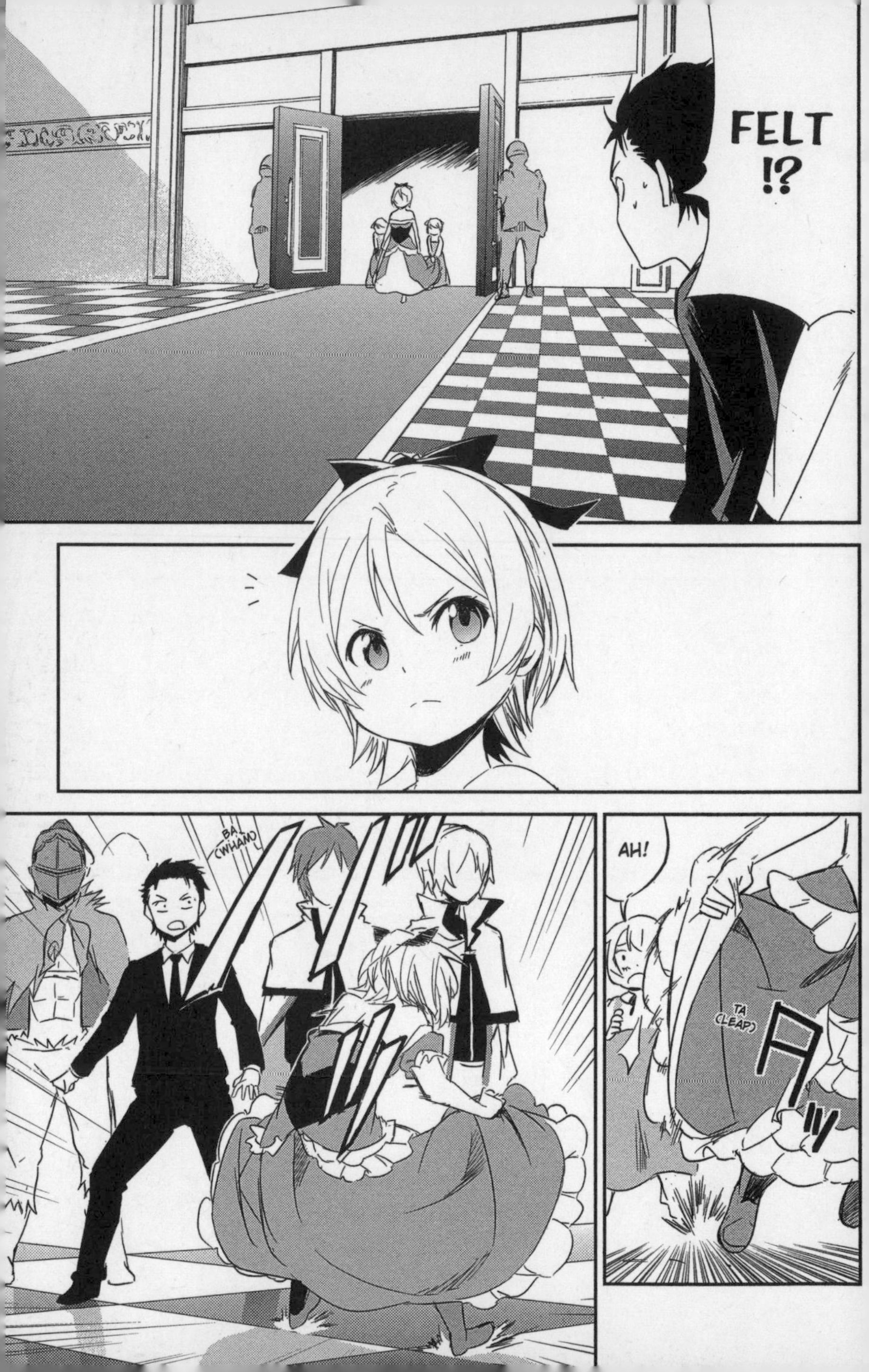
FELT !?
AH!
TA (LEAP)
BA (WHAM)

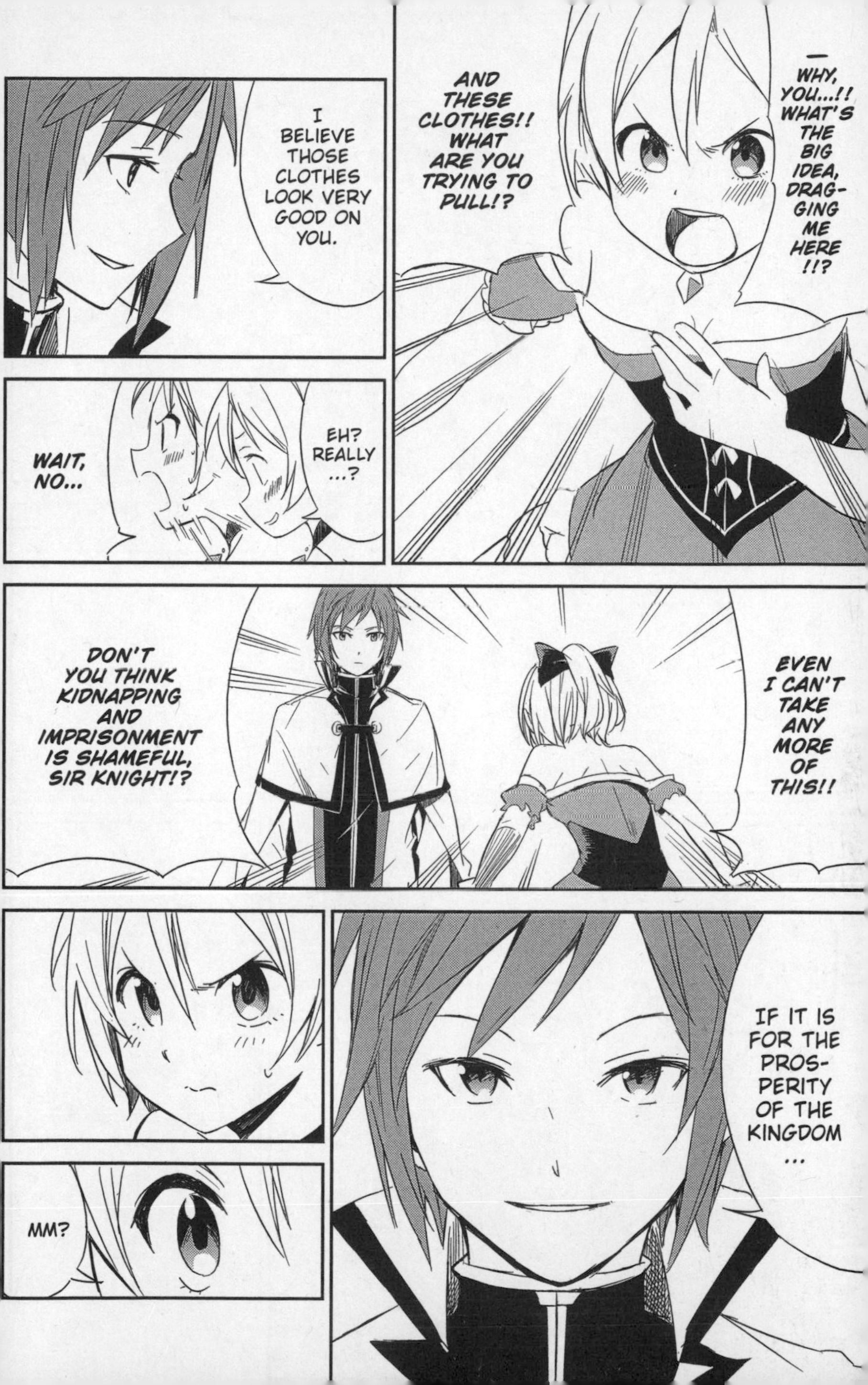
—WHY, YOU...!! WHAT'S THE BIG IDEA, DRAG-GING ME HERE!!?
AND THESE CLOTHES!! WHAT ARE YOU TRYING TO PULL!?
I BELIEVE THOSE CLOTHES LOOK VERY GOOD ON YOU.
EH? REALLY ...?
WAIT, NO...
EVEN I CAN'T TAKE ANY MORE OF THIS!!
DON'T YOU THINK KIDNAPPING AND IMPRISONMENT IS SHAMEFUL, SIR KNIGHT!?
IF IT IS FOR THE PROS-PERITY OF THE KINGDOM ...
MM?

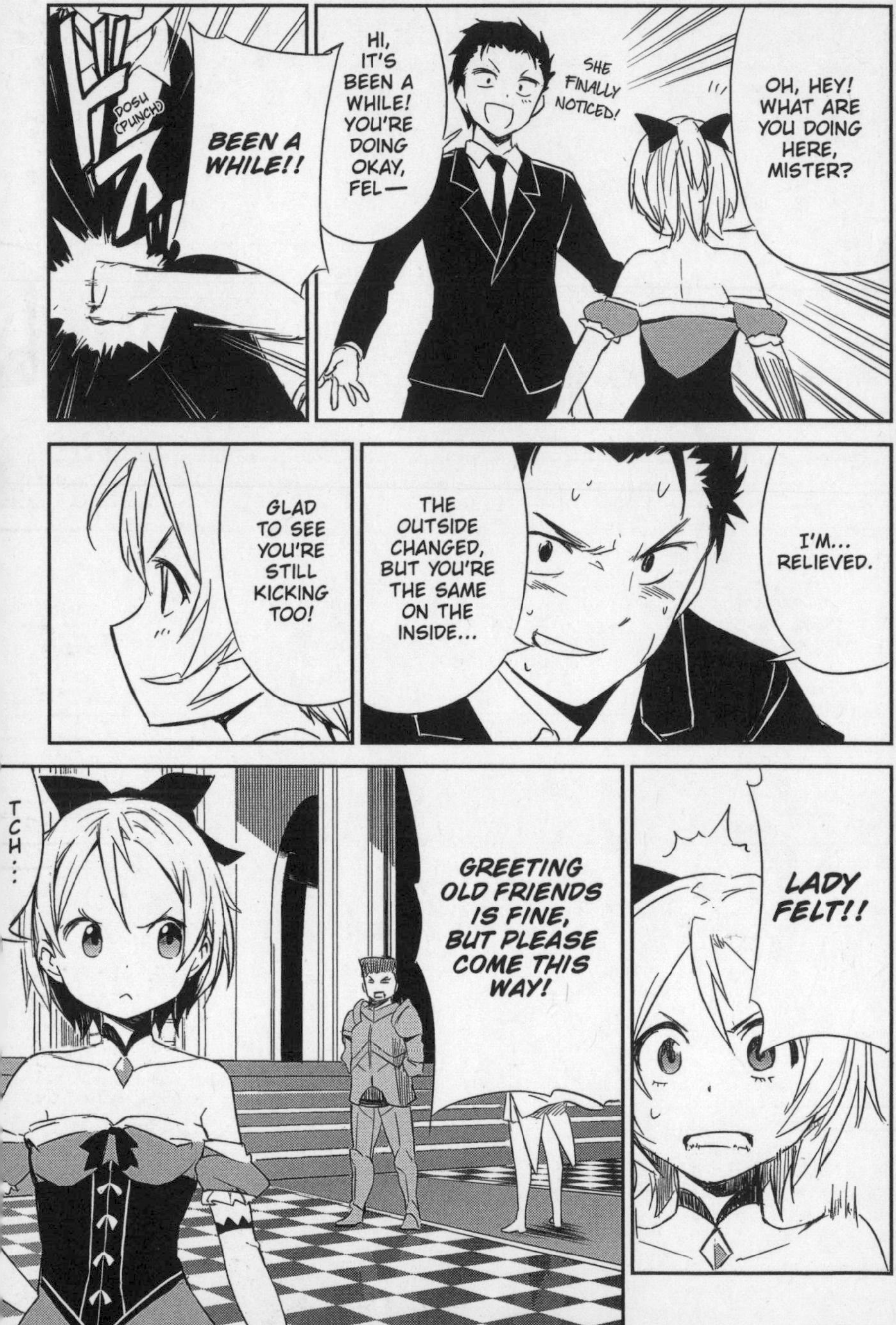
OH, HEY! WHAT ARE YOU DOING HERE, MISTER?
SHE FINALLY NOTICED!
HI, IT'S BEEN A WHILE! YOU'RE DOING OKAY, FEL—
BEEN A WHILE!!
DOSU (PUNCH)
I'M... RELIEVED.
THE OUTSIDE CHANGED, BUT YOU'RE THE SAME ON THE INSIDE...
GLAD TO SEE YOU'RE STILL KICKING TOO!
LADY FELT!!
GREETING OLD FRIENDS IS FINE, BUT PLEASE COME THIS WAY!
TCH...

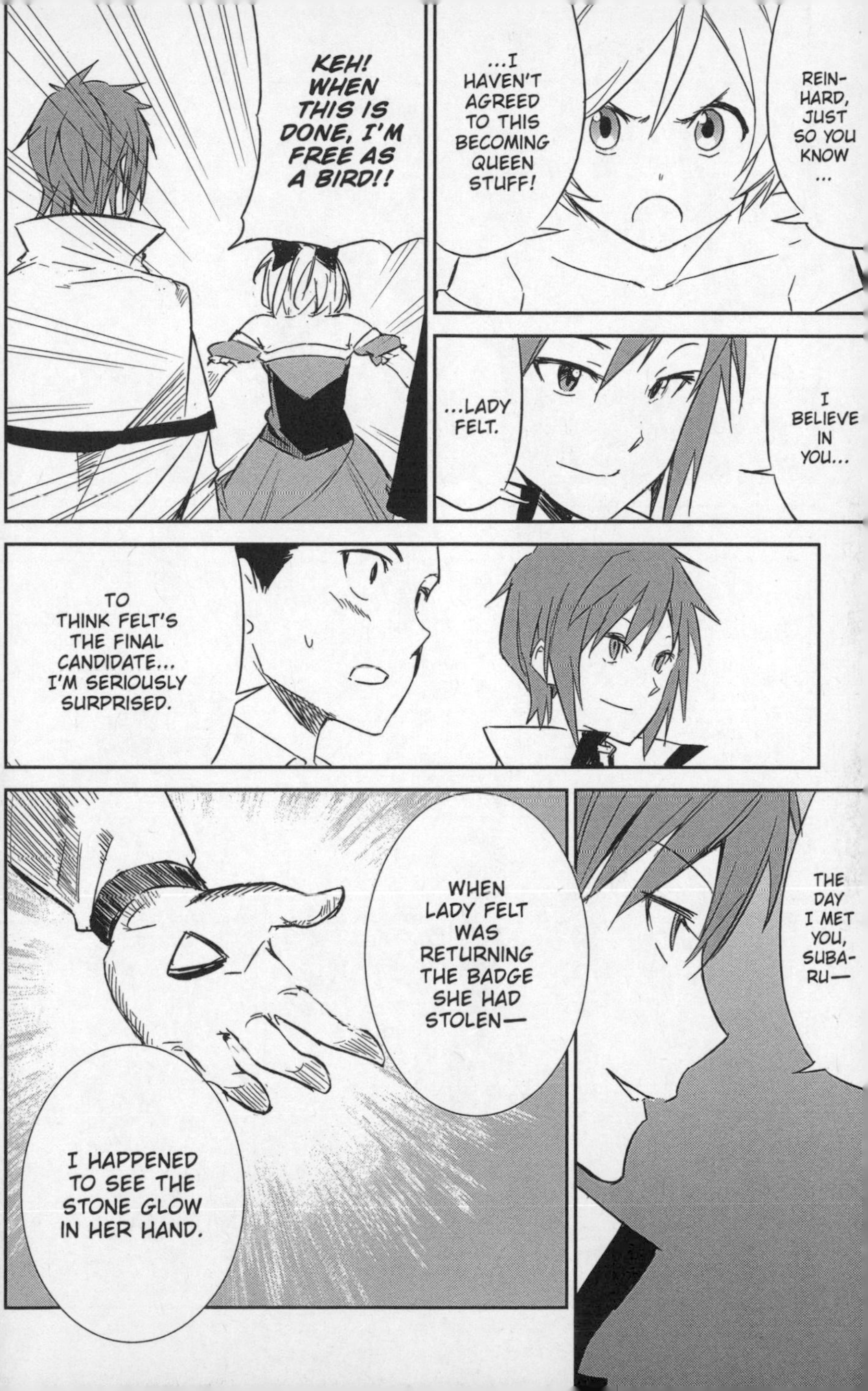
REIN-HARD, JUST SO YOU KNOW ...
...I HAVEN'T AGREED TO THIS BECOMING QUEEN STUFF!
I BELIEVE IN YOU...
...LADY FELT.
KEH! WHEN THIS IS DONE, I'M FREE AS A BIRD!!
TO THINK FELT'S THE FINAL CANDIDATE... I'M SERIOUSLY SURPRISED.
THE DAY I MET YOU, SUBA-RU—
WHEN LADY FELT WAS RETURNING THE BADGE SHE HAD STOLEN—
I HAPPENED TO SEE THE STONE GLOW IN HER HAND.

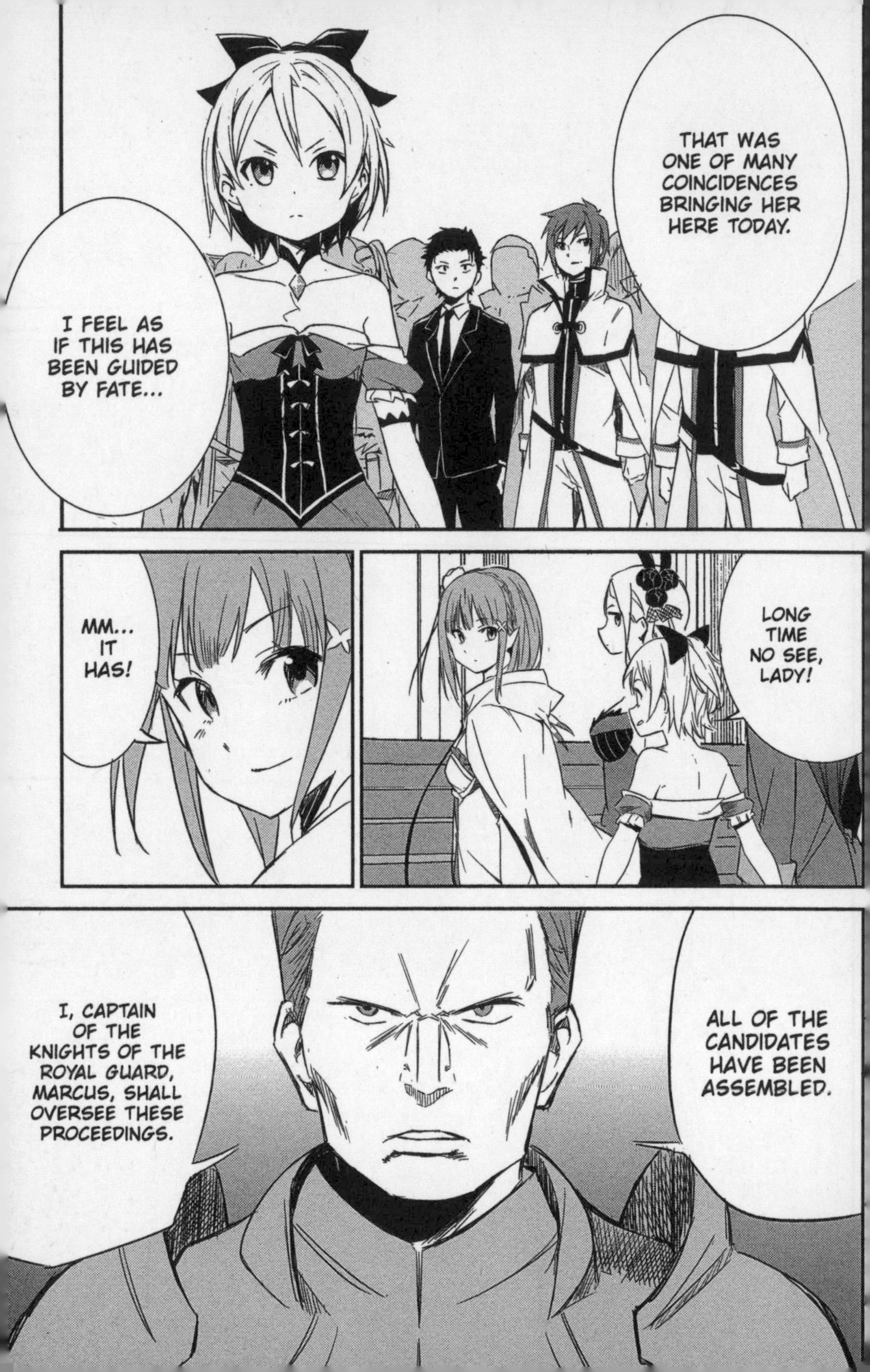
THAT WAS ONE OF MANY COINCIDENCES BRINGING HER HERE TODAY.
I FEEL AS IF THIS HAS BEEN GUIDED BY FATE...
LONG TIME NO SEE, LADY!
MM... IT HAS!
ALL OF THE CANDIDATES HAVE BEEN ASSEMBLED.
I, CAPTAIN OF THE KNIGHTS OF THE ROYAL GUARD, MARCUS, SHALL OVERSEE THESE PROCEEDINGS.

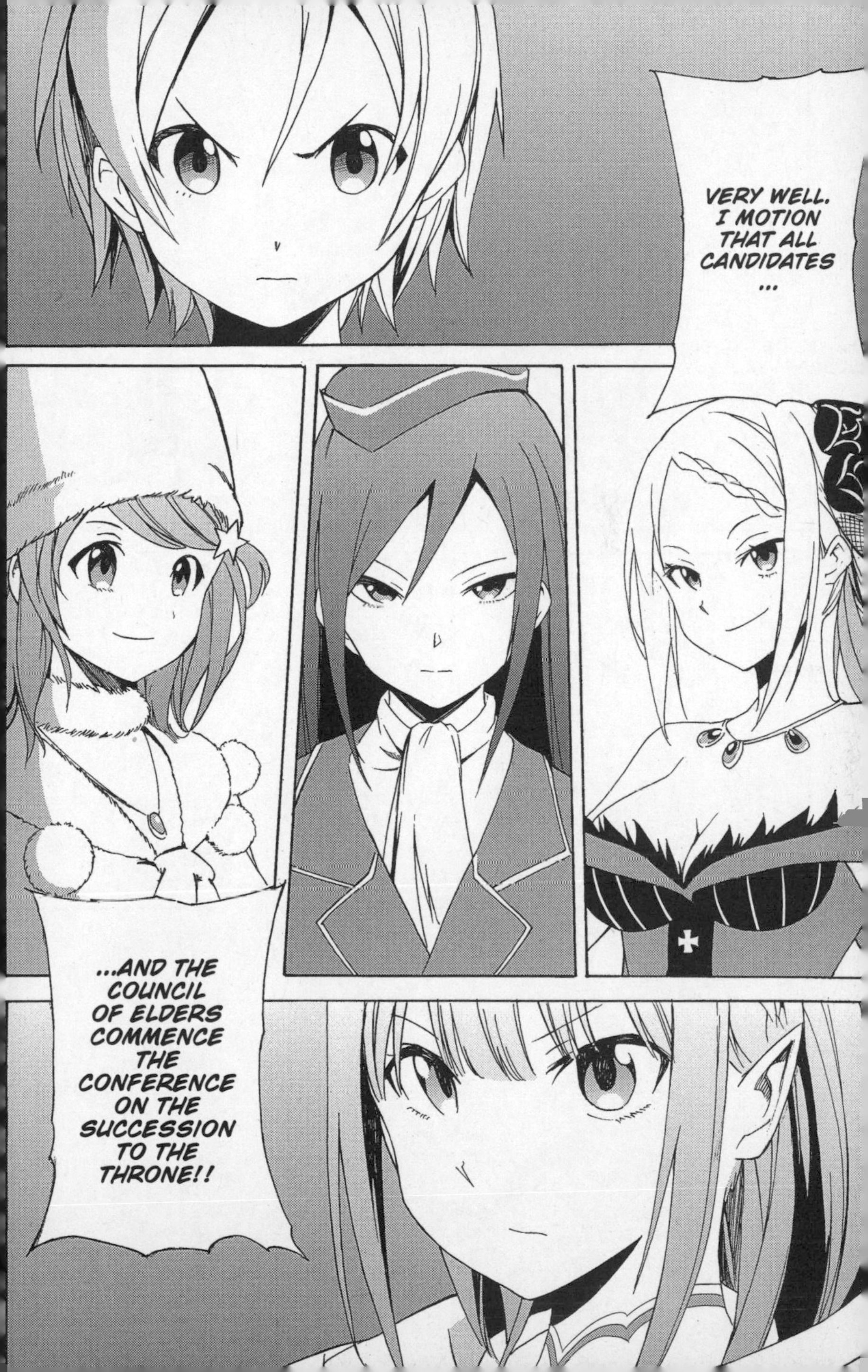
VERY WELL. I MOTION THAT ALL CANDIDATES ...
...AND THE COUNCIL OF ELDERS COMMENCE THE CONFERENCE ON THE SUCCESSION TO THE THRONE!!

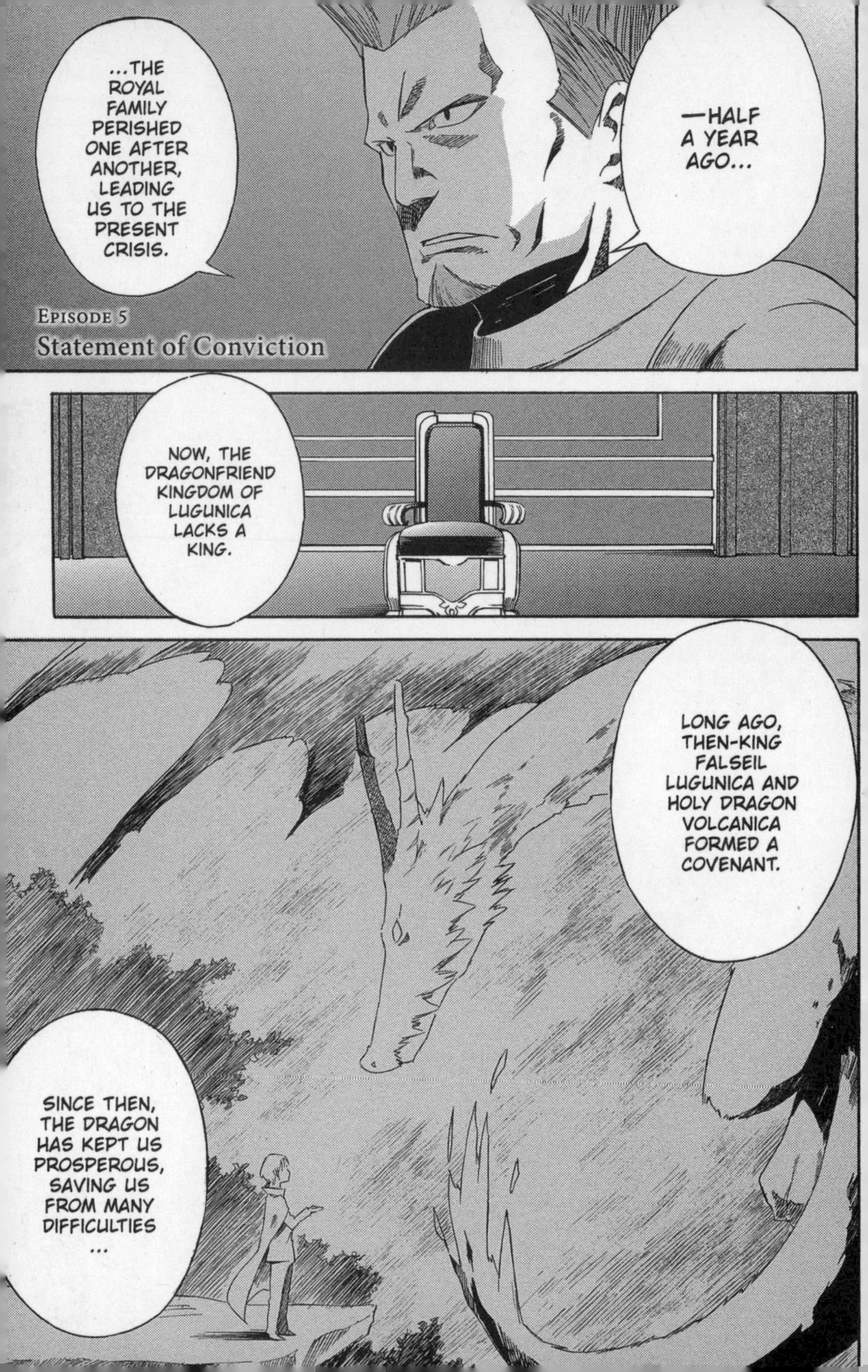
—HALF A YEAR AGO...
...THE ROYAL FAMILY PERISHED ONE AFTER ANOTHER, LEADING US TO THE PRESENT CRISIS.
Episode 5
Statement of Conviction
NOW, THE DRAGONFRIEND KINGDOM OF LUGUNICA LACKS A KING.
LONG AGO, THEN-KING FALSEIL LUGUNICA AND HOLY DRAGON VOLCANICA FORMED A COVENANT.
SINCE THEN, THE DRAGON HAS KEPT US PROSPEROUS, SAVING US FROM MANY DIFFICULTIES ...

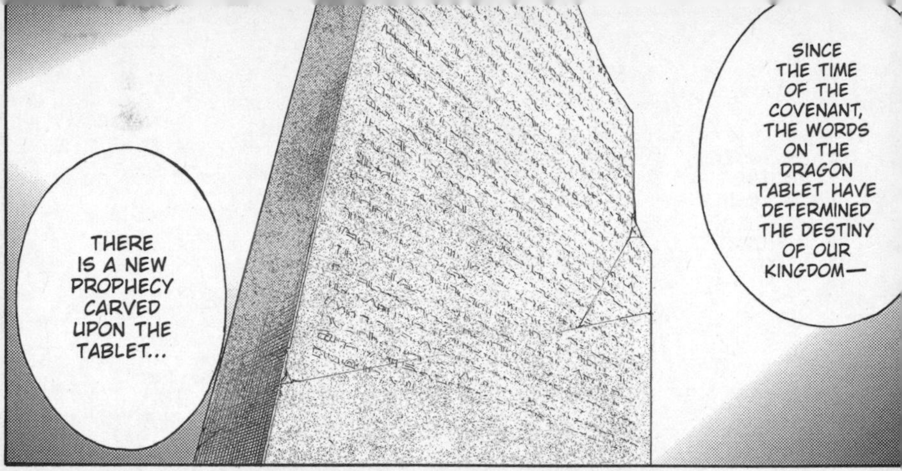
SINCE THE TIME OF THE COVENANT, THE WORDS ON THE DRAGON TABLET HAVE DETERMINED THE DESTINY OF OUR KINGDOM—
THERE IS A NEW PROPHECY CARVED UPON THE TABLET...

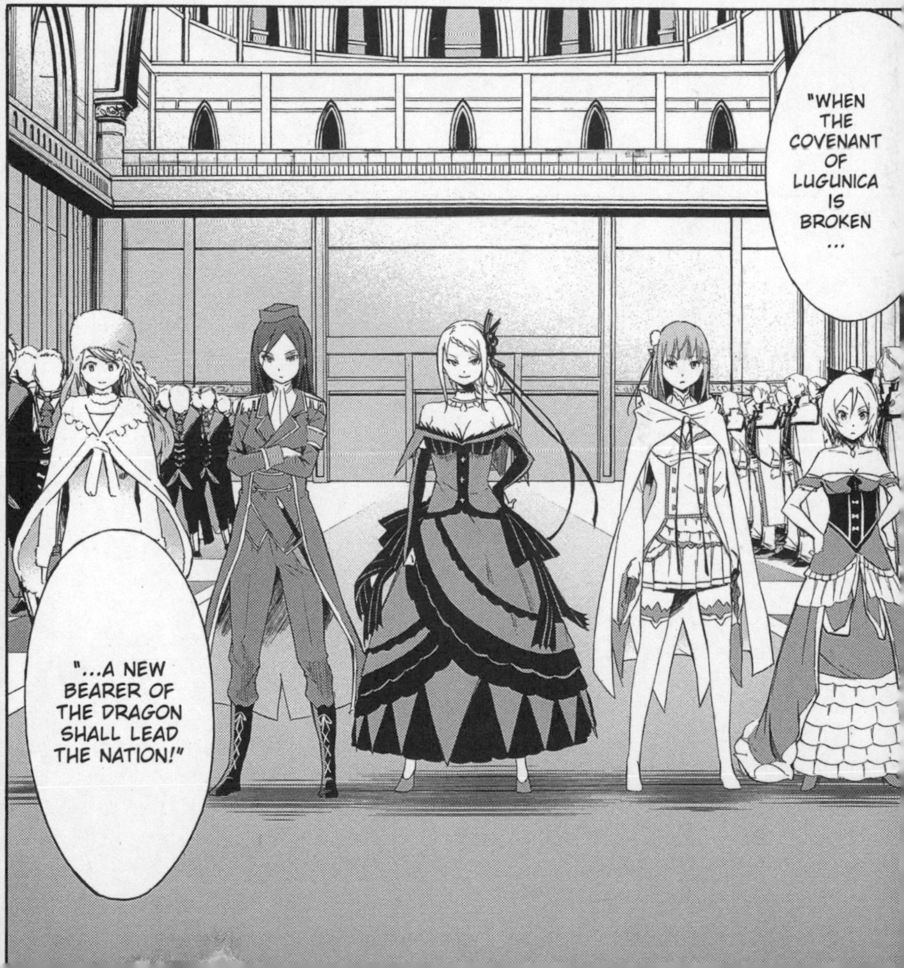
"WHEN THE COVENANT OF LUGUNICA IS BROKEN...
"...A NEW BEARER OF THE DRAGON SHALL LEAD THE NATION!"

REM

- A maid at Roswaal Manor and a fanatical Subaru sympathizer.
- A solicitous Super Maid, supreme in all domestic skills, but hasty decision-making is the flaw in her jewel.
- A member of the near-extinct "Oni" race, she grows a horn when she fights and swings around an iron ball on a chain. Also a water magic user at a fairly robust level.
- Normally, her personality is gentle, but she is prone to fierce emotional outbursts. She is the type to go above and beyond for those she cares about, which currently includes Ram and Subaru.
- Once hostile to Subaru, she has completely fallen for him and is his ally through thick and thin.
- Though she's dextrous in all areas, nothing stands out in particular, and this gives her a sense of inferiority relative to her older sister.
- Special skills: [Cooking], [Laundry], [Cleaning], [Sewing]
- Hobbies: [Appreciation of Theater], [Poetry]

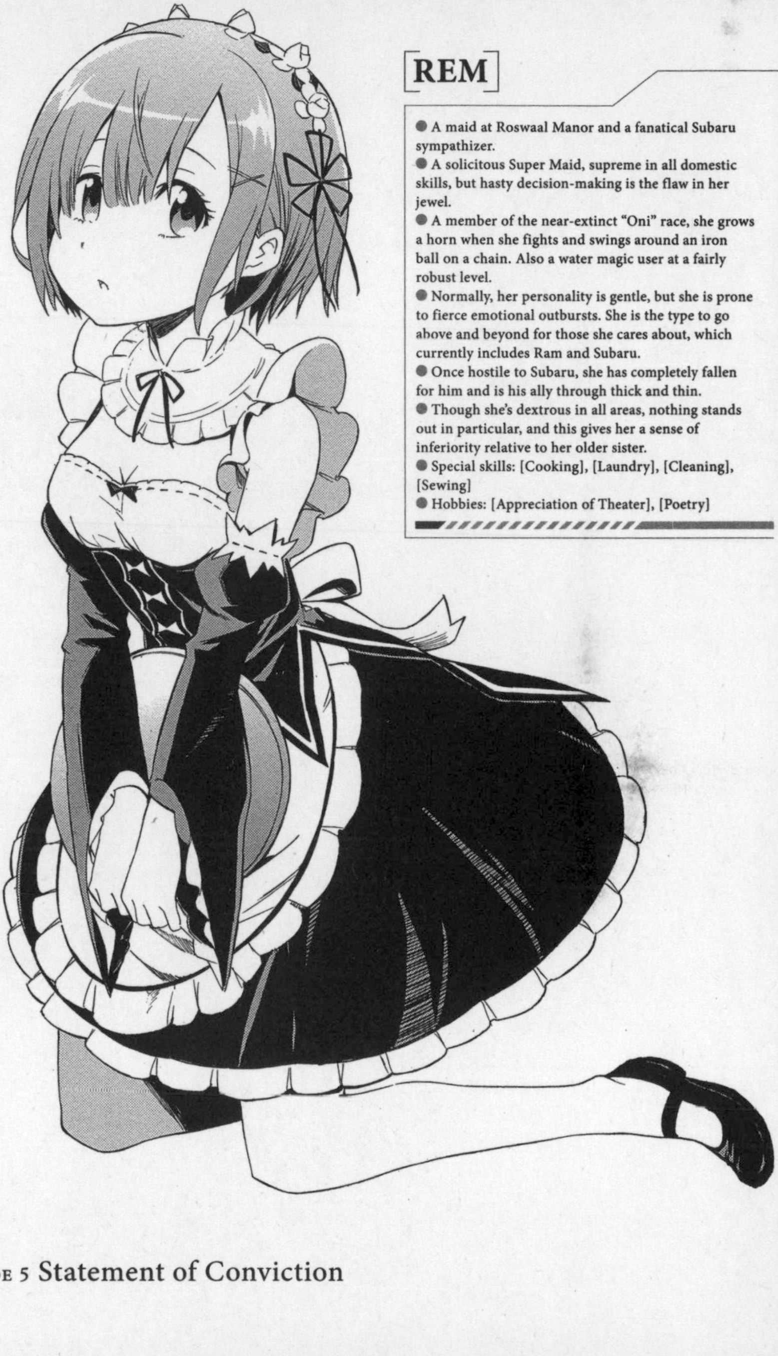

Episode 5 Statement of Conviction

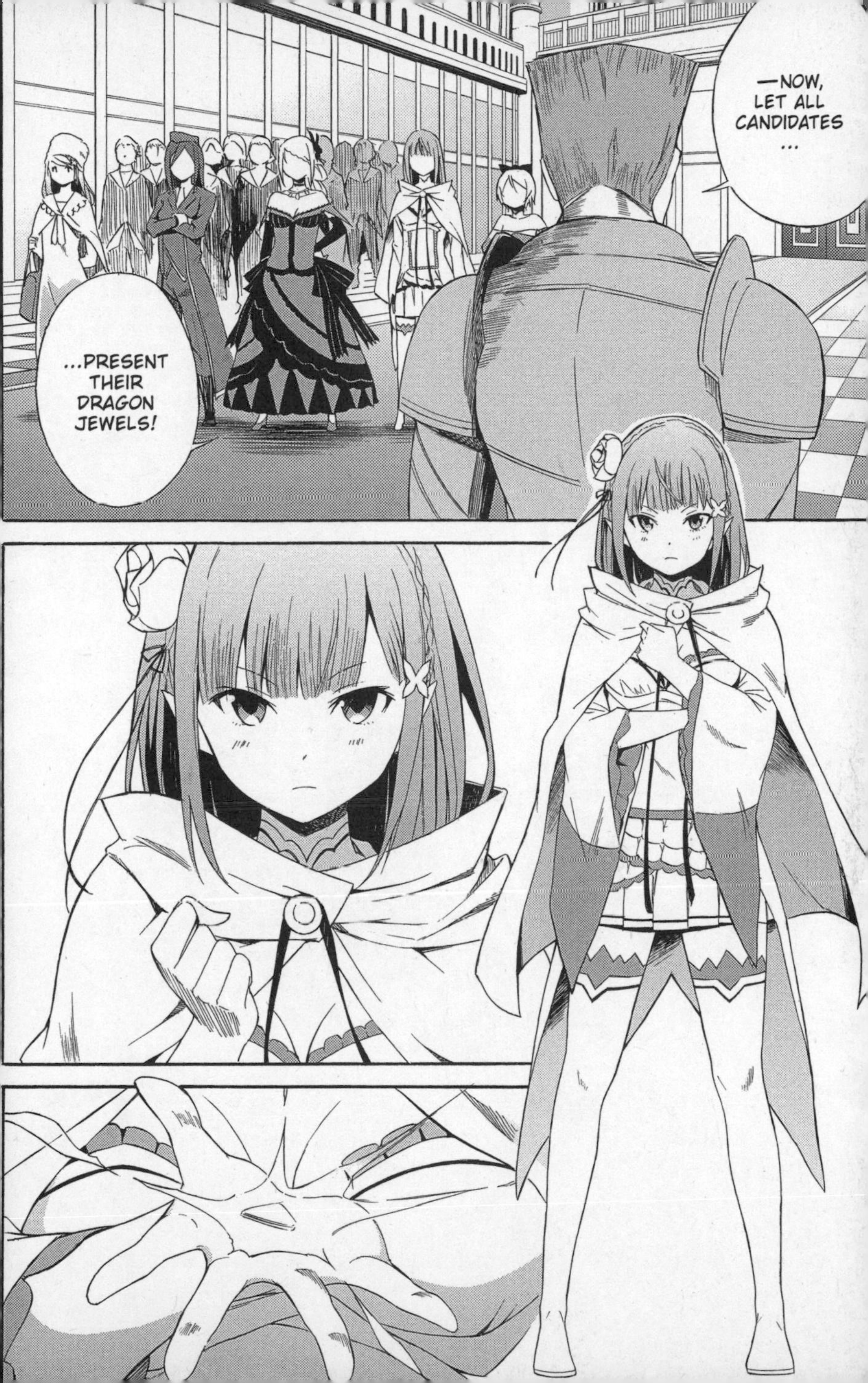
—NOW, LET ALL CANDIDATES ...
...PRESENT THEIR DRAGON JEWELS!

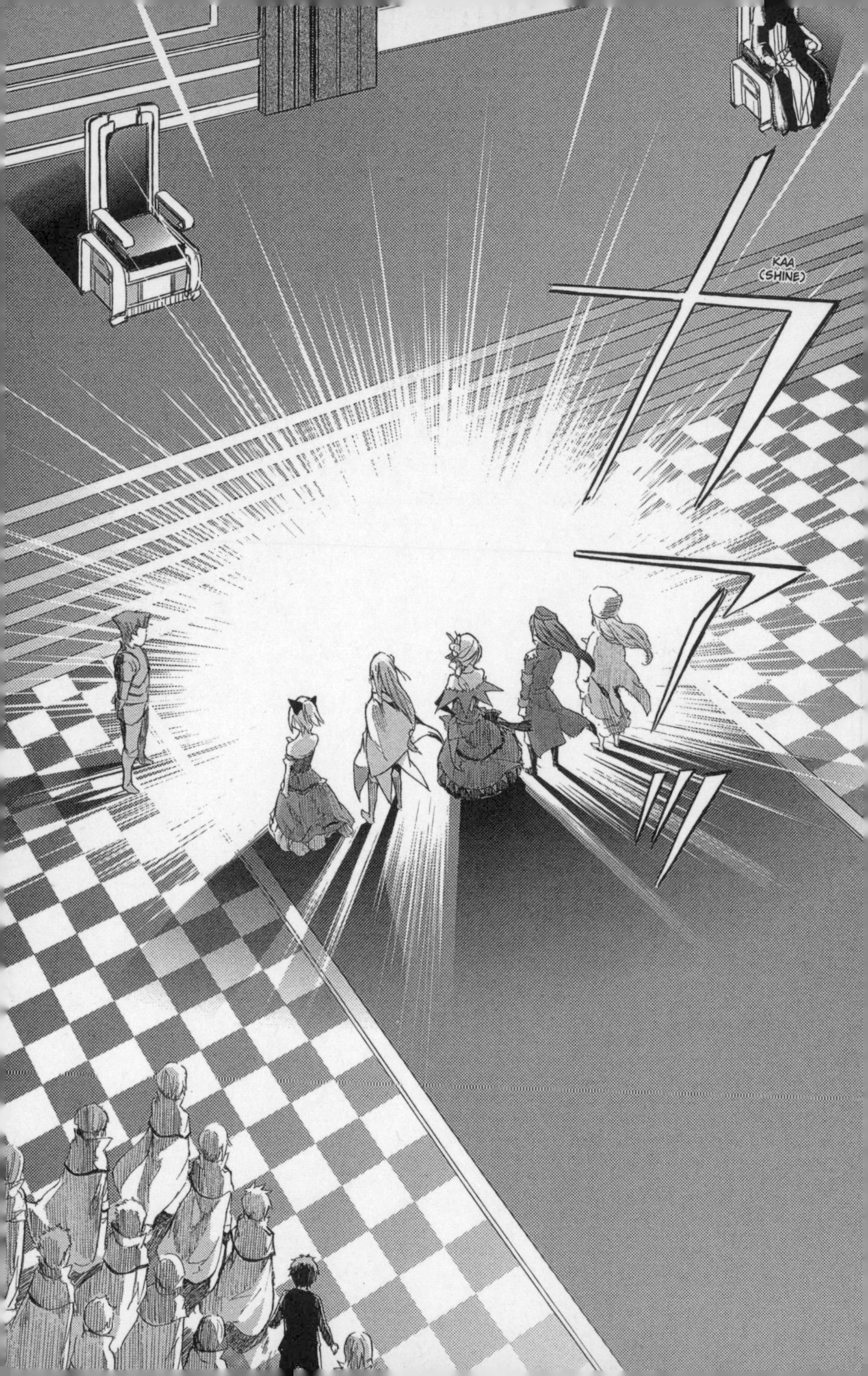
KAA
(SHINE)

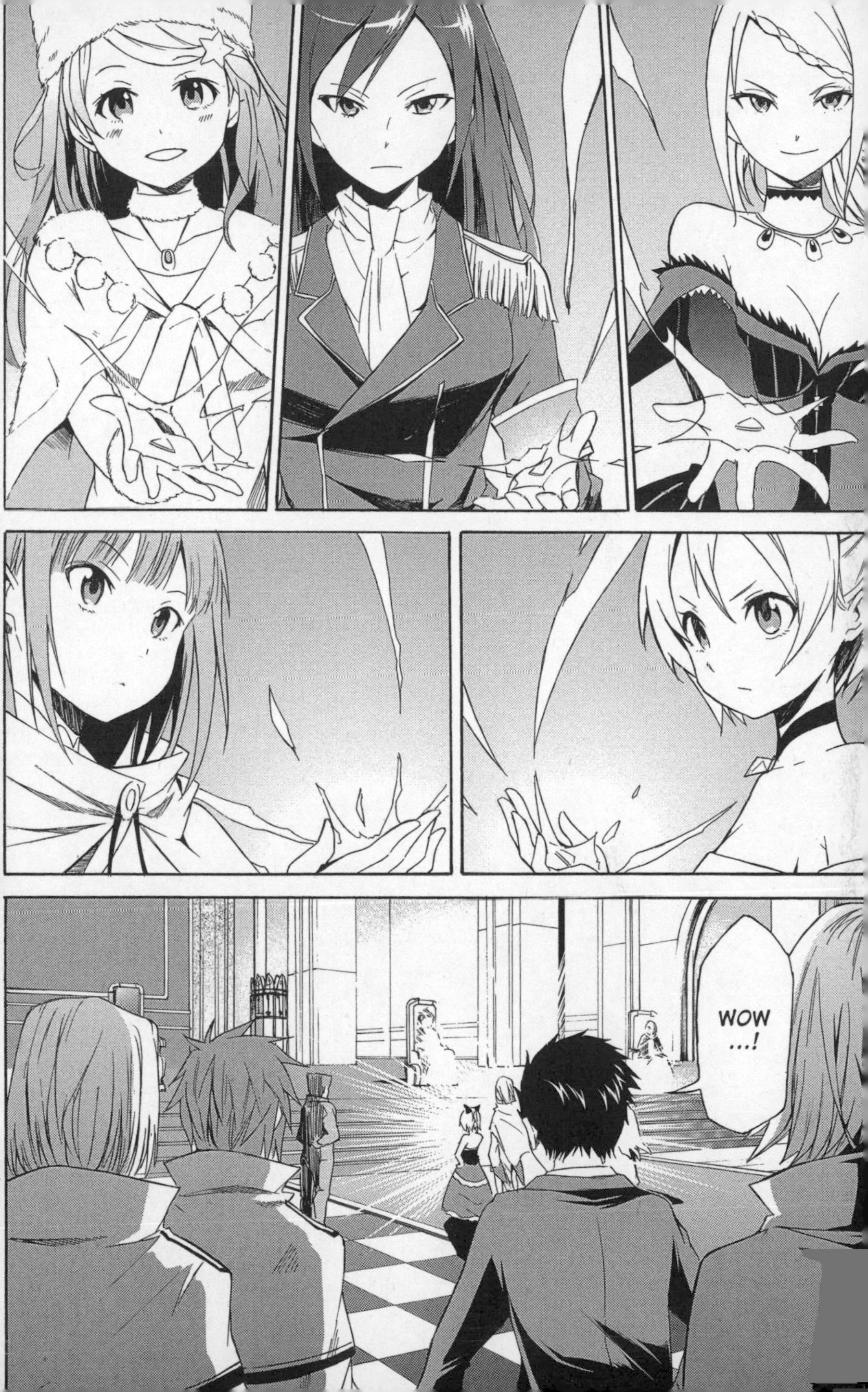
WOW
...!

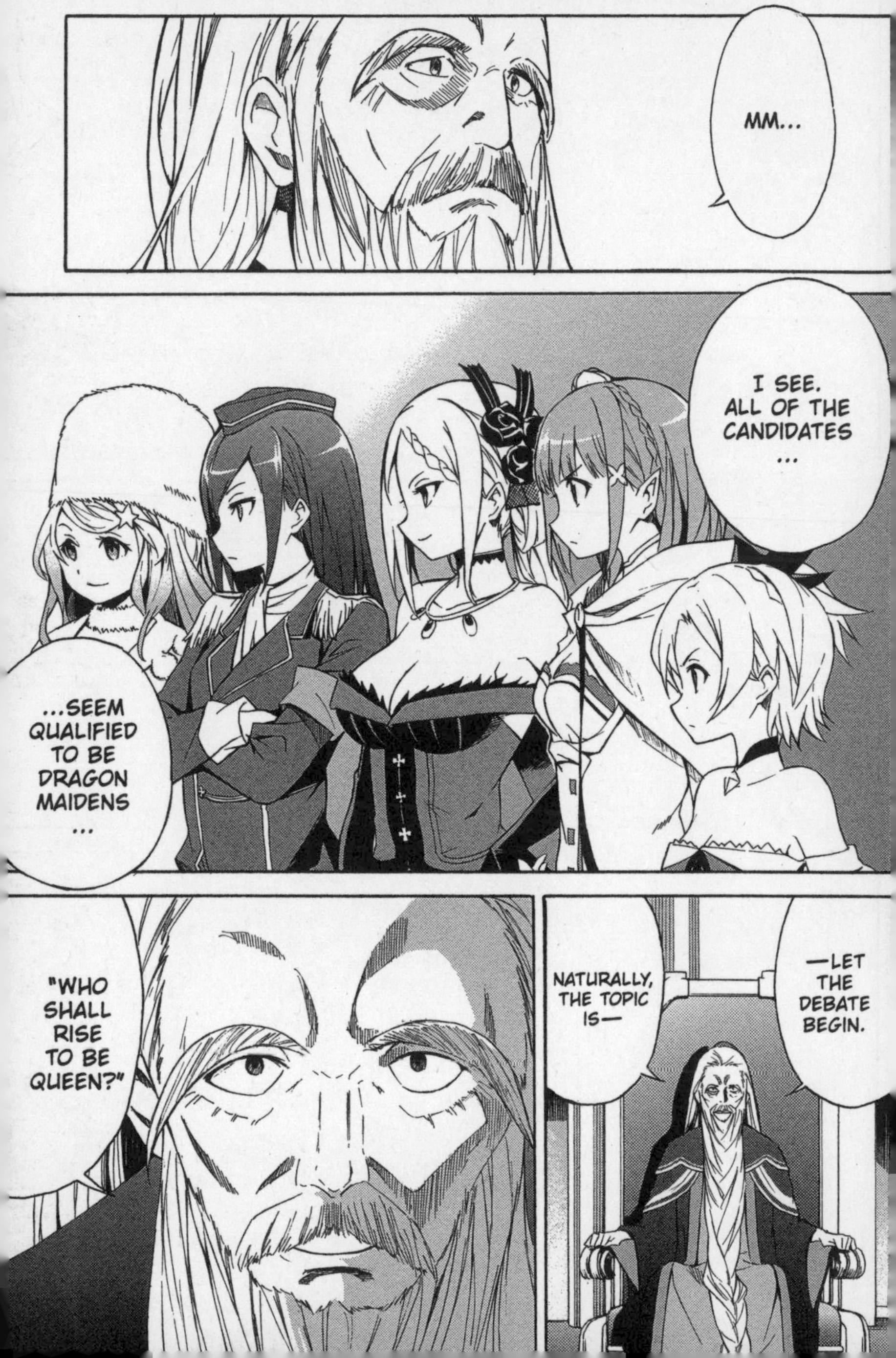
MM...
I SEE. ALL OF THE CANDIDATES ...
...SEEM QUALIFIED TO BE DRAGON MAIDENS ...
—LET THE DEBATE BEGIN.
NATURALLY, THE TOPIC IS—
"WHO SHALL RISE TO BE QUEEN?"

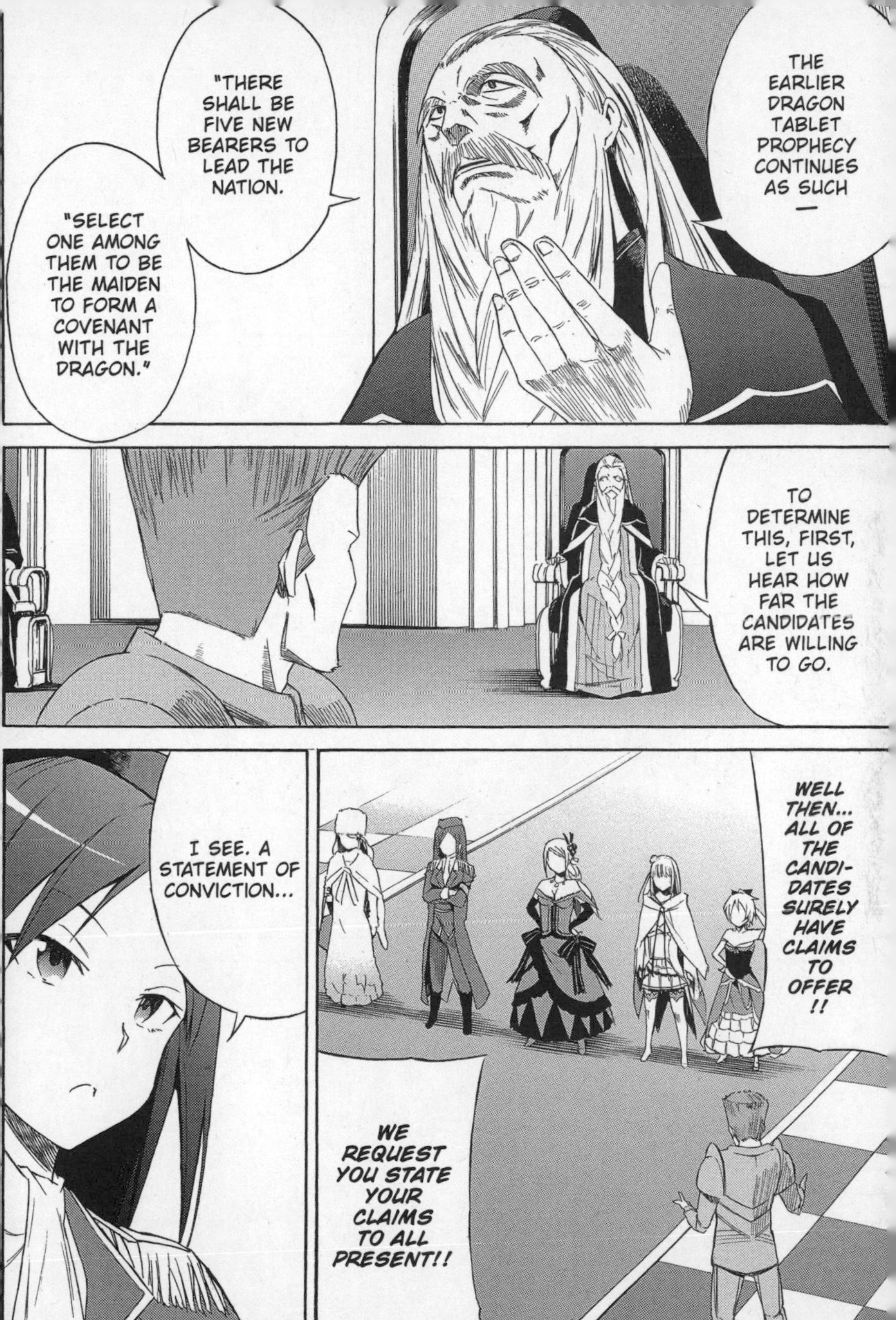
THE EARLIER DRAGON TABLET PROPHECY CONTINUES AS SUCH —
"THERE SHALL BE FIVE NEW BEARERS TO LEAD THE NATION.
"SELECT ONE AMONG THEM TO BE THE MAIDEN TO FORM A COVENANT WITH THE DRAGON."
TO DETERMINE THIS, FIRST, LET US HEAR HOW FAR THE CANDIDATES ARE WILLING TO GO.
WELL THEN... ALL OF THE CANDI-DATES SURELY HAVE CLAIMS TO OFFER!!
WE REQUEST YOU STATE YOUR CLAIMS TO ALL PRESENT!!
I SEE. A STATEMENT OF CONVICTION...

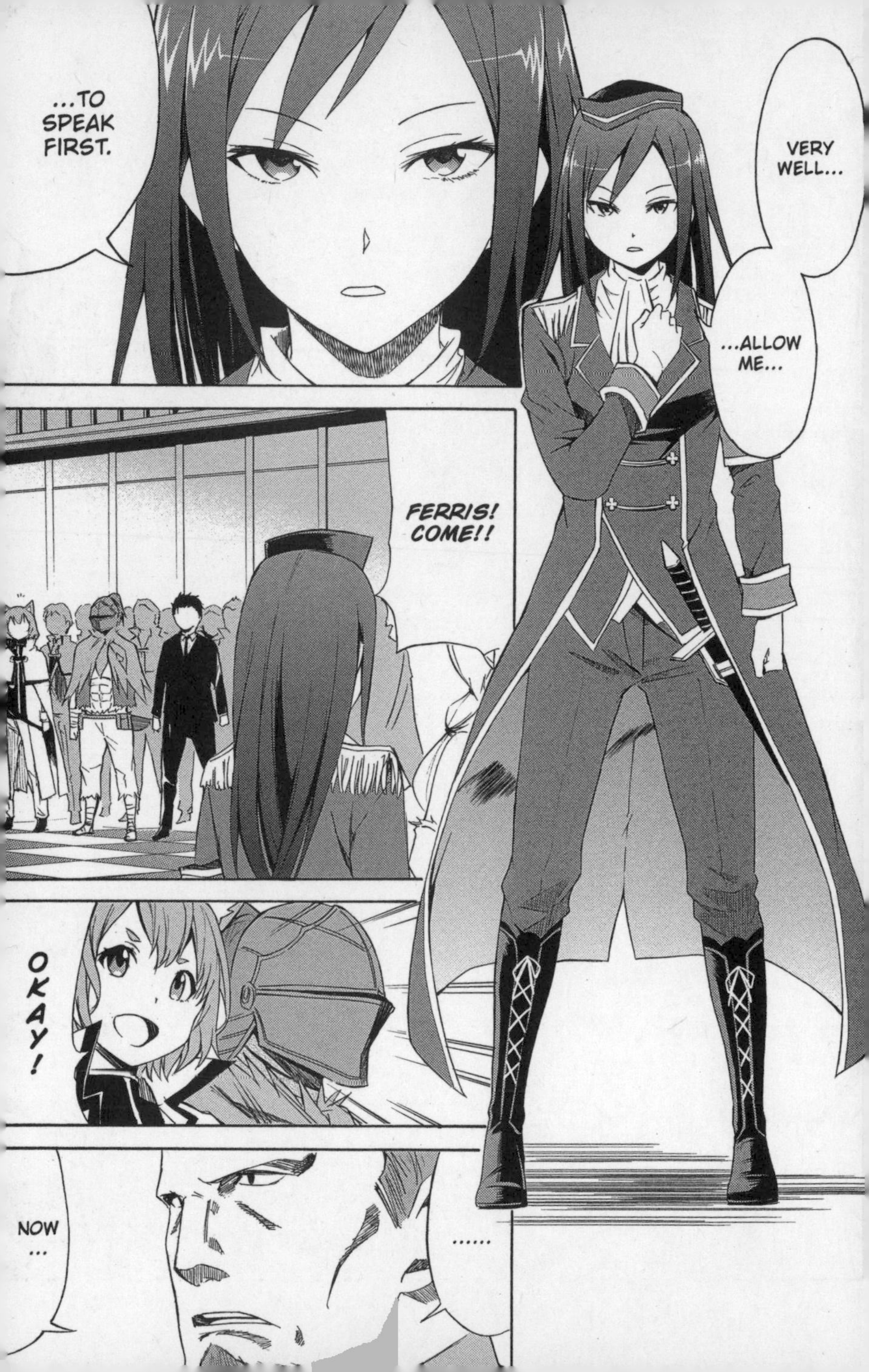
VERY WELL...
...ALLOW ME...
...TO SPEAK FIRST.
FERRIS! COME!!
OKAY!
......
NOW ...

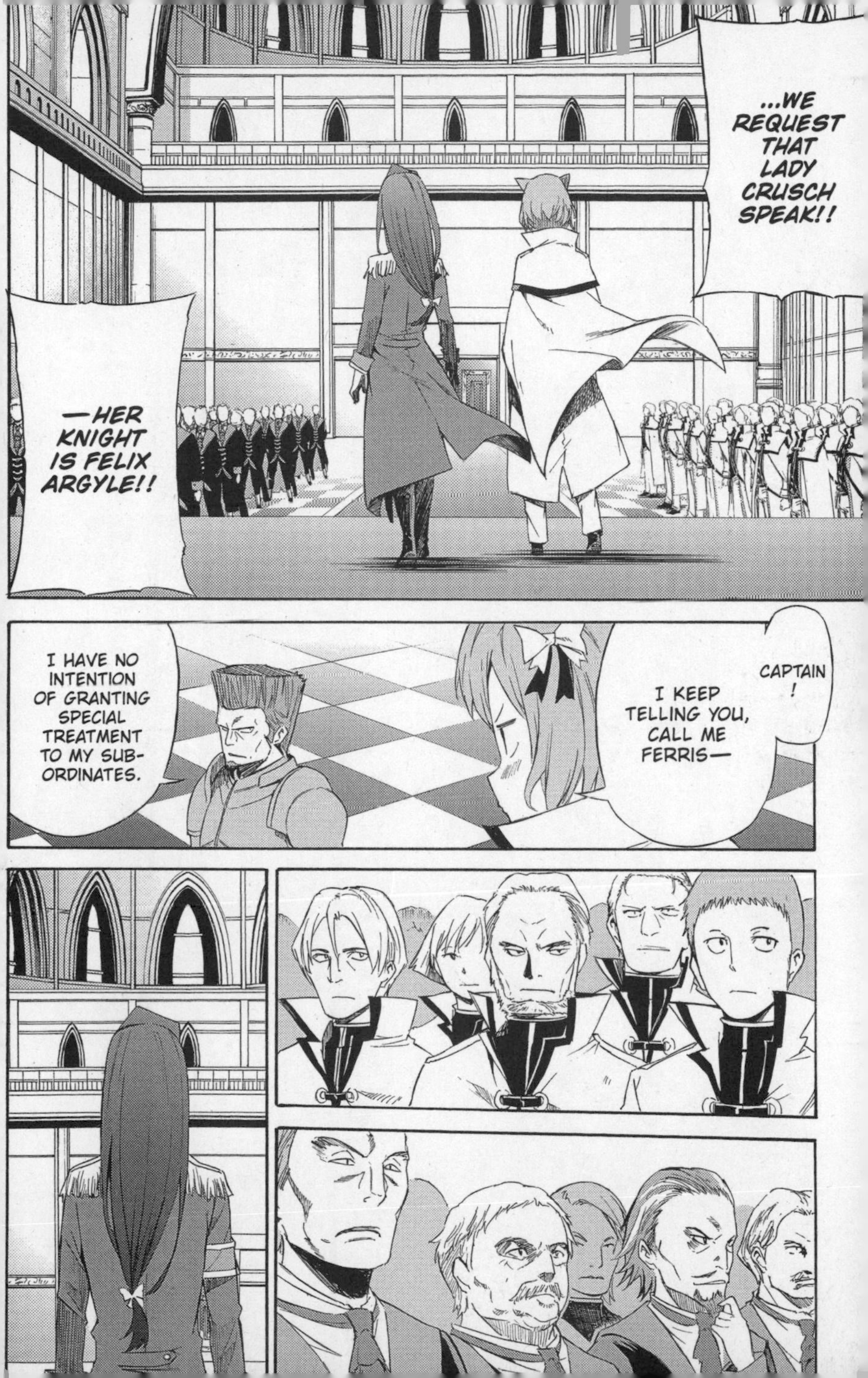
...WE REQUEST THAT LADY CRUSCH SPEAK!!
—HER KNIGHT IS FELIX ARGYLE!!
CAPTAIN!
I KEEP TELLING YOU, CALL ME FERRIS—
I HAVE NO INTENTION OF GRANTING SPECIAL TREATMENT TO MY SUB-ORDINATES.

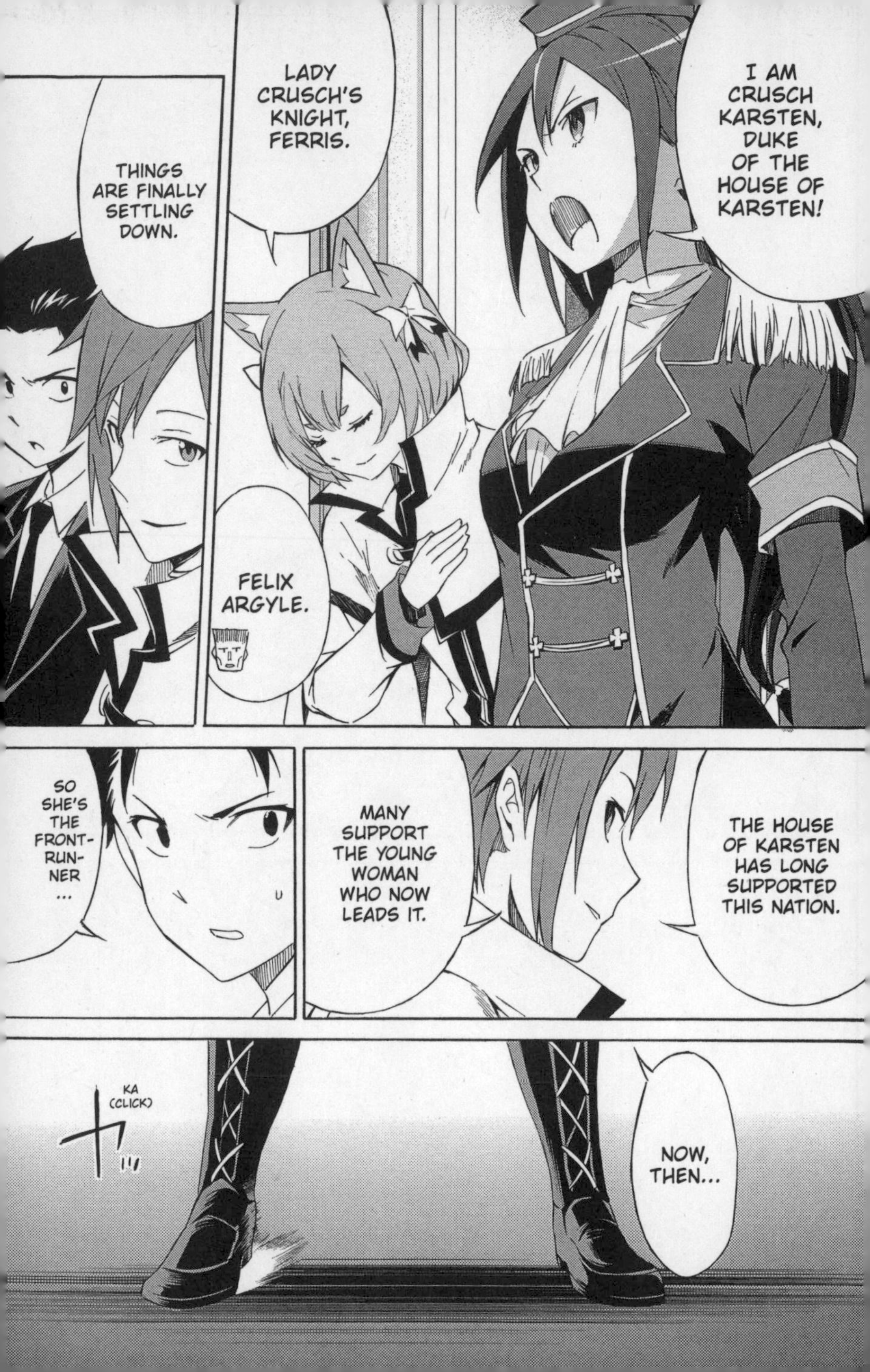
I AM CRUSCH KARSTEN, DUKE OF THE HOUSE OF KARSTEN!
LADY CRUSCH'S KNIGHT, FERRIS.
FELIX ARGYLE.
THINGS ARE FINALLY SETTLING DOWN.
THE HOUSE OF KARSTEN HAS LONG SUPPORTED THIS NATION.
MANY SUPPORT THE YOUNG WOMAN WHO NOW LEADS IT.
SO SHE'S THE FRONT-RUNNER...
NOW, THEN...
KA (CLICK)

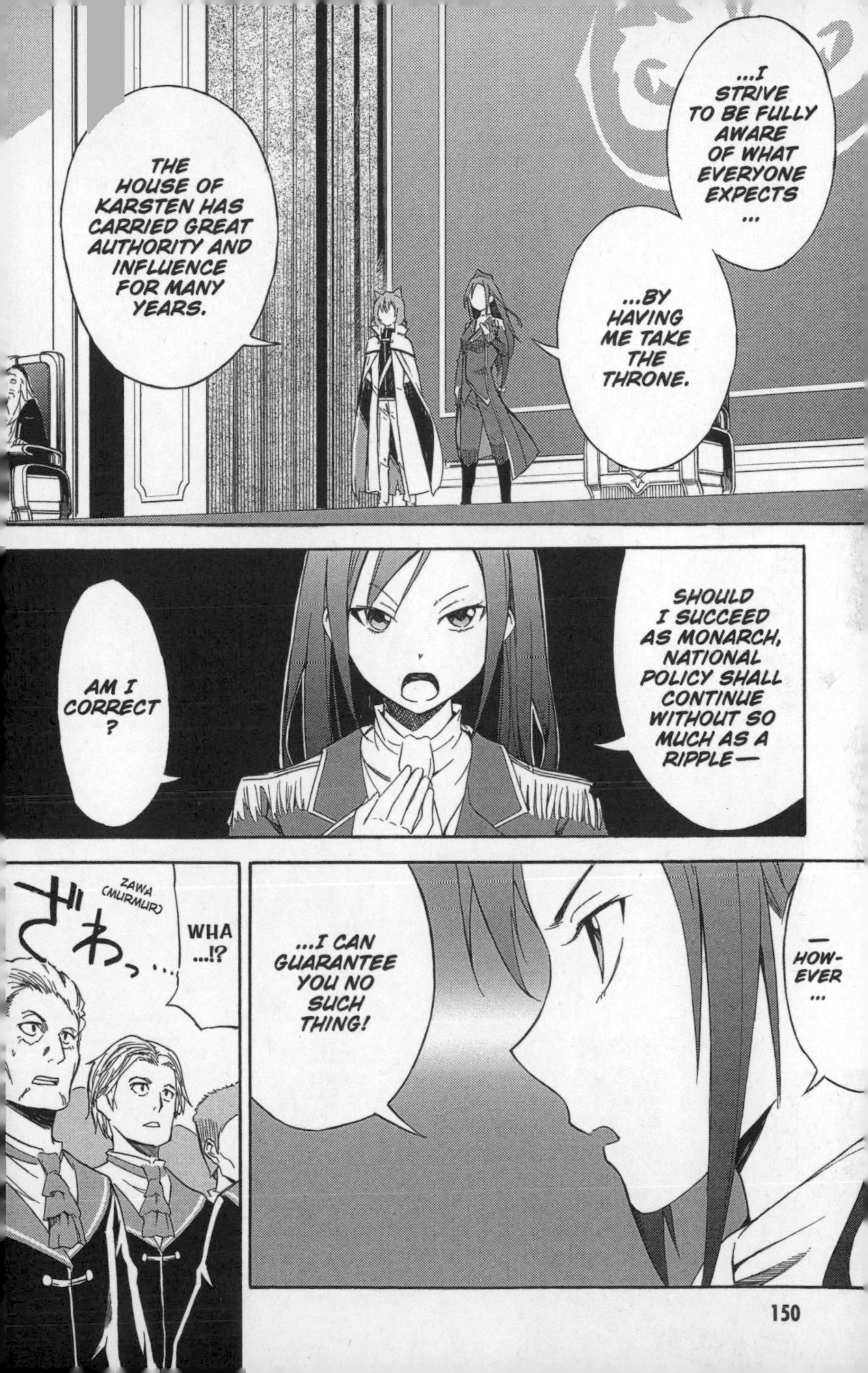
...I STRIVE TO BE FULLY AWARE OF WHAT EVERYONE EXPECTS ...
...BY HAVING ME TAKE THE THRONE.
THE HOUSE OF KARSTEN HAS CARRIED GREAT AUTHORITY AND INFLUENCE FOR MANY YEARS.
SHOULD I SUCCEED AS MONARCH, NATIONAL POLICY SHALL CONTINUE WITHOUT SO MUCH AS A RIPPLE—
AM I CORRECT ?
—HOW-EVER ...
...I CAN GUARANTEE YOU NO SUCH THING!
WHA ...!?
ざわっ...
ZAWA (MURMUR)

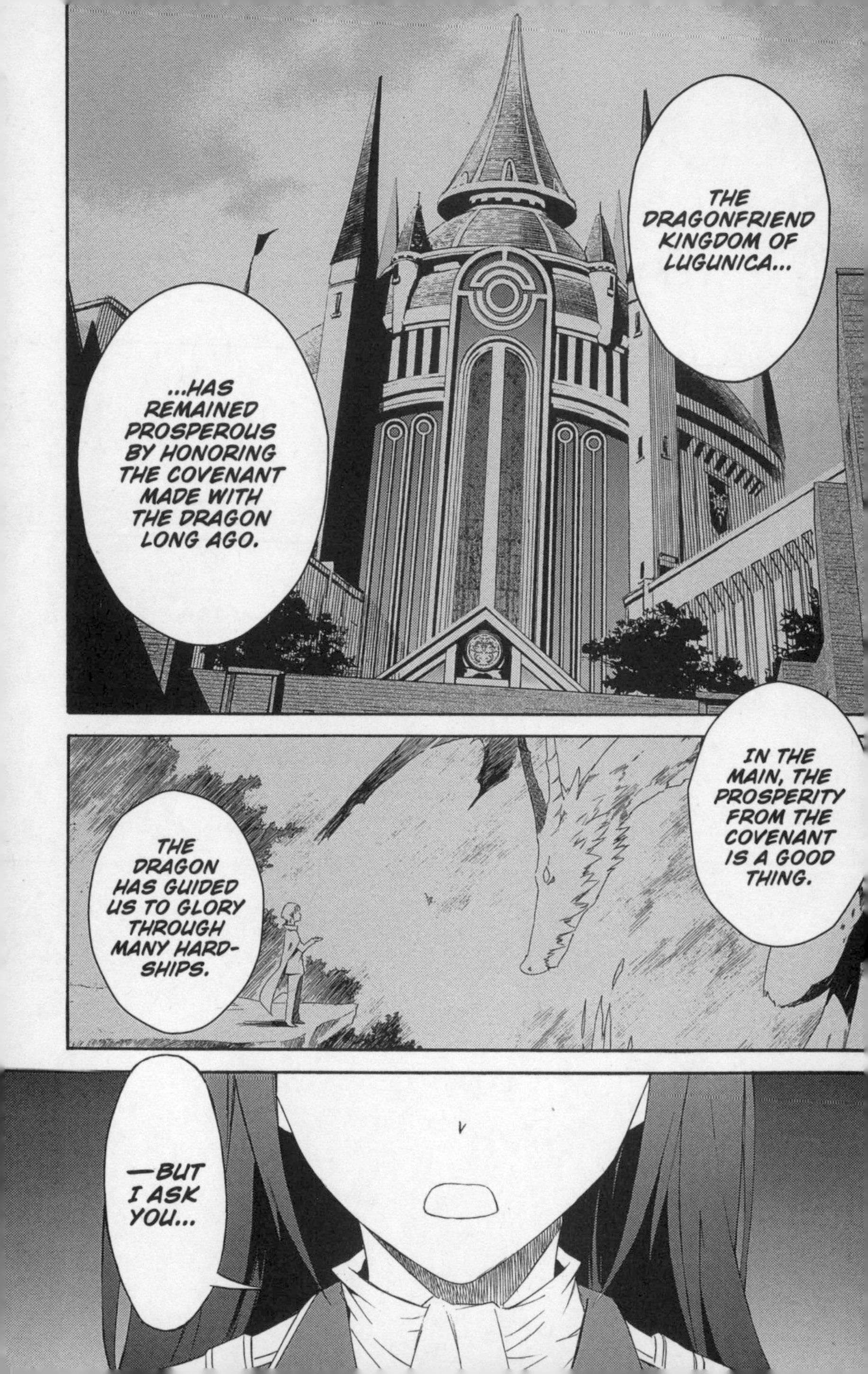
THE DRAGONFRIEND KINGDOM OF LUGUNICA...
...HAS REMAINED PROSPEROUS BY HONORING THE COVENANT MADE WITH THE DRAGON LONG AGO.
IN THE MAIN, THE PROSPERITY FROM THE COVENANT IS A GOOD THING.
THE DRAGON HAS GUIDED US TO GLORY THROUGH MANY HARD-SHIPS.
—BUT I ASK YOU...

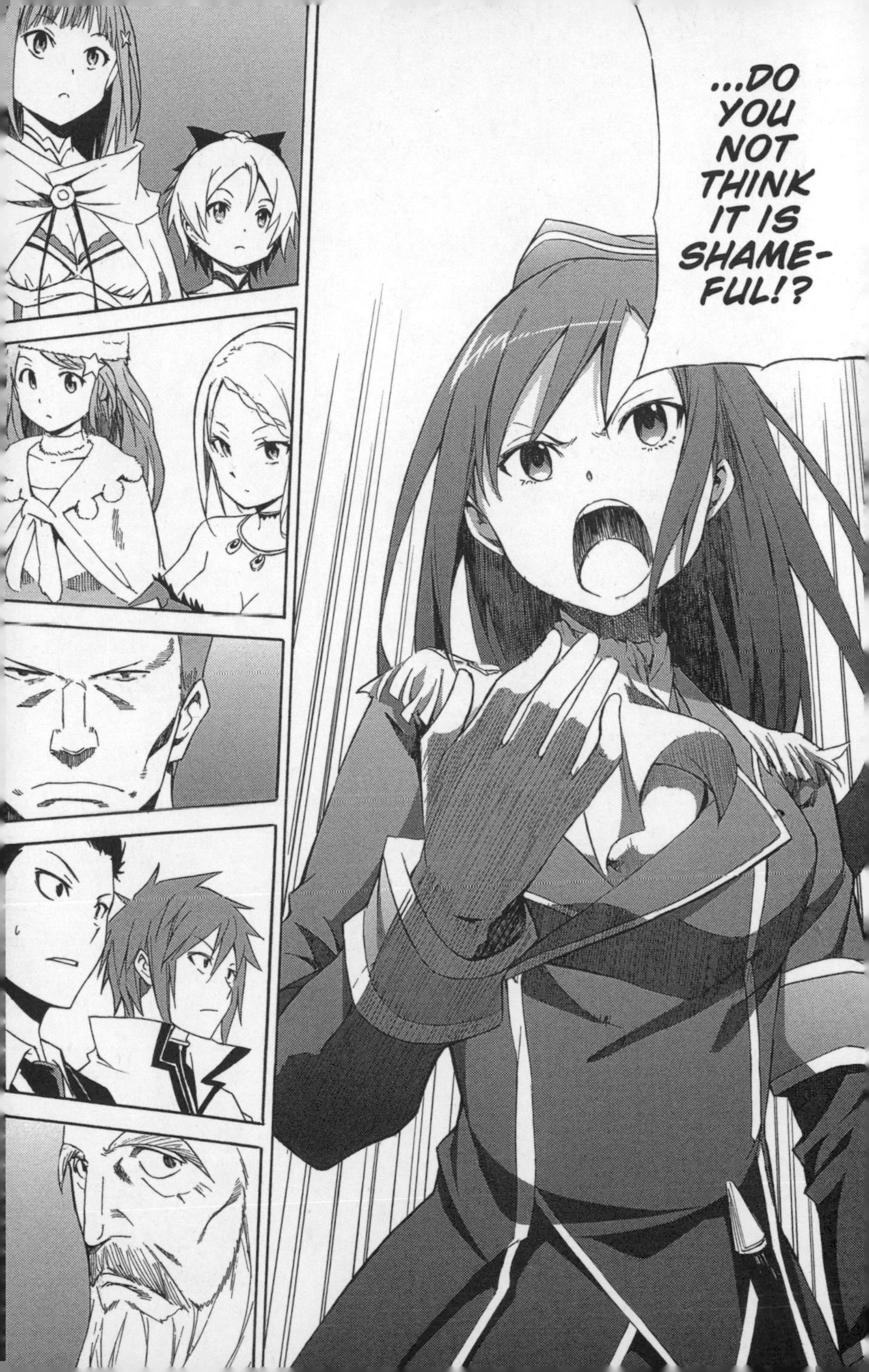
...DO YOU NOT THINK IT IS SHAME-FUL!?

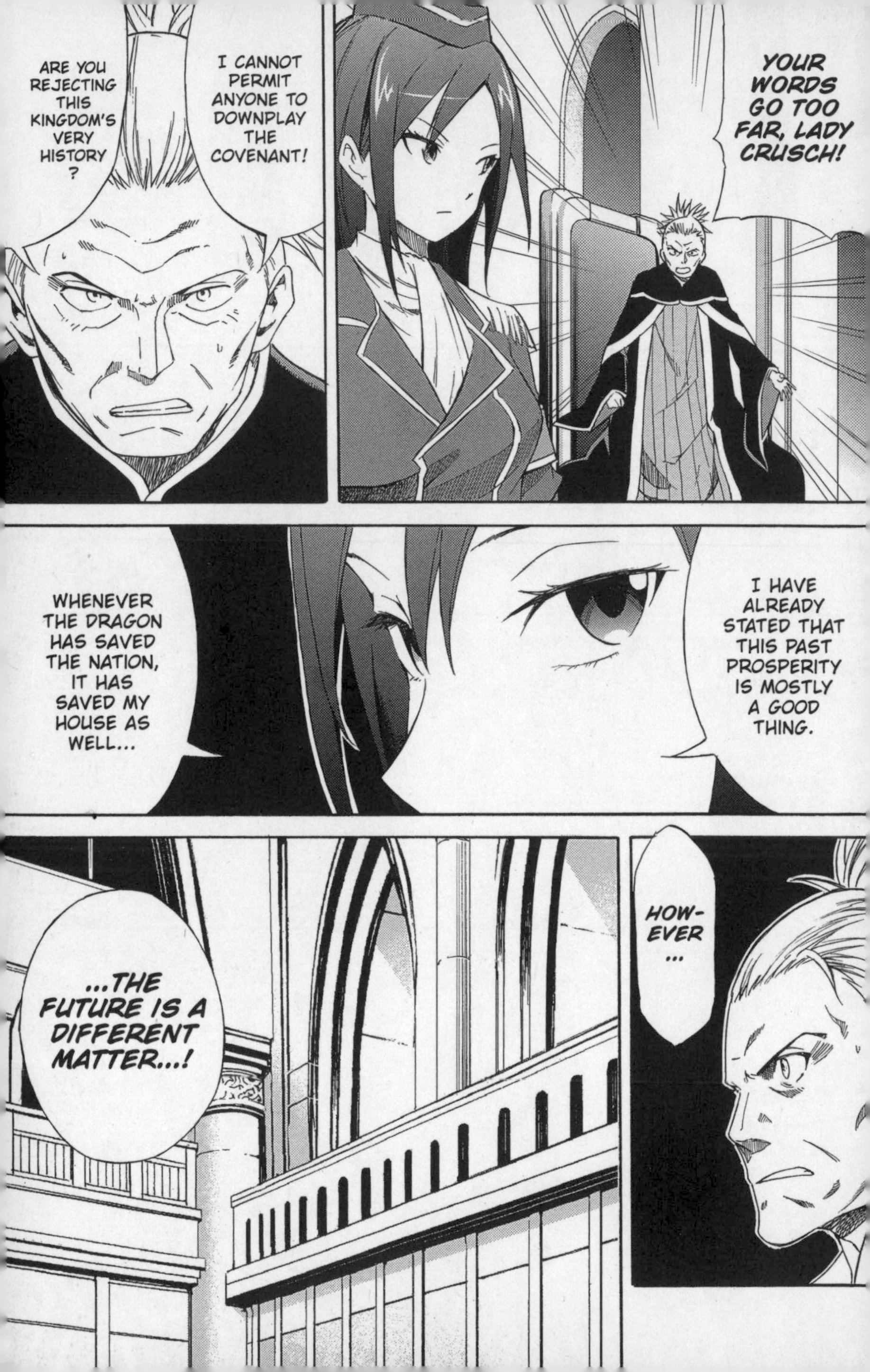
YOUR WORDS GO TOO FAR, LADY CRUSCH!
I CANNOT PERMIT ANYONE TO DOWNPLAY THE COVENANT!
ARE YOU REJECTING THIS KINGDOM'S VERY HISTORY?
I HAVE ALREADY STATED THAT THIS PAST PROSPERITY IS MOSTLY A GOOD THING.
WHENEVER THE DRAGON HAS SAVED THE NATION, IT HAS SAVED MY HOUSE AS WELL...
HOW-EVER...
...THE FUTURE IS A DIFFERENT MATTER...!

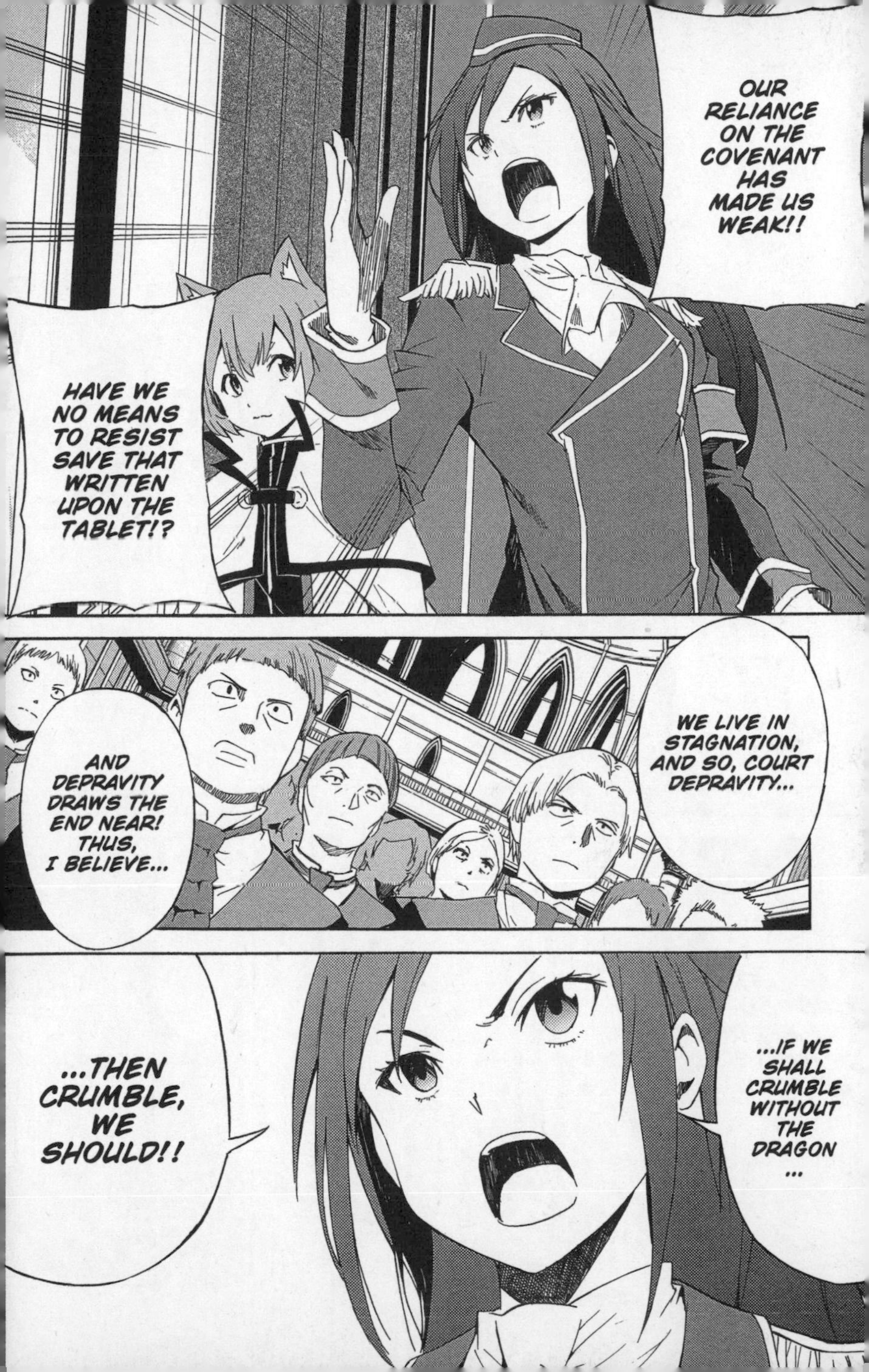
OUR RELIANCE ON THE COVENANT HAS MADE US WEAK!!
HAVE WE NO MEANS TO RESIST SAVE THAT WRITTEN UPON THE TABLET!?
WE LIVE IN STAGNATION, AND SO, COURT DEPRAVITY...
AND DEPRAVITY DRAWS THE END NEAR! THUS, I BELIEVE...
...IF WE SHALL CRUMBLE WITHOUT THE DRAGON ...
...THEN CRUMBLE, WE SHOULD!!

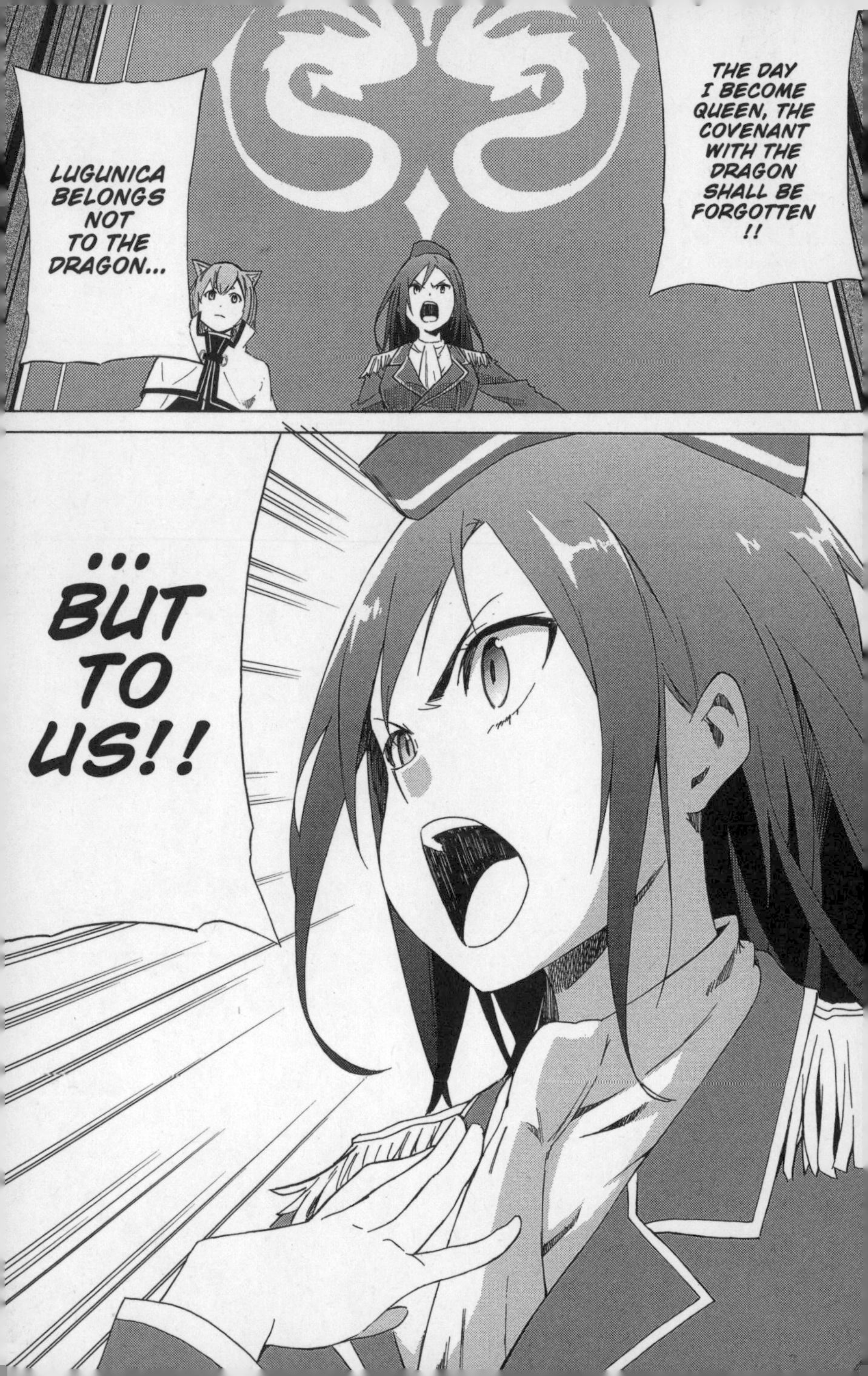
THE DAY I BECOME QUEEN, THE COVENANT WITH THE DRAGON SHALL BE FORGOTTEN!!
LUGUNICA BELONGS NOT TO THE DRAGON...
...BUT TO US!!

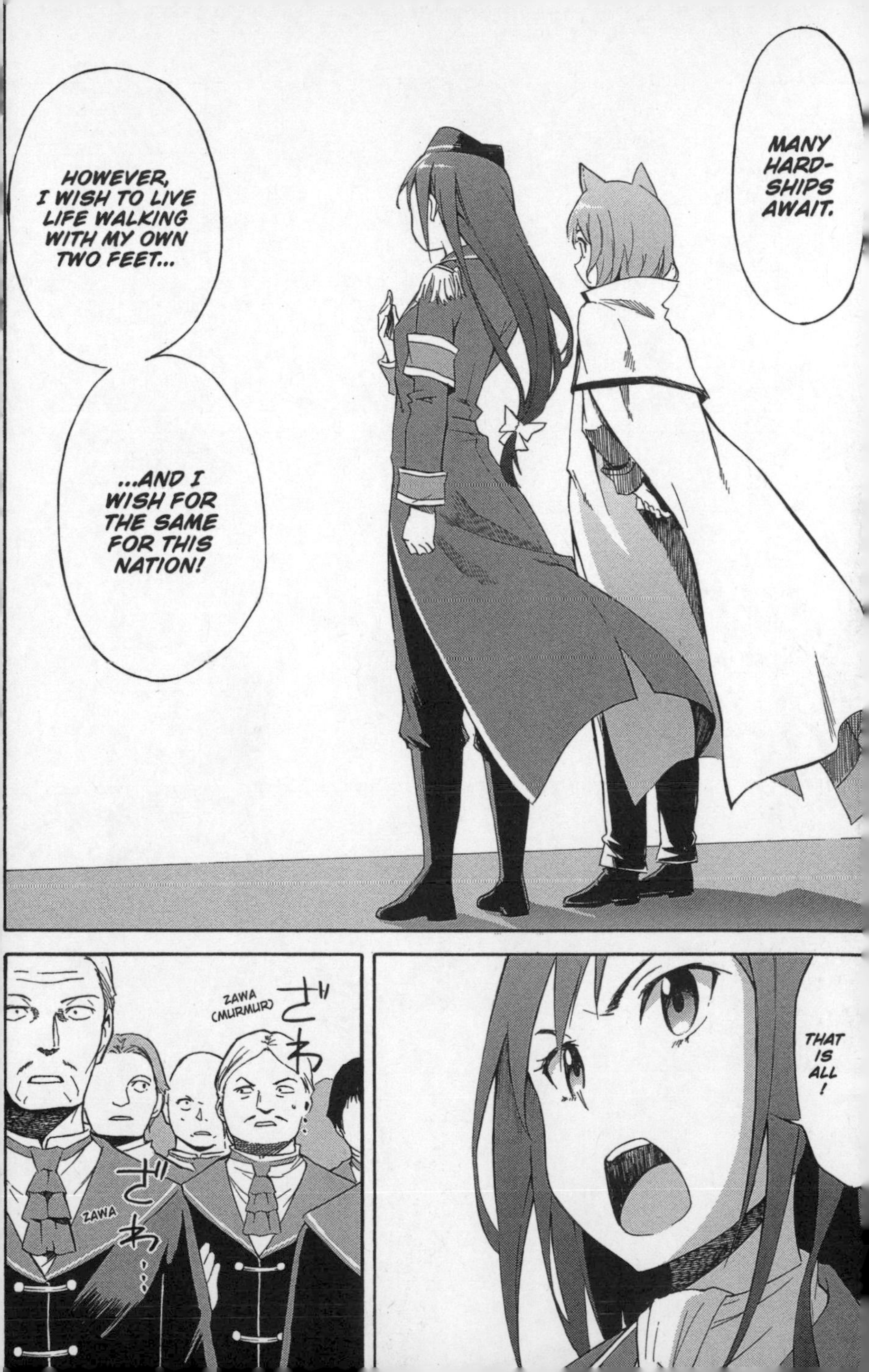
MANY HARD-SHIPS AWAIT.
HOWEVER, I WISH TO LIVE LIFE WALKING WITH MY OWN TWO FEET...
...AND I WISH FOR THE SAME FOR THIS NATION!
THAT IS ALL!
ZAWA (MURMUR)
ざわ
ざわ...
ZAWA

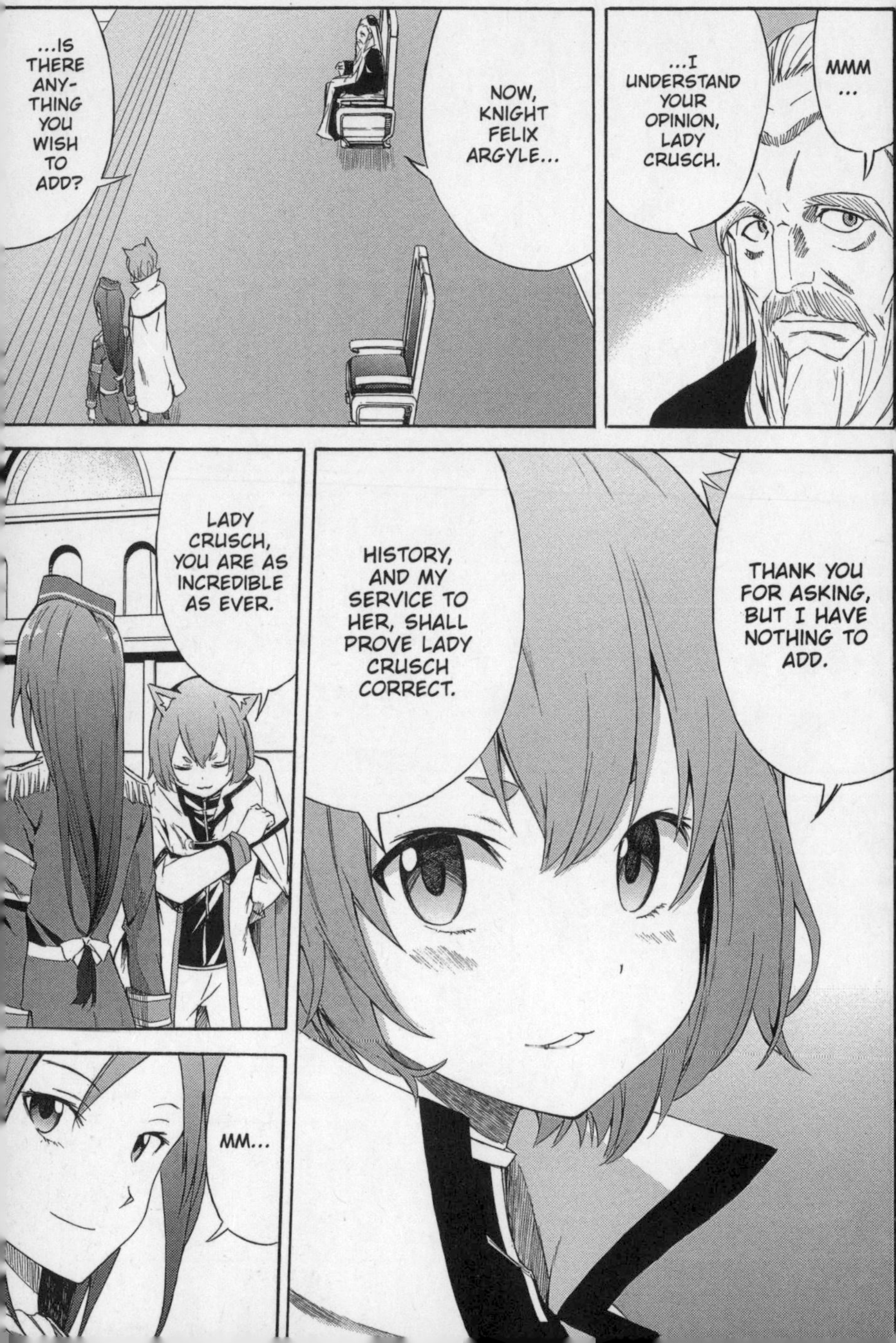
MMM...
...I UNDERSTAND YOUR OPINION, LADY CRUSCH.
NOW, KNIGHT FELIX ARGYLE...
...IS THERE ANYTHING YOU WISH TO ADD?
THANK YOU FOR ASKING, BUT I HAVE NOTHING TO ADD.
HISTORY, AND MY SERVICE TO HER, SHALL PROVE LADY CRUSCH CORRECT.
LADY CRUSCH, YOU ARE AS INCREDIBLE AS EVER.
MM...

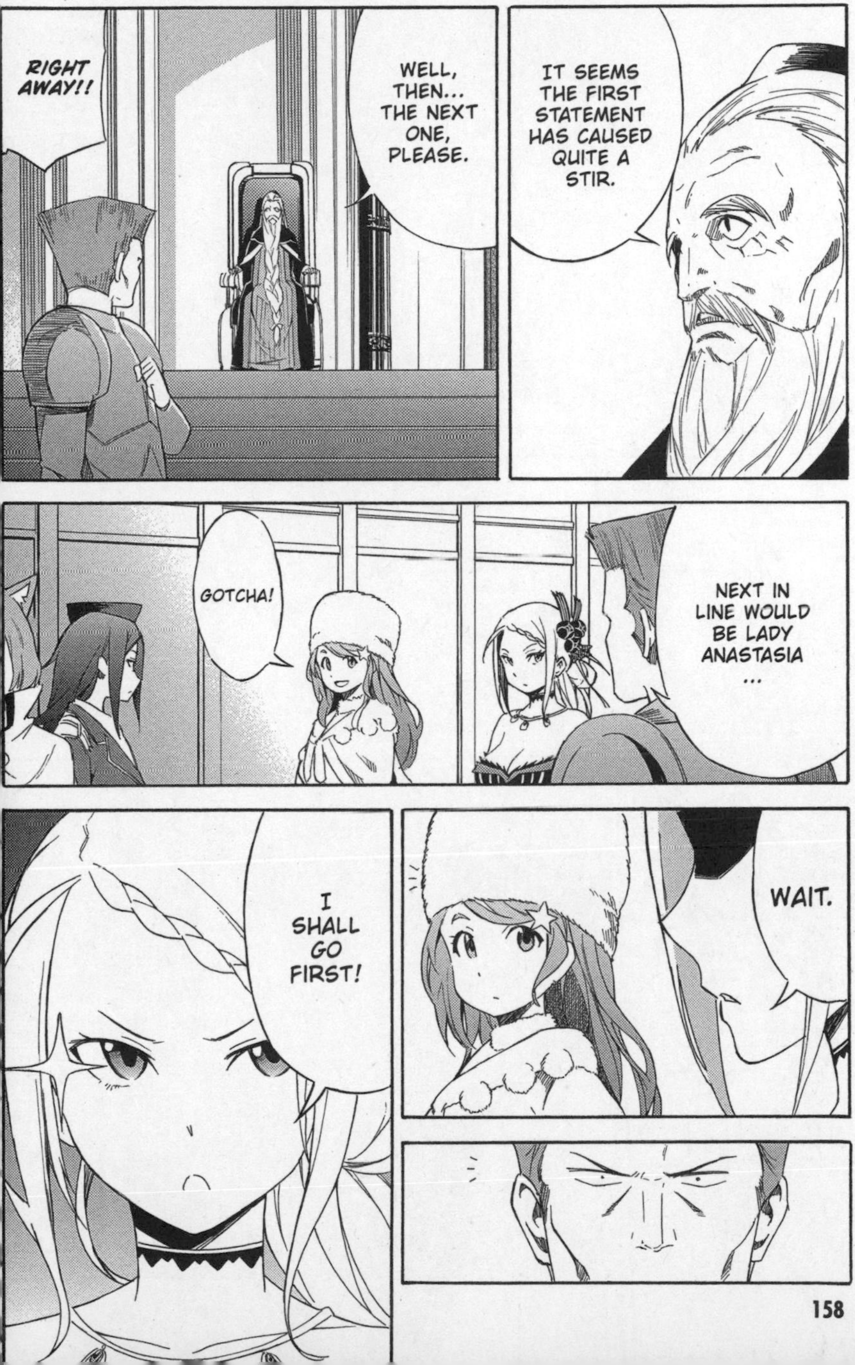
IT SEEMS THE FIRST STATEMENT HAS CAUSED QUITE A STIR.
WELL, THEN... THE NEXT ONE, PLEASE.
RIGHT AWAY!!
NEXT IN LINE WOULD BE LADY ANASTASIA ...
GOTCHA!
WAIT.
I SHALL GO FIRST!

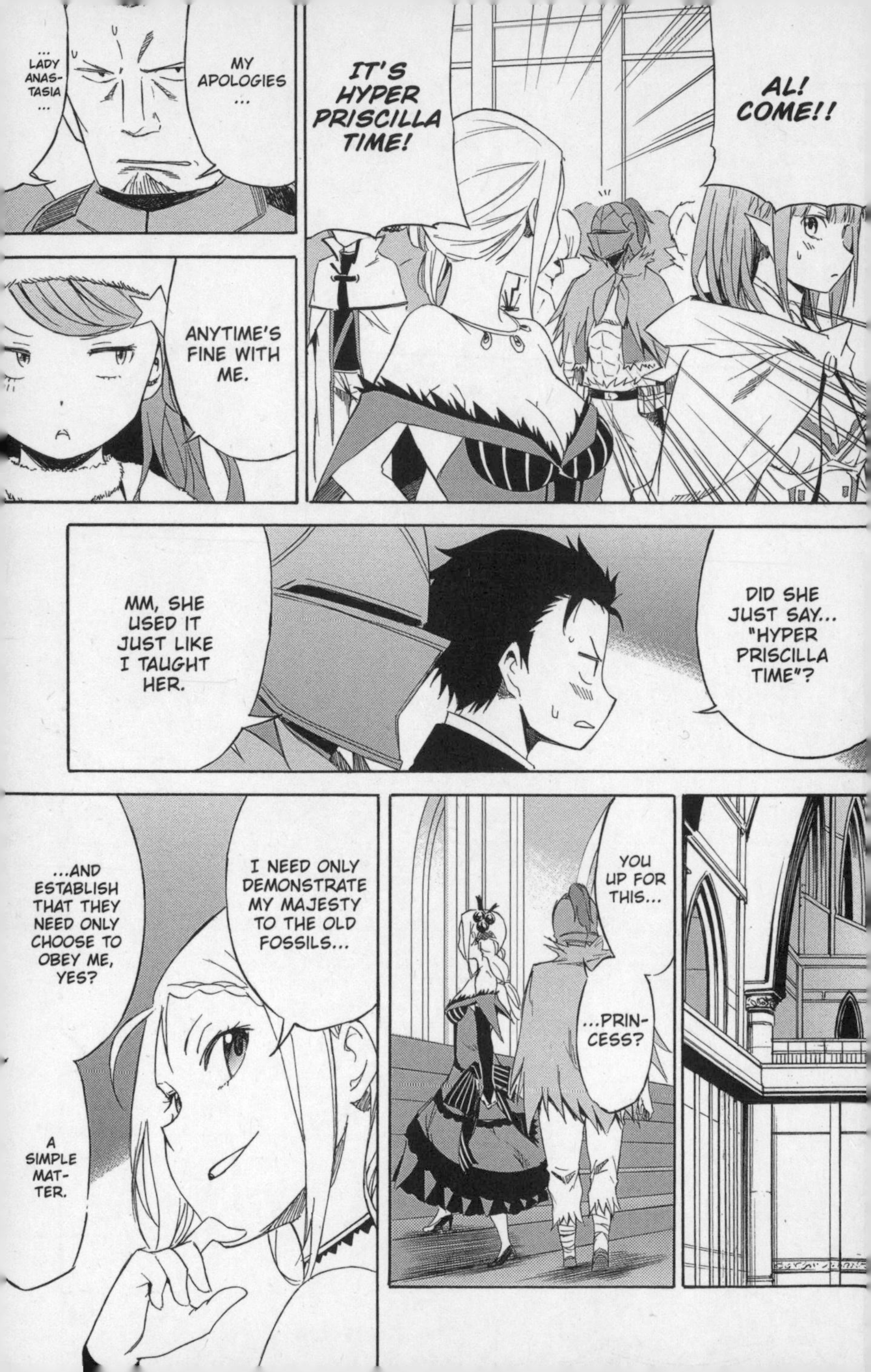
AL! COME!!
IT'S HYPER PRISCILLA TIME!
MY APOLOGIES ...
... LADY ANASTASIA ...
ANYTIME'S FINE WITH ME.
DID SHE JUST SAY... "HYPER PRISCILLA TIME"?
MM, SHE USED IT JUST LIKE I TAUGHT HER.
YOU UP FOR THIS...
...PRINCESS?
I NEED ONLY DEMONSTRATE MY MAJESTY TO THE OLD FOSSILS...
...AND ESTABLISH THAT THEY NEED ONLY CHOOSE TO OBEY ME, YES?
A SIMPLE MATTER.

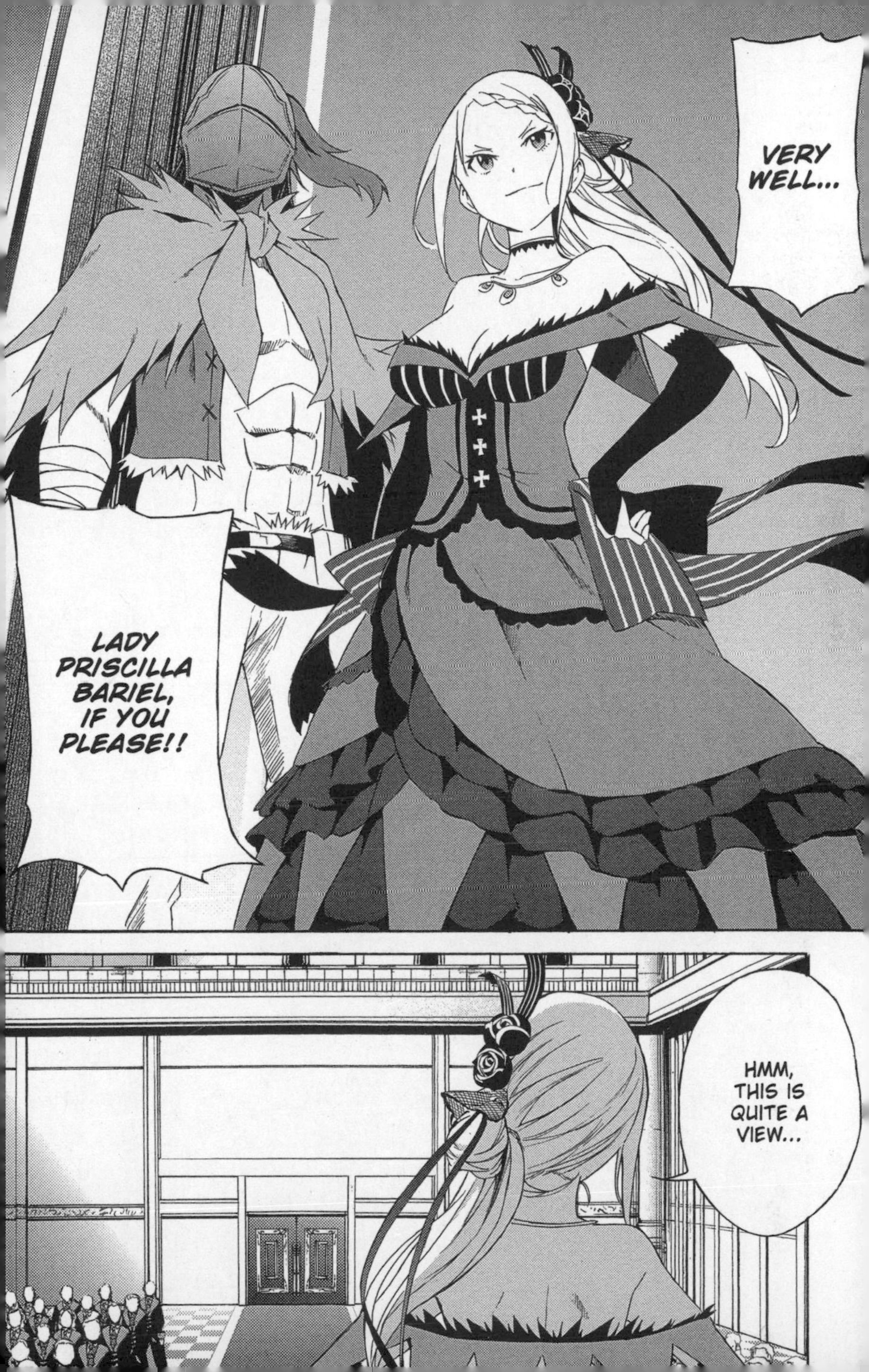
VERY WELL...
LADY PRISCILLA BARIEL, IF YOU PLEASE!!
HMM, THIS IS QUITE A VIEW...

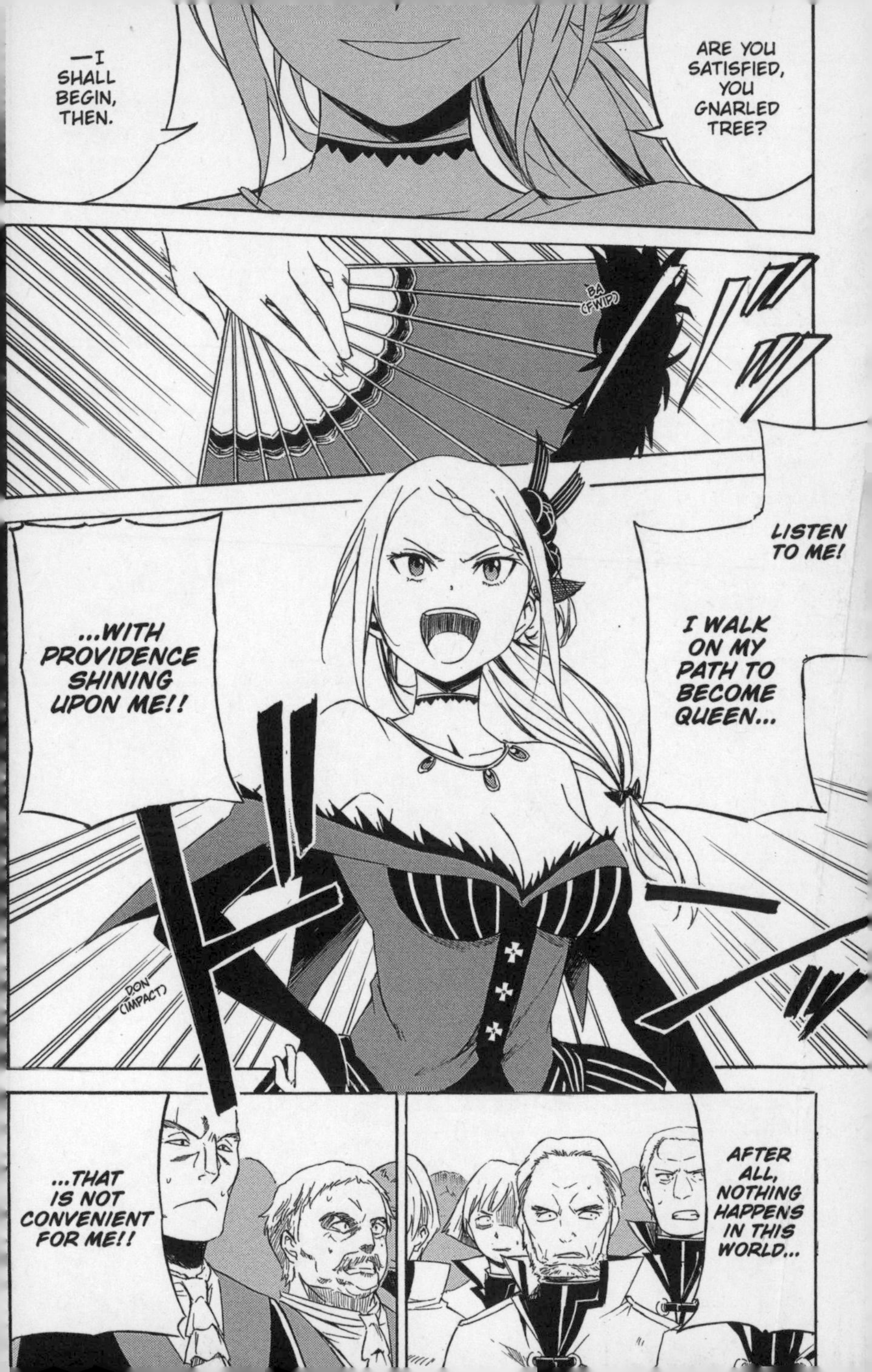
ARE YOU SATISFIED, YOU GNARLED TREE?
—I SHALL BEGIN, THEN.
BA (FWIP)
LISTEN TO ME!
I WALK ON MY PATH TO BECOME QUEEN...
...WITH PROVIDENCE SHINING UPON ME!!
DON (IMPACT)
AFTER ALL, NOTHING HAPPENS IN THIS WORLD...
...THAT IS NOT CONVENIENT FOR ME!!

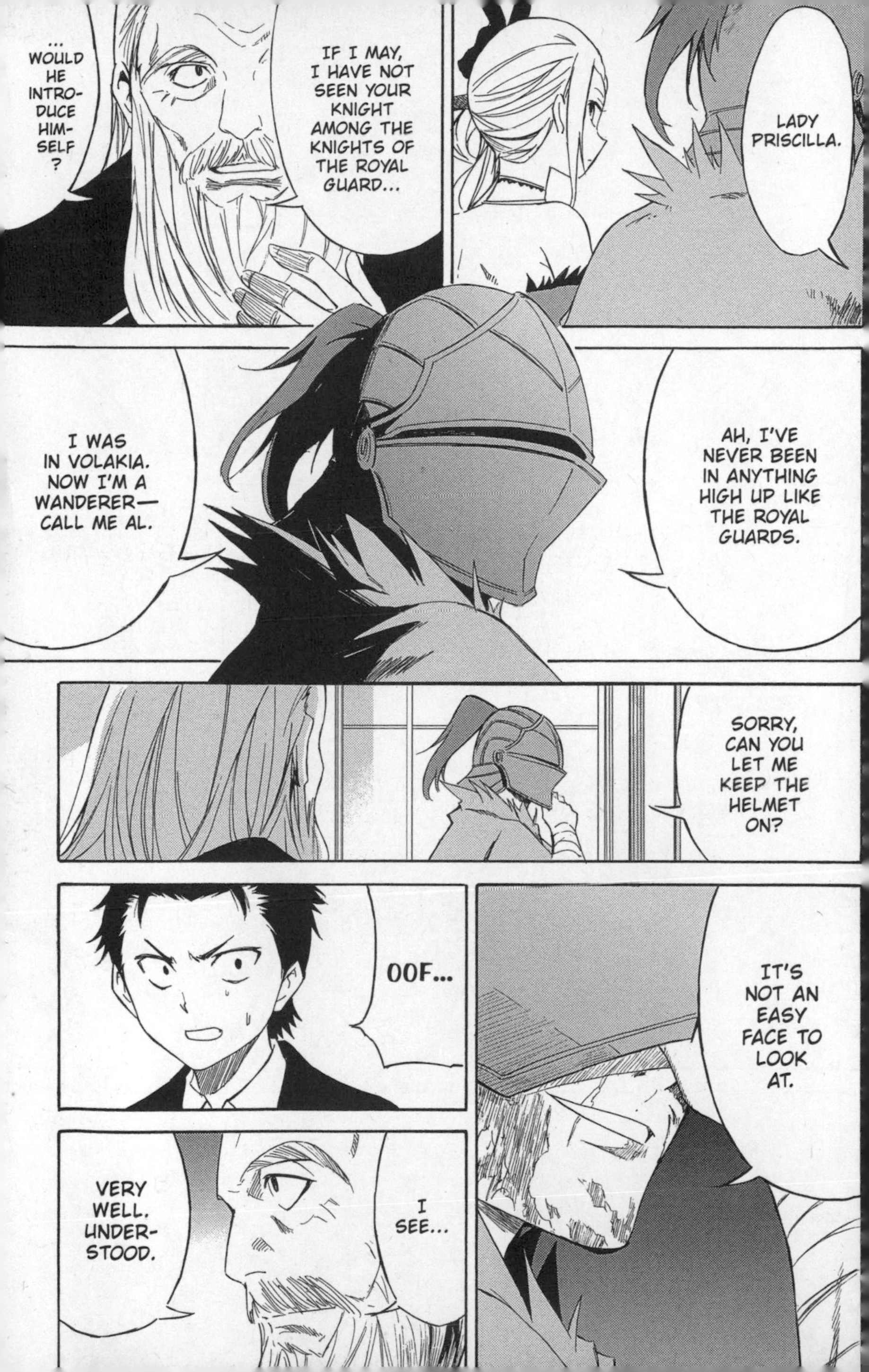
LADY PRISCILLA.
IF I MAY, I HAVE NOT SEEN YOUR KNIGHT AMONG THE KNIGHTS OF THE ROYAL GUARD...
... WOULD HE INTRODUCE HIMSELF?
AH, I'VE NEVER BEEN IN ANYTHING HIGH UP LIKE THE ROYAL GUARDS.
I WAS IN VOLAKIA. NOW I'M A WANDERER—CALL ME AL.
SORRY, CAN YOU LET ME KEEP THE HELMET ON?
IT'S NOT AN EASY FACE TO LOOK AT.
OOF...
I SEE...
VERY WELL. UNDERSTOOD.

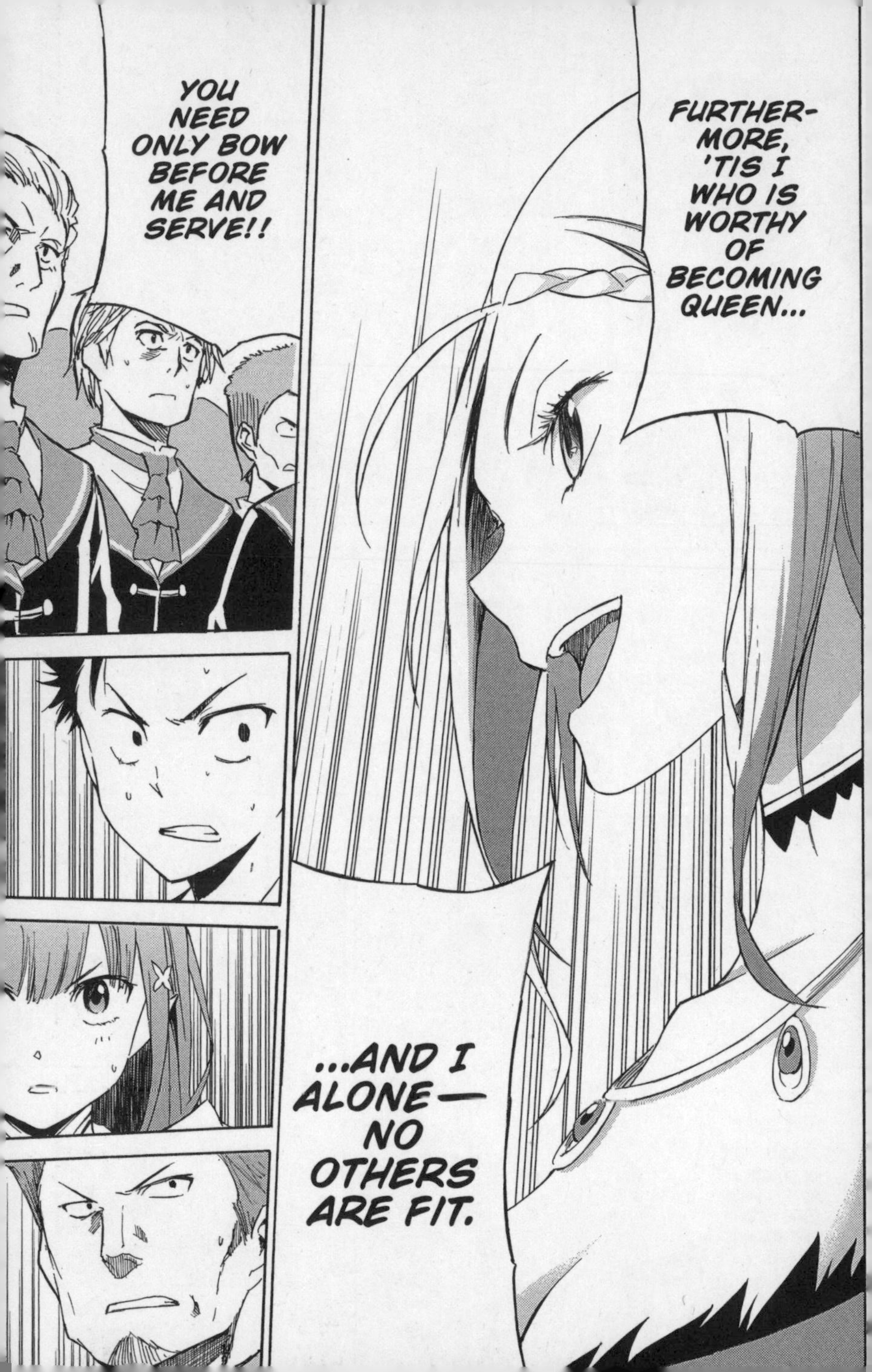
FURTHER-MORE, 'TIS I WHO IS WORTHY OF BECOMING QUEEN...
...AND I ALONE—NO OTHERS ARE FIT.
YOU NEED ONLY BOW BEFORE ME AND SERVE!!

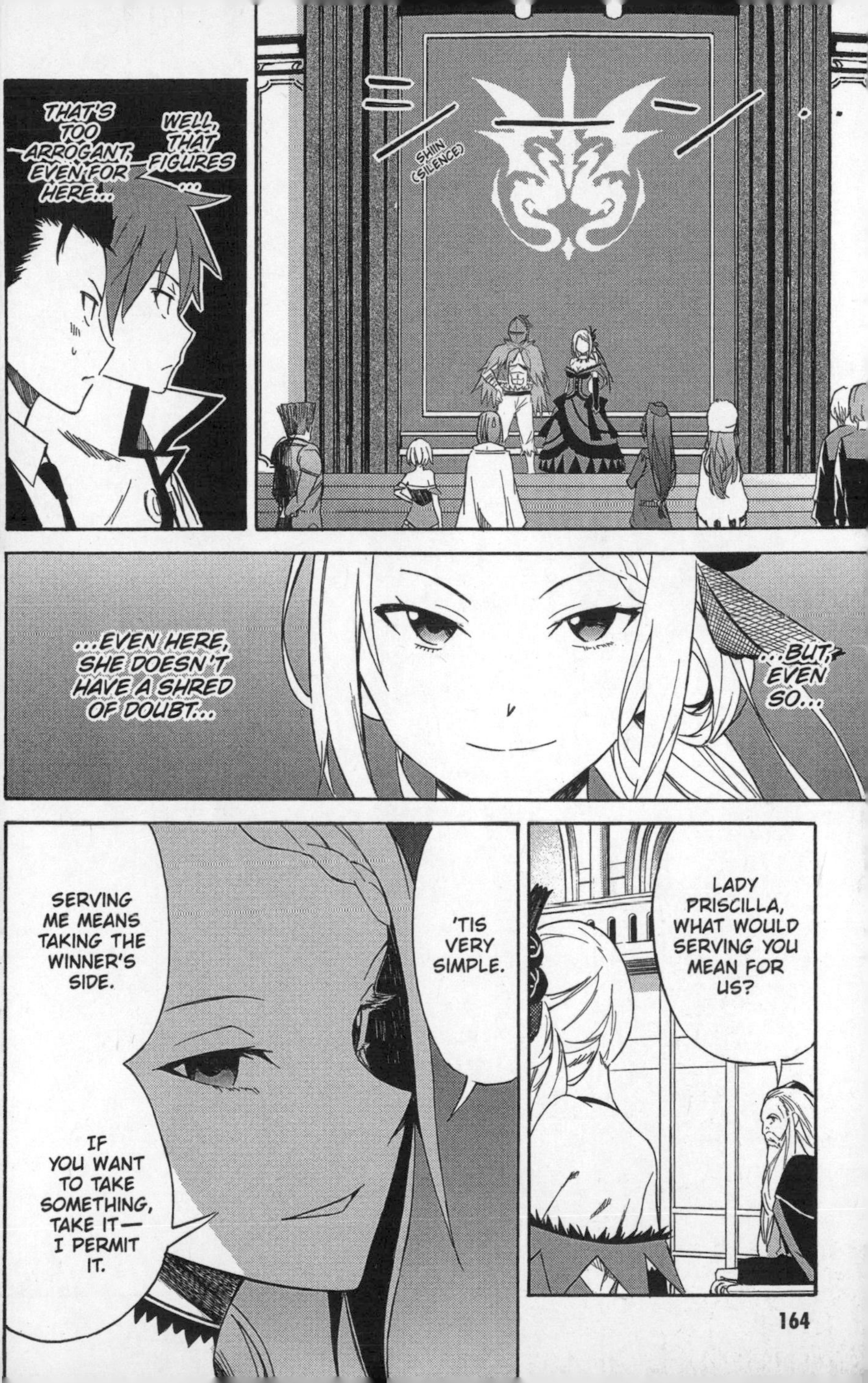
SHIIN (SILENCE)
WELL, THAT FIGURES...
THAT'S TOO ARROGANT, EVEN FOR HERE...
...BUT, EVEN SO...
...EVEN HERE, SHE DOESN'T HAVE A SHRED OF DOUBT...
LADY PRISCILLA, WHAT WOULD SERVING YOU MEAN FOR US?
'TIS VERY SIMPLE.
SERVING ME MEANS TAKING THE WINNER'S SIDE.
IF YOU WANT TO TAKE SOMETHING, TAKE IT— I PERMIT IT.

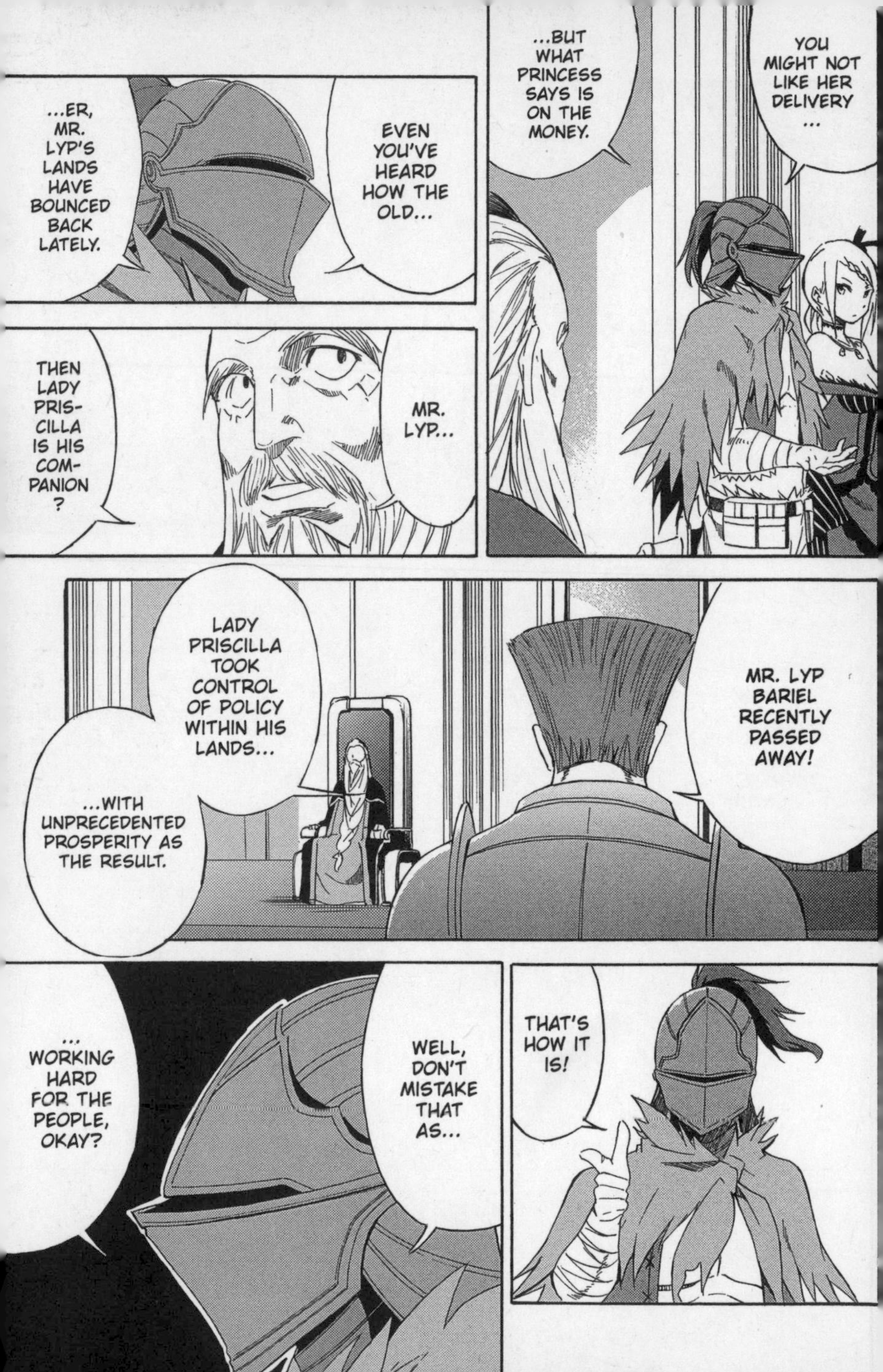
YOU MIGHT NOT LIKE HER DELIVERY ...
...BUT WHAT PRINCESS SAYS IS ON THE MONEY.
EVEN YOU'VE HEARD HOW THE OLD...
...ER, MR. LYP'S LANDS HAVE BOUNCED BACK LATELY.
MR. LYP...
THEN LADY PRIS-CILLA IS HIS COM-PANION?
MR. LYP BARIEL RECENTLY PASSED AWAY!
LADY PRISCILLA TOOK CONTROL OF POLICY WITHIN HIS LANDS...
...WITH UNPRECEDENTED PROSPERITY AS THE RESULT.
THAT'S HOW IT IS!
WELL, DON'T MISTAKE THAT AS...
...WORKING HARD FOR THE PEOPLE, OKAY?

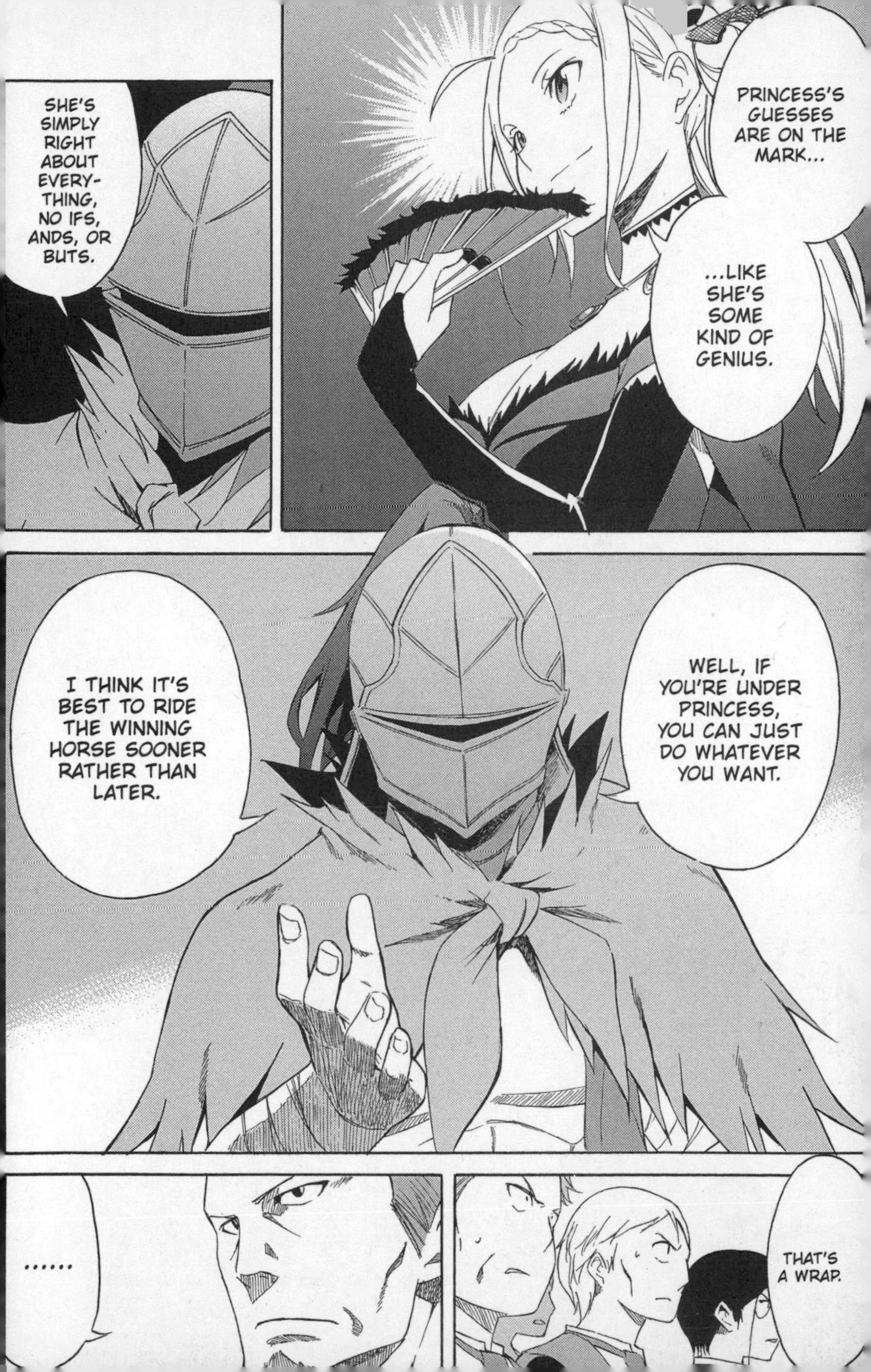
PRINCESS'S GUESSES ARE ON THE MARK...
...LIKE SHE'S SOME KIND OF GENIUS.
SHE'S SIMPLY RIGHT ABOUT EVERY-THING, NO IFS, ANDS, OR BUTS.
WELL, IF YOU'RE UNDER PRINCESS, YOU CAN JUST DO WHATEVER YOU WANT.
I THINK IT'S BEST TO RIDE THE WINNING HORSE SOONER RATHER THAN LATER.
THAT'S A WRAP.
......

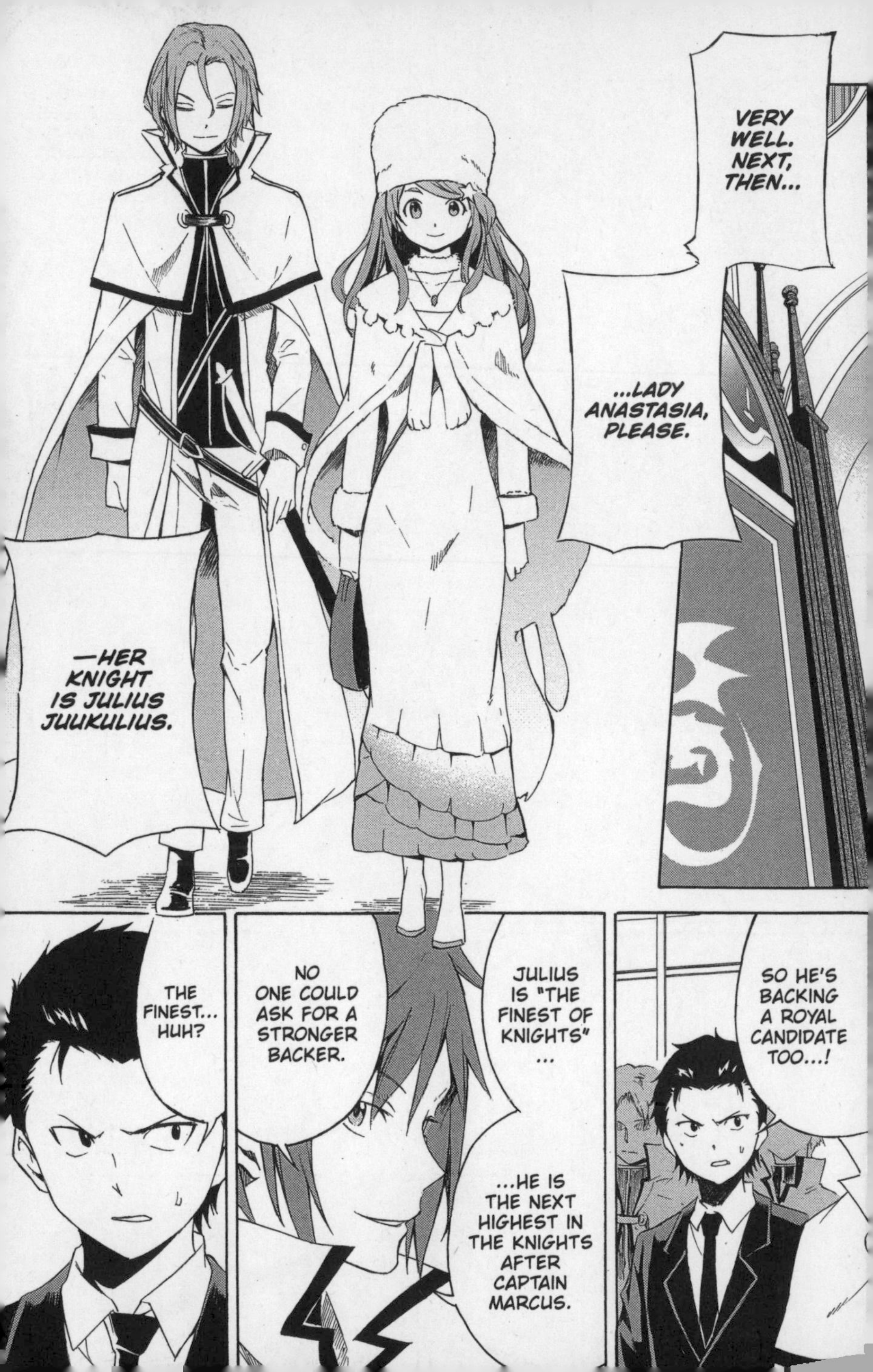
VERY WELL. NEXT, THEN...
...LADY ANASTASIA, PLEASE.
—HER KNIGHT IS JULIUS JUUKULIUS.
SO HE'S BACKING A ROYAL CANDIDATE TOO...!
JULIUS IS "THE FINEST OF KNIGHTS"...
...HE IS THE NEXT HIGHEST IN THE KNIGHTS AFTER CAPTAIN MARCUS.
NO ONE COULD ASK FOR A STRONGER BACKER.
THE FINEST... HUH?

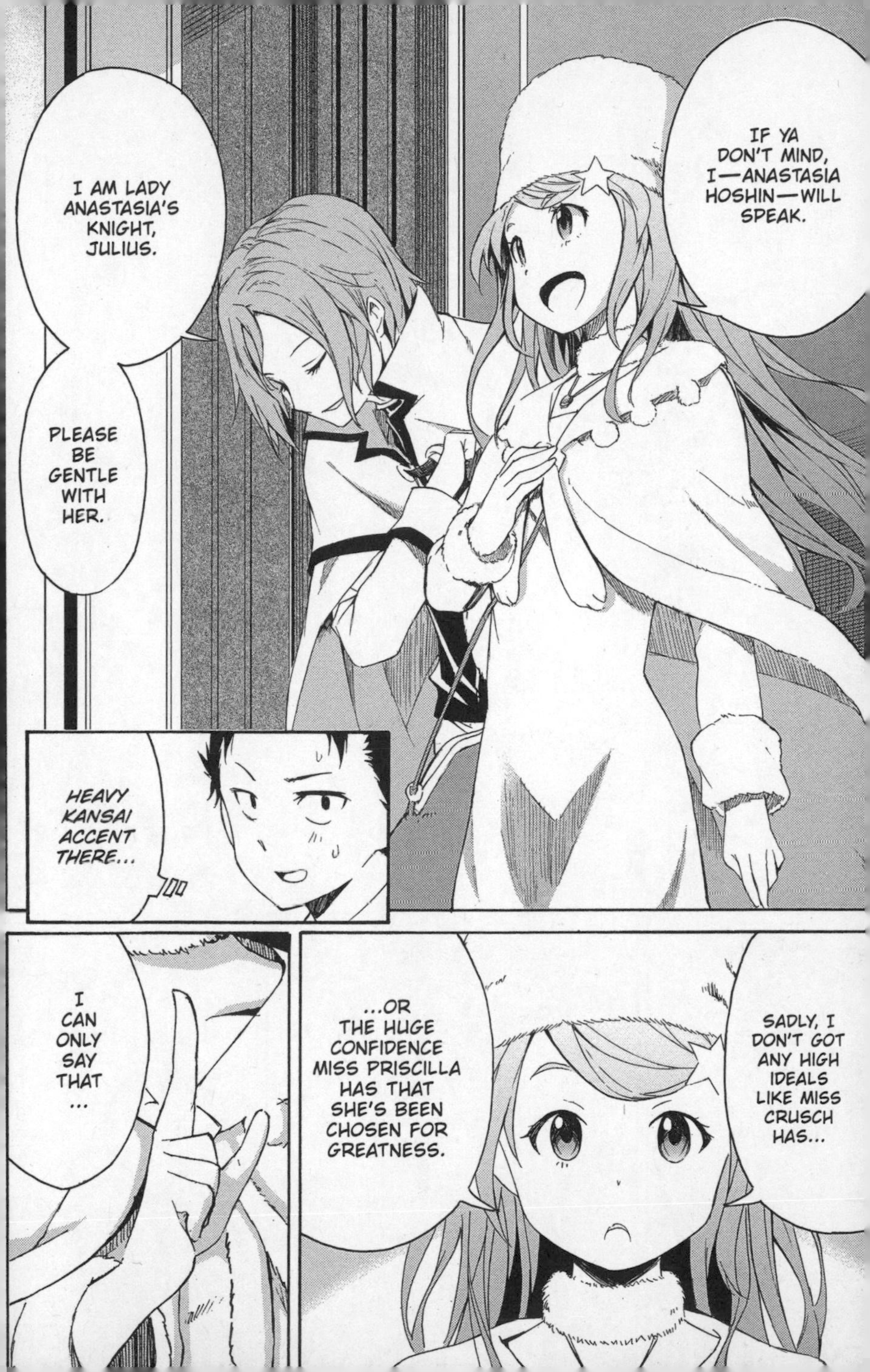
IF YA DON'T MIND, I—ANASTASIA HOSHIN—WILL SPEAK.
I AM LADY ANASTASIA'S KNIGHT, JULIUS.
PLEASE BE GENTLE WITH HER.
HEAVY KANSAI ACCENT THERE...
SADLY, I DON'T GOT ANY HIGH IDEALS LIKE MISS CRUSCH HAS...
...OR THE HUGE CONFIDENCE MISS PRISCILLA HAS THAT SHE'S BEEN CHOSEN FOR GREATNESS.
I CAN ONLY SAY THAT...

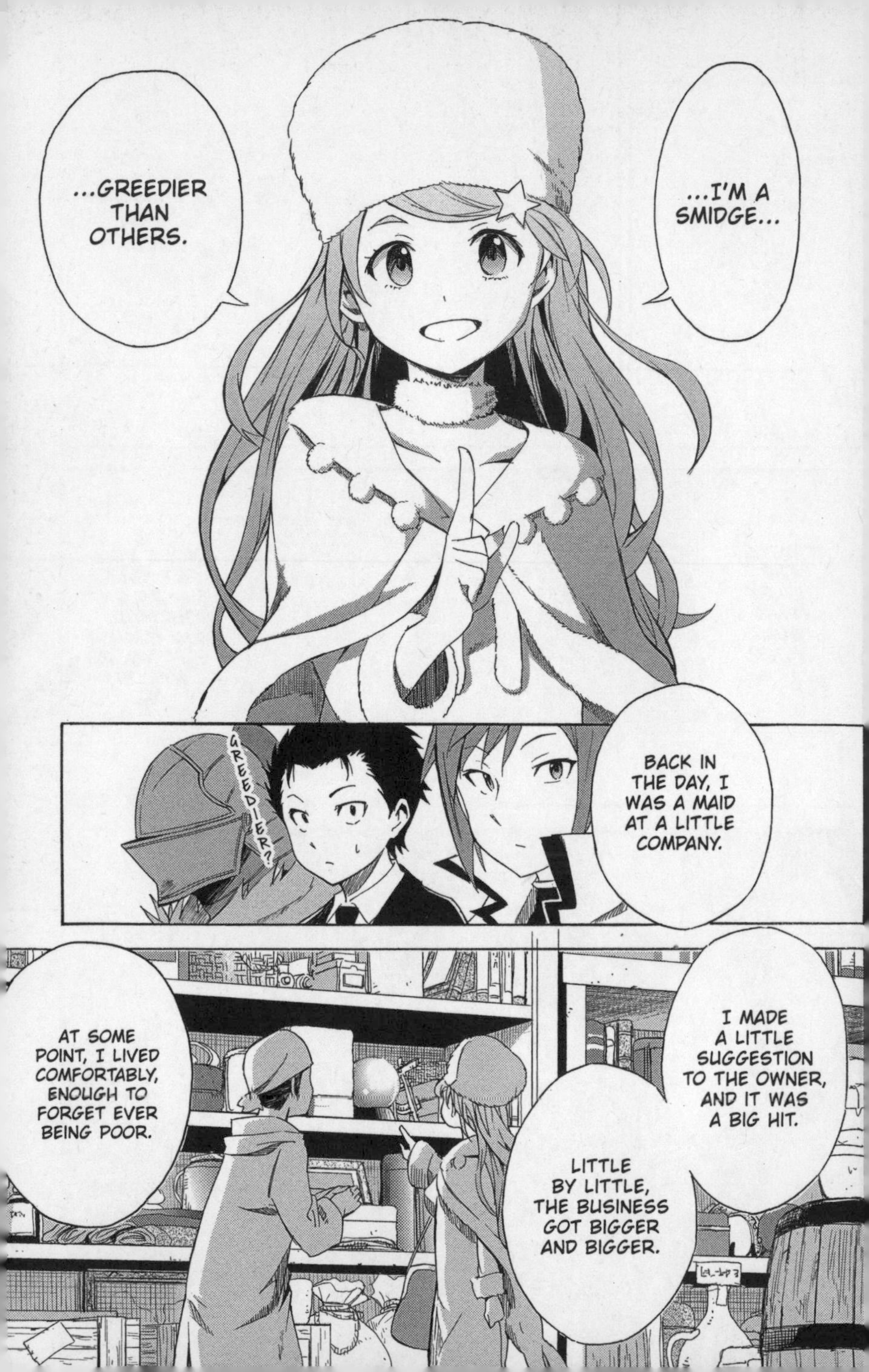
...I'M A SMIDGE...
...GREEDIER THAN OTHERS.
BACK IN THE DAY, I WAS A MAID AT A LITTLE COMPANY.
GREEDIER?
I MADE A LITTLE SUGGESTION TO THE OWNER, AND IT WAS A BIG HIT.
LITTLE BY LITTLE, THE BUSINESS GOT BIGGER AND BIGGER.
AT SOME POINT, I LIVED COMFORTABLY, ENOUGH TO FORGET EVER BEING POOR.

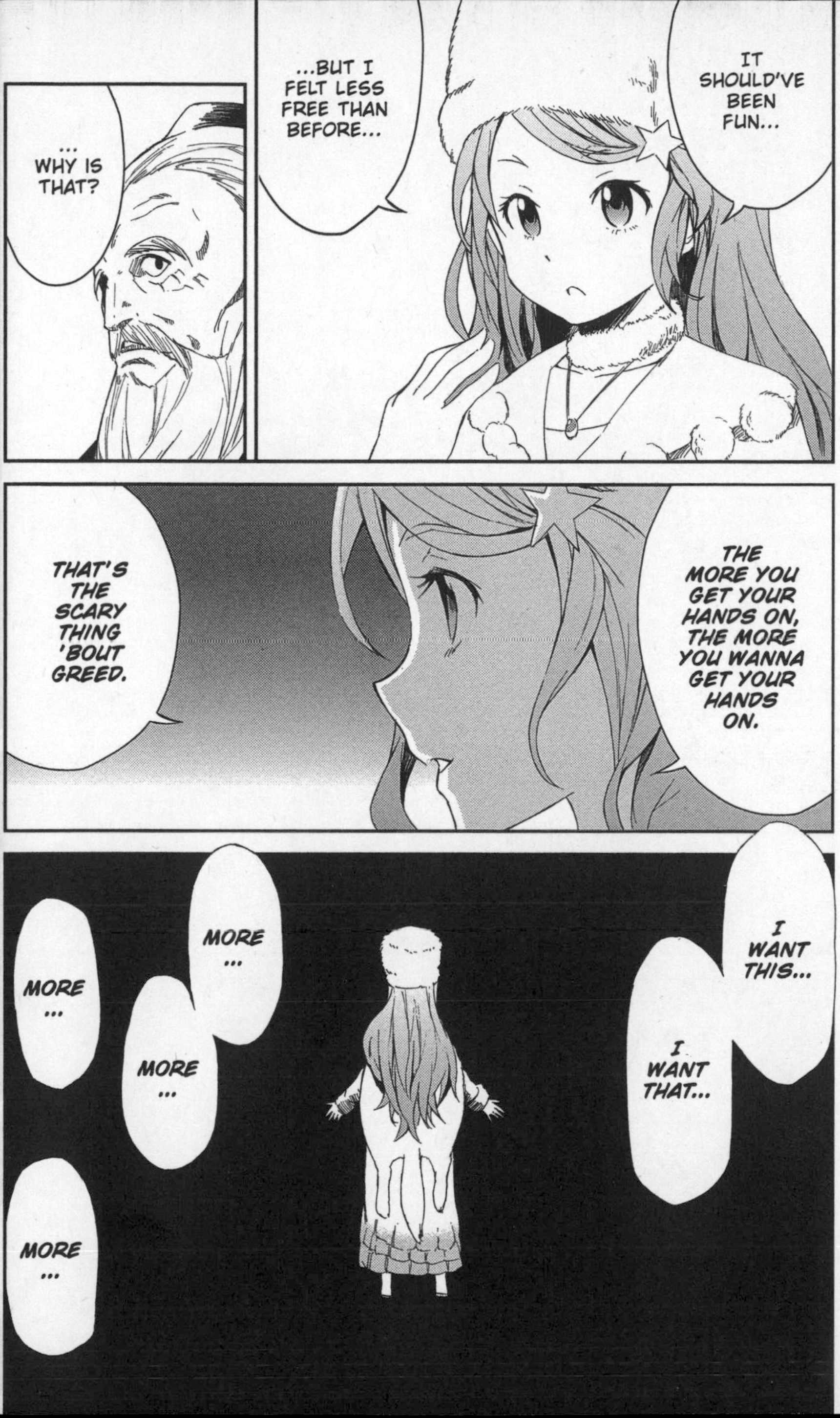
IT SHOULD'VE BEEN FUN...
...BUT I FELT LESS FREE THAN BEFORE...
... WHY IS THAT?
THE MORE YOU GET YOUR HANDS ON, THE MORE YOU WANNA GET YOUR HANDS ON.
THAT'S THE SCARY THING 'BOUT GREED.
I WANT THIS...
I WANT THAT...
MORE ...
MORE ...
MORE ...
MORE ...

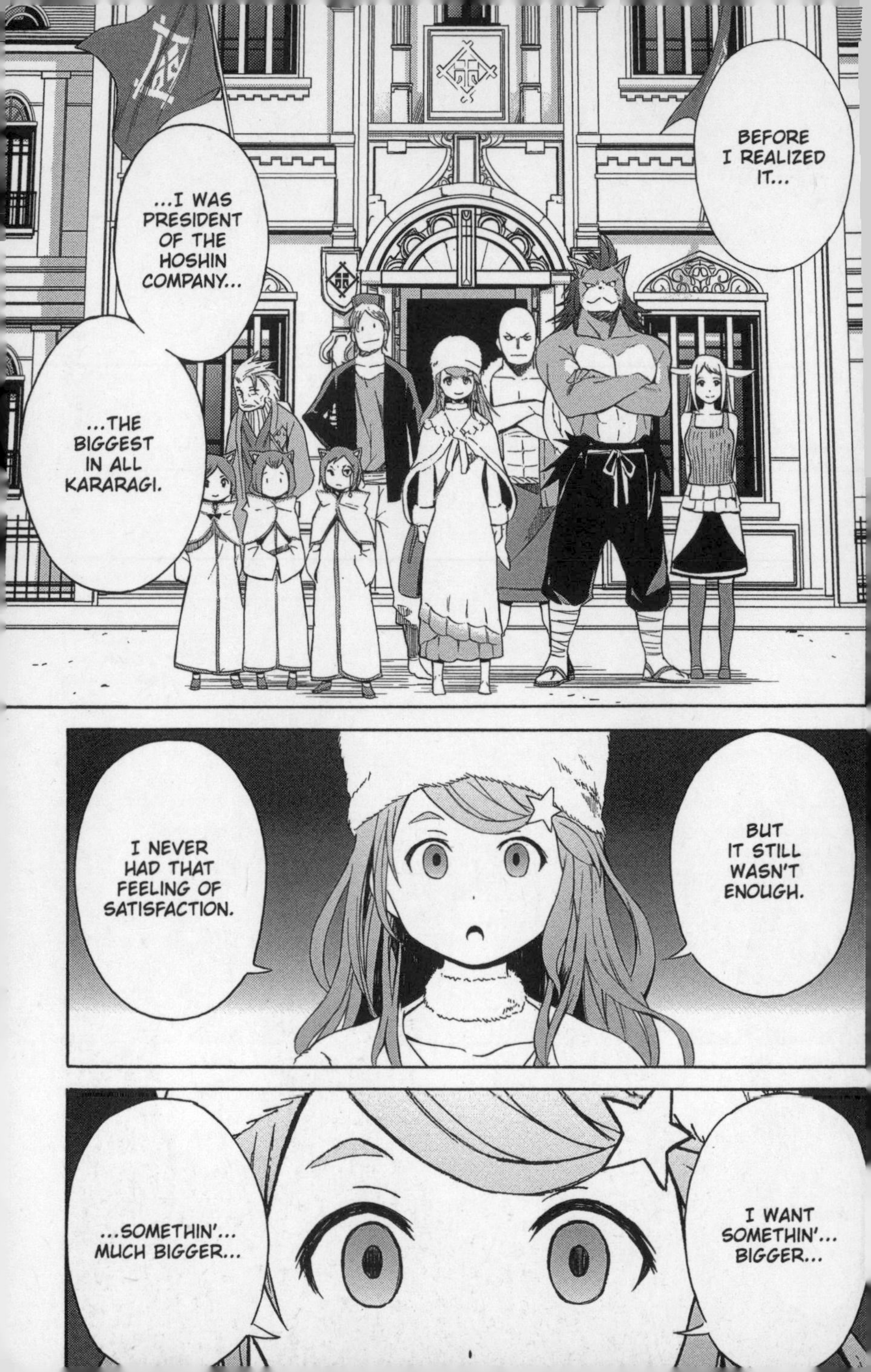
BEFORE I REALIZED IT...
...I WAS PRESIDENT OF THE HOSHIN COMPANY...
...THE BIGGEST IN ALL KARARAGI.
BUT IT STILL WASN'T ENOUGH.
I NEVER HAD THAT FEELING OF SATISFACTION.
I WANT SOMETHIN'... BIGGER...
...SOMETHIN'... MUCH BIGGER...

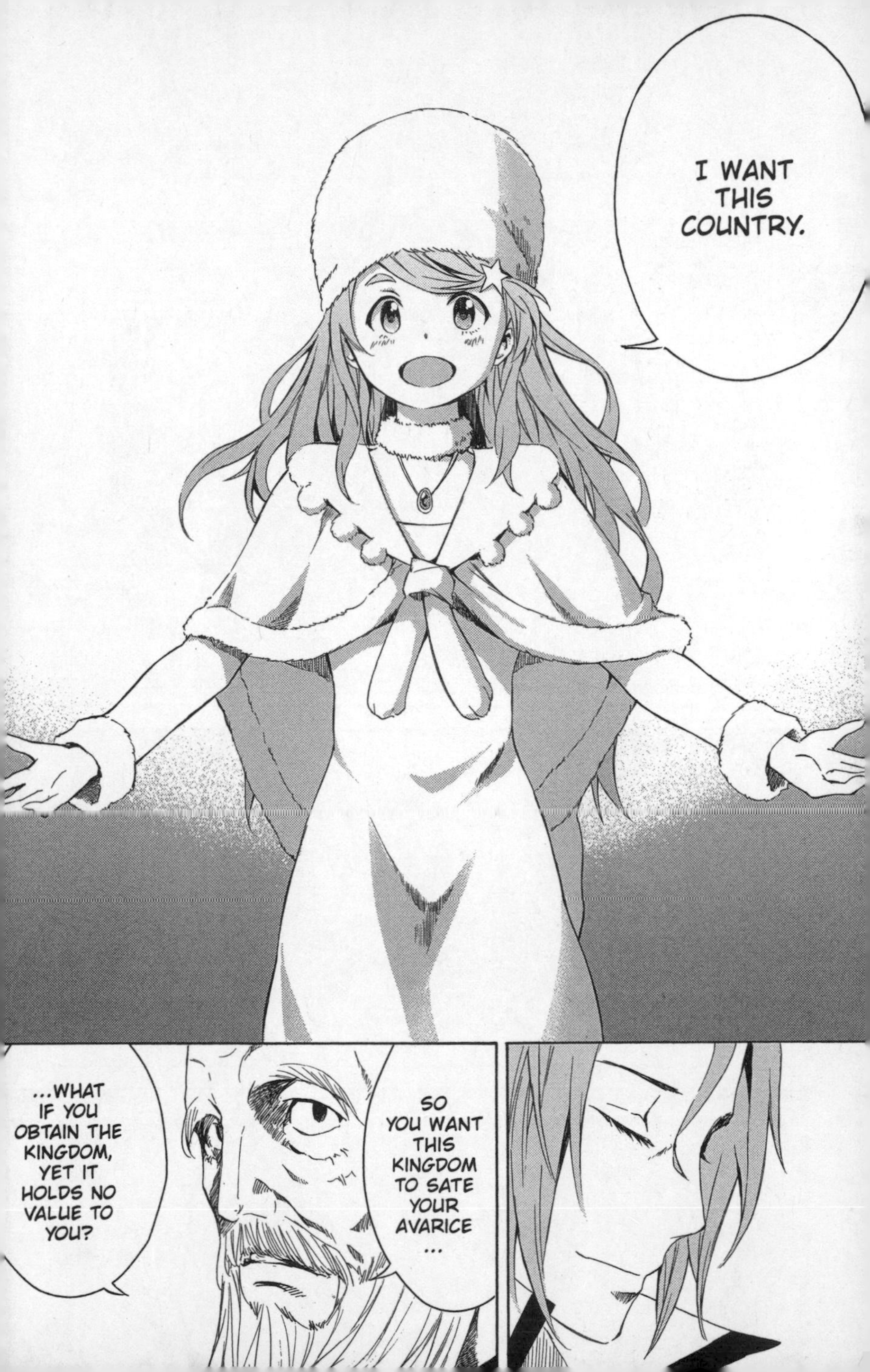
I WANT THIS COUNTRY.
SO YOU WANT THIS KINGDOM TO SATE YOUR AVARICE ...
...WHAT IF YOU OBTAIN THE KINGDOM, YET IT HOLDS NO VALUE TO YOU?

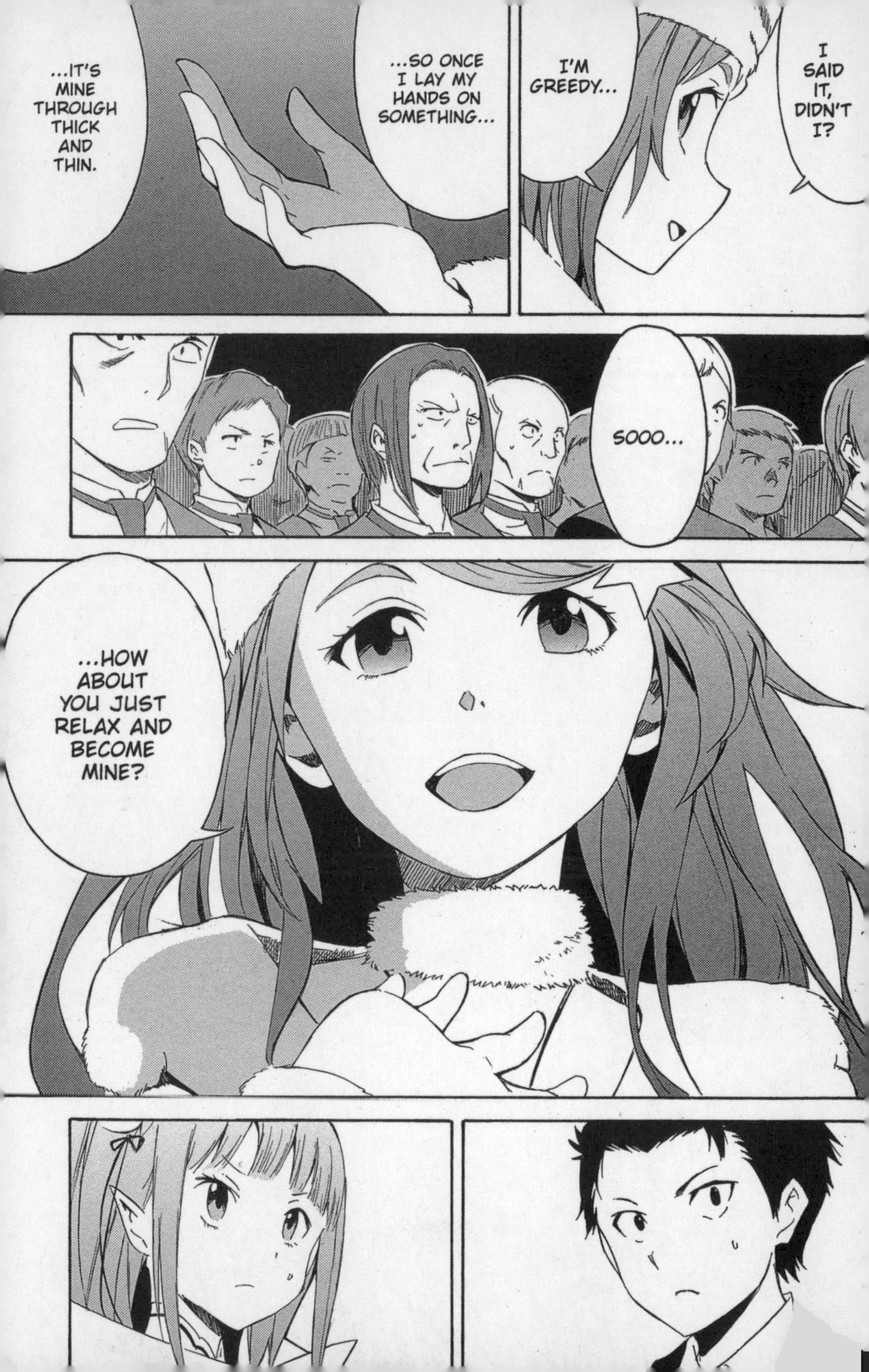
I SAID IT, DIDN'T I?
I'M GREEDY...
...SO ONCE I LAY MY HANDS ON SOMETHING...
...IT'S MINE THROUGH THICK AND THIN.
SOOO...
...HOW ABOUT YOU JUST RELAX AND BECOME MINE?

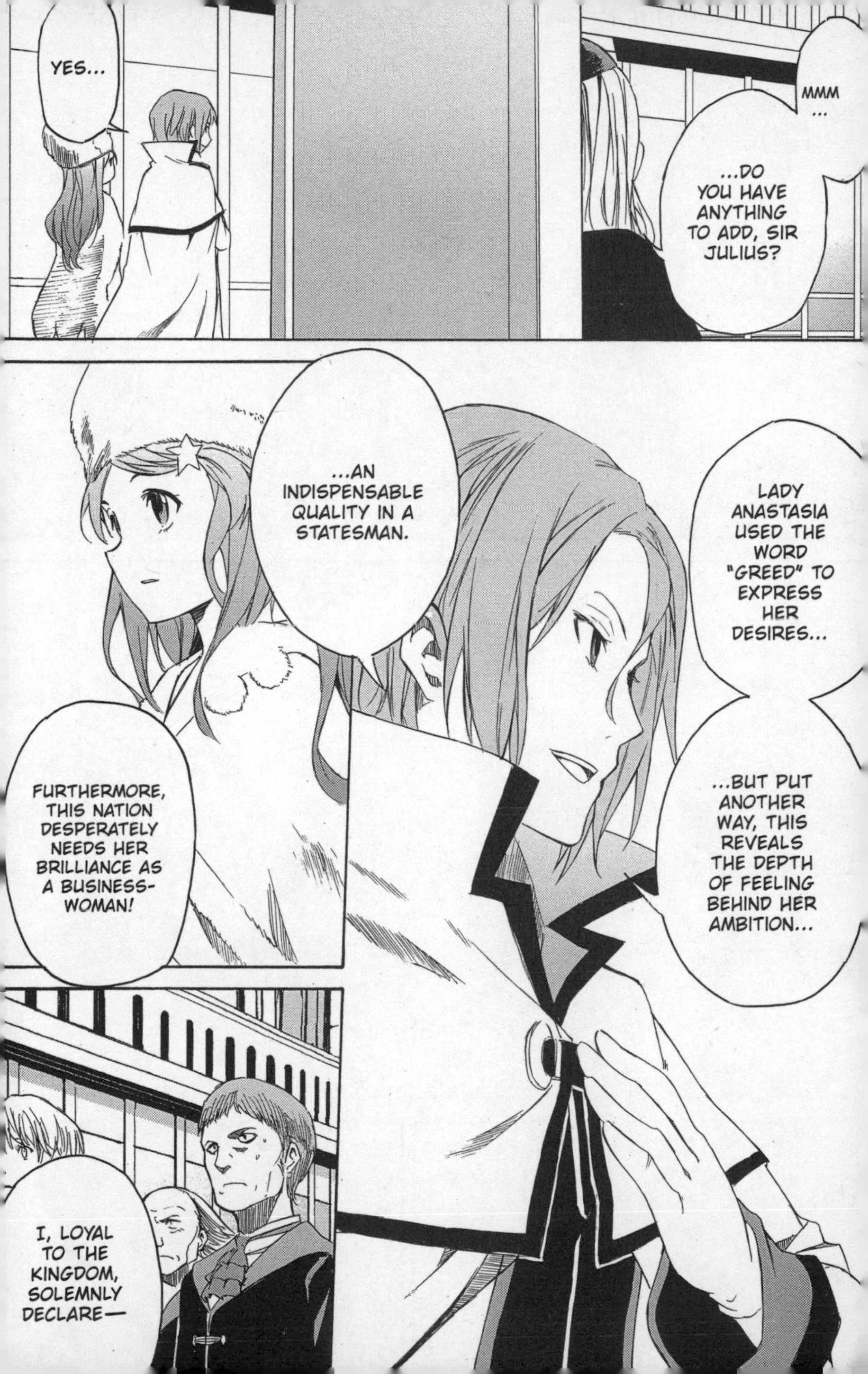
MMM...
...DO YOU HAVE ANYTHING TO ADD, SIR JULIUS?
YES...
LADY ANASTASIA USED THE WORD "GREED" TO EXPRESS HER DESIRES...
...BUT PUT ANOTHER WAY, THIS REVEALS THE DEPTH OF FEELING BEHIND HER AMBITION...
...AN INDISPENSABLE QUALITY IN A STATESMAN.
FURTHERMORE, THIS NATION DESPERATELY NEEDS HER BRILLIANCE AS A BUSINESS-WOMAN!
I, LOYAL TO THE KINGDOM, SOLEMNLY DECLARE—

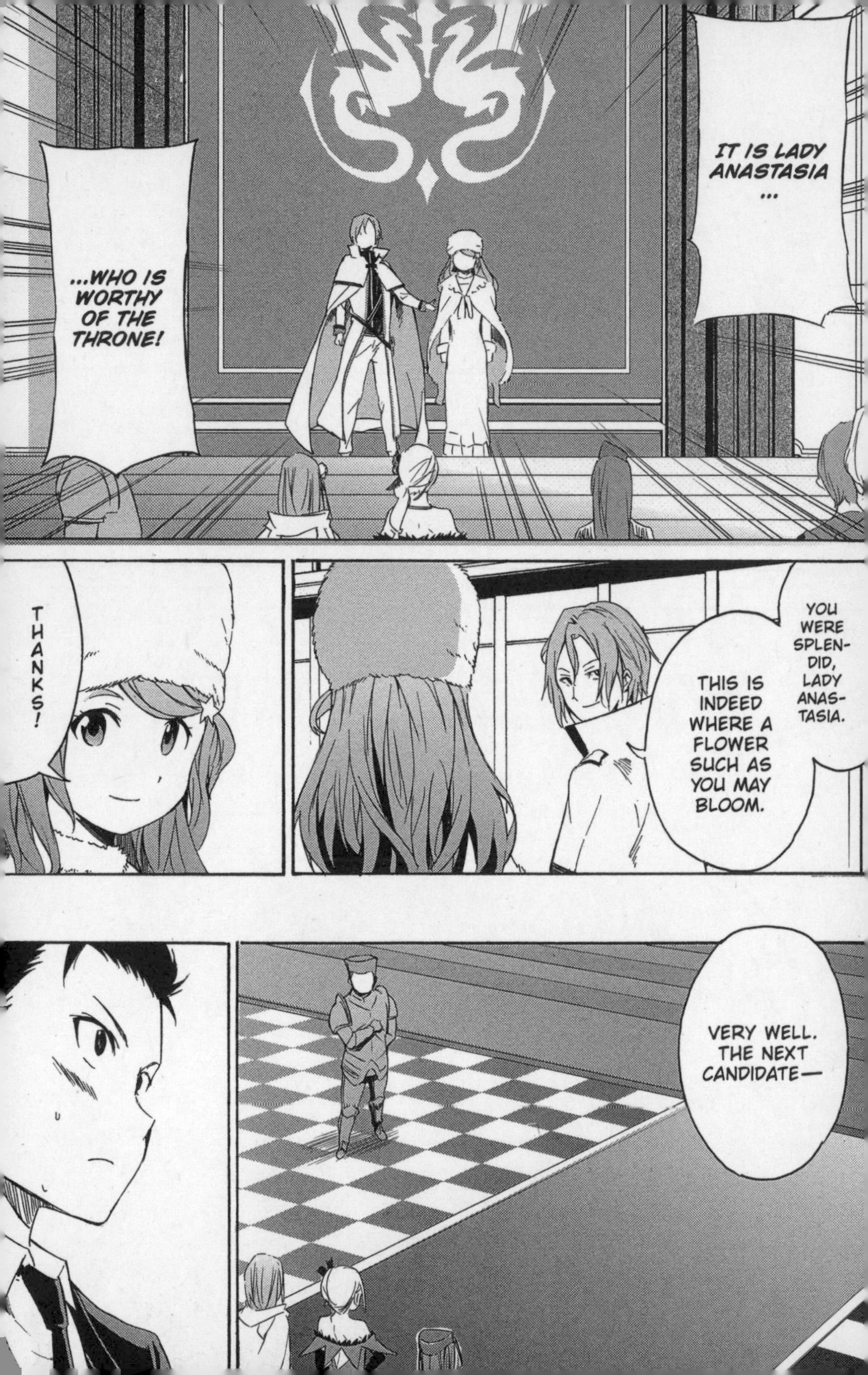
IT IS LADY ANASTASIA ...
...WHO IS WORTHY OF THE THRONE!
YOU WERE SPLEN-DID, LADY ANAS-TASIA.
THIS IS INDEED WHERE A FLOWER SUCH AS YOU MAY BLOOM.
THANKS!
VERY WELL. THE NEXT CANDIDATE—

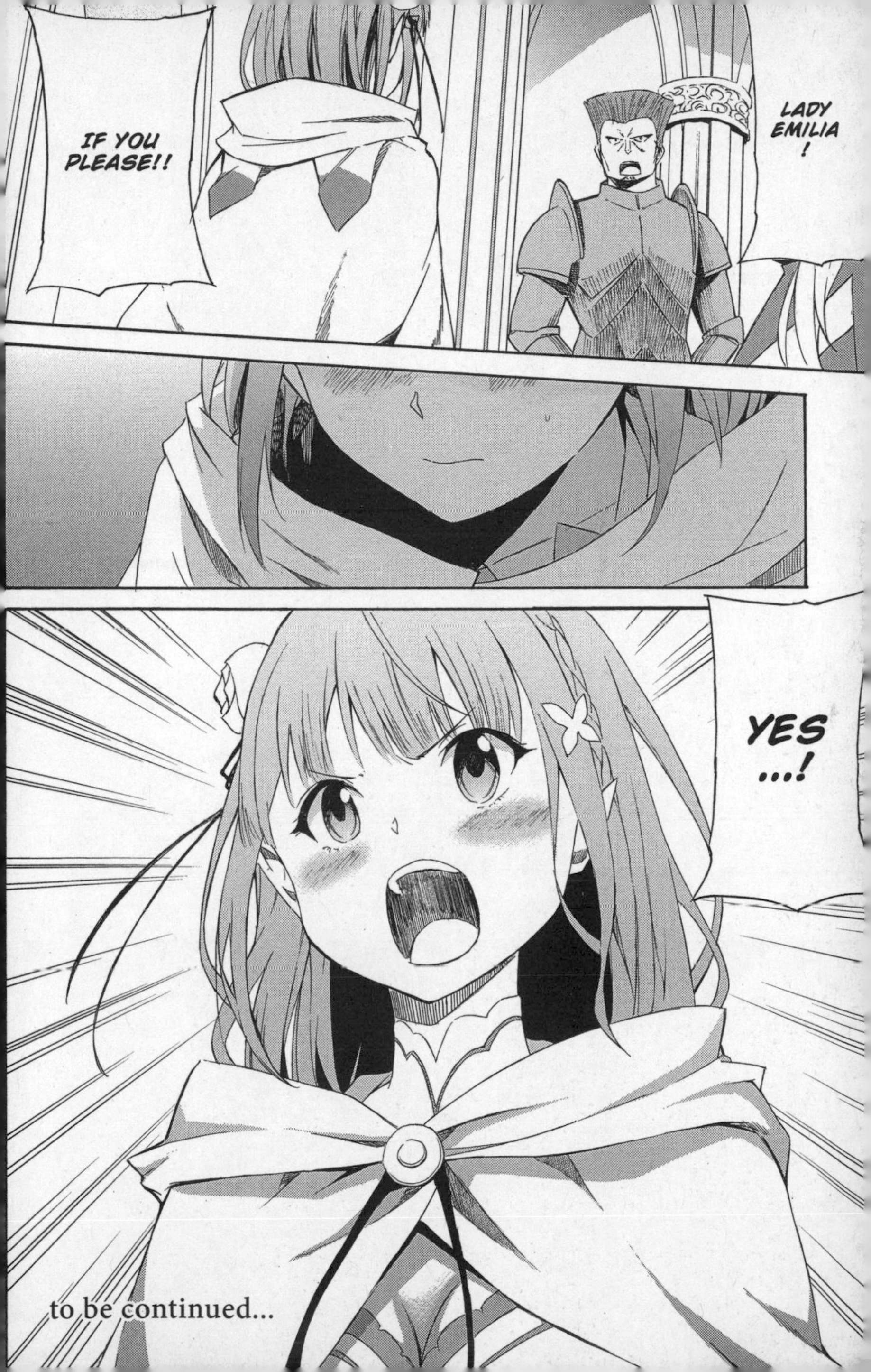
LADY EMILIA!
IF YOU PLEASE!!
YES ...!
to be continued...

Re:ZERO -Starting Life in Another World-

Truth of Zero

The only ability Subaru Natsuki gets when he's summoned to another world is time travel via his own death. But to save her, he'll die as many times as it takes.

Illustration by Shinichirou Otsuka (Character Designer)

Re:ZERO -Starting Life in Another World-

Supporting Comments from the Author of the Original Work, Tappei Nagatsuki

Daichi Matsuse-sensei,
congratulations on Volume 1 of the *Re:ZERO* comic going on sale! That statement gives me déjà vu…Or, rather, thank you for continuing the comic adaptation with Chapter 3! I haven't forgotten the moment I heard that the same Matsuse-sensei who drew Chapter 1 was handling the third one too. I pumped my fist and went, "Yes!!" Seeing the big increase in characters for the third arc, I'm grateful that you drew the various characters as cute as I expected…no, even more so. Chapter 3 is a tale built upon the great success of the first and the second. With so many hardships and twists awaiting, it'll be a lot of fun seeing how Matsuse-sensei will apply the power of his pencil and draw it all! With the anime due to air on television, more and more readers will be starting with the comics rather than the light novels. By all means, I'm very happy to have you with me, making *Re:ZERO* an even bigger success in the days to come! Now then, I greatly look forward to the next volume of Matsuse-sensei's version of *Re:ZERO*!

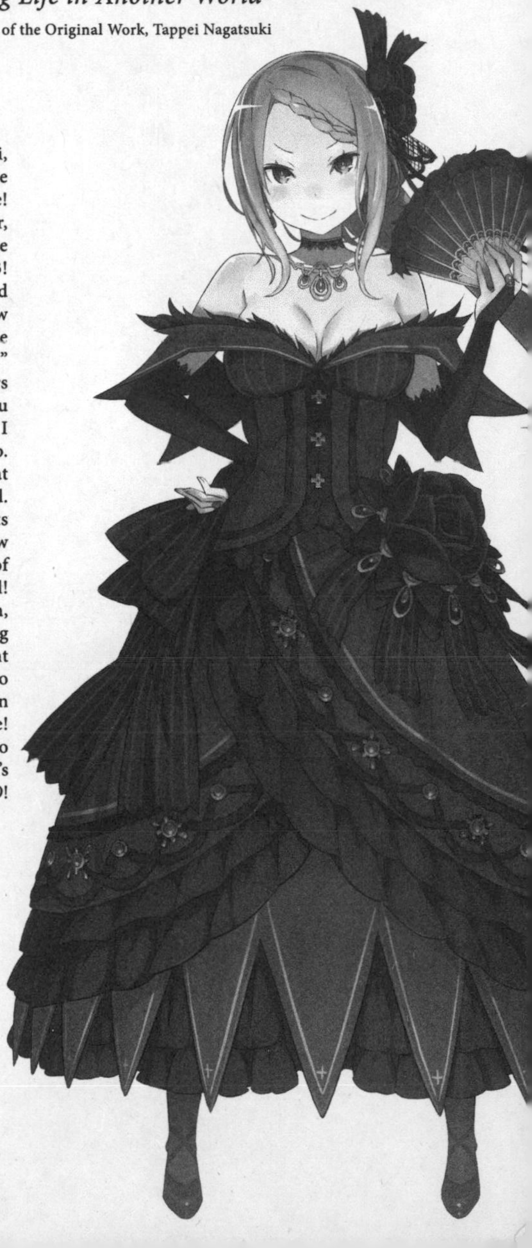